MEDIA IMAGES & ISSUES

MEDIA IMAGES & ISSUES

Donna Carpenter
Language Arts, English, and Drama Consultant
Halton Board of Education

Contributing Writer
Bill Smart
Head of English
Scarlett Heights Collegiate Institute
Etobicoke Board of Education

Consultant
Chris M. Worsnop
Coordinator of English
Peel Board of Education

Addison-Wesley Publishers Limited
Don Mills, Ontario • Reading, Massachusetts
Menlo Park, California • Wokingham, England • Amsterdam
Sydney • Singapore • Tokyo • Madrid • Bogotá
Santiago • San Juan

Senior Editor: Alan Simpson
Editors: Evlyn Windross, Lisa Guthro, Lynne Gulliver
Design: Many Pens Design Ltd.
Cover Photograph: Steve Hunt/The Image Bank
Typesetter: Alpha Graphics Limited

Addison-Wesley Publishers wish to thank the educators who have contributed to the development of this book. The publishers are especially grateful for the evaluations and suggestions of the following:
Derek Boles, Media Teacher, Thornlea Secondary School, York Region Board of Education
Donald Cassidy, Coordinator of Communications, Wentworth County Board of Education
Marty Woollings, English Department Head, London South Secondary School, London Board of Education

Credits for photographs appear on p. 376.

To my family with love and hope, and to Tedd for beginning it.
— Donna Carpenter

Canadian Cataloguing in Publication Data
Carpenter, Donna
Media — : images & issues

For use in schools.
Includes index.
ISBN 0-201-19207-1

1. Mass media. 2. Mass media — Problems, exercises, etc.
I. Smart, Bill II. Title.

P90.C37 1989 302.2′34 C88-094649-0

ISBN 0-201-19207-1

Printed and bound in Canada

C D E -BP- 93 92 91

Welcome to...

Media Images & Issues

Why Study the Media? A recent segment of ABC's *Viewpoint* presented the topic "Media Manipulation." For an hour and a half, panelists from the government and the media wrestled with such questions as: *Are journalists representatives of the general public?* and *Is it unpatriotic of news agencies to report events those in authority ask them not to?* The auditorium was packed with spectators, and the television cameras revealed lines of people stepping up to microphones to direct their own questions towards the panelists. People are concerned about the influence of the media in their lives – the images of themselves and their world reflected in the media, and the important issues confronting both the producers and the consumers of media messages.

There has been an overabundance of written commentaries and reports on the wide-ranging influence of the media, including Canadian Royal Commissions and U.S. Senate investigations – all with a common purpose: to seek answers to the troubling questions surrounding the media's impact on society and the individual. But the jury is still out. Few satisfying answers have been found to even basic questions, such as: *Do the media* shape *or* reflect *values, and to what degree?* Perhaps this very uncertainty is the most compelling reason for studying the mass media as part of your high-school curriculum. This book is designed to help you become more aware of the effects of the media in your life and your world – awareness that will help you make informed choices in the ways you consume, and use, the media.

This book will provide you with opportunities to examine critically articles written *about* the media – giving various points of view (You will find there can be as many points of view as there are issues in the media.); to analyze print ads and other examples *of* the media; and to create your own written, oral, and taped media products. You will be challenged to explore and draw your own conclusions about contemporary media images and issues.

Your investigation of the media will, perhaps, be the most personal of all the studies you will undertake in school this year. This is as it should be, for the media experience is essentially a private and personal one. In many ways, you are already an "expert" on the mass media; you have had a wide experience of print and electronic media – you are in fact a member of one of the first groups who have grown up with a very powerful electronic medium, television. This book will challenge you to work individually and collaboratively to reflect on your own experiences and beliefs; to ask questions and consider implications; to evaluate all that you hear, read, and see; and to experiment with creating your own "media messages."

Features of this book

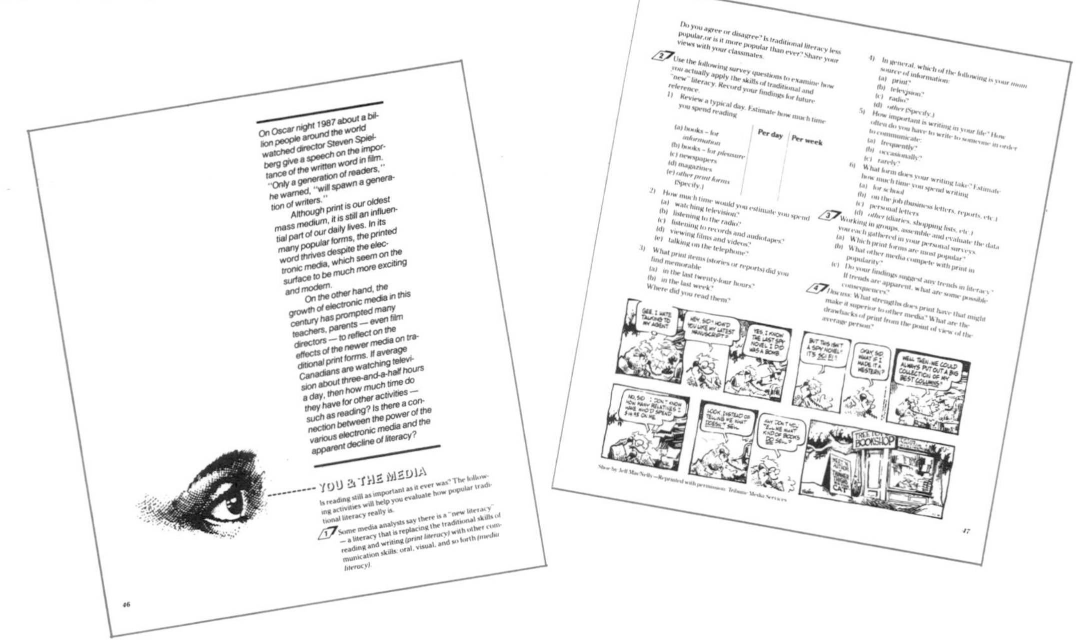

On Oscar night 1987 about a billion people around the world watched director Steven Spielberg give a speech on the importance of the written word in film. "Only a generation of readers," he warned, "will spawn a generation of writers."

Although print is our oldest mass medium, it is still an influential part of our daily lives. In its many popular forms, the printed word thrives despite the electronic media, which seem on the surface to be much more exciting and modern.

On the other hand, the growth of electronic media in this century has prompted many teachers, parents — even film directors — to reflect on the effects of the newer media on traditional print forms. If average Canadians are watching television about three-and-a-half hours a day, then how much time do they have for other activities — such as reading? Is there a connection between the power of the various electronic media and the apparent decline of literacy?

YOU & THE MEDIA

Is reading still as important as it ever was? The following activities will help you evaluate how popular traditional literacy really is.

1. Some media analysts say there is a "new literacy" — a literacy that is replacing the traditional skills of reading and writing (*print literacy*) with other communication skills: oral, visual, and so forth (*media literacy*).

46

Do you agree or disagree? Is traditional literacy less popular, or is it more popular than ever? Share your views with your classmates.

2. Use the following survey questions to examine how you actually apply the skills of traditional and "new" literacy. Record your findings for future reference.

1) Review a typical day. Estimate how much time you spend reading

	Per day	Per week
(a) books – for *information*		
(b) books – for *pleasure*		
(c) newspapers		
(d) magazines		
(e) *other print forms* (Specify.)		

2) How much time would you estimate you spend
(a) watching television?
(b) listening to the radio?
(c) listening to records and audiotapes?
(d) viewing films and videos?
(e) talking on the telephone?

3) What print items (stories or reports) did you find memorable
(a) in the last twenty-four hours?
(b) in the last week?
Where did you read them?

4) In general, which of the following is your *main* source of information:
(a) print?
(b) television?
(c) radio?
(d) *other* (Specify.)

5) How important is writing in your life? How often do you have to write to someone in order to communicate:
(a) frequently?
(b) occasionally?
(c) rarely?

6) What form does your writing take? Estimate how much time you spend writing
(a) for school
(b) on the job (business letters, reports, etc.)
(c) personal letters
(d) *other* (diaries, shopping lists, etc.)

3. Working in groups, assemble and evaluate the data you each gathered in your personal surveys.
(a) Which print forms are most popular?
(b) What other media compete with print in popularity?
(c) Do your findings suggest any trends in literacy? If trends are apparent, what are some possible consequences?

4. *Discuss:* What strengths does print have that might make it superior to other media? What are the drawbacks of print from the point of view of the average person?

Shoe by Jeff MacNelly—Reprinted with permission: Tribune Media Services

47

Content:

The 'What' and 'How' of Media Images & Issues

The articles, news items, and media products you will investigate in this book reflect a broad range of concerns and points of view surrounding the mass media. The majority have been written by and about Canadians and aim to focus your vision on the Canadian media scene.

But not only will you be responding to the materials in this text, you will also be examining print, radio, film, and television as an ongoing process – using survey questions and data sheets to collect information, observations, and opinions on the media as it affects and is part of your daily life.

You will be maintaining your own *Personal Response Journal* – your chance to reflect and comment on the media as you experience their images and issues. In addition, throughout the media program you will be creating, expanding, and reviewing personal and collective *Media Files* containing examples of print ads, photographs, and so on, that you and your classmates find interesting, informative, or otherwise noteworthy.

Suggested Activities:

A Focus of Investigation

Under the following headings, you will find various types of activities to help focus your investigation of the media.

You & the Media: Each unit begins with a brief introduction followed by activities that encourage you to examine your own experiences and beliefs *before* you explore the materials in the unit.

Exploring Ideas: After reading an article, or group of related materials, you will encounter a set of activities designed to prompt focused exploration and assessment of the ideas and opinions presented. You will share your observations, views, and conclusions through class and small-group discussions, journal-entry comments, and written or oral reports to the class.

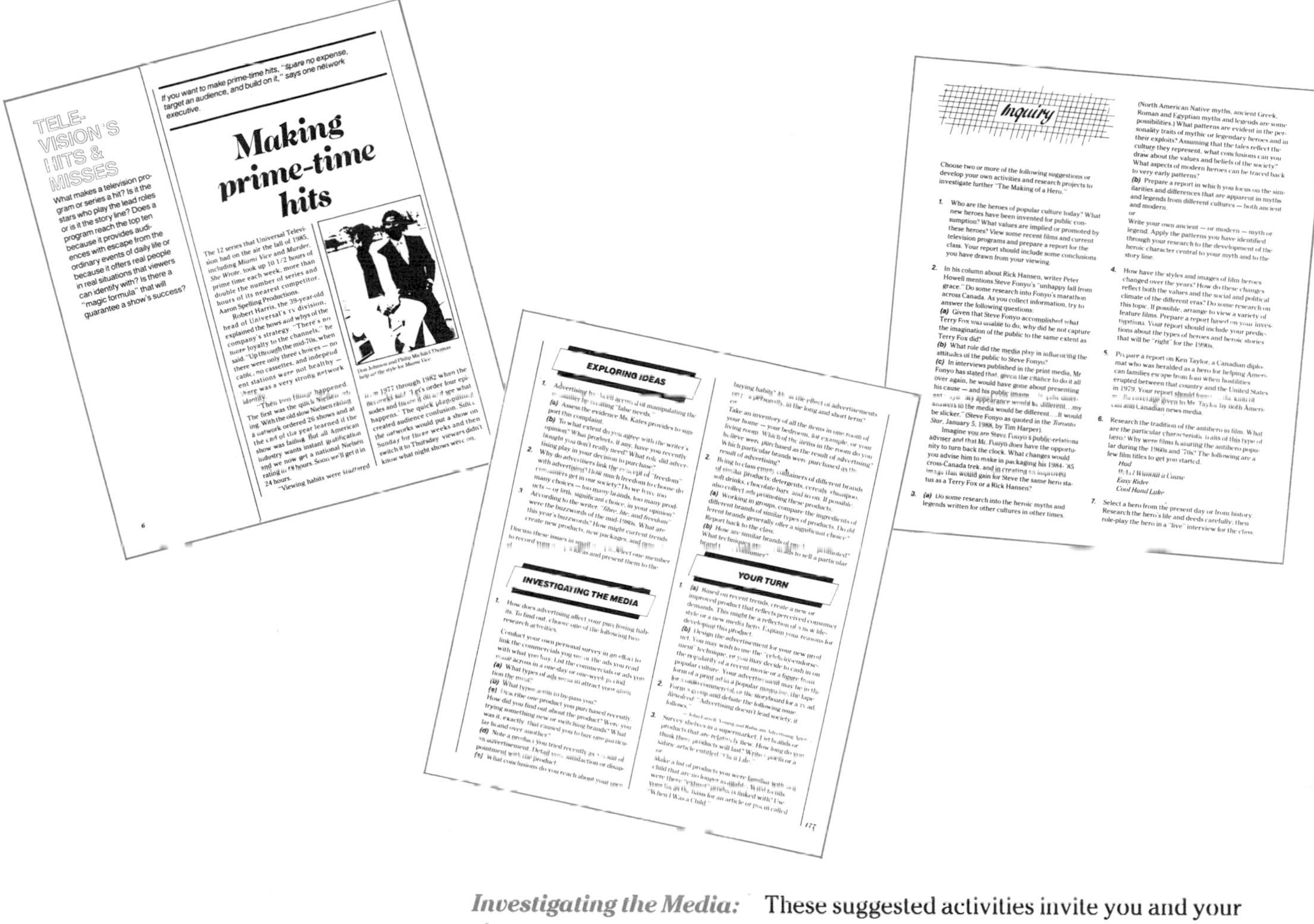

Investigating the Media: These suggested activities invite you and your classmates to examine and interact with the media in order to reflect and draw conclusions regarding images and issues related to the article(s) you have just read and discussed.

Your Turn: This section gives you opportunities to undertake individual or small-group projects that will encourage experimentation in creating your own media reports, presentations, and products.

Inquiry: Each unit ends with a number of suggestions for extended research and investigation. Based on your interests and abilities, you will choose individual and small-group projects that will allow you to pursue an in-depth examination of topics, themes, and issues introduced in the unit. Alternatively, you may decide to develop your own activities and research projects. The products of your inquiries will provide opportunities to develop and refine your skills in presenting in a variety of forms and formats.

Special *Media Facts & Techniques* sections provide practical background information on media terms, tools, and techniques.

The Units:

Eight Vehicles for Investigating Media

This book is organized around eight *units*, each of which focuses on a specific topic or theme related to media images and issues.

Unit 1–Television, Radio, and You: The selections in this unit take you through a range of topics associated with the electronic mass media. These include: assessments of what makes a program a hit on TV; the effect of ratings on program schedules and content; the influence of TV and radio on various audience groups; the future of radio as a communication medium.

Unit 2–The Future of Print: This unit invites you to explore a variety of print media, including newspapers, popular novels, and magazines. You will also examine the role of "traditional" literacy in relation to the so-called new, media literacy of the "information age."

Unit 3–Changing Focus: Photography and Films: You will be encouraged to examine and reflect upon the power of visual images, both still photographs and film – images that shape the way we perceive events and people around us and in distant "corners" of our world. You will also explore and experiment with the processes, tools, and techniques of photography and video.

Unit 4–Getting the Message: Advertising: This unit asks you to take a close look at the techniques used in designing ads, the issues and ethics of advertising, and advertising's influence on the consumer. The rights and powers of consumers regarding the content and presentation of advertising are explored.

Unit 5–The Public's Right to Know: Reporting the News: In this unit you will confront a number of questions related to the presentation of news in newspapers, newsmagazines, and on television. These questions include: *What constitutes "responsible" journalism?* and *How can journalists maintain a balance between the public's right to know and the individual's right to privacy?*

Unit 6–In Whose Image? Issues surrounding lifestyle and other images reflected in the media form the major focus of this unit. Topics include sex-role stereotyping, TV and children, and the image of Canada in film and on television.

Unit 7–The Making of a Hero: Do the media both promote and *create* fictional and real-world heroes? You will examine the media's role in shaping and re-shaping our images of heroism.

Unit 8–Futurewatch: You will conclude your investigation of the media by "looking into the crystal ball." What will be the impact of future trends in media technology – such as computer-assisted recording and video techniques, interactive television, desktop publishing – and what ethical questions will they present? You will examine how the "brave new world" of "future tech" is already changing the way you work, learn, play, and live.

Contents

Readings–List of Selections

UNIT 1–Television, Radio, and You

UNIT 2–The Future of Print

UNIT 3–Changing Focus: Photography & Films

UNIT 7–The Making of a Hero

UNIT 8–Futurewatch

MEDIA IMAGES & ISSUES

UNIT ONE:

TELEVISI RADIO,

> "The average Canadian watches 24.2 hours of television per week — but only 8.7 minutes of that is educational TV, Statistics Canada says. Instead, viewers spend most of their television time crying and laughing, watching 10.5 hours of drama and 3.5 hours of comedy. And on average, viewers take in only 8.4 hours a week of Canadian programming."

— Alan Toulin
The Toronto Star
April 25, 1987

Television arrived in Canada in the late 1940s. At first the only programs available were broadcast from stations in the United States; then in September 1952 Canadians viewed their first home-grown English-language broadcast: the children's program Uncle Chichimus.

Media "prophets" predicted the new medium would make radio obsolete — TV could entertain, provide information, and take us right into the sports arena. And, of course, television did it with pictures!

Viewers of early television broadcasts suffered through unreliable black-and-white pictures that were sometimes obliterated by "snow." Nevertheless, those in the new medium recognized that TV had great potential power.

In a brief time television has indeed become an important force in society; it is difficult for many of us to imagine life without TV. Exactly how has television transformed communication in our world? What are we watching and how does it affect us?

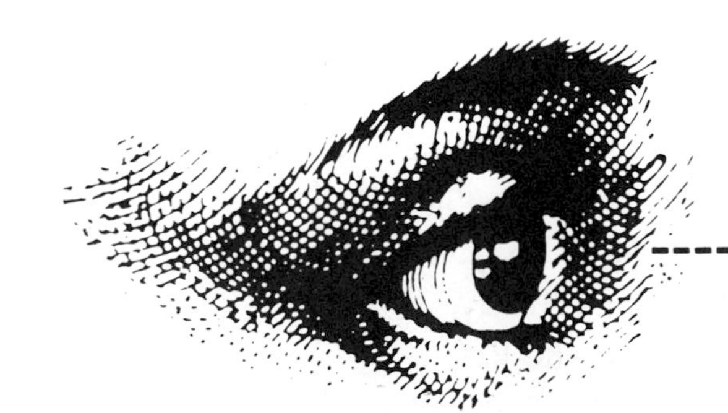

How influential is television in *your* life? The following activities will help you assess the power of the "box."

1. Share your opinions on the role of television in our society:
   - Why, do you think, is television such a powerful force in our society?

- What service does it provide for you and other groups in our society, such as the elderly and young children? How might your life be different *without* TV?
- On the whole, do you think TV's effect is positive or negative?

2 Conduct a survey of viewing habits in your class, using the following questions as a guide:

1) Estimate the number of hours you spend watching television per day.
2) Estimate the number of hours per day you spend
   (a) listening (to tapes, records, radio)
   (b) reading (books, magazines, newspapers, letters)
   (c) speaking (conversations with friends, family)
   (d) participating in other hobbies or interests (sports, etc.)
3) List three of your favourite television programs.
4) Identify your favourite types of television programs:
   - music
   - news
   - sports
   - action/adventure
   - interview/talk shows
   - movies
   - daytime soap operas
   - prime-time soaps
   - situation comedies
   - game shows
   - mysteries
   - specials
   - mini-series
5) Identify your favourite TV stars and characters.

Be sure to keep your responses to this survey for future reference.

3 Working in small groups, compile and summarize your findings. Then write a news report describing the viewing habits of the students in your class.

4 How accurate were your estimates? To find out, keep a record of the *actual* times and the number of hours you watch television, and the channels and programs watched. Maintain your record for between three to seven days, including one weekend. A chart like the following will help you keep accurate records of your viewing habits:

Time	Friday	Saturday	Sunday
7 am	Channel- Program-		
8 am			
Total			

At the end of the viewing period review your record sheet and respond to the following questions:

(a) Are you surprised in any way by what the record sheet reveals?

(b) How close are your findings to the statistics quoted *earlier*?

5 Maintain an ongoing journal during this unit. Use the journal for recording your personal responses to what you watch on television — thoughts about the performances, the social message or value of the program, the costumes and sets, and so on.

ALL WE EVER DO IS WATCH TELEVISION...

WE NEVER JUST SIT AND TALK ABOUT THINGS ANYMORE!

WHADDYER WANT TO TALK ABOUT?

MY PROGRAM STARTS IN TEN MINUTES.

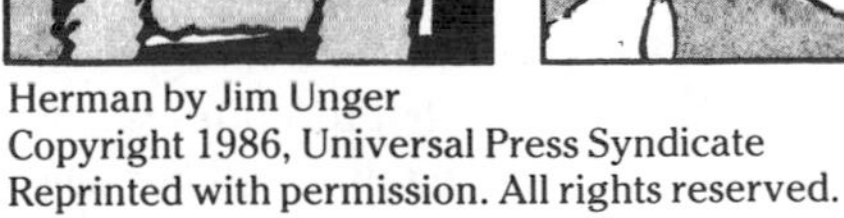
Herman by Jim Unger

TELE-VISION'S HITS & MISSES

What makes a television program or series a hit? Is it the stars who play the lead roles or is it the story line? Does a program reach the top ten because it provides audiences with escape from the ordinary events of daily life or because it offers real people in real situations that viewers can identify with? Is there a "magic formula" that will guarantee a show's success?

If you want to make prime-time hits, "spare no expense, target an audience, and build on it," says one network executive.

Making prime-time hits

The 12 series that Universal Television had on the air the fall of 1985, including *Miami Vice* and *Murder, She Wrote*, took up 10 1/2 hours of prime time each week, more than double the number of series and hours of its nearest competitor, Aaron Spelling Productions.

Robert Harris, the 39-year-old head of Universal's TV division, explained the hows and whys of the company's strategy. "There's no more loyalty to the channels," he said. "Up through the mid-70s, when there were only three choices — no cable, no cassettes, and independent stations were not healthy — there was a very strong network identity.

Don Johnson and Philip Michael Thomas help set the style for *Miami Vice*.

"Then two things happened. The first was the quick Nielsen rating. With the old slow Nielsen rating, a network ordered 26 shows and at the end of the year learned if the show was failing. But all American industry wants instant gratification and we now get a national Nielsen rating in 48 hours. Soon we'll get it in 24 hours.

"Viewing habits were shattered from 1977 through 1982 when the networks said, 'Let's order four episodes and throw it on and see what happens.' The quick plug-pulling created audience confusion. Since the networks would put a show on Sunday for three weeks and then switch it to Thursday, viewers didn't know what night shows were on.

"That coincided with the second thing. While the networks were juggling time periods, you had the growth of cable and cassettes and local stations whose graphics looked like the networks and who showed old network series in color."

In 1978, the networks had 95 per cent of the prime-time audience. Today, they have 78 per cent. And Universal is enticing viewers not with words or complicated plots but with the way a series looks. "We're dealing with the MTV generation, which is the *Sesame Street* generation," said Harris. "People are used to getting visually stimulated very quickly."

For example, *Miami Vice*, with its jump cuts and brilliant pastel colors, or *The Equalizer*, with its neon-lit, rain-slick New York streets.

Universal routinely runs a deficit of $250 000 to $500 000 an episode on *Miami Vice*. Each episode costs $1.2 million to $1.5 million. The average licencing fee paid by the networks for a first-year series is well under $1 million an hour. Only if the series stays on the air the four or five years it takes to make enough episodes to sell for syndication will the studio make money. And Universal's deficits are the highest in the industry.

"Our philosophy is that you've got to spend money to make money," said Harris. "For one episode of *Miami Vice*, we went to a place off the coast of Florida where the houses are built on stilts. When the cops were closing in on the dealers, our guys were in a shiny black speedboat. A yellow-and-black seaplane comes flying in against blue skies. That freeze-frame was like a painting. We stuck a camera in the boat, so you're with our guys in the boat. It costs a lot of money to go on water, go to location, rent a black-and-yellow plane, and put the camera in the boat."

"In the old days, you did a mystery in three rooms," he said. "*Murder, She Wrote* has as high a set-construction budget as *Miami Vice*."

Money is also spent on a stable of over 100 contract producers and writers, probably double that of any other studio.

Another part of the Universal philosophy is "to target a core audience and hope to build to a mass audience," said Harris. "The urban-male sophisticated-action audience that was our target for *Miami Vice* had deserted series television to watch movies. At first, the program only had a 22 share, but its core audience loved it."

"People see the ratings as a World Series with one winner," said Harris. "But it takes something very extraordinary to knock off a network leader. The networks are looking for series that improve their position."

Being second in your time period is sometimes success enough. Universal's *Equalizer* on CBS was a series that appeared at first glance to be a loser. A tough, gritty series about a world-weary ex-secret agent, *The Equalizer* was beaten each week by ABC's *Hotel*. In its one test against NBC's *St. Elsewhere*, *The Equalizer* came out ahead.

"*The Equalizer* is a self-starter," Harris said. "People come to it from nowhere. As a result, CBS ordered nine more scripts."

— Aljean Harmetz
New York Times Service

Every now and then a series comes along that takes a chance and wins audiences despite — or perhaps because of — the fact that it breaks established moulds.

What happens when TV tries a little risk-taking

No one will ever accuse the entertainment industry of living on the edge. Mention taking a chance and knees start knocking.

No wonder nearly all TV is soft-centered, thumb-sucking, and curled into a fetal position.

Which makes risk-taking episodes of NBC's *St. Elsewhere* and ABC's *Moonlighting* all the more amazing and admirable.

St. Elsewhere has had many superior episodes, but none bolder than one in which Dr. Wayne Fiscus (Howie Mandel) lingered in a deathly state between heaven and hell after being shot in the chest by the estranged wife of a patient.

Moonlighting plays Russian roulette almost every week.

Creator and executive producer Glenn Caron turned *Moonlighting* into the razziest, snazziest hit on TV by breaking rules. His series takes longer to write and shoot than most other hour programs. It is also more expensive (worth every penny, artistically) and more outrageous.

Occasionally it is a detective story, more often a people story defined by a near-lethal, almost-but-not-quite-yet romance between silky Maddie Hayes (Cybill Shepherd) and do-whopping David Addison (Bruce Willis).

Caron's stories usually do not climax, they just sort of ... stop, in mid-mood, often making you feel that you now understand David and Maddie just a little bit less than you did before. It is excruciatingly, exquisitely baffling.

"Everything is filled with enigma," Caron said. "I think enigma is kind of wonderful."

Most times, *Moonlighting* is just kind of wonderful. A recent hour — which revealed that the mysterious David had an ex-wife who left him for another woman — was extraordinary, let's-preserve-it-in-a-time-capsule TV.

You got shadings and half-tones and gleaming dialogue and a dream by Maddie that became a seven-minute dance sequence set to new Billy Joel music and inspired by an expressionistic number that Gene Kelly danced with Cyd Charisse in *Singin' in the Rain*.

A week later, *Moonlighting* pressed a different button, withdrawing to ye olde Middle Ages in a parody of Shakespeare's *Taming of the Shrew*. It was untamed TV and flawed, but you had to admire its vision and chutzpah.

Caron resists the "daring" label. "When we're taking risks, I don't know we're taking risks," he said. "We don't sit around each week and say, 'Let's do this, let's do that.' This is going to sound pretentious, but it's purer than that. We chase a central truth. Our characters tell us where to take them. I'll gladly take the credit, but it's not risk-taking. It's storytelling."

For someone who was hitless before *Moonlighting*, Caron got enormous freedom from ABC, even in his show's first season. That was when Caron decolored *Moonlighting* to create its most famous episode, a black-and-white spoof of 1940s movies.

Caron also loved the episode in which Maddie discovered her father was going out on her mother. "When Maddie leaves that show, there is a lot of pain and discomfort," Caron said. "Discomfort — that's what binds us all together."

Moonlighting is ever in danger of straying from its roots by centering on one character, and it always risks getting too cute.

When *Moonlighting* is on its game, "It's like being at a party with someone who is very witty," Caron said.

David and Maddie of ABC's *Moonlighting*—Their mixed-up relationship makes for "untamed TV."

"When we go too far, it's like being at a party with someone who's had too much to drink."

Meanwhile, he would like to buy rights to the 1925 silent film *The Lost World* and "mat" David and Maddie into its story about prehistoric beasts on a deserted island. "I'd also like to do a Godzilla film — Godzilla vs. King Kong, and have them save Tokyo," Caron said.

Exceptional TV is often costly TV, hence *Moonlighting* shares an "expensive" tag, along with such shows as *Miami Vice*, *L.A. Law*, and *St. Elsewhere*. But Caron does not like tags.

"TV is a ridiculous industry," he said, "where everyone works under the presumption that a particular hour of broadcast material should cost the same as any other hour. They say that an hour of TV should cost $900 000 (*Moonlighting* is said to often cost almost double that), as if you buy it by the yard. That's stupid TV."

The *St. Elsewhere* Fiscus-near-death episode looked very swanky.

It featured intermittent dreamlike sequences, cutting back and forth between a lifeless Fiscus on the operating table, being worked over by his colleagues, to a terrified and bewildered Fiscus drifting between heaven and hell.

The story began with Fiscus chasing fireflies in front of the hospital at night and finally capturing one in a glass jar. It was highly unusual, almost surreal TV, in which Fiscus's colleagues were personally renewed by restoring him to life.

Before that happened, though, Fiscus twice passed through hell, encountering two of his dead patients in addition to a murdered doctor-rapist-drug addict and some stripe-shirted, whistle-blowing football referees. "They never played the game," Fiscus observed. "They just pass judgment on real athletes."

He also found himself in heaven: a genteel lawn party attended by a deceased heart-transplant patient and God, an ordinary guy who looks and sounds like Fiscus. "I just create circumstances," said God, denying omnipotence. "I turn My head, things have changed...."

The risk-taking *St. Elsewhere* and *Moonlighting* are fireflies — flickering brightness in TV's night. Would there were more.

— Howard Rosenberg
Los Angeles Times
January 5, 1987

EXPLORING IDEAS

1. **(a)** Evaluate the factors the writers of the previous articles see as important in creating hits. Do you agree with their opinions? Explain why or why not.
   (b) Which programs currently running are hits? What do you think accounts for their success?
2. "*Universal is enticing viewers not with words or complicated plots, but with the way a series looks.*"
   (a) Do you agree or disagree that visual appeal is more important than plot or script? Explain.
   (b) Which of this season's television series have strong visual appeal? Which elements — for example, costumes, location — contribute to the visual appeal of these programs?
   (c) Which of this season's hits do not depend on visual appeal? What, in your opinion, accounts for their success?
3. "*No one will ever accuse the television industry of living on the edge.*" Do you agree? Is television too bland? What shows on television stand out in your mind as being "a little out of the ordinary"? Were these shows among your personal favourites?
4. Are popular programs necessarily *good* programs? Working in groups, develop a list of criteria for quality programs. Apply these to shows currently considered hits.

YOUR TURN

1. Be a critic. Using the criteria for quality programming you developed earlier, write a review of a series you watch often. Your purpose in writing is to recommend the series to others. Consider the series' setting, its plot line and pacing, and the characters.
   or
   Review one or two episodes of a series that is not doing well in the ratings this year. How do you explain the low ratings?
2. You are the head of a writing team that is developing a new TV series. It will be a "big-budget" production. You must create a show that will have a powerful visual impact on viewers.

   With a partner, decide on a "look" for the show that will make it distinctive. Briefly describe some of the elements (costumes, sets, locations, time period, and so on) that will contribute to the visual appeal of the series. Create an advertising poster that demonstrates the show's visual appeal.
   or
   You and a partner are the hosts of a televised entertainment magazine such as *Entertainment Tonight*. Script a segment of the program in which you discuss trends in this season's hits and flops — for example, a shift away from sitcoms to action/adventure series, or the rise of new types of heroes or stars. Videotape your segment *or* present it "live" for the class.

Media Facts & Techniques

The Ratings Game

Commercial television is a business, and like any business the major commercial networks (in Canada these include CTV, Global, and — to some extent — CBC; in the United States, ABC, NBC, CBS, and Fox) exist to make money. The success of commercial networks depends on you, the consumer and audience.

In commercial television the stations or networks use the revenues received from the sale of advertising time to purchase or produce programs. The audience for any given program determines the amount of money that can be charged for a 30-or 60-second ad. (Under Canadian broadcasting regulations there can be up to 12 minutes of advertising per hour.) Advertisers naturally want as many people as possible to see their ads.

Understanding the meaning of some basic terms will help you to appreciate the relationship between ratings, revenues, and program scheduling and content.

Demographics: the process of dividing the public into several groups with certain common characteristics (for example, males between the ages of 25 and 35 with a university education; females from 40 to 50 who have never worked outside the home).

Target Core Audience: the demographic group to which a program is designed to appeal.

Audience Share: the portion of the total television viewing audience that is watching a specific program at any given time. A *30 audience share* means that 30 per cent of all the people who were watching television in that hour were tuned to that program.

Audience Flow: measures the percentage of people who switch channels at the end of the program as well as which channel they turn to.

Prime Time: the hours between 8:00 and 11:00 in the evening, when television attracts the most viewers of all types. During Sunday evenings — which draw the largest audience — prime-time hours extend from 7:00 to 11:00 pm.

Nielsen Ratings: the ranking of television shows from the most to the least watched, based on an estimate of audience share. Nielsen ratings were originally obtained by having viewers fill out detailed questionnaires, called *diaries*. In the U.S. a mechanical recording device called an *Audimeter* was attached to the viewers' TV to record the times the set was turned on and the channels tuned. However, the Audimeter cannot give information about the individual viewer. The Nielsen company later introduced a computerized system called *The People Meter*, which can also record information about who is watching a particular channel. Together with the diaries, the Nielsen People Meter is used by the major U.S. networks and will be introduced in Canada in 1989.

WIZARD OF ID
BY BRANT PARKER & JOHNNY HART
SEVEN O'CLOCK AND ALL'S WELL!
...EIGHT O'CLOCK WILL BE MOVED TO NINE O'CLOCK...
....AND NINE O'CLOCK WILL BE HEARD ON TUESDAY
© 1987 North America Syndicate, Inc.
JUST WHAT I NEED.... A RATINGS WAR BETWEEN THE NORTH AND SOUTH TOWER

INVESTIGATING THE MEDIA

1. Do you like what you see on television? Use the following chart to record your opinions about different categories of shows on network TV.

   (a) Put a check beside each type of TV show on the list that you rate as either "very good" or "excellent."

   (b) Indicate in the second column whether you would like to see "more" or "less" of each type of show.

Type of Show	Personal Rating (Indicate with a check the types of shows you rate as "very good" or "excellent.")	Would you like to see "more" or "less" of this type of show? Why?
Sitcoms		
Soap Operas (Daytime)		
Nighttime Soaps		
Game Shows		
Network Shows		
Talk Shows		
Movies		
Sports		
Action/Adventure		
Crime/Detective		
Mini-Series		
Drama		

2. Working in groups, examine the content and style of programs scheduled in different selected time slots on different networks. Based on your observations, draft a description of the likely target core audience for the programs you watch. Present a brief report on your findings.
3. A 1982 survey conducted by the Television Audience Assessment Service produced the following findings:
   - Nearly half of all viewers are eating, washing dishes, reading, telephoning, or doing something else while "watching" television.
   - Half the audience leaves the room at least once during a show. And less than two-thirds of the audience for an average hour-long program watches to the end.
   - Viewers give full attention to only one-third of the programs they watch.

   Share your opinions on the following:

   (a) What do these findings indicate about viewers' attitudes towards television?

   (b) What do they suggest about the reliability of program ratings?

   (c) What influence might these findings have on
   - networks?
   - advertisers?

YOUR TURN

1. Working in small groups, prepare a proposal for a new television series. Your proposal should include the following:

   (a) a profile of the target audience for the show

   (b) a point-form outline for the show establishing the show's plot, characters, and setting

   (c) preferred placement in the network's schedule

   (d) possible sponsors who would specifically benefit from the target audience viewer group

   Role-play a presentation of your proposal, with other students acting as network executives and advertisers. Following the role-play, discuss the reasons why your proposal was or was not accepted.

Situation comedies have been part of network schedules since the early days of television. Their popularity fluctuates from time to time, but there has never been a year when TV did not offer a sitcom or two.

Today's Morality Play: The Sitcom

In the controversy over TV evangelism, no one seemed to have noticed that the most influential preacher in America was not Jim Bakker or Jerry Falwell or John Cardinal O'Connor. Rather it was Bill Cosby.

Every week his program and some others — *Family Ties*, *Growing Pains*, *Mr. Belvedere*, and *My Sister Sam* — present vivid and appealing paradigms of love to vast audiences. This love is disclosed by the resolution of family tensions in the lives of characters who have become as real as your next-door neighbors — the Huxtable family of *The Cosby Show*: Heathcliff, Claire, Sondra, Denise, Vanessa, Theo, and Rudi; *Family Ties'* Alex, Andy, Jennifer and Mallory and their "parents," Steven and Elyse.

So we learn, without even realizing it, how to live lovingly in families. The popularity of family situation comedies is so great, in fact, that in 1987 *The Cosby Show* and *Family Ties* became, respectively, the first and second most-watched programs in the history of television.

We laugh at the familiar pattern of conflict and tension created by family conflicts, trivial and not so trivial, like the possibility that an overstudious young woman will skip a grade; an engagement announcement; a 50th birthday; a big telephone bill; a fight between young lovers; a decision by a boy that he wants to take flying lessons; a wedding anniversary of grandparents; the divorce of two friends; an assault of flu on the family. As we laugh we see the virtues required for conflict resolution: such frequently honored but difficult qualities as patience, trust, sensitivity, honesty, generosity, flexibility, and forgiveness.

• • •

The shows rarely draw explicit moral conclusions for us. Usually they do not insist on hammering home ethical principles. Rather they hint lightly at the skills and traits that sustain love.

A modern version of the medieval morality play has slipped into prime-time television almost without anyone noticing it.

There are exceptions to the general restraint about moralizing and preaching: After the final commercial in an episode of *Growing Pains*, Kirk Cameron, who plays Mike, steps out of character to emphasize the importance of saying "no" to cocaine, addressing the young people in the audience directly. In an hour-long episode of *Family Ties* in which Alex — Michael J. Fox — mourns for a dead friend, he faces squarely problems of life and death, meaning and belonging, faith and despair.

But *The Cosby Show* rarely attempts to preach directly on the need for family love. It doesn't have to. Albert Bergesen, a sociology professor at the University of Arizona and a student of popular culture, argues that the appeal of *The Cosby Show* is to be found in the intensity of family love "into which we slip when the program begins. It is like a Franklin stove radiating warmth around which we crowd on a cold winter night. We know about rising divorce rates, single-parent families, abortion, incest, spousal abuse, teenage pregnancy, but when the Huxtables are on screen we absorb their affection of a functioning intact family and feel good. When the program is over, we are more hopeful for families and for our own family. It isn't merely the gentle moral lesson. It's the appeal of love."

An escape?

When I listen to Sir Georg Solti and the Chicago Symphony it's an escape too. But it's also a renewal. *Cosby* reached No. 1 because it has mastered the art of renewing hope for the family. Your family.

The Cosby Show, then, provides moral paradigms and displays warm and renewing love.

Family life has been the raw material of much of Bill Cosby's humor from the beginning of his career, and it has always been a humor of love. Perhaps his doctorate in education has made him more reflective about what he is doing, more conscious of the moral and religious issues he is tackling; but he has always been in his own way a minister of the word.

Portrait of family love—*The Cosby Show*'s Huxtable family

This program and the others are based on the insight that implicit ethics and religion in a matrix of humor are highly commercial in a country where meaning and belonging are as important as they have ever been and where those institutions traditionally charged with meaning and belonging — churches and schools — are failing to deliver sufficient amounts of either.

Critics of both the Right and the Left have been attacking the family comedies lately, as they will do when something is extraordinarily successful. The programs, it is said, are shallow and superficial. They do not depict the anguish and suffering of many families or the discrimination against many black families. They ignore the misery and unhappiness that plague many husband-wife and parent-children relationships. They deal only with intact upper-middle-class families. The characters are wimps, never wanting to get away from the family and go to a Bulls game.

Like much media criticism, these comments are the result of the fallacy of misplaced genre. A half-hour TV program is not a three-hour Broadway production. A miracle play is not a sociological report or an ideological indoctrination. It paints with quick, broad strokes and says to us not "this is the way all families are" or "this is what you must do" but rather "these are the skills needed to make intimacies work."

Those who demand that *Cosby* be more "militant" fail completely to understand the subtle boundaries that separate genres and the damage you do when you blur these boundaries. Should *The Cosby Show* be turned into an ideological platform, its fragile magic would be destroyed.

The basic objection to *Cosby* et al. is that they are about intact middle class families, a social institution that many Americans in the cultural elite (and this includes not a few clerics) think (or would like to think) is obsolete.

What's wrong with a few programs about intact families?

Television viewers in America, including many who are not intact families, seem to disagree with that cultural elite. Based on the popularity of these shows, the public apparently believes that an intact family is better on the whole than an unintact family. Sometimes it may be necessary to be a single parent, but on the whole it is better to be a married parent. Because single parents and broken families are increasing, it does not follow, the public seems to think, that the intact and affectionate family is any less the ideal or that familial love, even in unusual situations, is any less important.

The appeal of the shows is their portrait of family love, whether the family be intact or not.

— Andrew Greeley
The New York Times
May 17, 1987

EXPLORING IDEAS

1. Do you agree with the writer that family shows should demonstrate "the skills needed to make intimacies work"? Or, as the critics suggest, should they more accurately reflect "the way things are"? Support your point of view.
2. What qualities and characteristics would the "ideal" TV sitcom about family life have, in your view?

INVESTIGATING THE MEDIA

1. Examine other types of shows; for example, a game show, an action adventure, a rock video. Pay particular attention to the setting, the personality of the characters, the plot line. In small groups, discuss: *What values do these shows promote?*
2. For your next two or three journal entries, comment on the way in which conflicts are resolved in the programs you watch. How realistic are the solutions? What alternative solutions can you suggest? Share with a partner the journal entry you like best.

YOUR TURN

1. In small groups, brainstorm a list of everyday family situations that have potential for humour — for example, meeting your boyfriend's/girlfriend's parents for the first time.

   Select one of the situations and improvise the dialogue that might occur. Then script a brief scene from a family sitcom. Present your scene on videotape or "live" for the class.

“They’re one of the most scorned aspects of popular culture, but soap operas remain one of TV’s most enduring and influential forms.”

— Bill Anderson
“Why Soap Operas Wash”

Why, do you think, do critics love to hate soap operas? Which side are you on? If you’re a fan, why do you watch? If you’re not a fan, why not?

Soap opera ‘disease’ claiming more victims

A friend whose taste in popular culture rarely sinks lower than the occasional James Bond flick became a dedicated follower of the sci-fi escapades on the TV soap opera *General Hospital*. Another whose only serial indulgence used to be a Sunday morning fix of *Coronation Street* ran out to buy a video recorder to tape seven-year-old, weekday afternoon segments of the same show — as well as *General Hospital* and *Ryan’s Hope*. A student friend confessed to a particular weakness for CHCH’s humorous soap opera commentator, Vic Cummings.

The same week, *Newsweek* and TIME ran stories on a new disease, “General Hospitalitis,” and *Rolling Stone* ran a preppies’ guide to the soaps. A Toronto fraternity threw a *General Hospital* party ($4 admission; $3 if one dressed as a character from the show), while 600 fans from across Canada and the United States flew to Los Angeles and paid $25 a head to catch a glimpse of the cast of the top-rated serial.

Two actors on *General Hospital* flew to Chicago to do *Phil Donahue* and were treated with the respect usually reserved for former First Ladies and Academy Award-winners. And then, speaking of Academy Award-winners, Elizabeth Taylor *asked* to do a guest appearance on her favorite daytime show, *General Hospital*. What next? Well, there’s a rumor making the rounds that Mick Jagger will pop up on *As the World Turns* ...

Television producer Carol Burtin-Fripp of TVOntario first became interested in the soaps “long ago” when she was in university. “I took sociology as one of my courses and there in the required reading was how soap operas are put together,” she says. “What interested me was how they put so much thought into who played whom, how the characters should look, at what point people should be punished, and the tremendous amount of market research done to gratify the needs and wishes of the audience.”

That’s to be expected. Compared to the costs of prime-time television, soap operas are relatively cheap to produce and earn tremendous profits for the networks, but they are a long-term investment. It is not easy to create a new daytime drama and build a new audience, but it is easy to lose viewers by killing off the wrong characters or introducing irritating ones.

Listening to the viewers has paid off, with huge audiences for the top programs, more male viewers, and certainly a more dedicated following among younger viewers. All this Miss Burtin-Fripp finds somewhat disconcerting. “According to the evidence I’ve seen, soap operas do indeed shape how we interact in the world," she says, "whether it's a question of how safe our streets are, how good our doctors are, and so on."

Prime-time programs deliver many of the same messages as daytime shows do, but the context is different. The effect of the daily routine of soap opera and heavy emotional content is that "the viewer, especially the unsophisticated viewer, can't tell the difference between reality and what he sees on the screen," says Mark Freiman, a University of Toronto professor who teaches a course on culture and media in Canada. TVOntario quotes him as calling soaps "video Valium."

The entire appeal of soap opera, Freiman says, is in the display of suffering. "So, one of two very undesirable things happens. Either the viewer is entertained by watching the suffering, or the viewer learns that to suffer is the human condition."

His course spends less than a week a year on daytime drama and Freiman follows none of the 13 programs on the air, but he is cynical about the networks' claims of technical and dramatic advancements in the past few years. The much-heralded remote location tapings, which take viewers out of the studios to such faraway spots as the Caribbean, South America, or a Long Island beach, Freiman dismisses as opportunities "to parade female actors around in skimpy bathing suits." As for the proud claims of Agnes Nixon, creator of *All My Children* and other shows, that daytime TV now has social relevance and can be used to teach viewers about such problems as diabetes, spousal abuse, and alcoholism, Freiman retorts, "You can't make a marshmallow fudge sundae nutritious by sprinkling crunchy granola on top."

Freiman speaks calmly but with passion about soap operas — he doesn't watch them now, but he was hooked in the past. "When I was 7 and home from school for the summer holidays, I was hopelessly addicted and had to watch two hours a day." The experience was a formative one and images have stuck. "I still remember death row scenes where the heroine was saved in the nick of time by a confession, and I imagine that some of my expectations of art and culture have been formed by those early experiences."

On the other side of the debate is another born-again video professor. "I didn't even know what a soap opera was," says Dr. Mary Cassata of her familiarity with the genre, before she started teaching a 1977 seminar on soaps at the State University of New York at Buffalo. "My mother never watched soap operas or listened to them on the radio."

As Miss Cassata began to explore the field, she real-

Academy Award-winner Elizabeth Taylor—She *asked* to do a guest appearance on the TV soap opera *General Hospital.*

ized that most communications research focused on prime-time programming. "Nobody was paying attention to what was going on in daytime, and it was dealing with some very mature themes which would be censored right off the air in prime time." So she created Project Daytime, an effort co-ordinated with 19 other communications professors in the United States, Great Britain, and the Netherlands. Cassata has learned a great deal about the afternoon audience, and would classify it as loyal rather than addicted.

"My own theory is that people who watch soap operas are watching *programs*, are very involved and not apathetic at all in their viewing, whereas people who watch prime-time TV tend to be watching without being as deliberate ... Daytime people will not substitute one soap easily for another."

Viewers have seen tremendous changes on daytime in the past few years — more location shooting; fantastic, science-fiction adventure stories; characters drawn in shades of grey; and certainly more youth-oriented plot lines. "It's away from the hospital and the bedroom and the interpersonal relationships," Miss Cassata says.

The potential power of the soaps' influence, Miss Cassata says, is both "good and bad." One of the soaps' underlying messages that disturbs her is "that money will buy anything. Money is a very corrupting force in daytime ... a terrible message to give young people." But, as in the great instalment tradition of Dickens and the Bible, Miss Cassata sees soap opera as tremendously entertaining and an excellent vehicle for worthwhile stories about the human condition. In fact, she and two former students have been putting together an outline for a continuing drama that would incorporate various social themes, and two of the American networks have expressed interest in seeing their proposal.

— Hester Riches
The Globe and Mail
November 1981

EXPLORING IDEAS

1. Mr. Freiman states: *"The effect of the daily routine of soap opera and heavy emotional content is that the viewer, especially the unsophisticated viewer, can't tell the difference between reality and what he sees on the screen."* Do you agree or disagree with his opinion? What evidence can you offer to support your point of view?
2. Evaluate Dr. Cassata's views on daytime soaps.

INVESTIGATING THE MEDIA

1. Working in groups, develop a list of examples from soap operas to support or dispute the claim that "daytime TV now has social relevance." What messages do these soaps present? Prepare a report based on your observations and conclusions.
2. Critics have suggested that some prime-time series have borrowed elements of soap operas to achieve their success. Which series currently on TV demonstrate this borrowing from soaps? What elements do they have in common with daytime drama?

YOUR TURN

1. Imagine you write for a soap-opera digest. Prepare a report on your favourite soap or one that you "love to hate." Focus your report on the plot and the social commentary you feel the writers are trying to inject into the story line. The tone of your article can be serious, critical, or humorous.
   or
   Develop an outline for a soap opera set in your own school or community. Outline the characters, setting, and possible plot complications. Then write a TV listings entry for the first episode.
2. Develop a plot outline for an episode of your favourite television sitcom or soap opera. Work with a partner or in small groups.

CAN CANADIAN TELE-VISION COMPETE?

"Ninety-six per cent of the drama programs available on Canadian television represent the imaginary world of another people.... (Culture) is what makes a people interesting, worthy of attention by the rest of the world. A strong Canadian culture lies at the heart of political sovereignty."

— Pierre Juneau, president of the CBC, in *The Burlington Spectator* June 4, 1987

Our government and members of the media industry in Canada continually stress the need for more Canadian content on radio and television. Does the Canadian public share this view? Consider the comments in the following articles.

America wins ratings game

Every week, the Bureau of Broadcast Measurement sends out press releases announcing the Top 10 shows on Canadian network TV.

And every week, there's something funny about the BBM's 10 most-watched shows on Canadian television.

Almost all of them are American.

Of the Top 10 shows on Canadian TV during the first week of April 1987, only two were Canadian: *Hockey Night in Canada* and ... wait for it ... *NHL Hockey Playoffs*.

Each year, the federal government shells out millions of tax dollars to support Canadian programming on television. The importance of Canadian culture is a constant theme in free-trade talks. The Canadian Radio-television and Telecommunications Commission demands that Canadian content play a vital role in the program schedules of all Canadian television stations.

And yet, given a free choice, Canadian viewers have crowned Bill Cosby the undisputed king of Canadian television.

The Cosby Show attracted more than 5 million viewers on the first Thursday in April 1987. That's about 2.3 million more than the top-rated Canadian show — *Hockey Night in Canada*'s April 4 telecast of the game between the Toronto Maple Leafs and the Chicago Blackhawks — managed to pull in.

The following is BBM's list of Canada's Top 10 English network TV shows for the week of April 2 to April 8, 1987.

1. *The Cosby Show* (CTV) – 5.15 million viewers.
2. *Family Ties* (CTV) – 4.445 million viewers.
3. *Cheers* (CTV) – 3.064 million viewers.
4. *Hockey Night in Canada*: Chicago Blackhawks vs. Toronto Maple Leafs (CBC, April 4) – 2.886 million viewers.
5. *NHL Playoffs*: Toronto Maple Leafs vs. St. Louis Blues, Game 1 (CBC, April 8) – 2.766 million viewers.
6. *Dallas* (CBC) – 2.642 million viewers.
7. *Moonlighting* (CTV) – 2.450 million viewers.
8. *Sunday Movie: Daddy* (CTV, April 5) – 2.183 million viewers.
9. *MacGyver* (CTV) – 2.154 million viewers.
10. *Night Court* (CTV) – 2.151 million viewers.

— Eric Kohanik
The Burlington Spectator
May 1, 1987

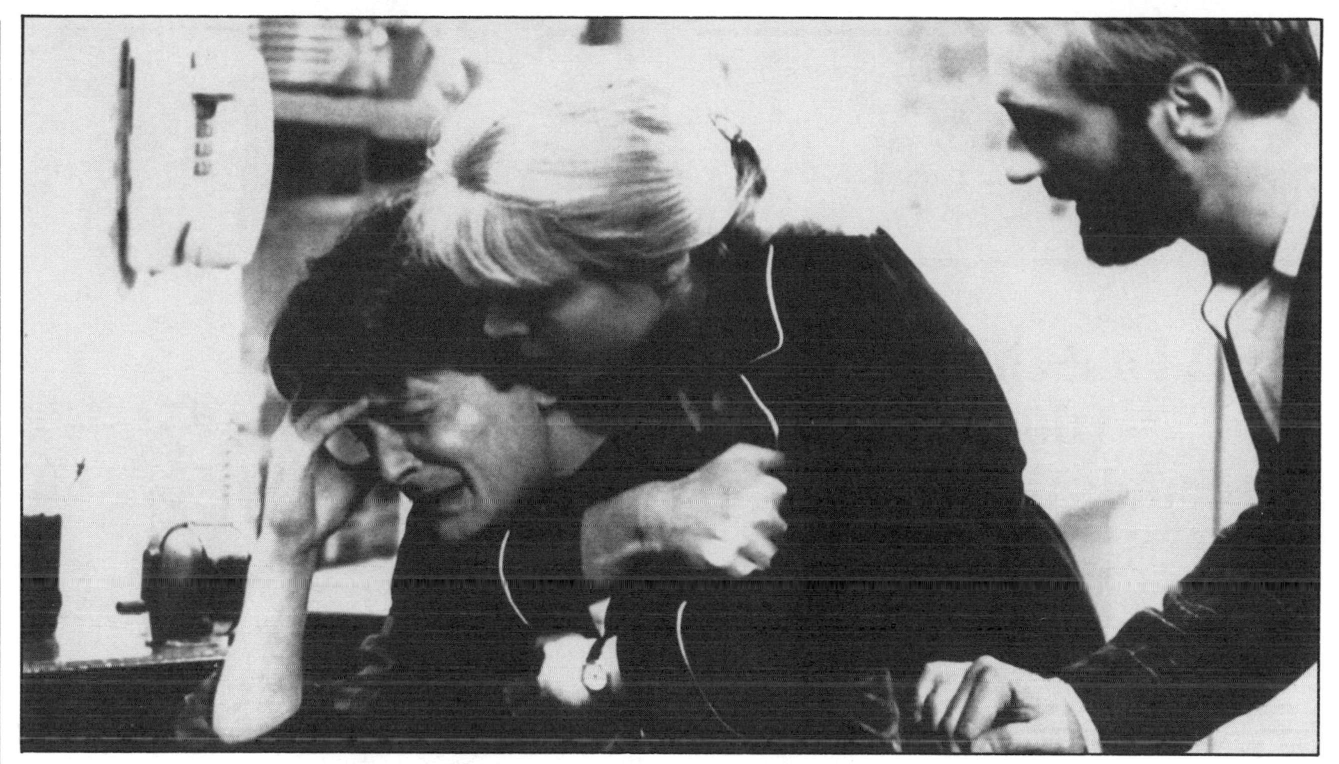

Alex (Michael J. Fox), Elyse (Meredith Baxter Birney), and Steven (Michael Gross) of *Family Ties*—The American sitcom is one of the Top 10 shows on Canadian TV.

Tough times for the CBC

For 50 years, the Canadian Broadcasting Corp. has been the principal sword and shield for Canadian culture in the face of steady bombardment from U.S. broadcasters. As the 1990s approach, the undiminished clutter of American programs on our private TV networks, cable and pay-TV hook-ups is persuasive evidence that a strong CBC is as vital as ever to our national identity.

Despite severe assaults on its budget by successive governments, the CBC still gets 40 per cent of Ottawa's culture money. Yet these are dark days for public broadcasting. In 1985 and 1986, the CBC had to lay off 425 employees, and cut nearly 1100 positions. A further 400 jobs had to be eliminated in 1987. Its plans to beef up Canadian content are on indefinite hold.

We wonder why the Tories, who created the CBC in the depths of the Great Depression, seem so reluctant to use it to stop the American takeover of our culture. In the fall of 1986, the Caplan-Sauvageau report reminded us that 98 per cent of our English-language TV drama is foreign in content, most of it American.

Criticizing private networks for this dearth of Canadian shows, Caplan-Sauvageau pointed out that "it is upon the CBC that we must rely for an abundance of compelling radio and television programs — by, for, and about Canadians."

— *The Toronto Star*
February 23, 1987

EXPLORING IDEAS

1. In the survey you did earlier, how many of the television programs identified by your class as "personal favourites" were *Canadian* productions? How do you account for the results?
2. To what extent do you agree with this statement from the editorial: *"A strong CBC is as vital as ever to our national identity"*?

   Do you agree or disagree that the Americans are taking over our culture? Support your opinion.

In the next article Mr. Bawden expresses his views on the differences between the American and Canadian television industries. Why do you think Canadian audiences prefer U.S. programs?

A long-time critic (finally) counts the reasons U.S. TV beats all

Jim Bawden, long-time TV critic

"Why isn't Canadian TV as good as American TV?" It's a question I've been fielding for the past decade as a TV critic. Industry insiders continually ask it of one another. The general public wants to know why Canadian TV can't produce anything as popular and slick as *Dynasty*. Heck, even the CRTC has devoted dozens of hearings and millions of words to the perplexing problem of why Canadians seem to prefer a steady diet of American TV fare.

On a recent flying visit to Hollywood all the factors that make up the sum total of my answers suddenly seemed to come together. Let's itemize them in descending order of importance.

• The American Big Three networks are so rich they can cope with a failure rate of 90 per cent and still make the huge profits necessary to survive. That may not be the case in the future, with narrowcasting cable networks eating into the general audience, but for now even the lowest-rated show guarantees the networks some profit.

Several seasons ago there was only one new hit, *Falcon Crest*, and it made it through the back gate by being positioned behind front-running *Dallas*. To get that one hit, CBS spent $70 million on program development — money spent on producers, script development from first draft to shooting, stage and pilot shooting. Some of the projects wound up as special TV-movies. But the majority of funding was spent on ideas that never reached the filmed stage. Give the CBC drama department $70 million a year to play around with and you'd wind up with just as many slick productions as CBS.

• American networks love stars; CBC distrusts them. When *King of Kensington* became a surprise hit (and CBC's only popular sitcom since the days of *The Plouffe Family*), it was largely because of the popularity and professionalism of its star, Al Waxman. CBC should have grabbed him and developed another series, banking on his high TV visibility. Truth to tell, there were talks, but Waxman finally tired of CBC's desultory interest. He's now in Hollywood co-starring in an American cops-and-robbers saga, *Cagney & Lacey*. The Al Waxman saga has been repeated dozens of times. Either CBC doesn't understand how to nurture talent, or it doesn't want to.

• A one-hour drama can cost as much as $800 000 to produce in today's market, far more than the cost of an entire season's worth of a CBC series. But networks do not pay the studios nearly enough (for the licence fee of one run and one repeat) to make ends meet.

Grant Tinker, when he was president of MTM Productions, used to joke he was mortgaged to the Crocker Bank. When *Mary Tyler Moore* hit syndication, the windfall started — stations in New York and Los Angeles were paying about $100 000 for each episode (at six runs). *Laverne & Shirley* and *M*A*S*H* will each make more in reruns than *Star Wars* ever garnered at the box office. If a half-hour comedy lasts five seasons it is virtually guaranteed vast profits in the rerun market. CBC shows are rarely rerun (*The Beachcombers* is a notable exception).

So far, Canadian producers seem to lack the entrepreneurial skills to score in the lush U.S. market.

• Finally, for all our addiction to U.S. sitcoms, don't we agree it's better to at least try for some balance? The U.S. has PBS, but it is woefully underfunded. If Canadian TV sometimes reeks of American cultural pollution, that's merely the forces of the marketplace at work. The Americans are richer and craftier when it comes to fashioning mass-appeal, low-brow entertainment series, that's all.

— Jim Bawden
Starweek

EXPLORING IDEAS

1. *"The Americans are richer and craftier when it comes to fashioning mass-appeal, low-brow entertainment series."* Do you agree? If not, what factors do you think account for the success of U.S. series? Cite specific examples to support your opinion.
2. Canada is one of the most "cabled" countries in the world — viewers have access to programs produced in other countries and a tremendous range of choice on television. Is this a positive or negative situation? Debate this issue informally in class.
3. Should Canadian TV try to compete in the area of mass entertainment? Explain.

INVESTIGATING THE MEDIA

1. In groups, prepare a chart like the following. Use your summary as a basis for comparing Canadian and American television. Focus your discussion on the programs that are likely to have stronger audience appeal. What causes one program to be more popular than another? Have you found any differences not mentioned in the article? Does your group agree that American TV beats all — every time? Be prepared to share your group's findings and ideas with the class.

Type of Program	Canadian	American	Description/ Characteristics
Game Show	Definition	Wheel of Fortune	
Sitcom			
Mystery/Drama			
Crime/Drama			
Special			
Documentary			
News			

2. Compare a typical evening of prime-time TV on the CBC with that of a commercial U.S. network. Are you satisfied with the amount of Canadian content on the CBC? Prepare and present a report based on your observations and conclusions.

In this article one of the stars of the sitcom Airwaves explains why she believes the program was a distinctly Canadian creation.

Roberta says mom doesn't know best

Jean Lipton (Roberta Maxwell) is a 40ish radio journalist and single mother who's happily proving that the family unit — by whatever definition — is alive and well. The clan includes daughter Zoe (Ingrid Veninger), grandfather Bobby (Roland Hewgill), and Jean's nephew Matt (Christopher Bolton), spending time with his aunt while his own folks are off to work in Saudi Arabia.

While critics grapple with definitions for *Airwaves*, calling it everything from a situation comedy to high drama, Maxwell believes it's unique to television. "It's a great combination of wit, humor, and intelligence," she says. "It's not a stereotype of an American sitcom. I think the airwaves of Canada need another clone of an American sitcom like they need another dose of acid rain."

When the comedy in sitcoms often relies on the conflict of stereotypical characters and attitudes, the characters on *Airwaves* are anything but one dimensional. "It really attempts to break new ground. I think people are willing and are interested in new creations," says Maxwell.

The humor exists within a dramatic framework where Jean has dealt with the death of her husband and welcomed her widowed father into her home, making for a unique three-generation living arrangement. Dear old dad does most of the cooking and keeps busy taking courses. Daughter Zoe, on the other hand, has forfeited university to pursue more artistic endeavors while she waits tables at a trendy bistro.

But Maxwell insists it isn't a show where mother knows best. "Quite frankly, mother doesn't know best. But mother knows something and it's an enlightened point of view."

The series was produced by Janice Platt for Atlantis Films Limited. Platt says *Airwaves* differs from other TV series because there's no laugh track forcing guffaws every 15 seconds. And if *Airwaves* looks different than other TV shows, it's because it was shot like a film in a 360-degree setting where viewers see every room in the house from every imaginable angle.

The 1987 season not only brought Jean's nephew Matt to the show but a new co-worker at the radio station named Dale Campbell (Patrick Rose). Producer Platt says the preppy Matt and the oh-so-vain Dale provide more dramatic tension and comic relief to the show. Similarly, the 1987 episodes dealt with smaller issues and everyday situations rather than the broad social concerns that proved too unwieldy for a half-hour format.

Maxwell, primarily a stage actress who has done everything from Neil Simon comedy to Shakespearean tragedy, credits the popularity of *Airwaves* to Atlantis's belief that television audiences are more intelligent than many presume.

"*Airwaves* comes from Canadians. It comes from their consciousness and it can't fit into the Hollywood stereotype. It has a distinct Canadian style. The sooner we have faith in it, the better."

— John Tanasychuk
The Burlington Spectator
May 2, 1987

EXPLORING IDEAS

1. "Airwaves *comes from Canadians. It comes from their consciousness and it can't fit into the Hollywood stereotype. It has a distinct Canadian style. The sooner we have faith in it, the better.*"

   As a class, discuss the validity of this statement. Is the Canadian consciousness different from that of Americans? In which ways? If *you* were producing a Canadian television show, how would you reflect these differences in the content and style of your program?

INVESTIGATING THE MEDIA

1. If possible, arrange a viewing of one or two episodes of *Airwaves* or another Canadian sitcom. Evaluate the program in comparison with American sitcoms currently on television; *is* it different from the U.S. series? Which do you prefer, *Airwaves* or Hollywood sitcoms? Why?

YOUR TURN

1. Design an outline for a Canadian dramatic series that would, in your opinion, be superior to existing Canadian television programs. In developing your outline, consider the following:
   - characters — identity, basic personality
   - target audience
   - typical story lines, conflicts and resolutions
   - production elements such as settings and costumes

   or

   Imagine you are part of a group creating an advertising campaign for a new CBC series. Your purpose is to attract a large audience share for the first episode.

   (a) Begin by reaching agreement in your group about the type of program you will be advertising, general story lines, and the time the program will be scheduled for broadcast.

   (b) Check TV listings so that you are aware of the programs scheduled by competing networks on the day and time you have advertised.

   (c) Decide how you will advertise the new series.

   (d) Present your campaign ideas to the class.

   When you present your ideas, the rest of the class will serve as network executives. Their job will be to evaluate your suggestions and decide whether to accept, reject, or ask for changes in your campaign.

Jean Lipton (Roberta Maxwell) of *Airwaves*—Mom combines wit and intelligence in this distinctly Canadian sitcom.

There are always two sides in every debate. Canadians have indeed created some excellent (and successful) television programs, as the writer of the next article explains.

Searching for God in the soul of Man

On the television screen, a patient at a Hamilton, Ont., psychiatric hospital is about to receive electroshock therapy. Terrified, she struggles against the calm-voiced hospital personnel and shrieks, "Don't take my heart out!" Same time, same channel, but on a different Wednesday night: Canadian citizens Israel and Frania Rubinek, Jews who survived the Nazi Holocaust, return to Poland for the first time in more than 40 years. There, they have an emotional reunion with the farm family that sheltered them for 28 months in a cellar, and they recall how they survived the war through what Frania describes as "so many miracles."

Both stories are recent episodes from the CBC's eclectic, nondenominational religious affairs program, *Man Alive*. Now in its 20th season, the show that wrestles with the angels of contemporary ethics has won more than 50 international awards. Its audience of one million viewers per week ranges from letter-writing zealots who are frequently outraged by the program's open-mindedness, to a Langley, B.C., minister who has distributed "Watch *Man Alive*" bumper stickers to his flock. Yet *Man Alive* squeaks by on $15 000 per half-hour episode.

The show takes its name and broad mandate from a quotation by a second-century French saint, Irenaeus, who observed that "the glory of God is in man fully alive." In the course of two decades, the show's producers have profiled such important figures as Mother Teresa and South Africa's Desmond Tutu, then bishop of Johannesburg. In a candid 1985 profile, Tutu described how his boyhood heroes, baseball player Jackie Robinson and singer Lena Horne, showed him that Blacks could achieve greatness.

Man Alive has addressed issues ranging from the nuclear threat to the Vatican bank scandal of 1982 — a program that prompted testy letters from such prominent Roman Catholics as Toronto's Gerald Emmett Cardinal Carter. The show has scored several journalistic triumphs, including an audience with the Dalai Lama of Tibet, and an exclusive interview with Susan Nelles, the nurse who was charged with — and then exonerated from — having murdered four babies at Toronto's Hospital for Sick Children in 1981. But its biggest coup to date was the episode that opened its 1986-1987 season on Oct. 8: an interview with the Aga Khan, spiritual leader of the world's 15 million Ismaili Muslims.

The Aga Khan had already declined to appear on the CBS network's current affairs show *60 Minutes*. Instead, after a year of correspondence with *Man Alive's* producers, the articulate, soft-spoken billionaire gave his first formal television interview for a North American audience to the low-budget Canadian program. Although producer Katherine Smalley's exhaustive preliminary research on the Ismailis did much to persuade the Aga Khan to appear on *Man Alive*, the religious leader admitted that he was also impressed by the interviewing style of Roy Bonisteel, who has hosted the show since its inception.

With his resplendent white hair and earnest gaze, Bonisteel is often mistaken for a minister. He is in fact a journalist who once described religion as "a fascinating beat." He got his start in religious broadcasting at a St. Catharines, Ont., radio station in 1953 and produced syndicated radio shows for the United Church of Canada in the mid-1960s. In 1967 CBC executive producer Leo Rampen and the network's religious adviser, Rev. Brian Freeland, asked him to host a proposed new television show to be called *Man Alive*. Now, after more than 30 years of interviewing religious leaders from a multitude of faiths, Bonisteel concedes, "If someone said to me today, 'Go out and join a church,' I wouldn't know which one to choose."

Providing programming that has meaning for people of all faiths — and even for agnostics and atheists — is the secret of *Man Alive's* longevity. During the show's first season Toronto critic Nathan Cohen praised it as "an attempt to make religion an issue of vital concern rather than a matter of formal, official dogma." But organized worship is only one aspect of humanity

A Canadian coup—The Aga Khan (*right*) gives his first formal TV interview for a North American audience to Roy Bonisteel (*left*).

explored on *Man Alive*. Some of the shows best-received episodes have focused on how handicapped individuals meet the challenges of daily life. The profile *David*, which aired in 1980, chronicled the achievements of a mentally handicapped youth who had starred in a CBC television drama special, *One of Our Own*. Produced by Tom Kelly, the profile captured David McFarlane's inspiring determination and sense of humor as he struggled to memorize his lines. It won several international awards, including first prize at the 1980 American Film Festival in New York.

The show's award-winning episodes have been sold to 24 countries around the world, including Sweden, Israel, and Thailand.

Despite its increasingly stringent budget, *Man Alive* must maintain high ratings. Broadcast Wednesday nights at 9:30, the show has had to shift its focus to keep a 15-percent share of the viewing audience. Said Louise Lore, *Man Alive's* executive producer since 1980: "We're doing more controversial material than ever, but we're doing fewer shows on strictly theological issues. We came on the air in the wake of all the excitement and idealism of Vatican II — a time of incredible ferment and clergy activism. But the environment has changed. We can't get the ratings we need to survive in prime time with a show on [dissenting Swiss Catholic theologian] Hans Küng."

Shows in the 1986-1987 season reflected *Man Alive's* aggressively varied programming. They ranged from a documentary on Canada's decision to resume sending aid shipments to El Salvador to a fresh look at unidentified flying objects. The Jan. 14 episode, *Penetang — By Reason of Insanity*, examined life inside a maximum security psychiatric hospital. Although *Man Alive* has broadened its scope, its producers argue that it is as much a spiritual odyssey as a current affairs program. Said Lore: "I think of it as a religious program for a post-Christian age, and that's not the same thing as secular age. People may not go to church as often as they once did. But they still seek faith."

— Pamela Young
Maclean's
January 12, 1987

EXPLORING IDEAS

1. **(a)** What factors seem to account for the enduring success of CBC's *Man Alive*?
   (b) Develop a profile of the target audience for *Man Alive*.
2. Which other Canadian programs are also "enduring successes"? Explain the factors that account for the success, in your view.

YOUR TURN

1. Roy Bonisteel and the producers of *Man Alive* are interested in attracting an audience in your age group. At the same time, everyone working on the show wants to maintain the basic style and tone that have made it so popular over the years.

   With a partner, develop a list of topics and people to be interviewed on the program. Present a brief explanation of how these topics and people will meet the stated requirements.

TV'S EFFECTS ON SOCIETY

Statistics show that many of our waking hours are devoted to viewing programs on television. What are the consequences? Does watching television have any effect at all on the viewer? Can TV shape our attitudes and values, or influence our behaviour?

Does TV serve or enslave the family? George James attempts to answer that question in the next article, as he examines the impact television has on children and families.

Stay Tuned

Among the many elements that shape the growing child television is the most widely used and routinely condemned. Studies show that pre-school children watch four or more hours of TV a day. In less than 50 years television has passed out of the hands of its inventors and into almost every home with electricity. According to Statistics Canada 98.6 per cent of Canadian households own at least one TV. Almost half have two or more sets. In fact, it's no longer unusual for a home to have as many televisions as it has family members.

• • •

In 1985, Claudine Goller, an elementary teacher who specializes in the media, wrote a guide to TV literacy for use in Scarborough, Ontario schools. Goller is convinced that many parents and teachers underestimate television's influence. "The TV set has become a new member of the family," she says. "It sits in the corner and talks to anyone and everyone who cares to listen. It is never too busy to be good company, doesn't give orders, and is dependable. It has become so firmly entrenched that adults as well as children are unable to imagine what life would be like without it."

Apprehensive about television's effect on children, Goller has held seminars and workshops for teachers and given six-unit lessons to students from Kindergarten to Grade Eight on how to watch TV wisely. "Children should be taught that much of what they see on television is not real," she explains, "and because it is not real, it should be treated in the same way as other fantasy."

Many experts agree with Goller, despite some studies which suggest that even very young viewers are surprisingly skeptical of TV and try to square the wizardry of what they see with what they know to be true. These studies mirror what many parents already believe: that not every child will climb out of his bedroom window to see if he, like Superman, can fly, although most will probably test the idea out on the sofa.

This is not to say that children can easily separate reality from fantasy.

They may be skeptical of Superman, but they tend to believe in James Bond stunts and high-tech cars. To the average eight-year-old the home computer and the technology of the 22nd century are one and the same. As Murray, a Grade Four student remarks, "They have all that stuff already."

Yet television cannot be blamed for blurring the difference between fantasy and reality. Like all theatre it is based on the assumption that the audience must suspend its disbelief in order for the entertainment to work. After all, the moment Hamlet looks at his watch the illusion is lost.

It's because television is so successful technically — at blurring fantasy and reality that children, especially, are subject to its influence. But it isn't simply a case of seeing is believing, even if the young audience does believe much of what it sees. TV's effect on children appears to have a behavioural as well as a conceptual dimension. For example, research in the United States has shown that TV violence leads to a rise in aggressive behaviour in children. This isn't surprising. Aggression is the first language of childhood; by age two, most children have mastered its many nuances.

But television does more than show violence. By seldom presenting it truthfully — as random, squalid, and painful — TV bestows upon it an abstract legitimacy. When the hero decides to give the villain one last punch, even though the villain has surrendered, we applaud.

That punch, in any case, is achieved with a blend of camera angle, dubbed sound and crisp editing, and the result is not so much fantasy as exaggerated reality. A TV punch on the jaw SOUNDS like a punch on the jaw. A real-life punch, if heard, sounds like nothing much at all. Fourteen-year-old Roy, who recently witnessed an armed robbery, comments, "I didn't even know there had been shots. It sounded like a car back-firing."

According to Kate Moody in *Growing Up on Television*, by age five, the typical child in the United States has seen over 200 hours of violent images, "and the average 14-year-old has witnessed the killing of 13 000 human beings — usually without pain, funeral, or grieving relatives."

Such estimates are probably true of Canadian children, many of whom are familiar, as are children the world-over, with American programmes. In the late 1960s studies showed that Saturday morning children's television had six times the violence of adult prime time. If those figures are no longer true, it isn't because children's television has dramatically improved; but rather because adult programming is now setting the trend.

To be fair, Canadian children's programming isn't as "action-packed" as American TV. In most provinces the Canadian Broadcasting Corporation's (CBC) morning line-up (admittedly, intended for VERY young viewers) is exemplary. Outside of the news, parents would be hard-pressed to find ANY violence on that network. But then, the CBC is subsidized, which shields it from the harsher whips of free enterprise. Private broadcasters must juggle the need for advertising revenue with appropriate programming for children, although no spokesperson for CTV or Global was able to say precisely where the balance lies.

Understandably, many parents are concerned about the level of violence on TV. In 1976, the government of Ontario, under pressure from the public, established a Royal Commission on violence in the communications industry. The Commission's findings weren't surprising: there is too much violence on TV. With Ontario the most heavily cabled province in Canada, and most of the cable services offering rich diets of American-made programmes, it's no wonder that, ten years later, the issue has not gone away.

As for Canadian broadcasters, there are guidelines set by the Canadian Radio-television and Telecommunications Commission (CRTC) and the individual networks and stations concerned. Larry Schnurr, programming manager for CHCH TV in Hamilton, Ontario, explains: "The CRTC is concerned about violence. CHCH can purchase a programme and air it without CRTC clearance. However, we can be approached directly or held up at the licence review by CRTC if the programme doesn't adhere to the CRTC code." The CRTC admits, however, that since 1968, when the commission was established, no station has had its licence revoked.

Ultimately, how much violence children are exposed to on TV depends on how often and how indiscriminately they watch — which, in turn, depends on how concerned their parents are about what programmes they see. With many Canadian homes receiving a dozen or more channels, it isn't practical to assume that no violence will be shown during the hours children normally watch TV. Some stations will schedule such shows *knowing* that preteens will watch along with their parents. This pleases advertisers who want to reach adult audiences at less than prime-time rates.

Short of pulling the plug on the family TV, parents are advised to be aware of, if not actually watch, all the programmes their children see. As Claudine Goller says, "Parents can talk about television, about the programmes their children watch, about the amount of time they spend watching TV, about what they are learning from TV, values as well as ideas, and about the techniques that serve to convey messages."

There really is no substitute for parental supervision. The problem with TV violence isn't just knowing that it exists and that it influences children; it's knowing how to apportion to governments, broadcasters, advertisers, and ourselves the appropriate share of blame.

If TV does influence children, what about the commercials they see? Is there a strong moral argument for not allowing TV commercials intended for children at all, as the Quebec government decided in 1980? Nationwide, the CBC doesn't air commercials during children's programming, but because it's subsidized, the CBC, unlike private broadcasters, can afford its commercial-free policy. The bottom line for all TV is that somebody, somewhere, pays: the consumer or the taxpayer.

In fact, CBC's policy on advertising to children isn't as straightforward as it seems. Programmes such as the *Muppets* and *Fraggle Rock* are classified as "variety shows" and are therefore subject to the same commercial breaks as are other programmes. More to the point, it can be argued that the *Muppets* is an extended commercial itself. As David Owen says in his penetrating and compelling article *Where the Toys Come From* (*Atlantic Monthly*, October 1986), "The Muppets' creator, Henson Associates, is on almost everyone's list of top-quality producers, but the Muppets support a profitable stable of more than 500 licensed products, many of them toys. Henson even has its own New York toy store, called Muppet Stuff. Henson Associates, whatever else it is, is an extremely successful toy business, and Henson's shows, whatever else they are, are programme-length commercials."

Susan Burke, director of the standards division of the Canadian Advertising Foundation, a self-regulator organization which administers the broadcast code for the CRTC, admits that many parents are concerned about commercials aimed at children. "They are particularly worried about certain aspects of commercials such as the availability of combat and violent toys and how they are portrayed," she says. Asked about the current code for advertising to children, she adds, "It's under review."

According to Burke, 95-98 per cent of American commercials are rejected for use in Canada. "Each year, about 20 or 30 come up which are total washouts, violating almost every one of the code's regulations." Canadian advertisers fare much better. "Most are cleared at the first review," she says, "because many are submitted in script form and changes can be made before filming begins."

There are, of course, arguments on both sides for airing children's commercials. Certainly, no one defends the blatant hard sell, and there are various federal and provincial regulations to prevent it. But some experts, including many parents, say that children aren't capable of assessing *any* product's value, and therefore shouldn't be asked to. To this the manufacturers reply that good products (for children or adults) need to be advertised.

In fact, the Quebec government's 1980 ban on TV advertising directed at children was successfully challenged by Irwin Toy Ltd. in April 1981 in the Court of Appeal. Although the ban is still in effect, a decision on its constitutionality is expected by the Supreme Court of Canada in the spring of 1988.

But we aren't just talking about constitutional rights. The right to advertise is one issue. The opportunity to teach lifestyles to our children is another.

Nutrition is just one example. Broadcasters can hardly claim to provide their young viewers with a balanced diet. According to Kate Moody in *Growing Up on Television*, when a New York watchdog committee monitored TV advertisements, they found that "the most frequent commercials were for cereals, followed by candy and gum and then cookies and crackers, non-carbonated 'fruit' drinks, spaghetti and macaroni, cakes, pies, pastry, desserts, citrus, carbonated soda pop, ice cream, etc."

How television affects children isn't confined to the programmes and advertising they see. According to some researchers, just watching it, whatever the quality of the programme, may have negative physical effects on young viewers. Certainly, the more TV children watch, the less time they have for other activities, such as reading and imaginative play, but the research suggests that a heavy diet of TV, inhibiting as it can the acquisition of language, may also inhibit brain development. As Marie Winn says in *The Plug-In Drug*, "There *are* certain aspects of brain development that may be significantly affected by regular exposure to the television experience."

Nor should parents overlook that, while their children are watching TV, they aren't *doing*. In most cases they aren't even thinking. Television does the talking, doing, and thinking for them — and four hours of television a day is equivalent to one third of the pre-schooler's awake-time.

Coming to the defence of television, some will argue that it's a great educational tool, that children learn from it, and learn faster than they would otherwise. Doesn't *Sesame Street* teach children their numbers? And what about *Wonderworks*, *Owl* TV, and *Mr. Dressup*? Can't something be said in their favour?

The answer is: yes, of course it can. Compared to most children's TV, these programmes (and others) are fountains of delight.

But how effectively *do* they teach? All the indications are that children learn most, and retain knowledge longest, by *experiencing* the world directly. Unless it's constantly repeated, as are some songs and jingles, most children quickly forget what they learn from TV. As Moody says, "There are factors in the perceptual development of children that make them quite unready to take on TV viewing as a major experience. They need time for reflection in order to absorb and process experience, and they need lots of human interaction in order to learn optimally."

There's also the problem of sex stereotyping on TV. Though not as blatant as it was, it still exists. Creative Research, a company specializing in commercial research for government, manufacturers, and retailers, says that there are clear differences between what boys and girls watch on TV. In a pamphlet outlining a 1981 survey, the company says that girls are more likely than boys to be aware of shampoo and chocolate-bar commercials, with boys showing a preference for, among other things, hockey and cars.

Whatever else it's doing, TV is reinforcing perceived gender differences.

In fact, some experts contend that TV stereotypes the family, too, leading children to have unrealistic expectations about what their parents can be. "Even more serious," says Kate Moody, "is what TV does to family living patterns." Far from bringing them together, as was TV's early promise, the family is becoming increasingly fragmented and isolated. With programming targeted exclusively at either children or adults, what tends to happen is the television stays on from morning to night, while different family members take their turn in front of the set. According to Moody, "Even the illusion of togetherness is lost."

It's fashionable, of course, to criticize TV; it has been ever since the first sets brought their flickering, incandescent images into the family home. Our parents warned us not to sit too close to the screen, scolded us for watching too often, and then swore when the vertical hold lost its grip on Ed Sullivan. If, at the outset, TV was a member of the family, it was the baby, prone to every hiccough.

But perhaps that was part of its charm. In those days, TV was as fickle and unpredictable as any person. We rarely watched it much because it rarely worked; and when it did work we saw, even in mid-summer, a raging snowstorm.

Those were pioneering days. Today's children can zap through 40 channels, all in crisp, computer-locked colour, at the press of a button.

If our parents worried about radiation from television, we worry about the *habit* of TV. Of the families who stop watching TV altogether (and there aren't many who have) few seem to miss it once they are over the initial withdrawal symptoms. As Marie Winn says, "A feeling of pride that sometimes borders on the self-satisfied often characterizes the no-television-ever family. Though sometimes guilty of smugness, no-television-ever families may well have something to be smug about."

But, for most parents, giving up TV isn't a practical option, or even a wise one. To use a metaphorical pun, the issue of watching TV isn't black and white. For all its faults, television brings people and countries closer — a cry in China is a cry in Canada's suburbs.

Without it many children wouldn't learn about the horror of war or witness the spectacle of professional athletics. They might never see a play, an orchestra, parliamentary debate, or Charlie Chaplin.

The list is endless as we might expect. TV is too broad an industry to be labelled all good or all bad. It never has, and probably never will, sit comfortably with any sweeping generalizations. The programmes parents watch on TV and how often they watch will influence their children at least as much as the overall quality of television. In any case, the issue isn't about excellence or quantity. It's about who's in charge: us or the bright-eyed magician in the corner.

— George A. James
Today's Parent
March 1987

EXPLORING IDEAS

1. Discuss the following in small groups. Appoint one member to record and present your group's ideas to the class.
   (a) *"(Children) may be skeptical of Superman, but they tend to believe in James Bond stunts and high-tech cars."*
   - Do you agree or disagree with this observation? Support your view.
   - What reasons other than those presented by the writer can you suggest to explain this behaviour?
   - If we accept this comment as valid, which of this season's television programs are most likely to blur reality and fantasy for younger viewers?

   (b) *"By seldom presenting (violence) truthfully — as random, squalid, and painful — TV bestows on it an abstract legitimacy."*
   - Evaluate this comment.
   - Should television portray violence more "truthfully"? Why or why not?

   (c) *"...children aren't capable of assessing any product's value, and therefore shouldn't be asked to."*
   "...good products (for children and adults) need to be advertised."
   - Compare these two comments. Which best summarizes *your* opinions on advertising for children? Explain your position.

   (d) *"...for most parents, giving up TV isn't a practical option, or even a wise one."*
   - What would happen if *your* family became one of the "no-television-ever" families?
   - Would you consider it a wise decision to give up TV? Explain.

   (e) *"TV is too broad an industry to be labelled all good or all bad."*
   - What are some of the positive effects of watching television? Expand on those suggested in the article.

2. *"Competition for mass audiences and revenues means crime dramas have been staples of U.S. prime-time television because they are a proven method for getting and keeping audience ratings."*
   — The Ontario Royal Commission on Violence in the Communications Industry, 1976

   "Violence is a part of life. If the mass media are to reflect real life, then violence must logically be part of that reflection."

   (a) Evaluate, in a class discussion, each of the two preceding statements.
   (b) Do you believe there is a cause-and-effect relationship between the amount of violence on TV and behaviour in real life? Has television simply become a scapegoat for conditions within society that are difficult to identify or change?
   Share your opinions on these questions. What are *your* views on violence and TV?

INVESTIGATING THE MEDIA

1. *"...while children are watching TV, they aren't doing. In most cases, they aren't even thinking."* Is this a valid assessment of all children's programming? Watch several television programs designed for young audiences. Which ones encourage passive viewing? Which encourage active participation by the viewer? What techniques are used to encourage involvement? Prepare a report based on your observations.
2. *"Whatever else it's doing, TV is reinforcing perceived gender differences."* How valid is this judgment? Watch some television programs that are popular with children. What evidence is there to support or refute this claim? Prepare a report based on your observations.
3. ***(a)*** List five of your current favourites on television. Indicate with an asterisk those TV programs that contain scenes of violence. Be honest with yourself — is it the violence that makes the movie or program one of your favourites?
   (b) How much violence is there on television? Watch a variety of programs on different networks and at different times. Use a chart like the one below to record your observations.

Program Title	Time	Type of Violence	Consequences of Violence

Prepare a brief report based on your findings. Your report should include your personal conclusions about whether there is an excessive amount of violence on television programs.

YOUR TURN

1. Form a small group of students and stage — or choreograph — a fight scene. Select two people from the group to act as camerapeople. As you design the scene, imagine how you would shoot it on film. Consider such aspects as distance from the actors and camera angles. Plan the filming in two ways:
(a) to minimize the violence in the scene
(b) to heighten or glamorize the impact of the violence
Prepare a demonstration of the scene for the class. "Freeze" the action at appropriate moments and describe how you would show it on film.
or
Prepare a slide presentation of your fight scene as you have rehearsed it. Compose a commentary to be taped or given orally as the slides are shown.

2. Draft a class letter to a television network, local TV station, or the Canadian Radio-television and Telecommunications Commission (CRTC) in which you express your concerns about television and offer suggestions for improvement.

A list of addresses follows. (Local TV stations can be found in your business directory or phonebook.)

- *ABC*, 1330 Avenue of the Americas, New York, N.Y. 10019
- *CBS*, 51 West 52nd Street, New York, N.Y. 10019
- *NBC*, 30 Rockefeller Plaza, New York, N.Y. 10020
- *PBS*, 475 L'Enfant Plaza, West, S.W. Washington, D.C. 20024
- *CBC*, Box 500, Station A, Toronto, Ont. M5W 1E6
- *CTV*, 42 Charles Street East, Toronto, Ont. M4Y 1T5
- *Global*, 81 Barber Greene Road, Don Mills, Ont. M3C 2A2
- *TVOntario*, Box 200, Station Q, Toronto, Ont. M4T 2T1
- *Radio-Canada*, C.P. 6000, Station A, Montreal, Que. H3C 3A8
- *CRTC*, Central Building, Terrasses de la Chaudière, Room 561, Promenade du Portage, Hull, Que. K1A 0N2

The writer of the previous article stated that television is neither good nor bad — how we use it determines whether TV has a positive or negative influence on our views of life. The next article presents some suggestions for turning television viewing into a positive experience.

10 steps to better family TV viewing

Even TVOntario — respected among children's televison programmers — still recommends parents establish time and quality control on their children's television viewing.

But they're not saying what it should be.

"It's up to the parent to decide what is the limit," says Ruth Vernon, head of Ontario's educational network's children's programming.

According to a 1985 Gallup poll, the average Canadian teenager watches three hours of television a day, while children between 2 and 11 watch 2 1/2 hours daily.

It's not how much TV children watch that's important, says Vernon, but how much of their time it takes up. If TV is just one of many activities, then it should not be harmful, she says.

"Television is one of the best teachers in the world and a lot of children automatically know this," she says. "TV can stimulate the imagination and encourage them to play more creatively. The problems occur when parents let them watch programs not designed for children, such as soap operas in the day."

But Vernon believes that children often don't pick up the full impact of some of the so-called adult programs.

"That program *Three's Company* that runs at suppertime — 9-year-olds love it because it is slapstick comedy. Often the shows are loaded with all kinds of values we think are terrible but the kids may be just watching the fun," she says.

But Vernon believes parents must limit what and how much their children watch.

"Putting limitations on the number of hours makes a child choose what he has to watch. He makes a logical choice."

Watching television with children is one way to take control, and turning off the television when the program is over is another.

Vernon suggests parents keep a log for a week or so to determine who in the family is watching what, then set up a viewing-control system: Children could use tokens to 'pay' for shows; or use up less points for worthwhile shows, more points for questionable shows, and no points to those off-limits; or have viewing licences spelling out what shows are allowed and what aren't; or tape programs on the family videocassette recorder for playing when homework, hockey practices, and other activities are over.

In a TVOntario publication called *Television & Your Children*, which Vernon co-ordinated, she recommends 10 steps to take for better viewing. They are:

- Treat television as only one activity among many.
- Choose a place for the TV that shows it isn't the focal point of life.
- Establish the ground rules for watching TV.
- Choose what's watched by planning ahead, consulting television listing guides, and talking to family members.
- Discuss special shows ahead of time. Get background information to get the most out of the program.
- Watch with the kids as often as possible.
- React to, and talk about, what is being seen.
- Turn off the set when the program is over.
- Follow up shows with related activities the family can do together.
- Don't be afraid to watch. There's nothing wrong with using TV to unwind. After all, it is there to entertain.

— Cathy Dunphy
Toronto Star
April 28, 1986

EXPLORING IDEAS

1. In small groups, share your thoughts on the following:

(a) Which of the recommendations in the article are realistic and workable in families today? Record the reasons why your group accepts or rejects each recommendation.

(b) Does your group have some ideas of its own on this issue? If so, add your group's recommendations to the list of rules for household viewing.

Select one member to report your group's conclusions to the class. Are there any recommendations your whole class agreed on?

YOUR TURN

1. Imagine you are a parent; write a policy for television viewing in your home. Mention specific programs you would allow your children to watch and programs you would prohibit.
or
You are the director of a children's TV program such as *Sesame Street*. Create a new puppet character that will appeal to children and promote positive values. Script a pilot segment to sell your concept to the program sponsors and producers.

2. "It isn't fair" to ban television in the home. Create a poem or paragraph on this theme. You may wish to begin by listing reasons why banning TV wouldn't be fair, as a basis for your finished product.

CAN RADIO COMPETE?

When people began to flock to buy television sets, experts predicted that radio was finished. Of course, radio did not die. It did change however. Before television, the radio was often the centre of entertainment in the home. Radio dramas thrilled children and parents alike. People were kept informed through news and current affairs programs. All of the "big games" were broadcast live for the benefit of those who couldn't get to the sports stadium or arena. Certainly radio lost in the competition with television in many aspects of programming; but as radio stations adapted, listeners continued to tune in.

Radio has been adapting to change for 60 years. Now it must deal with new media and a flood of new stations. The writer of the next article shows how radio is changing to ensure its survival.

Radio: The Great Survivor

Radio is not only the oldest of the electronic entertainment media, it is also the most flexible. Radio has adapted to competition from movies, records, and television, and recently, cable, home video, and the Walkman. Today there are more radio stations, formats, program suppliers, and networks drawing larger total audiences and profits than ever before. Revenues have consistently grown by 10 to 15 per cent in each of the last five years. According to industry figures, radio now reaches 96 per cent of all Americans 12 years and older during a typical week, with an average tune-in time of 25 hours per person — only five hours less than television.

But now radio must adapt to a new set of internal pressures — the proliferation of stations, decline in AM listeners, and increased competition from financially powerful media. The industry is essentially an odd assortment of small to medium-sized businesses (receiving three quarters of their revenue from local ad sales). Few stations have the financial resources that television broadcasters or big cable operators can pour into programming and promotion. The resulting experimentation has produced a dizzying turnover in formats, personnel, and promotional strategies.

MARKETPLACE: With more than 10 000 stations on the air (9000 commercial and 1300 non-commercial), formats have become more and more specialized, targeting ever-narrower demographic groups. This endears radio to advertisers, who realize that television, even in the cable age, can never afford to specialize as effectively as radio.

Predictably, as the "baby boom" generation gets older and more affluent, advertisers — and therefore radio stations — are competing more aggressively for its attention. Fewer stations are catering to teenagers (Top 40) and seniors (beautiful music and news/talk). Contemporary hit radio, meanwhile, has become the hottest format. CHR, as it is known in the trade, is an upscale version of Top 40, relying heavily on punchy jingles, fast-talking disc jockeys, and frequent repetition of

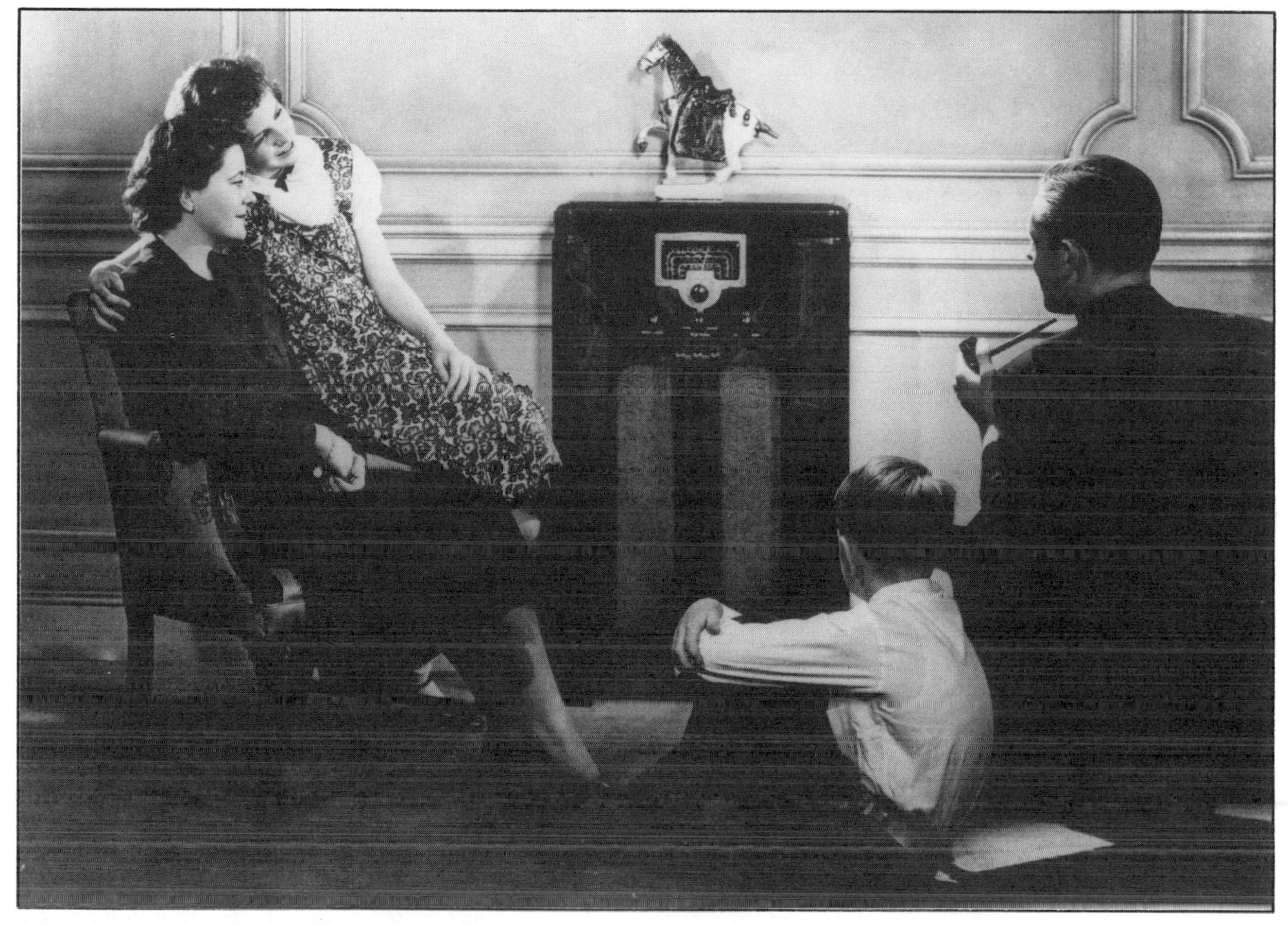

Before television—In the 1930s and '40s radio played a central role in entertaining and informing North Americans.

popular songs by artists as diverse as Lionel Richie and Bruce Springsteen. Album-oriented rock, the format associated with the heyday of '60s music, has gone into decline. Country music, the hardy perennial, remains the staple for the largest percentage of stations.

The rock format has split into dozens of variants, as have other music genres, such as country and black-oriented. Stations are also reacting to the enormous popularity of music videos, simulcasting television concerts or music-video programs.

The younger generation has virtually abandoned AM for the high fidelity and music emphasis of FM, though new techniques for broadcasting AM stereo may come to its rescue. At present AM stations have been left to specialize in news, talk, religion, and ethnic fare.

Cost pressures and competition have forced some small stations to cut staff and reduce expensive services, such as local news. Satellite-delivered networks, providing polished announcers and up-to-date music selections for a fraction of a staff disc jockey's salary, have been the salvation of many struggling outlets. Barter syndicators are lining up as many as 700 similarly formatted stations, giving them free programs in exchange for some of the commercial time.

TECHNOLOGY: Radio networks and many syndicators have completed the transition from costly landlines to inexpensive satellite transmission. At least 20 nationwide networks, dozens of regional syndicates, and scores of specialized program services are now available to the station with a satellite receiver. Program directors can "cherry-pick" particular music, news, features, and specials that match the station's image.

— Richard Mahler
Channels

EXPLORING IDEAS

1. *"(Radio)...is also the most flexible (medium). Radio has adapted to competition from movies, records, and television, and recently, cable, home video, and the Walkman."*

   How well, do *you* think, has radio adapted to change? Share your opinions with the class.
2. Advertising is critical to the future success of radio. What unique qualities might radio offer the advertiser? Why might he or she choose it over other media, such as television or newspapers?
3. ***(a)*** How have videos influenced your listening habits? How does viewing a video differ from listening to music on radio?
   (b) Do you think video will surpass radio as a showcase for new music? Support your opinion. How might radio further alter its programming to stay competitive?

INVESTIGATING THE MEDIA

1. As an individual or in small groups, complete the following survey on your radio-listening habits:
   1) List the AM and FM stations available in your area.
   2) Listen to these stations and regroup them according to the kinds of music they play:
      (a) Rock 'n' Roll – Easy Listening
      (b) Rock 'n' Roll – Heavy Metal
      (c) New Wave – Experimental Rock
      (d) Pop/"Beautiful Music" – Easy Listening/ Middle of the Road
      (e) Country and Western
      (f) Rhythm and Blues/Funk
      (g) "Golden Oldies" – '50s and '60s Rock/Pop
      (h) Classical
      (i) Jazz
      (j) All Talk (Little or No Music)
      (k) *Other* (specify)
   3) (a) Listen to a continuous hour of broadcasting on your favourite station at different times of the day over a period of a few days, including a weekend. Keep careful notes on the amount of time devoted to each of the following:
      - music
      - news
      - weather
      - traffic reports
      - open-line programs
      - sports reports
      - sports-event broadcasting
      - station promotion
      - commercials
      - public affairs
      - time checks
      - DJ talk
      - *other* (specify)

      (b) Summarize your findings in a chart, graph, or other visual representation.
      (c) What conclusions can you draw about the content of a typical hour of this station's broadcasting?
   4) (a) What are your favourite stations on FM? AM?
      (b) Who is your favourite radio personality? Describe this person's style.
      (c) What products or services are frequently advertised on your favourite station? How many of these do you purchase/use?
      (d) Who listens to radio most frequently in your household?
2. What does radio offer listeners that other media do not? Discuss this as a class or respond in your journal.

YOUR TURN

1. Be a radio programmer. Outline the "log" for an hour of broadcasting *you* would like to hear on radio. How would your programming compare with the content you noted in the survey above? Compare your choices with your classmates'.

“If the Canadian record industry produced 150 Anne Murrays, radio stations would play 100 per cent Canadian content.”

— Radio executive
Toronto, Sept/86

For many people, Canadian content is as great a concern on radio as it is on television. As the next writer explains, the music industry in particular relies on content guidelines to provide exposure and support for Canadian artists.

Radio broadcasting less and less Canadian content

Pulse racing? Cold sweat forming on the brow? Hellish visions of sugarplum snowbirds winging through your head? If not, check in with the rock'n'roll doctor. Immediately.

The essential problem with the wisdom quoted above isn't necessarily the intriguing concept of our Ms. Murray singing her sweet-heart out 25-hours-a-day — although that's a nightmarish fate far worse than anything even such horror masters as Stephen King have yet dreamed up.

No, the trouble lies with the convoluted and dangerous thinking that would result in such a scary, scary statement.

To give it context, it was the final salvo in a discussion that took place during a meeting of the Canadian Independent Record Production Association (CIRPA), which represents those music-makers who subsist outside the multinational (read: American) record companies.

The debate circled around one fact: over the past few years, Canadian radio has broadcast less and less Canadian music. Naturally, CIRPA members weren't happy; it largely being their records that were collecting dust. Voices were raised; blood-pressure soared. Finally, the radio spokesman dealt his ace; there simply wasn't enough “world-class” Canadian music to keep the listening audience listening. Anne Murray was his definition of “world-class,” although he could just as well have cited Bryan Adams or David Foster.

To grasp the implications of all this, a little background is in order.

Let's start with Canadian content, for that's the nest in which this country's music biz was hatched and the forge upon which it was hammered into shape.

Harken back to the Sixties and a Canada that feared for its identity, a shy and unformed character in danger of being swallowed whole by the cultural Cronus known as the United States of America.

Twenty years ago everybody was flushed with the Canada-first national-

Without Canadian content rules, would Canadian listeners have heard the recordings of such homegrown artists as Luba and Bryan Adams?

ism of our 100th anniversary. The successive Liberal governments of Lester Pearson and Pierre Trudeau were erecting legislative barriers to keep the American wolf at bay. Their objective: to allow the arts in Canada to survive and, in time, permit a distinctive national character to evolve. Trade barriers had historically worked for Canadian industry. The logical extension was that protectionism could do a fine job for the cultural sector as well.

Like its fellow arts, Canadian music didn't enjoy the support of anything that could remotely be described as an "industry." A handful of independent labels sustained a small core of folk, country, and rock artists. The record business was ruled by U.S. branch-plant operations (CBS, Warners, Capitol, etc.) whose job it was to manufacture foreign product for sale here, not develop Canadian talent. For its part, radio played the hits of the day — American and British, natch. They could only go so far with Paul Anka, the Guess Who, and Gordon Lightfoot, our only real stars of the Sixties.

All this changed overnight in June 1970, when the Canadian Radio-television and Telecommunications Commission (CRTC), a government body that regulates and governs broadcasters, announced a radical and controversial policy: Effective six months hence, all Canadian radio stations would be required to play set amounts of Canadian music during their broadcast day. In the case of the dominant medium at the time, AM radio, that level was a whopping 30 per cent. From maybe a 1:10 ratio at best, Canadian songs would be heard at a clip of almost one in three.

Broadcasters suddenly needed Canadian music. Record companies responded. "Can con," as it soon became known, initiated the first great Canadian gold-rush, led by Lighthouse, April Wine, and the Stampeders. Not only did the guidelines create a home base for our composers, lyricists, performers, and producers, it also gave them a launching pad for international careers and U.S. success.

Okay, you may be thinking, Canadian content rules are a strict and somewhat unnatural remedy to the apathy of the Sixties. Surely, Canadian artists could have survived on their own?

But ask yourself this: without Can con, would we have ever heard from Adams, Corey Hart, Platinum Blonde, Gowan, Luba, and Honeymoon Suite? Would radio have given these acts that all-important first exposure? All enjoy major label support, but would these companies have signed them if there wasn't a built-in guarantee of radio airplay? Look at the pre-1970 environment and you'll have your answer.

The guidelines still exist. But today the 30 per cent standard has slipped, with many stations now being allowed to play 25 per cent, 20 per cent, and sometimes even 15 per cent Canadian content.

The CRTC has bought the Anne Murray scenario. Radio programmers say their average listener — not you, the teenager, but adults aged 25-49 — won't stay tuned to anything but state-of-the-art pop, the kind of glossy productions delivered by Lionel Richie, Tina Turner, Rod Stewart, and that calibre of top gun.

To get a million-dollar sound requires just that — lots and lots of loot. Canadian labels are only rich enough to finance a few big-budget albums each year. Of recent vintage, you can toss Corey Hart's *Fields of Fire, Tom Cochrane and Red Rider,* and Honeymoon Suite's *The Big Prize* into this category.

So, in his own matter-of-fact way, our radio friend is correct. In his terms, there isn't enough "world-class" Canadian music available. But his definition is certainly a subjective one. What, one must ask, is so amateurish about such homegrown acts as Eye Eye, Double Dare, Haywire, Jane Siberry, Bruce Cockburn, Scott Merritt, Erroll Starr, 54-40, Chalk Circle, Zappacosta, and Body Electric? In 1986, all turned out first-rate tunes. And while they received some airplay, it wasn't nearly as much as the songs warranted.

Fortunately, the CRTC is still committed to its original principles and is eager to see radio return to the 30 per cent mark. As a result, the government in September 1986 approved an $18-million aid package to be distributed to record and video makers over the next five years. The idea is that this money will undercut the arguments of the broadcasters, and provide them with enough quality Canadian material.

Even without this money, Canadian music has what it takes to fill 30 per cent of the airwaves. With it, radio's lame excuses won't have a leg to stand on.

— Geoffrey Clinton
Teen Generation
October 1986

EXPLORING IDEAS

1. **(a)** What does the term "world-class music" mean to you? As a class, develop a definition or a list of descriptors for the term.
   (b) Compile a list of Canadian recording artists who fit the definition you have created.
2. Is there enough quality Canadian music to fill the 30 per cent quota stipulated by the CRTC? Debate this issue informally in class.
3. Write a journal entry in which you respond to the following statement: *"Radio programmers should be free to play whatever music they feel that you, the listener, would like to hear, no matter what the country of origin."* In small groups, compare your responses.

YOUR TURN

1. Create a series of promotional spots for radio designed to boost the career of a Canadian musical group that is just breaking onto the scene. Tape your spots and play them for the class.

Industry experts acknowledge that "baby boomers" are the primary target of new programming strategies in radio. The writer of this article speculates on the effects this trend might have on you, the younger listening audience.

Golden Oldies in the Year 2017

The story is told of the two old people who stumbled into one of those places where teenagers dance, if you can call it dancing. Shocking sights greeted the old people, the most shocking being their own faces in the mirror. And shocking sounds greeted them too, the most shocking being the music the teenagers were dancing to. It was the music of 20 years ago. It was the same music the old people once danced to, if you could call it dancing.

The children dancing to the old music seemed to be having a good enough time. They bounced around, looked silly, and knew all the words, the way young people in those places always have.

Having made good their escape, the old people turned on the car radio and found more of the same music. They changed the station and found still more. They kept playing with the radio until they found a solitary little FM station playing a song they hated and couldn't understand. They figured it must be the music of today and quickly changed the station, because they knew the music of today is supposed to sound strange and awful to other generations.

That has always been the way one generation approached another generation's music. What is different now is that the music of today is in scarce supply, because the generation of yesterday isn't. The generation that rules the marketplace also rules the airwaves.

All over North America, young people are travelling up and down the AM and FM dials looking for the music of today, only to find the music of their parents. (Occasionally, they find The Music of Your Life, which is the music of their parents' parents.)

Some of the children find the search frustrating. They wonder why they can't have their own music on the radio when all previous generations did. But the parents of today — that is, the teenagers of 20 years ago — find the situation comforting, somehow. Their kids are liking good music, the old people think — forgetting that it is only rock 'n' roll, a type of music people once grew out of when they reached a certain age. No one worries about the plight of a culturally disenfranchised generation, forced by the laws of economics to listen on the radio to the music their parents liked when they were in high school.

And no one sees the consequences, which should be obvious to anyone who can look 30 years down the road....

Noteworthy are the magnificent senior citizens' residences that line the streets. The residences are called Boomer Haven and Woodstock Lodge and Yuppie Manor, all uses of the word "sunset" having been banned. Together the residences are known as The Lodges, and all political and economic power is concentrated here.

Each day The Lodges are visited by a steady stream of delivery trucks from gourmet takeout joints, bringing avocados, kiwi fruit, pasta, and two-toned chocolates shaped like 1967 Chevrolets.

From the sidewalk, the faint sound of a radio can be detected. It is playing — yes: "Sergeant Pepper's Lonely Hearts Club Band." That's funny. We just heard that on the radio coming over. In fact, it was on two stations at once.

Now we remember. "Sergeant Pepper's Lonely Hearts Club Band" is going to play all day on all the stations. It was announced from The Lodges. Yesterday it was "Bad Moon Rising"; tomorrow it's "I Heard It Through the Grapevine." Next week's schedule hasn't been released yet.

Inside The Lodges, the residents are playing backgammon, taking dancing lessons (today: the Watusi), and watching television. The TV schedule includes *Laugh-In*, *The Man from U.N.C.L.E.*, and reruns of reruns of *Leave It to Beaver*. The commercials have to do with receding gums, cleaning agents for false teeth, and stomach powders.

Sports fans are watching the 1975 World Series again. Most stations play the 1975 World Series most of the time. A few years ago The Lodges decided that Game Six was the best game ever — the "Sergeant Pepper's Lonely Hearts Club Band" of sports events. New baseball games ceased to be played in the mid-1990s, when a consensus emerged that nothing could improve upon the old games.

It was about the same time that the recording industry stopped putting out new records, other than by Bob

The Beatles—Their classic album "Sergeant Pepper's Lonely Hearts Club Band," and other examples of the music of yesterday, often gets more radio airplay than the music of today.

Dylan and Bruce Springsteen, whom medical science vowed to keep alive for as long as they were needed.

Interest in the present has largely disappeared, although newspapers and magazines have not. They pay considerable attention to the weather, but the main reason for their survival is the detailed coverage they give to those most exciting years of the 1960s and 1970s. More up to date are the columns of music criticism analysing and re-analysing the contributions made to world culture by such figures as The Monkees. There are, in addition, health tips, recipes, and financial advice of interest to the aging baby-boom generation. And in the classified pages, long-lost nannies can be traced. Since the future can never be better than the past, the newspapers carry no horoscopes.

It is the best of times for historians, the worst of times for fortune-tellers.

The newspapers also give token coverage to the

whinings of the younger generations, who say that they are tired of "Sergeant Pepper's Lonely Hearts Club Band."

The more radical of the young people — that is, the under-65s — are threatening to return to the punk styles and attitudes of the most recent revolt against the values of the majority. The Lodges have answered the threat with a press release saying that the boutiques and hairdressing salons of The Lodges are always on the lookout for any outrageous new fad.

The message is clear. The Lodges are threatening another wave of repressive tolerance.

It may not be enough this time, however. Tired of sacrificing huge chunks of their meagre paycheques to finance the lavish pensions of the boomers, the younger generations are planning bold measures. The first step will be to seize the radio stations.

At The Lodges, the first sign of trouble will be when the elites are suddenly unable to dance to the music coming from the radio. Other points of resistance will quickly crumble. When the revolution is finally over, the new leaders will marvel at the arrogance of a generation that thought it could defend a fortress covered with skylights.

— Charles Gordon
Maclean's
January 12, 1987

EXPLORING IDEAS

1. *"The music of today is in scarce supply on radio."* To what extent do you agree with this statement? What is your reaction to the music of the '60s?

2. Mr. Gordon claims that today's youth are "culturally disenfranchised" by radio. Discuss this statement.

(a) Do you agree or disagree? What evidence can you offer to support your point of view?

(b) What, in your opinion, is the most effective medium for your generation to experience and promote your own culture?

(c) What evidence is there that other media are catering more to baby boomers than to you?

3. If Mr. Gordon's assessment of the situation is in any way accurate, what are the implications or consequences for your generation? Write a response to this question in your journal.

INVESTIGATING THE MEDIA

1. Working in small groups, arrange to listen to a number of different radio stations. (You will have gathered some of this information in your earlier survey of radio programming.) Based on the type of music played, the products advertised, the personality of the DJs and so on, draft a description of the likely target audience for each station. Which stations can be identified as stations for today's teenagers?

or

What evidence, beyond the type of music being played, is there to support the opinion that we live in the age of "Yuppie Radio"? For example:

- Does the language used by the on-air personalities seem to appeal to a particular audience group?
- What do the DJs talk about between musical selections?
- What types of products are advertised?

Prepare a group report based on your findings.

YOUR TURN

1. Draft a proposal for the CRTC describing a new station for people your age.

Your proposal should outline

(a) the type of music programs

(b) *other* types of programs (career information, interviews, etc.)

(c) the personality of the program hosts and DJs

Choose two or more of the following activities that interest *you*. Alternatively, develop your own activities and research projects to investigate further the images and issues associated with radio and television.

1. *"Stations with clear, distinctive music policies will grow stronger in status and ratings...."*

   — Henry Mietkiewicz, *The Toronto Star*

   Contact your local radio station and arrange an interview with one of the on-air personalities or music programmers. Find out how recordings are selected and who selects them. How much influence, if any, do advertisers have on the choice of music that is played?

   How much freedom or direction does a DJ have? Do many listeners complain about the music played on the station? How are complaints handled? How important is popularity to DJs? Write or tape your interview to present to the class.

2. Research the relationship between government and broadcasting. What regulations has the CRTC (Canadian Radio-television and Telecommunications Commission) imposed on radio and television? How have these affected broadcasting? What role does the government play in encouraging new broadcasting strategies? new technology? How could government policies be changed to serve the public better? Prepare a documentary or news report based on your research. You may wish to videotape your report.

3. Investigate careers in radio or television. Some possibilities are sales, station manager, DJ, news announcer, sports announcer, music programmer. Interview men and women whose jobs you'd like to know more about. Find out how they got started in a career in radio or television. What qualities or characteristics should a person have in order to succeed? What background or training is required? Use the information to prepare a handbook for students interested in careers in radio or television.

4. If you live in a city or town close to a cable or network television studio, arrange a visit to gain a first-hand look at the behind-the-scenes technology. Use your experiences as a basis for a report or a "live" or videotaped class presentation.

5. Do additional research on the subject of violence on television. What claims do people in the industry, psychologists, sociologists, parents make regarding this controversial issue? What evidence do they offer to support their claims? Prepare a report including conclusions and recommendations based on the evidence you have studied.

6. Enlist members of your household or a group of friends to help you conduct some personal research. Everyone involved should agree to the following:
   (a) *not* to watch any television for a specified period of time
   (b) to maintain a brief daily journal in which thoughts and feelings are recorded
   (c) to meet with you at the end of the experimental period to share experiences

   Prepare a report based on your research. Below are some suggestions that may help you focus your report:
   - What "withdrawal symptoms," if any, did people experience?
   - What changes, if any, occurred in normal daily routines and habits? For example, did people spend more time reading, talking on the phone, and so on?
   - Were there any times when people felt left out of a conversation because those around them were discussing what they had been watching on television?

UNIT TWO: THE FUTURE OF

PRINT

"I think it's time to renew our romance with the word."
— **Steven Spielberg**

On Oscar night 1987 about a billion people around the world watched director Steven Spielberg give a speech on the importance of the written word in film. "Only a generation of readers," he warned, "will spawn a generation of writers."

Although print is our oldest mass medium, it is still an influential part of our daily lives. In its many popular forms, the printed word thrives despite the electronic media, which seem on the surface to be much more exciting and modern.

On the other hand, the growth of electronic media in this century has prompted many teachers, parents — even film directors — to reflect on the effects of the newer media on traditional print forms. If average Canadians are watching television about three-and-a-half hours a day, then how much time do they have for other activities — such as reading? Is there a connection between the power of the various electronic media and the apparent decline of literacy?

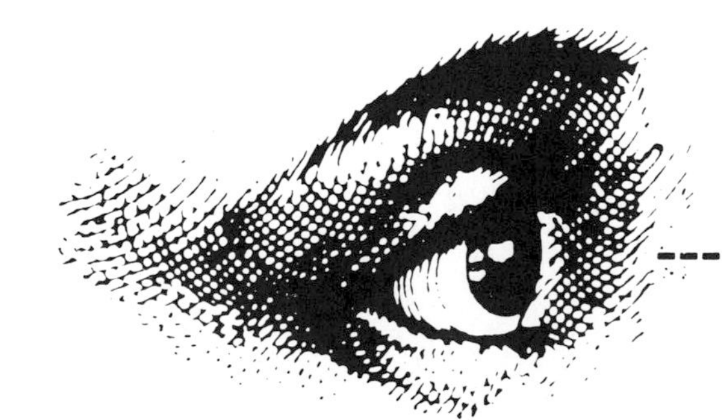

YOU & THE MEDIA

Is reading still as important as it ever was? The following activities will help you evaluate how popular traditional literacy really is.

1. Some media analysts say there is a "new literacy" — a literacy that is replacing the traditional skills of reading and writing *(print literacy)* with other communication skills: oral, visual, and so forth *(media literacy).*

Do you agree or disagree? Is traditional literacy less popular,or is it more popular than ever? Share your views with your classmates.

Use the following survey questions to examine how *you* actually apply the skills of traditional and "new" literacy. Record your findings for future reference.

1) Review a typical day. Estimate how much time you spend reading

	Per day	**Per week**
(a) books – for *information*		
(b) books – for *pleasure*		
(c) newspapers		
(d) magazines		
(e) *other print forms* (Specify.)		

2) How much time would you estimate you spend
   (a) watching television?
   (b) listening to the radio?
   (c) listening to records and audiotapes?
   (d) viewing films and videos?
   (e) talking on the telephone?
3) What print items (stories or reports) did you find memorable
   (a) in the last twenty-four hours?
   (b) in the last week?
   Where did you read them?
4) In general, which of the following is your *main* source of information:
   (a) print?
   (b) television?
   (c) radio?
   (d) *other* (Specify.)
5) How important is writing in your life? How often do you have to write to someone in order to communicate:
   (a) frequently?
   (b) occasionally?
   (c) rarely?
6) What form does your writing take? Estimate how much time you spend writing
   (a) for school
   (b) on the job (business letters, reports, etc.)
   (c) personal letters
   (d) *other* (diaries, shopping lists, etc.)

3 Working in groups, assemble and evaluate the data you each gathered in your personal surveys.
(a) Which print forms are most popular?
(b) What other media compete with print in popularity?
(c) Do your findings suggest any trends in literacy? If trends are apparent, what are some possible consequences?

4 *Discuss*: What strengths does print have that might make it superior to other media? What are the drawbacks of print from the point of view of the average person?

Shoe by Jeff MacNelly—Reprinted with permission: Tribune Media Services

IS LITERACY IN DECLINE?

Do people read as often as they used to? What is happening to traditional reading skills in the wake of the "new literacy"? Some commentators believe a serious problem is threatening the future of young people and our society as a whole. They call this important issue the "decline of traditional literacy."

The following article presents some surprising findings of a recent survey on the question of literacy in Canada.

Literacy in Canada: One in four Canadians functionally illiterate

OTTAWA — Five million Canadians can't read, write, or use numbers well enough to meet the literacy demands of today's society — and one-third are high school graduates, an exclusive nationwide survey has disclosed. Among the findings of the survey:

- Illiteracy increases from west to east, rising from a low of 17 per cent among adults in British Columbia to an astonishing high of 44 per cent in Newfoundland. Two-thirds of illiterates live in Ontario and Quebec.
- Illiteracy is higher among Francophones than Anglophones — 29 per cent to 23 per cent — but the gap is biggest among the oldest and vanishes among the young.
- Nearly half of the 4.5 million functional illiterates identified in the survey are 55 or older, even though this group accounts for only 29 per cent of the total population.
- More than half of the 4.5 million illiterates said they went to high school and one-third claimed to be high school graduates. One in 12 — 8 per cent — who claimed to be university graduates still tested as functionally illiterate.
- More men than women were identified as functional illiterates — 53.5 per cent to 46.5 per cent for a projected national difference of 300 000 between the sexes.

The findings show that Canada's rate of 24 per cent is considerably worse than the global rate of 17.6 per cent.

The Southam survey's definition of functional literacy was the ability to use printed and written information to function in society. Experts agree this approach is more relevant today than the traditional definition of just being able to sign a name or read a simple sentence.

The survey tested 2398 Canadians on their reading, writing, and numbers skills with a battery of more than 40 literacy-related questions selected by a national advisory panel.

— Peter Calamai
The Toronto Star
September 12, 1987

For the millions who can't read
Give the gift of literacy
More than four million adult Canadians can't read well enough to fill out a job application or understand the directions on a medicine bottle. You can help. Give money, volunteer with a literacy group, write to your MP, and read to your children.
For more information, contact:
Canadian Give the Gift of Literacy Foundation
34 Ross St., Suite 200,
Toronto, Ont. M5T 1Z9
(416) 595-9967

EXPLORING IDEAS

1. ***(a)*** What reasons can you offer to explain the following?
   - Canada's comparatively high illiteracy rate (24%)
   - The high concentration of illiteracy in Ontario and Quebec
   - The fact that illiteracy is higher among adult males than females in Canada

   (b) Which facts, if any, in this national survey do you find particularly surprising? Give your reasons.
2. Do you think illiteracy in Canada is as widespread as this survey claims? Support your point of view.
3. Is the situation likely to improve or become worse in the future? Explain why you think so. What effects on society might this situation have?

The following article suggests that the blame for what the author sees as the "growing problem of illiteracy" in North America lies with the "media distractions" of our society.

The End of Meaning

A number of writers, broadcasters, and journalists have recently been expressing concern over the widespread and growing problem of illiteracy in our society. CBS's *60 Minutes* has aired a report on the complete functional illiteracy of some college graduates who went through university on sports scholarships. Scarcely a week passes without an article appearing in a magazine or newspaper, often with a sensational headline, giving a similar story. (On June 16, 1980, the Montreal *Gazette* carried a story headed "At 19, he can barely read or write.") A recent government-sponsored report in Canada estimated that five million Canadians are functionally illiterate.

Even among the literate it is clear that the ability of the average person to express himself clearly, simply and precisely, in writing and in speech, has declined in recent years. A glance at the letters page or the "Dear Abby" column in any newspaper should be enough to convince anyone that the average person's writing ability is quite inadequate, even for such a relatively undemanding task as the composition of a letter. The same is true of speaking ability, as one meets more and more people who are even unable to construct a coherent, grammatically correct sentence, seeking instead the comforting support of such meaningless conjunctions as "you know," "sort of," "I mean," "like," and the repetition of a small number of appallingly overworked all-purpose words such as "uptight," "hassle," "upbeat," and the like.

Whereas not long ago the average North American was estimated to have a working vocabulary of only a few thousand words, today he appears to get by with only a few hundred, including those few just mentioned that recur with the maddening monotony of a scratch on a record. (T.W. Lawson, head of the English department of

Trinity College School, in Port Hope, Ontario, tells of a typical Grade 11 student who did not know the meaning of *conciliate, deter, enthrall, exhaustive, haphazard, hilarious,* or *naive.*) The English language is one of the richest and most powerful in the world, and has been developing in scope, color, and precision since the time of Chaucer. Yet today we see less of it than a mariner sees of an iceberg.

What are the reasons for this drop in our standard of literacy? To say that people do not write as much as they used to is to beg the question, why don't they write as much? The same question may be asked about reading.

The fact that ours is what Hugh MacLennan calls "the age of distraction" no doubt has something to do with it. Since the end of the war we have had to live with a growing number of diverse and insistent media distractions, all of which have helped rob us of our concentration and fill our minds with trivia. TV brings its message of uniformity into nearly every living room in the land; the radio blares its concentrated bursts of sound into the home, the car, the garden, the beach, the street, and 1000 other places; piped-in music invades the restaurant, the hotel lobby, and even the dentist's waiting room; often vulgar advertising messages intrude into our line of vision from billboards and the sides of buses, subway walls, and even cereal boxes; and every day a gargantuan pile of printed matter is delivered in the mail, left on the doorstep, or just allowed to fall out of a swollen newspaper onto our laps. Everyone clamors for our attention, be it only a glance at a full-page color advertisement costing thousands of dollars or an even more cursory look at a 20-second burst of concentrated sales talk in prime time costing much more.

Nor is this all. Even the ubiquitous telephone has played its part; more than anything else it may be held responsible for the loss of the art of letter writing. The advent of computer-corrected multiple-choice exams in schools and universities has meant that it is now possible for many people to go through life without knowing how to write in anything but block capitals, assuming they know how to write at all, which it would appear many do not. Today, it is simply no longer considered to be fundamental to develop the ability to express oneself in writing.

The fact that writing is a discipline and, as such, is not easy to learn has only compounded the problem, for the direction of modern society is to escape the tedious and time consuming. This is the age of the labor-saving device and the electronic gadget. We have instant coffee, fast food, and everything else "while you wait"; books tell us how to do things "without really trying"; we have cameras that give us instant pictures, photocopying machines that give us instant copies, and TV that gives us the news "as it happens." Why should we spend time learning how to write?

Indeed, of all the distractions of our age, none has had so great an impact on the standard of literacy as television. No other single invention so rules the average North American's hours of leisure as does TV, and no other invention makes such a mockery of that most versatile, awesome, and mysterious gift with which we have been endowed: the mind. Concentration, creativity, subtlety of thought, and development of imagination — all are sacrificed before the electronic altar in the living room. And the viewing of television is a seductive pastime because no active participation, either mental or physical, is required on the part of the viewer; he is the passive recipient of one-way communication, and it is inevitable that after a while his mind, growing sluggish, will lose the quickness and resilience that comes from communication that is an *exchange*. The viewer is often not even a sounding board, but a human black hole, into whom communication disappears without a trace.

The validity of this claim may be tested by asking the average viewer how many TV programs that he saw more than a few days before he can remember. In most cases it would be surprising if there were any. The reason for this may be that the medium gives the viewer no time to reflect on what he sees, assuming it's *worth* reflecting on. Everything, even the viewer's emotions, is orchestrated in the studio (think of canned laughter). Small wonder that in his book *1984*, George Orwell placed a two-way TV screen in every room.

Conversation is an art that benefits the mind in a unique way. No other activity is so useful in developing powers of verbal self-expression under conditions that demand mental reflex and agility. In its most developed form conversation is intellectual combat, the art of verbal self-defence. It is mental exercise without equal, and as such plays a key role in the development of the literate functions.

Reading is equally as important, but it too is much less common a pastime than it used to be. With it are being lost such positive side effects as the exercise of the memory and the development of the powers of concentration and imagination. It may not be too farfetched to link the increase in television viewing to the increase in the use of drugs; one of the reasons drugs are commonly used is that they give release to the imagination, an effect that watching TV does not have.

That TV does not require the viewer to exercise his imagination is perhaps the worst indictment that can be brought against the medium, for our imagination is not only unique to the human race, but is possibly the greatest gift with which we have been provided. It is from imagination that have come all the world's great literature, music, architecture, and works of art; it is imagination that has set us free from the bonds of the material world and allowed us a glimpse of the transcendent. It was this feeling that Father Alphonse Déquire expressed when, shortly before he was tortured and executed by the Nazis in 1944, he wrote: "When the prison door closes, my mind flies out through. . .the window to freedom."

But reading is not easy, if by reading we mean more than just deciphering printed symbols. It is a habit that requires a long period of cultivation before its benefits are reaped. These benefits include a range of experience of other cultures and peoples, understanding of human nature, independence of thought and strength of conviction, not to mention an awareness of the beauties of the English language, with all its great literature and poetry. Those who do not read eventually become such that they cannot read because they do not know how. They have lost the ability to concentrate and use their imagination in order to derive more than just immediate benefit from the factual information conveyed by the words.

Children who see their parents read grow up accepting it as a natural activity and form the lifelong habit of reading. But how many parents read and have discussions of any complexity or duration with their children about what they have read? And today, as the number of illiterate, or semiliterate, school-leavers indicates, it seems to be equally as hopeless to expect children to develop reading habits at school. Whereas at one time literacy skills formed an integral part of education, today they are no longer stressed; indeed, it has been noted that standards of literacy among teachers themselves have been declining.

The young generation is frequently referred to as "the television generation," and one young math teacher tells of the way in which the full significance of this epithet struck him. One day, while explaining something to a class from the board, he became aware that, though they seemed attentive, most of them were wearing facial expressions of almost hypnotic blankness and detachment. He suddenly realized how easily their minds were able to slip into a state of passive reception, which after a time became a sort of mental inertia, rendering them unwilling (and eventually unable) to undertake any sort of mental or physical activity. He describes how even lifting a pen became to them a task of almost agonizing proportions. He says he felt they appreciated his histrionics and mathematical ability, and were prepared to watch him and be entertained, but that it was impossible to elicit any sort of response from them. They had become less and less able to *do* things, and more and more used to *watching* things being done. Considering that the average schoolchild watches from two to five hours of TV a day, this is hardly surprising.

That there is a reaction against the direction in which all this is leading us may offer some small hope to those who might otherwise despair. As well as catching the interest of a number of observers in the media, the phenomenon of creeping illiteracy has recently become a cause of concern among educators. More and more, they are calling for corrective measures to be taken to try to reverse the decline of literacy in our society.

In this regard, it would be helpful if teachers, writers, broadcasters, journalists, and anyone else whose spoken and written words reach the larger audience were more concerned in a practical way with seeing that the precision of the English language is preserved and appreciated by those who use it. Some already are, but for the most part they tend to submit too readily to the mediocrity of common usage. There is too much at stake; we cannot afford to go on having the unique qualities of our minds suffer any more abuse.

It is also disappointing and ironic that the inability of the average person to communicate comes at a time of widespread interest in the theoretical study of communications. Communications "experts" may reply that there is more to communication than writing and speaking, and there is even a small band of thinkers (communicators?), whose oriflamme was hoisted by Marshall McLuhan in the 1960s, who hold that the printed word is dead and that we are entering the age of "total communication" and the supremacy of the visual image. In spite of their theories, written and spoken forms of communication still are, and seem certain to remain, the most fundamental forms there are. They certainly are the most common forms of communication in everyday use, and are basic to the very nature of human political, business, educational, and social relations. Even the "total communicators," as Bernard Levin, formerly of *The Times* of London, has waggishly pointed out, chose to announce their theories that the printed word was finished in a succession of books.

— A. Stephen Pimenoff
Quest
October 1981

MEMBERSHIP IN THE COALITION FOR LITERACY
HELPS FIGHT ILLITERACY

To 27 million Americans this scene is a fairy tale. You can help make America aware and involved in the problem of adult functional illiteracy by joining the Coalition for Literacy in sponsoring the national literacy awareness campaign. Become a one-time, two-year member. Choose a category of membership and make your check payable to COALITION FOR LITERACY.

SPONSORING MEMBER $1,000 and more

Membership in this category makes you a visible partner in the fight against illiteracy.

GENERAL MEMBER $500, $100, $50 & $10

This is a supporting membership.

The Coalition for Literacy operates under the fiscal management of the American Library Association. Send your tax deductible membership check to: COALITION FOR LITERACY, 50 East Huron Street, Chicago, Illinois 60611.

Coalition for Literacy

A literate America
is a good investment.

EXPLORING IDEAS

1. **(a)** Share your views on the factors Stephen Pimenoff claims are to blame for a decline of literacy in our society.
   (b) Do you agree that students today *are* lacking in the communication skills they really need — or are they developing different types of skills to meet the needs of a changing society?
2. The author states that educators more and more are "*calling for corrective measures to be taken to reverse the decline of literacy in our society.*" Do you believe that "corrective measures" are needed? What policies would you recommend with regard to education, child-raising, and government involvement? Discuss these questions and present your suggestions to the class.
3. **(a)** Now that you have read the two articles, do you agree with the experts' definition of *literacy*? How do *you* define this term?
   (b) Do you think there is a connection between good grammar, good spelling, and literacy? Support your opinions.
   (c) How will literacy be defined in the future — for *your* children, for example? Explain.

YOUR TURN

1. How are the media changing our language? In groups, brainstorm a list of words and expressions that have been added to our language from the non-print media — radio, television, film, and so on. Use your ideas to create a display for the classroom.
2. Working with a partner, consider some ways the non-print media could play a role in *improving* national literacy. Explain. Present a written or oral report to the class.
3. Working in a small group, present a panel discussion to the class on the topic of literacy testing.

   Discuss: Should all high-school students be required to pass a literacy test before being granted a diploma?

Recently publishers have begun to re-define "the book." Do you believe that innovations such as the following might take hold?

Talking Books

So there I was, driving down the highway, reading *Prizzi's Honor* and... Wait a minute. You were driving down the highway **reading** *Prizzi's Honor*!

Yes, and it's great.

But why would you be reading *Prizzi's Honor* while driving down the highway?

Because I already read *Farewell My Lovely.*

Okay, okay, I wasn't actually *reading* while driving.

The book was *talking* to me.

Now before you start whistling for the chaps with the white coats, give a listen to my most recent discovery, books on cassette, which, incidentally, is one of the fastest-growing segments of the entertainment industry.

You're driving to work (or jogging, gardening, painting, you-name-it) and you slip a cassette into your tape deck. Instantly, the worst of traffic jams disappears as you listen to the mellifluous tones of Michael Moriarty reading *One Flew Over the Cuckoo's Nest* or Robert Vaughn acting out *The Manchurian Candidate.*

I thought it was nutsy when I first heard of it. Even when my cousin in Los Angeles sent along some early tapes, I continued to resist.

Like a lot of folks, I thought it was a lazy man's way of reading. I had long been a voracious reader even though I haven't found as much time as I like in recent years. But — ecch — having someone read to me?

"Most people say that initially, but think about how you originally learned to read," said Terry Durkin, president of Listen For Pleasure and the chap who originally introduced commercial talking books to North America.

"You got into it with somebody reading you stories. We're doing the same thing only making it more entertaining. Our tapes aren't meant to compete with books. We're an alternate form of entertainment. And a lot of people find themselves reading even more."

That's me. Once I relented, I was hooked. I now "read" an average of two or three new titles a week on cassette. I also continue my actual reading habits. So instead of cheating myself, I'm ahead of the game.

What makes these cassettes most attractive are the length — generally three hours — and the reader. A good story needs a good storyteller. In print, that's the author. On cassette, it's the reader and some of the people on these tapes are nothing less than wonderful.

Jack Nicholson was great in the movie, *Prizzi's Honor*. Paul Sorvino is incredible reading it. I wanted more and more. The same with Moriarty.

"Most of the people we use to read are good at it because this is their chosen profession," said Durkin. "They're actors and they go into the studio to act out these scripts. And occasionally we get someone like John le Carré. Here's a guy who gets $4 million for writing a book and he calls us to read."

Talking books aren't a new phenomenon. They've been around for years to assist the blind, seniors, and others with handicaps. But those leaned towards the classics or plays and were read by volunteers.

That all changed when the British-born Durkin got into the act in 1979 while running Library Sound Service, which specialized in distributing recorded literary classics. Acquiring a handful of best-sellers on cassette, he was blown away by the quality of the product.

"There were about 20-30 pieces available from Thorn-EMI, the giant British media conglomerate, which had launched talking books the previous year. I arranged a deal to become their distributor in North America."

Listen For Pleasure started small, but Durkin soon realized to make it he would have to manufacture his own tapes. He arranged a royalties deal with Thorn-EMI and the latter provided the masters. Before long, he had also established a U.S. base.

"It was a slow process and we had to build step by step. And it was frustrating because people thought we were for the blind. Gradually, it began to change."

Now people know who they are and what they sell. In fact, Listen For Pleasure (LFP), which is considered the Cadillac of the spoken word, has a network of about 5000 stores.

The total books-on-tape market, which runs the gamut from fiction to business to How To instruction tapes, is estimated at between $200-$300 million and climbing.

So it was no surprise to Durkin when some of the major New York publishing outlets like Random House, Simon and Schuster, Bantam, and Warner Communications jumped into the marketplace. "We used to have a 60% share, but when the others joined us we dropped down. However, we're climbing again."

LFP is interested only in quality, which is why they spend between $15 000 and $20 000 to turn out the average tape. Still involved with Thorn-EMI, the Canadian firm produces about half of its 250 tapes.

When seeking out a title, Durkin looks mainly for something that has a long shelf life and some movie or TV tie-in. "We want strong authors. And we shop around for good readers as well."

Reading usually takes a full day in the studio and readers get about $2500 plus a share of royalties. The tapes sell for about $14.95 both here and in the U.S.

Basically, they are looking for strong books that can be easily abridged without losing the story. Long books with complicated plots are out, which means people like Robert Ludlum and James Michener are passed over.

"Abridgers are instructed to cut out anything that doesn't directly advance the plot," says Durkin. "Sex scenes are also among the first to go unless they are absolutely essential.

"And, unlike some of our competitors, we don't bother with sound effects or music. We don't want anything to take away from the storyteller or the story."

Not surprisingly, the talking books have become popular among educators, particularly those dedicated teachers who were reading books into tapes and playing them for their students.

That's what convinced LFP to start its new Read-Along series, which is designed to tackle teenage and adult illiteracy as well as help others in school build and improve reading skills. The program combines the tapes with word-for-word transcript books. For schools, it includes a teacher's guide and student exercises.

"We've only been in the market with Read-Along (mostly classics) since October; but we're now selling to most European and South American countries. We're in school boards and libraries here and we're looking at the prison system. We're even talking to Russia and China."

The best example of its benefits came from a woman whose 10-year-old nephew was pulling a D-minus in reading. She gave him tapes of *Tom Sawyer* and *Huckleberry Finn* and the boy is now reading at an A level.

"For many people we're opening the door to the world of good books for the first time," said Durkin. "That's a good feeling."

Amen.

— Jerry Gladman
The Sunday Sun

EXPLORING IDEAS

1. Assess the advantages Jerry Gladman sees in the "talking book." What other advantages do you see in this approach? What might be some of the disadvantages?
2. In the future would you purchase such a product for your own children? Summarize your ideas in a paragraph or a journal entry.

INVESTIGATING THE MEDIA

1. When we talk about "reading" a book, an audiotape, or a computer program, in each case are we talking about the same kind of reading?
   (a) Discuss this in small groups; then make a journal entry in which you reflect on your own various kinds of "reading."
   (b) Next, conduct a "read-around" of these journal entries in class. As a class, what conclusions can you draw about the nature of "reading" today?

YOUR TURN

1. Design a poster or advertisement to promote the "Gift of Literacy." You may wish to submit your ideas to the Gift of Literacy Foundation.
2. Which book or story would you select for a talking-book cassette? Form groups to select and rehearse a story for presentation on tape. Compile and record your stories to create a class tape library. Design and produce posters or ads to promote the stories in your library.
3. Debate the following:

   Resolved: Print and print literacy in Canadian society are doomed.

   You may wish to use some of the findings from your *You and the Media* survey as evidence to support your arguments.

THE PAPERBACK REVOLUTION

Mass-market paperback is the term used for the rack-sized paperbound book that was introduced by Pocket Books in the United States in 1939 and sold for twenty-five cents, principally through periodical distributors in drugstores, chain stores, bus stations, and airport terminals — that is, the mass market.

Before these inexpensive, widely distributed books came along, only the rarest of books sold more than a hundred thousand copies; a million-seller was a real phenomenon. Bookstores were for the elite "carriage trade" of sophisticates, mostly in big cities; public libraries, few and far between, were not much better. Overnight, the paperback changed that. Suddenly, a book could reach not hundreds or thousands of readers but millions, many of whom had never owned a book before.

— Kenneth C. Davis
from the preface to *The Two-Bit Culture*

Paperback Best-Sellers: The First 25 Years

18.5 Million
Baby and Child Care by Benjamin M. Spock, M.D. (1946)

15.5 Million
The Merriam-Webster Pocket Dictionary (1947)

10 Million
Peyton Place by Grace Metalious (1957)

8 Million
God's Little Acre by Erskine Caldwell (1946)

6.5 Million
Webster's New World Dictionary of the American Language (1958)

6 Million
University of Chicago English-Spanish, Spanish-English Dictionary (1950)
In His Steps by Charles Sheldon (1960)

5.5 Million
Exodus by Leon Uris (1959)
To Kill a Mockingbird by Harper Lee (1962)
Roget's Pocket Thesaurus (1946)
The Carpetbaggers by Harold Robbins (1962)

5 Million
How to Win Friends and Influence People by Dale Carnegie (1940)
Return to Peyton Place by Grace Metalious (1960)

4.5 Million
The Pocket Cook Book by Elizabeth Woody (1942)
Profiles in Courage by John F. Kennedy (1947)
The Big Kill (1951), *I, the Jury* (1948), *My Gun Is Quick* (1950) by Mickey Spillane
1984 by George Orwell (1950)
Thunderball by Ian Fleming (1962)

4 Million
The Dell Crossword Dictionary by Kathleen Rafferty (1951)

— Kenneth C. Davis
from *The Two-Bit Culture*

EXPLORING IDEAS

1. Look carefully at each of the best-sellers on the list. What do some of these reveal about our society? What do they tell you about the times during which different titles were popular? (For example, consider the publication date of the best-selling paperback.)
2. Based on your examination of the list, what factors do you think contributed to making each a best-seller in the 1940s and '50s? What factors, do you think, contribute to making a best-seller today? Share your observations and opinions with the class.

INVESTIGATING THE MEDIA

1. Working in groups, discuss paperbacks you have recently purchased. What were some of the factors that made you purchase each paperback? Consider cover design, bookshelf displays, and so forth. Draft a set of guidelines for marketing paperbacks and present your ideas to the class.
2. ***(a)*** Obtain an up-to-date list of paperback best-sellers. Try to account for the popularity of each. Which books could be classified as "trash"? as potential "classics"? Which are fiction, which are non-fiction?
   (b) Conduct a class survey of titles that are currently popular with students, and produce your own list of Top-Ten Best-Sellers.
3. Bring to class one of your favourite paperback novels. Write or give an oral report in which you outline the strengths of this book — the reasons why you think others would like it. Consider the following:
   (a) *the plot*: How does the author keep the reader turning the pages?
   (b) *the characters*: Is the portrayal of the main characters stereotypical or realistic?

Harlequin Books was founded in 1949 in Winnipeg, by Canadian publisher Richard G. Bonnycastle. In its early years Harlequin's strongest sellers were reprinted British romance novels — typically featuring young nurses and governesses being pursued by handsome millionaires in exotic locations.

Today one out of every two paperbacks sold in North America is a romance. Toronto-based Harlequin is the world's largest publisher of romance fiction, publishing in 100 countries and 17 languages. (In 1986 Harlequin sold over 206 million books worldwide, with revenues of $300 million.)

The explosive growth of Harlequin Books is often credited to merchandising methods that are unique in the publishing industry. In the following interview Katherine Orr, Director of Public Relations for Harlequin Enterprises, discusses some of the factors behind the successful marketing of romance.

Packaging Romance: The Harlequin Story

Q1. Harlequin's success is often credited to its unique merchandising methods. What are some of those methods?

A. Well, Harlequin was the first publisher to apply packaged-goods marketing to books — to sell them like you would toothpaste or soap. We put books where women are — and that is in the supermarkets, convenience stores, drugstores, and so on. We created displays that were readily identifiable at about 100 paces — you always knew where the Harlequins were. And we promoted the brand name — Harlequin — over and above the name of the author or the story, so that we would achieve brand loyalty.

Q2. Who is the target audience for Harlequin romances? What have you discovered about them, and how do you shape your books to meet the tastes of your audience?

A. First of all, our books are written *by* women *for* women, so our audience is all women — of any age. Girls start reading them at 13, and continue until they're 100. I think the main thing they're looking for is a romantic fantasy with a "happily-ever-after" ending. The predictability of our books is their biggest selling feature. When you pick up a book, you know exactly what you're going to get — the heroine will fall in love with a wonderful man and in the course of the story he is going to promise her love forever. Not many people have that guarantee or reassurance in real life.

Q3. I'm interested in the profile of the Harlequin Romance heroine that you outline in your editorial guidelines. She is "inexperienced" and "need not have a career." What is the rationale behind that profile?

A. We do editorial guidelines mainly to delineate the different Harlequin lines — Harlequin Romance, Harlequin Presents, and so on. If you're going to write for, let's say, the Romance line, the heroine is rather young and inexperienced. She has to be a little less worldly than the hero so that there is a more common identification for the reader. In some of our more sophisticated lines, the heroine is more mature, and established in an interesting career.

Q4. Are you assuming that the reader of Harlequin Romance is also less experienced? Is the idea to create the heroine in the image of the reader?

A. Yes and no. With some women it's a recollection thing. The woman who's reading in her 30s or 40s has likely had her first love, but she's recalling it through that heroine.

Q5. How have your heroines changed over the years?

A. We used to be known for nurse, doctor, and governess stories, but now we have heroines that have a job like mine or they could be in radio or TV; they could be a lawyer or even a plumber; they're likely to be professionals meeting the man on the same level or perhaps above him.

Q6. How would you respond to the criticism that Harlequin romances perpetuate stereotypes of women and relationships?

A. Romances are no more detrimental to a woman's mental health than a man wishing he quarterbacked the most recent football victory. We *all* have dreams, male or female. Harlequin sells dreams; after all, we are in the entertainment business. These are positive books, which leave the reader with an uplifted feeling that happy endings perhaps could, and very often do, happen in real life.

Q7. Is setting a particularly important element in your books?

A. Our readers often say that they travel through our books. Toronto or Calgary or Winnipeg may not be exotic cities to Canadians, but they are to the woman who's reading in Japan or France. Boise, Idaho is pretty exotic if you're reading about it in Germany.

Q8. Who are your writers?

A. We have about 600 authors around the world — about 75 in Canada. It's part of my job to look after them. We make them feel very much a part of the Harlequin "family" by sending them a newsletter, birthday cards, valentines, and presents. They are generally over 30, because it's difficult to write about a love encounter if you haven't had one yourself. They're married with kids, their husbands are working. They're very much your average woman. Some have PhDs, some have fulltime jobs. Over half our writers write under a pseudonym. We do have a couple of male authors, but it's difficult for a man to describe a woman falling in love. Of course, the same is true for a woman trying to describe a man falling in love.

Q9. Do your Canadian authors have a favourite location?

A. The Canadian image has changed. There always used to be a western frontier — always the Manitoba rancher — but now our image has become more cosmopolitan. Now it's the sailing magnate in Vancouver, the fast-track banker in Toronto...

Q10. What advice would you give to a potential author?

A. There's about 3 or 4 key things. You've got to write about what you know, so don't try to write a book that's set in Afghanistan or Toronto if you haven't been there. Create a hero that not only you could fall in love with, but a man your reader could love too. Pace the story so that there is this wonderful love that's happening — there's confusion, there's conflict, then there's a resolution. The happy ending is essential. How you resolve a story is the best part of being a writer and the best way to have fun with what you're writing. That is, how do I get these two together? The formula — there isn't one. We provide guidelines as a recipe, but you have to have the cook in you to make the story sizzle.

Q11. How do you advertise Harlequin romances? What is the theme or message of your campaign?

A. Right now our advertising signature line is "Harlequin is romance," but we're looking at revamping that. In the '70s and '80s we wanted Harlequin to become a generic term — if you said "romance book," you'd say "Oh, Harlequin." We mainly advertise in women's consumer magazines so now we're looking at what our message will be.

Q12. How important is the cover to sales? What do you hope your cover will accomplish?

A. The cover design is defined by imprint, because we're selling the Harlequin lines over and above individual titles. Of course, the Harlequin diamond is on every book as well as the name of the imprint. The cover art always involves a couple in a "clinch." The colours tend to be pastel — very warm and inviting. The back-cover blurb is the enticing part — the window on the book. It tells you where the book's going to be set, what the characters' names are (the reader may have a friend with the same name), and what the conflict is. That's going to make the reader wonder what the resolution will be.

Q13. In an age when the electronic media are reputedly threatening print, how do you account for Harlequin's success? What features of the books do you think give them an advantage over television?

A. Well, the media confronts you with the real world. Harlequins are a relief — a bit of a haven from the

10/88 Harlequin Romance

Why had it become a battle of wills?

Berry Baker, popular hospital radio DJ, couldn't understand how her plan to raise money for a children's ward at St. Luke's Hospital had turned into a contest for control—between her and Julian Vyse, the senior medical consultant.

Was it because her youthful appearance and bouncy personality made her seem incapable of real responsibility? Or was it because Julian was just too accustomed to running the show?

Or had Berry thrown up battle lines because Julian had flirted with her, kissed her and threatened to crack her protective shell?

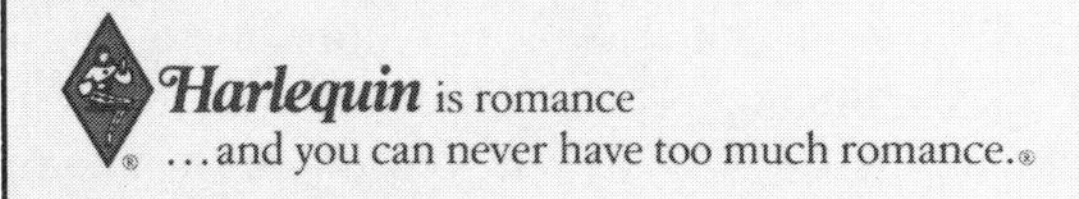

Harlequin is romance
...and you can never have too much romance.

ISBN 0-373-02938-1

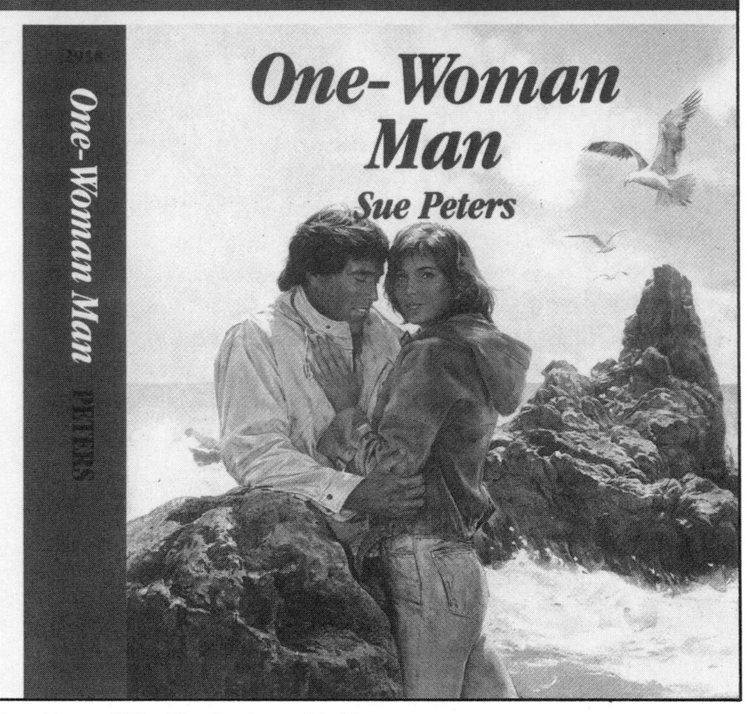

One-Woman Man
PETERS
One-Woman Man
Sue Peters

A Harlequin cover—an invitation to romance. In 1986, Harlequin sold over 206 million books worldwide.

rest of the world. And, there is also escape on television. If you isolate any love story in *Dallas* or *Dynasty*, it could be a Harlequin. *Love Boat* is a similar formulaic kind of plot. It's contrived — the happy ending is guaranteed. But the format of Harlequins offers distinct advantages over television: they're very portable, and they are not passive like television. The books are lightweight, you can read them in an hour-and-a-half to three hours, depending on your reading speed, and you can pick them up and put them down at your convenience.

Q14. What do you see as the future of mass-market romances? What innovations can we expect to see in the future?

A. I think women will always read romance because it's *in* us just as adventure is *in* men. But the series concept will change as the times change. With the return today back to traditional values, our stories may focus more on family. We are living in fearful times and we need this security in real life as well as in books. We've never dealt with issues such as divorce, religion, politics — we've always focussed on the man and woman. Well, we might spread out. There may be futuristic romances — sci-fi romances. We have an author who's working on this concept right now.

A line of video movies based on Harlequin romances has recently been launched. Called "A Harlequin Romance Movie," they are seen on the Showtime Cable TV Network (U.S.), First Choice/The Movie Channel (Canada), and are also available in video stores through Paramount. The first Harlequin movie was called *Love With a Perfect Stranger*. The movies are adapted by screenplay writers from Harlequin and Silhouette novels.

HARLEQUIN ROMANCE Editorial Guidelines

Length: 50 000 – 60 000 words.

Many aspiring romance writers believe that writing a Harlequin Romance, our original and longest-running romance line, is easy — simply follow the traditional "formula," employ a pleasant writing style, and you're there. This kind of thinking, however, is a mistake. A book written to "formula," one that only "makes the right noises," is readily obvious to an editor — and to readers. What we *are* looking for are romances with a spark of originality, imagination, a freshness of approach and strong believable characters, not stereotypes; stories that center on the development of the romance between the heroine and hero, with the emphasis on feelings and emotions, not necessarily only the heroine's.

Harlequin Romances are often referred to as "sweet" and "gentle," adjectives that differentiate them from our other lines. "Sweet" and "gentle" are broad terms that encompass many things: a light story, not filled with "heavy" realism; perhaps some touches of humor; warm, believable characterizations, stories that are sincere, heartwarming and charming. These are the qualities we are seeking.

Plot:

Story lines may be relatively simple, though there must be enough complexity to maintain interest for the required 50 000-plus words. Subplots that add elements of mystery, suspense or adventure are fine, as long as the emphasis remains on the central romance. This central romance should fulfill readers' fantasies of ideal love and meet a high moral standard. The plot should not be too grounded in harsh realities — Romance readers want to be uplifted, not depressed — but at the same time should make the reader feel that such a love is possible, if not probable.

Style:

Generally light and natural; humorous, but only if you have a bent for humor and humor fits naturally into the story. Do not allow long passages of narrative unbroken by dialogue. Dialogue should reflect the way people actually speak, but keep "strong" language (swear words) and highly provocative, sensual language to a minimum.

Heroine:

Generally, younger than the hero and *relatively* inexperienced. She should hold *traditional* (not to be equated with old-fashioned) moral standards. Unlike other romance lines, the heroine need not be a career woman, nor even a woman with a fascinating, different job. If the plot calls for her to be either of these, fine; otherwise, she may hold just an average job, earning average income; she may be unemployed. If she works in a traditional woman's job —

HARLEQUIN Fun Facts

• In 1986, Harlequin sold over 206 million books worldwide — reflecting a sale of almost six books a second, and almost two books to *every* woman in the United States.

• In 1985, Harlequin shipped its one billionth book in North America. To date, Harlequin has shipped nearly *two billion* books around the world.

• If you set out to read all the Harlequin books sold over the past ten years, averaging a little over two hours per book, you would be reading for the next quarter of a million years.

• If all the Harlequin books sold *in a single day* in 1986 were stacked one on top of another, the pile would be 16 times as high as New York's World Trade Center.

• If placed *end to end*, Harlequin books sold in 1986 could run along both banks of the Nile, both banks of the Amazon, and one bank of the Rio Grande.

• The weight of all Harlequin books sold in 1986 would equal the maximum carrying capacity of more than 169 Boeing 747 cargo planes.

• If all the words of all the Harlequin books sold in 1986 were laid end to end, they would stretch 1000 times around the earth or 93 times to the moon. That's a distance of halfway to the sun.

— *source*: Harlequin Books

HARLEQUIN'S Interesting Facts About...

Romance Readers (in general)

- Women, age 15 or older.
- 40% are college educated.
- 35% are employed full-time.
- 30% have an average family income in excess of $30 000.
- 20% read one romance book a day.
- 40% read one romance book every two days.
- The average romance reader spends up to $30 per month on romance books.

— *source*: Harlequin Books

secretarial, nursing, teaching, etc. — that's okay, too.

Despite her relative inexperience, she should not come across as weak, though she may be a bit naive. Her character should have depth and a likable, interesting personality readers can easily sympathize or identify with.

Hero:

He should be older, more mature than the heroine, probably late 20s to mid-30s. But try to avoid excessive age difference; for instance, the 17-year-old heroine and the 37-year-old hero. He should be very attractive, worldly, and successful in his field.

Setting:

Anywhere in the world as long as there is some romantic atmosphere conveyed. An "exotic" setting is desirable, but *only* if described naturally, blended with the plot, not fitted into the story like copy from a traveler's guidebook!

— *source*: Harlequin Books

EXPLORING IDEAS

1. How would you define "escapist" entertainment? What programs that you watch on TV would you define as "escapist"?

   Share your opinions on the following:

   (a) What, if anything, is wrong with escapist entertainment?

   (b) What purpose does escapism serve?
2. It would appear that the majority of writers and readers of this type of novel are women. In your view, why is this the case? Is there an equivalent of the "romance novel" for men?
3. Apparently, this traditional type of novel is changing to suit changing reader tastes and lifestyles. How might the romance novel continue to change in Canada — in the next century, for example?
4. Debate in class the following issue:

   Resolved: In view of their popularity, romances should be part of the English curriculum.

INVESTIGATING THE MEDIA

1. The tradition of romance in literature has created a number of enduring romances as well as popular romances in every era. What sets a classic apart from popular fiction?

   Prepare a report in which you compare a popular romance with a classic such as *Lorna Doone* or *Wuthering Heights*. What are the similarities in plot, characterization, format, etc.? What differences are there?

YOUR TURN

1. Working alone, or with a partner, write a description of an exotic location that could serve as a setting for a romance novel.

   or

   Write a description of the leading character for a romance novel. Choose a suitable title for the novel.
2. If you are a fan of romance novels, you might enjoy writing a tongue-in-cheek article entitled "Lessons to Be Learned from Reading Romance."

Teenage readers have been responsible for the success of many paperback novelists. S.E. Hinton, for example, is a writer whose novels enjoy enormous popularity in the teenage market. (Several of her novels have been translated into successful films.) Anyone who insists that teenagers have entirely rejected reading for other media is unaware of the impact that writers like S.E. Hinton have had on millions of young readers.

In the following interview, Ms. Hinton discusses her career as a novelist — a career that began when she published her first book, The Outsiders, *at the age of 18.*

S.E. Hinton

Interviewed by William Walsh

W.W. How does a sixteen year-old come to write a novel that is such a best seller and such a popular novel?

S.E.H. I'd been practising writing for eight years. I started in grade school, and I had written a couple of other novels before *The Outsiders.* It was just the first I ever tried to publish.

W.W. Tell us the story of why you sent this one out, when you hadn't sent any others.

S.E.H. The mother of a girlfriend of mine writes children's books, and she read *The Outsiders* and liked it. She said she would give me the name of her agency and told me to send it to them to see what they could do with it. Finally, I thought it would be worth a try, and I did send it.

W.W. Did this inspire you to burn the midnight oil?

S.E.H. Oh, no. It inspired me so greatly that I was unable to write for four years. I had a super case of "first-novel block." I could not write for four years. I could not use the typewriter, even to write a letter, even though I taught myself to type when I was in the sixth grade. I love to write, but for four years, I could not. I was a teenage writer, which is very similar to being a teenage werewolf. People are always watching you for signs of "things." I was put in the spotlight. I can understand complications people have who are suddenly famous overnight. Even though the amount of fame I got was very small, compared to that of a lot of people at the same age, it was enough to really bother me.

W.W. Where did you get the material to write the story, *The Outsiders?*

S.E.H. Well, it dealt with a situation I had in high school: The Socialist-Greasers thing, which is a very small part, because I went to a large high school and everybody divided up into different camps. The Socialists and the Greasers were actually just the extremes. There were all kinds of middle groups like the "artsy-craftsy" people; the "student council" people; "greasy socialists," and "socialist-greasers." It was a complicated social situation. I thought it was a very dumb situation, on top of that.

W.W. Did you belong to one of these groups yourself?

S.E.H. No. Even the nonconformists would not have me, because I wouldn't conform. But I had friends from all different groups. I thought it was dumb; but nobody questioned it.

W.W. You were accepted, though, by people in all the different groups?

S.E.H. Yes. Well, everyone looked at me sort of strangely, but I was accepted. I was a pretty good fighter; I did not scream when the police chased us; and I had a pretty good-sized switchblade knife that everybody liked. I was treated as one of the guys. I got my tooth chipped when I was hit in the face with a bottle. I had an interesting adolescence.

W.W. There's a crucial scene in the book where Johnnycake is dying in the hospital. He sees PonyBoy and he says, "Stay gold, PonyBoy; stay gold." Now, we remember, earlier on, that they were taught Robert Frost's poem, "Nothing Gold Can Stay." Did you have anything in mind beyond that?

S.E.H. Not really. While I was writing the book, I had no idea of plot structure — I still don't, I can't plot my way out of the Safe-Way Store — but I know my characters. And, during the book, I would go so far as to say to my friends, "I'm writing a book; this is what's happened so far. What should hap-

Best-selling novelist S.E. Hinton

pen next?" And they would tell me something, and I'd stick it in. The fire scene was something somebody told me ("Hey! Make the church catch on fire!" "Okay, I'll do that."). But, as far as the poem goes, I was working on my book in a creative writing class (which I made a "D" in because I was writing my book and not doing my class work), and I read the Robert Frost poem. I enjoyed it, and thought it was appropriate for my book and I stuck it in. I liked the feeling of it, the enthusiasm and the innocence and everything you lose as you get older. You lose your emotional commitments and I think that's what Frost had in mind. That's what I had in mind, even though I probably could not have articulated it at that time.

W.W. Was there a PonyBoy Curtis? I mean, I know you say there was a general situation, but...

S.E.H. Not really. I couldn't point out any kid that I knew as a child and say that that was PonyBoy; but he was very much like I was at that age. Maybe a lot of things happened to him that happened to different friends of mine. Not all of his experiences were one person's experiences. I just incorporated them. I've learned as a writer that any character you write is going to turn out to be some aspect of yourself, so there's an awful lot of me in Dallas Winston as well as PonyBoy Curtis. I don't think as a writer you can really, truthfully, say this person is so-and-so; it has to be filtered through your mind, so it is some part of you.

W.W. You said before that you couldn't plot your way out of Safe-Way and that, very often, others suggested elements of plot that you would put into the novel. Were the characters the same way? Do you have a clear idea of the character?

Cast of the film version of *The Outsiders*—S.E. Hinton worked with director Francis Coppola to bring the book to the screen.

S.E.H. I have an absolutely clear conception of my characters. If they walked through the door, I wouldn't be surprised. I know their birthdays, what they like to eat for breakfast; I know what kind of dreams they have; I know their hair color, their eye color. One thing I cannot stand. It happened when I was reading one of Harold Robbins' books. I got halfway through the book, and he switched his character's eye color on me, and I just shut the book. I thought, "If the man doesn't know his character well enough to know what color his eyes are, I don't really care to read his work." I'm a very strong character writer, but that is only myself. There are other writers, like Ray Bradbury, who are idea writers; there are people who are atmosphere writers; people who can do intricate plots. Everybody has his own strong point. Mine is character.

W.W. When you wrote *That Was Then*, did it also come out of some personal experience?

S.E.H. It's hard to say because you mix up things that have happened to other people with your own experiences, and you take what your own experiences might have been and dramatize them into something completely different. You get your characters from different places. Like Mark, one of the main characters in *That Was Then*. His personality was taken directly from a cat I had (people think this is a cute, funny, little writer-thing you say). I actually got his personality from a cat, as much as I can get a personality from a human being. Later, I was talking to my sister (who is also a cat-person) and told her I had gotten Mark from Rabbit — my cat — and she said, "Oh, yes. I see that." Rabbit had beautiful beer-colored eyes that I had to incorporate into the character. And he's a completely amoral little animal. What was good for him was good; what was bad for him was bad. He had no judgments, so far as how his actions might affect other people.

W. W. This mixing up your life with other people's and then sorting it out in a book, does that help you understand yourself or your experiences better?

S.E.H. Sometimes. But it takes several years to look back on it and see what you were actually saying; I feel the theme in *That Was Then* was "growth is betrayal" and, even though I knew that was what I wanted to say, when I got through with it, I was not satisfied that I had it said. I still could not put it into words until four or five years later.

W. W. You said it better than you knew. I think many writers have that experience. A lot of what you're doing is unconscious or subconscious.

S.E.H. It is completely subconscious; and later you can look back and say, "I did this," or "I did that." Like in *Rumblefish*, I had somebody remark upon the color symbolism I used (black-and-white motif) and I didn't realize that I had done it until I looked back and saw; not only with the color blindness of the motorcycle boy, but the different things of black and white and black and white and black and white that go throughout the story.

W. W. The feeling you get from reading *Rumblefish* is quite different from the feeling you get from *The Outsiders* and also from *That Was Then*. They are all first-person narrations, and it seems that it is the narrator who is changing in each case, and the world appears different, as each person sees it.

S.E.H. I try to do that. I could take PonyBoy Curtis and change his name to "Jim Smith" or something and write another book from the same person's point of view; but that's not stretching yourself as a writer, and I want to do that. At the same time, I still want to reach my own audience. I write for kids who don't usually read a book, so I feel that *Rumblefish* is written on two different levels, when it's one. Just a simple, straight story, a little action thing, how Rusty James couldn't let go of the good old days of the gangs, and how that destroyed him. But I still feel, at least from the letters I've gotten from kids, they realize there's something else there, even if they don't know what it is. They think, "I've got to think about that. Maybe I don't know what it means, but it's something to think about and maybe I'll come back to it later." I think I accomplished what I set out to do with *Rumblefish*.

W. W. Do any of the youngsters who write to you ask you about their own writing?

S.E.H. Yes, they do. A lot of them want to write and don't know where to begin. I always say that, first of all, they've got to read. Just read everything. I never studied writing consciously. But if you read a lot, like I did, subconsciously, structure is going to drop into your head, whether it's sentence structure, paragraph structure, chapter structure, or novel structure. Pretty soon, you're going to know where things go — where the climax is supposed to be, where the ending's supposed to be, how to get there, how to describe people. You can absorb it subconsciously. I, personally, never tried to copy any one person's style because I feel you should write the way you think. But reading lots of different styles will expose you to different ways of thinking. My big recommendation is to read and then practise. Write yourself. I wrote for eight years before I wrote *The Outsiders*. I advise writing for oneself. If you don't want to read it, nobody else is going to read it. Once you do that and get somebody else's opinion, just start sending it away.

W. W. All of your character-narrators are first-person, male.

S.E.H. I can't write from a female point of view. I've tried it, but I can't do it. It's just that when I was growing up, all my close friends were guys. I identified with the male culture; I was a tomboy; and, while I realize now I used to think I had a male mind, I think I just had a female mind that didn't conform to the female culture at that time. It's just a thing I feel very comfortable with, and I realize I reach all my audience that way. While girls will read boys' books, boys very often will not read girls' books; so one can appeal to both of them that way. It's very likely I will continue to write from the male point of view.

W.W. You don't think there's a great deal of difference, then, between the point of view of a fifteen-year-old boy and a fifteen-year-old girl?

S.E.H. Not as much as you would think, really. It's amazing the similarities among the letters I get from guys and girls. If they could just realize that this artificial barrier between them is almost just socially set up, that their wishes, their dreams and everything are very similar, they could communicate a lot better.

EXPLORING IDEAS

1. S.E. Hinton draws on her high-school experiences in her writing. Would a novel of today reflect similar experiences? If *you* were writing a novel about today's teenagers, what kinds of experiences would you draw on? Share your ideas in a class discussion.
2. **(a)** Ms. Hinton talks about "character writers," "idea writers," and "atmosphere writers." In your creative composing which of these labels best describes your writing style?

   (b) Can you identify with any of S.E. Hinton's writing processes and techniques? How well have these worked for you?

   Are there any of her techniques you would like to try out to "stretch yourself" as a writer? Share your ideas in small-group writers' "workshops."
3. To what extent do you agree with the following statement?

   "*If they could just realize that this artificial barrier between them (guys and girls) is almost just socially set up, that their wishes, their dreams, and everything are very similar, they could communicate a lot better.*"

   Discuss as a class.
4. "*I write for kids who don't usually read a book...*"

   How do you account for the popularity of Ms. Hinton's novels with today's teens? In what ways can you foresee the market changing for such novelists? Discuss this issue in small groups, appointing one member to report your observations, conclusions, and predictions to the class.

INVESTIGATING THE MEDIA

1. Read one or two novels by *other* writers whose books are targeted to readers aged 13-18. Write a review of each novel, noting especially why it would — or would not — be appealing to young readers.

YOUR TURN

1. Be a publisher. Design a line of paperbacks targeted to readers your own age. Develop editorial guidelines outlining the types of characters, plots, settings, etc., these books might feature. Select a "brand" name for the line and an advertising slogan or signature line. Create a cover and a back-cover "blurb" for one of the novels. After viewing displays of paperbacks in stores, design your own display.
2. Could anyone be another S.E. Hinton? Several writers have gained overnight success by writing the best-selling paperback novel. In fact, some of these best-sellers have been group efforts.

   Work in groups and make a list of some of the stock formulas for the best-seller under the following headings: plot, setting, characters, themes. Begin writing your own "mini-romance" or action-adventure. Appoint one or two editors who will select and add material, copy edit, and proofread. Others in the group will serve as a marketing team to plan strategies such as cover design, format, advertising, and sales.

READ ALL ABOUT IT: NEWSPAPERS

If you had to pinpoint one aspect of newspapers that made them different from all other media, what would it be? Many analysts insist that the unique aspect of this print form is the newspaper page itself. The front page, for example, throws many diverse items at the reader all at once in a visual display. It tries to catch us "on the street corner" with, of all things, its words.

The newspaper is one of the oldest forms of print media, yet despite growing competition it remains the largest advertising medium in Canada. It has survived by adopting strategies that suit the changing tastes of its readers. If you have any doubt, compare the following front page from *The Globe and Mail*, July 1, 1867, with the 1967 edition (on page 69).

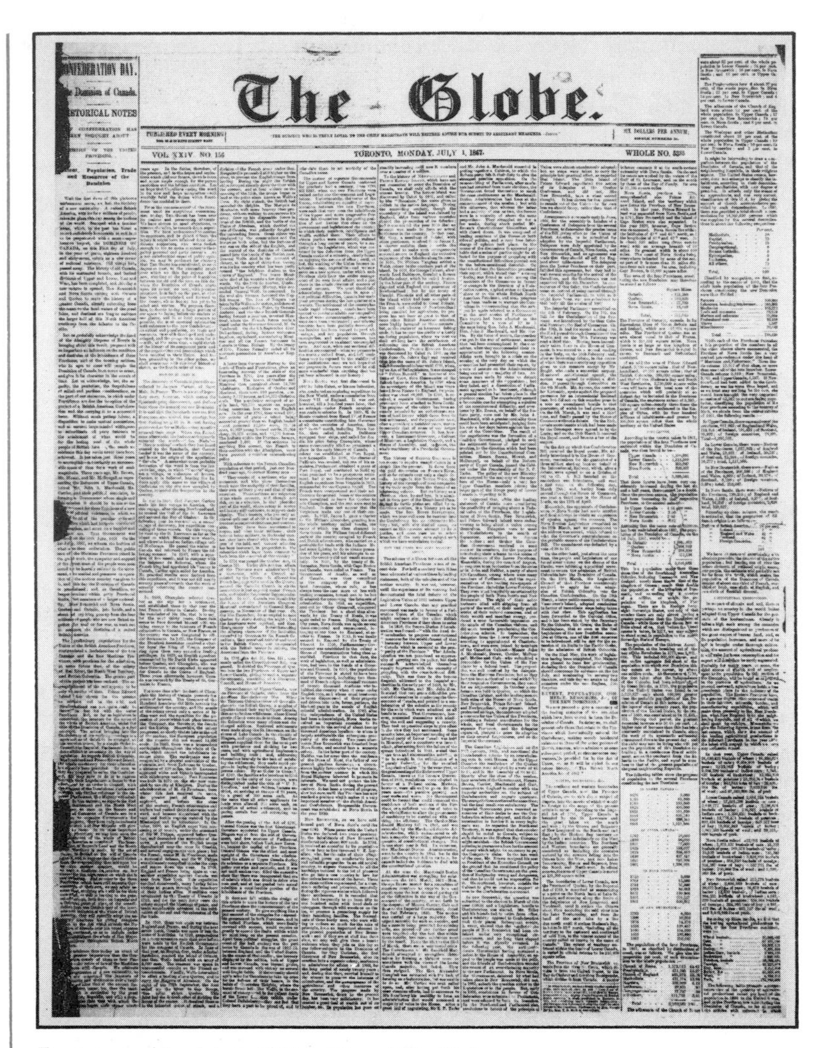

The Globe.

VOL. XXIV. NO. 156 — TORONTO, MONDAY, JULY 1, 1867.

Front page of the July 1, 1867, edition of *The Globe*

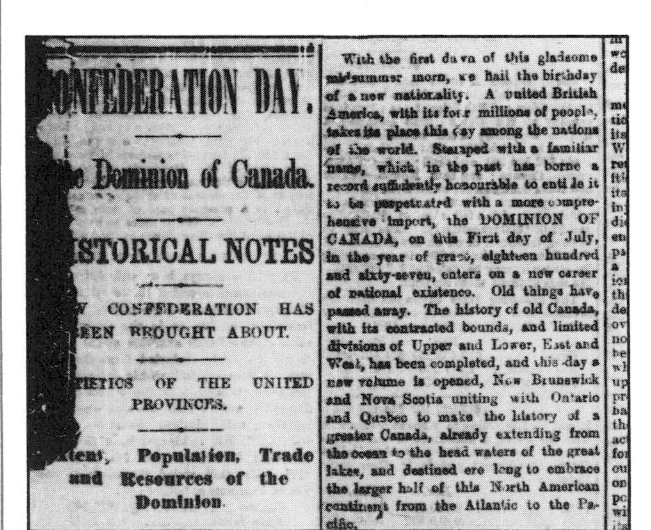

ONFEDERATION DAY.

he Dominion of Canada.

ISTORICAL NOTES

W CONFEDERATION HAS
EEN BROUGHT ABOUT.

TISTICS OF THE UNITED
PROVINCES.

tent, Population, Trade
and Resources of the
Dominion.

With the first dawn of this gladsome midsummer morn, we hail the birthday of a new nationality. A united British America, with its four millions of people, takes its place this day among the nations of the world. Stamped with a familiar name, which in the past has borne a record sufficiently honourable to entitle it to be perpetuated with a more comprehensive import, the DOMINION OF CANADA, on this First day of July, in the year of grace, eighteen hundred and sixty-seven, enters on a new career of national existence. Old things have passed away. The history of old Canada, with its contracted bounds, and limited divisions of Upper and Lower, East and West, has been completed, and this day a new volume is opened, New Brunswick and Nova Scotia uniting with Ontario and Quebec to make the history of a greater Canada, already extending from the ocean to the head waters of the great lakes, and destined ere long to embrace the larger half of this North American continent from the Atlantic to the Pacific.

Detail of the 1867 front page—Compare the treatment of the big story of the day with that of today's headline news.

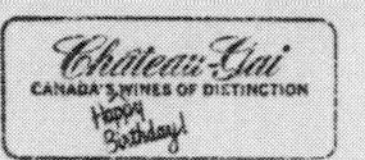

Château-Gai
CANADA'S WINES OF DISTINCTION
Happy Birthday!

The Globe and Mail

SERVING CANADIANS SINCE 1844
CANADA LIFE
Scattered showers
Toronto high 80
Details on page 2

124th YEAR, No. 36,674 METRO EDITION TORONTO, SATURDAY, JULY 1, 1967 56 PAGES TEN CENTS

WEEKLY

FIRST SECTION

Toronto 2067

High-rise living and instant suits. Page 7

SECOND SECTION

Johnny Wayne

He should have been born on July 1. Page 21

THIRD SECTION

The Canadian Open

Art Wall leads after two rounds. Page 37

THE CONFEDERATION GLOBE

A reproduction of the July 1, 1867, edition. Pages 27-30

Births, Deaths	54	Contract Bridge	55	Religion	32
Business	42	Crossword Puzzle	55	Stamps, Coins	55
Comics	55	Editorial	6	Women's	18

PM says it for all of us

'THIS DAY IS CANADA'S'

Queen laughs at skit

By SCOTT YOUNG
Globe and Mail Reporter

'Ours is a good land, resolve to better it'

From the Ottawa Bureau of The Globe and Mail

OTTAWA — In a special Dominion Day statement, Prime Minister Lester Pearson calls for continued work to fulfill the hopes and aspirations of the Canadian people.

His statement:

"This day, the 100th anniversary of the beginning of our Confederation; this day, our Centennial birthday, belongs to every Canadian.

"Those of us whose privilege it is to represent in public office the people of this country will play our formal roles in the pageants of this historic day.

"But the history and the heritage we celebrate are the possession of all Canadians, whatever our origin, whatever our occupation, wherever we live and work.

"Every one of you, and every Canadian before you, has had some part, however humble and unsung, in building the magnificent national structure of Confederation that we honour and salute today.

"As the world, to survive the nuclear future, must become a community of peace for all mankind, so must our country be a true homeland for all Canadians as it moves into its second century.

"The Fathers of Confederation, and those who followed them, have built a strong foundation for this Canadian home.

"As we begin our second hundred years, we must continue the work of furnishing it so that it will fulfill the hopes and aspirations of all our people for a good life.

"This is a memorable day for Canada.

"Ours is a good land. Our Centennial resolve must be to make it better for our children and our children's children.

"God bless our country."

Bells in foggy Halifax, dancing on N.B. wharf greet 100th birthday

Shower damps opening of city's first ceremony

Buffalo Bisons shift 6 games to Niagara Falls

8 of 1,137 teachers leave resignations in

Will not allow O'Keefe Centre to close its doors, Allen says

Your morning smile

Globe and Mail will publish on Monday

300 fired-up expatriates Down Under get a headstart on Centennial

The Aussie strike that couldn't stop partying Canadians

By IAN MOFFITT
Special to The Globe and Mail

Garden party draws Russians

Front page of the July 1, 1967, *Globe and Mail*—How has the format changed to suit the times?

EXPLORING IDEAS

1. What does the format of the news for July 1, 1867, tell us about the 19th century reader? Judging from this page, in what ways would you say the reader then was different from the reader today?
2. Study the front page dated one hundred years later. Some of the same news is being reported, but how has the format changed? What does this tell us about ourselves — about the way we want the news to "come at us"?
3. Brainstorm a list of format decisions that go into the design of the modern front page. Which decisions do you consider the most consequential?

YOUR TURN

1. Can you make any predictions about the front page of *The Globe and Mail*, July 1, 2067? Try it. Working in groups, design a front page for an edition in the twenty-first century.

Although the function of the newspaper is to report the news as completely and as accurately as possible, sometimes readers overlook that publishing a newspaper is a business. Like any other business, yearly profit is essential, as Walter Stewart points out in the following excerpt.

The News Business

A modern newspaper is an expensive undertaking. The *Montreal Star* was reputedly purchased for $100 before 1900, and the *Edmonton Bulletin* was started up for $21. In 1978-79, the *Star* managed to lose more than $10 million, and its presses and building were valued at more than $16 million. Today, a single portable Teleram machine for transmitting copy to newspapers costs $3500, and the word processors found on newsdesks can cost more than $10 000.

At one time, newspapers were run by people who specialized in words; now they are the property of those who know how to work the tax laws for maximum benefit. The peripheral activities of a newspaper like the *Toronto Star* — its real estate ventures, its holdings in weekly chains, its Harlequin romances publishing company — bring in more money and cause less grief than the newspaper itself. Newspapers still editorialize as if they thought they were providing a public service — it is part of their standard pitch when lobbying for legislative breaks — but in fact they are run very like any other business, and return, on the average, better profits than the steel industry.

Their activities are easier to understand in the context of business than journalism. What makes a modern newspaper tick is not the curiosity of its editors, or the conviction of its reporters, but the count of advertising lineage. In an earlier age, advertising was important, but today, when a newspaper represents an investment of twenty million dollars or more, advertising is crucial. If one newspaper can gain an advertising advantage over another within the same market, the first will live and the second will die. The day when half a dozen papers could survive side by side is gone; modern technology has produced a vicious circle. The presses and computers and trucks and all the other capital outlays required demand a constant high turnover of funds, which can only be generated by extensive advertising. In turn, the advertising determines the shape of the newspaper, as well as its quality. Wednesday newspapers are fat because they carry the grocery ads; Saturday papers are fatter still, because they carry all the weekend ads and supplements. On many large newspapers, the Saturday edition alone generates fifty per cent of all revenue. The reason you get to read long background stories in the Saturday paper is not because editors want to bring you the week's rich panorama of events, but because the Saturday ad lineage requires the paper to put on more pages, and that creates more space. Editors cope with this onslaught of advertising by increasing the proportion of ads to news. At one time, a balance of sixty per cent news to forty per cent ads was regarded as respectable, but the balance has shifted until today many papers carry seventy per cent ads to thirty per cent news. If the ads were all full-page, there might be no requirement for news whatsoever. No, I exaggerate; advertisers like their copy to appear surrounded by news stories — providing they are not rude — so there will always be a place, albeit shrinking, for news in newspapers.

Advertising is sold on the basis of circulation, and newspapers are in exactly the same kind of ratings war as the television networks. A newspaper with more readers can attract more ads, make more money, afford to improve the product, and thus attract more readers — and so it goes. At one time, an advertising edge meant merely that one newspaper made more money than another. Today, such an edge spells doom for the one and triumph for the other.

— Walter Stewart
from *Canadian Newspapers: The Inside Story*

Newspapers Remain the Largest Advertising Medium in Canada

With over $1.5 billion in advertising revenues in 1985, daily newspapers are still by far the largest advertising vehicle in Canada. The next largest competitor, television, had just over two-thirds of newspaper sales.

Magazines 4.1%
Weekly Newspapers 5.7%
Daily Newspapers 25.1%
Television 17.1%
Radio 9.4%
Outdoor 5.8%
Catalogues, Direct Mail 22.5%
Other Print 10.4%

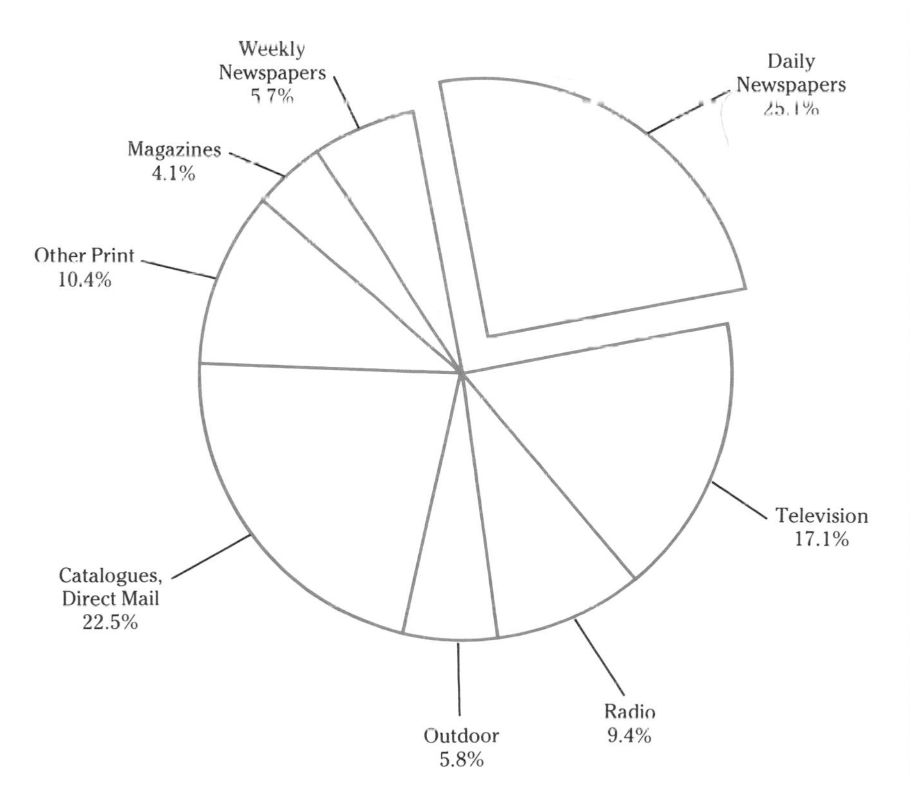

source: Maclean Hunter Research Bureau

EXPLORING IDEAS

1. According to Mr. Stewart, several factors in the "news business" are changing the form and content of newspapers today. In a class discussion, evaluate the validity of his assertions.
2. Examine the graph that accompanies the article. What facts are surprising to you? *Why* might daily newspapers be the largest advertising source in Canada? What can a newspaper do for an advertiser that, for example, television cannot? What types of businesses would likely put money into advertising in newspapers?
3. If it is true that the success or failure of newspapers hinges on advertising revenues, then how might this affect the story content and the appearance of newspapers?

INVESTIGATING THE MEDIA

1. "*Advertising determines the shape of the newspaper, as well as its quality.*" Test Mr. Stewart's arguments by studying a typical week of your daily newspaper.

   (a) Record the percentage of advertising to news for the same newspaper in relation to the days of the week. On which days does the newspaper contain the highest percentage of advertising? Why, do you think, is this so?

   (b) What relationship do you see between the quantity of advertising and the quality and quantity of news on various days?

   Report your findings and conclusions to the class.

Today there are two main types of front-page format: the traditional broadsheet and the newer and smaller tabloid. Both of these formats often carry the same news on the same day, but they structure their news differently.

The Look of the News: Formats

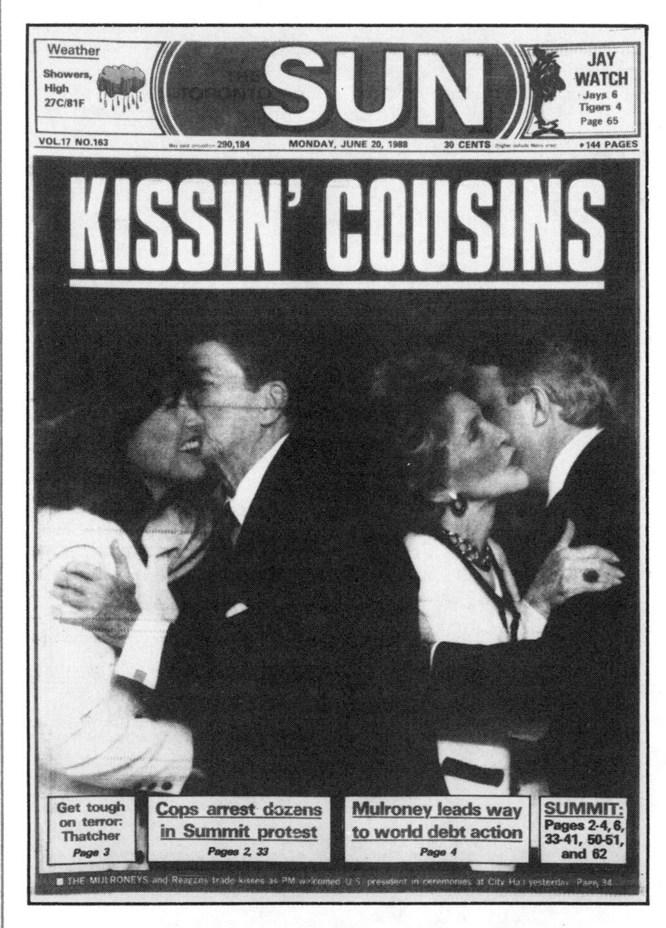

Weather
Showers, High 27C/81F

SUN

JAY WATCH
Jays 6
Tigers 4
Page 65

VOL.17 NO.163 | 290,184 | MONDAY, JUNE 20, 1988 | 30 CENTS | •144 PAGES

KISSIN' COUSINS

Get tough on terror: Thatcher
Page 3

Cops arrest dozens in Summit protest
Pages 2, 33

Mulroney leads way to world debt action
Page 4

SUMMIT: Pages 2-4, 6, 33-41, 50-51, and 62

■ THE MULRONEYS and Reagans trade kisses as PM welcomed U.S. president in ceremonies at City Hall yesterday. Page 34

The lead story: coverage of Toronto's Economic Summit, June 20, 1988. Evaluate the effect created by the front page of a tabloid (*above*) with that of the broadsheet (*right*).

59% IN CANADA FAVOR LIMITS ON ABORTIONS *Page A3*

SEXUAL ASSAULT CENTRE ANSWERS NEED *Page C1*

TILT MY HALO GETS A SCARE BUT WINS OAKS *Page D4*

MUGABE'S AMNESTY AVERTS WAR IN ZIMBABWE *Page A24*

LITERACY PROGRAM AIDS HOMELESS *Page A4*

Metro Weather
Partly sunny.
High 29C.
Details, A2
Car lights on 9.34 p.m., and off 6.07 a.m. tomorrow.

THE TORONTO STAR

Established 1892

Monday, June 20, 1988
30 CENTS
(higher outside Metro Toronto and surrounding suburbs)
May/88 Monday-Friday paid circulation 534,952

METRO EDITION ★

Leaders favor arms control deal

LEADERS: At The Hunt club from left are Jacques Delors, Ciriaco De Mita, Margaret Thatcher, Ronald Reagan, Brian Mulroney, Francois Mitterrand, Noboru Takeshita and Helmut Kohl.

Former Haitian leader escapes house arrest, overthrows president

PORT-AU-PRINCE (AP-Special) — Former Haitian military leader Lt.-Gen. Henri Namphy broke out of house arrest last night and his troops seized the presidential palace, overthrowing civilian President Leslie Manigat.

Manigat had fired Namphy Friday during a power struggle that split Haiti's military dictatorship.

The military ran the January balloting widely criticized as rigged that saw Manigat elected.

In Toronto, a senior Canadian official said Prime Minister Brian Mulroney learned of the coup following his dinner with the other world leaders attending the Economic Summit.

Canada's ambassador to Haiti has been called and told to report on the circumstances as soon as possible, the official said.

An Uzi sub-machinegun in his right hand, Namphy — wearing military fatigues and helmet — declared on state-run television early today that the army was in control. He spoke from the palace, which was taken in a gun and grenade battle.

"The army will lead the country this way," Namphy shouted, raising his weapon.

Government sources said Manigat was taken by ambulance from his home eight kilometres (five miles) north of the palace to a military hospital. There was no word on his condition, but a journalistic source close to the military said the president would be expelled today to an unspecified destination.

Namphy, surrounded by soldiers and speaking in Creole said during his seven minute speech, "We will not speak of what happened. We are looking ahead. We love the army, the regular army, the army loves the people and the country."

Namphy, 55, looked fatigued and said he was ailing.

Foreign Minister Gerard Latortue, Information Minister Roger Savain and several diplomats with close connections to Namphy and Manigat confirmed the coup, the Los Angeles Times reports.

Two majors of the 1,000-man Presidential Guard, whom Manigat in a sweeping reorganization of the armed forces had attempted yesterday to shift to powerless staff jobs, led the Namphy rescue and the palace seizure.

Earlier yesterday, Manigat retired the Port-au-Prince police chief and transferred about two dozen officers, including the head of the Presidential Guard.

A Western diplomat said the Presidential Guard had battled troops of the 700-man Dessalines Battalion, commanded by Lt.-Col. Jean-Claude Paul, whom Namphy tried to reassign last week to an administrative job.

Haiti's other combat-equipped infantry battalion, the Leopards, joined the Namphy forces against Paul's troops, according to diplomatic sources. Latortue told the Los Angeles Times he believed the Manigat government was "finished."

Ben Wicks

"Can't you see I'm busy?"

137 arrested in tight summit security

By Bob Hepburn
Toronto Star

The seven world leaders at Toronto's Economic Summit last night strongly endorsed U.S. President Ronald Reagan's efforts to conclude an arms control agreement that would eliminate all land-based, intermediate-range missiles.

[illegible] with Soviet leader Mikhail Gorbachev last December in Washington.

Canadian officials, briefing reporters after the summit leaders dined last night at the Toronto Hunt club, said the seven agreed relations with the Soviet Union are "reasonably positive," adding that Gorbachev is viewed as a reformer in the Soviet regime.

Meanwhile in Moscow, Gorbachev repeated in a message in East Berlin today to an international meeting on nuclear-free zones that the Kremlin is ready to scrap all its nuclear arms if other nuclear powers agree to do the same.

"The Soviet Union is fully prepared to eliminate its status as a nuclear power — and as soon as possible — together with the other countries possessing nuclear weapons," the Kremlin leader said.

Apartheid talks

At the Toronto summit, External Affairs Minister Joe Clark pressed his counterparts attending a separate dinner at the University of Toronto's Hart House to take a tougher stance against South African apartheid.

Clark reportedly told the foreign ministers that the situation in South Africa has deteriorated in the last year, especially after the recent government clampdown on protests.

Canadian officials, who refused to be identified, said the South African issue will be discussed today by Prime Minister Brian Mulroney and the other leaders.

After months of preparation, the Economic Summit opened yesterday amid massive security, lavish welcoming ceremonies and bitter squabbling among the seven world leaders over agricultural subsidies, one of the most crucial summit issues.

Police arrested [illegible] people as an anti-summit demonstration raged on University Ave.

Near the end of the 2½-hour rally, protesters threw large caricatures of the summit leaders on to a [illegible] to burn a tattered American flag.

Mulroney, in an upbeat assessment of the opening session, claimed that "there was a productive and spontaneous" debate among the leaders as they kicked off the three-day summit at the Metro Convention Centre.

"The leaders have had an excellent and free-wheeling discussion," Mulroney said as he ended the first meeting.

Despite Mulroney's optimistic report, the summit's opening day was marked by Canada's failure to wring an agreement from the leaders on how to deal with the controversial issue of agricultural subsidies.

Mulroney managed, however, to get the seven leaders — from the United States, England, France, Italy, Japan, West Germany and the European Community — to agree that the Canada-U.S. free trade deal "is a strong signal" that two countries can reduce trade barriers.

But the statement fell far short of a full endorsement for the free trade accord, which is still winding its way through Parliament and the U.S. Congress.

As a pipe and drum band played,

See REAGAN/page A19

TORONTO SUMMIT

Eight-page pullout section Pages A11 to A18

- Hang tough on economic policies, Reagan says A12
- Muskoka would have been better, Gwyn says. *A13*
- Italy demands tough war on drugs *A13*
- Thatcher sees Toronto *A15*
- Mila's style [illegible] media *A19*
- American TV coverage better than Canada's *C8*

Police launch all-out manhunt IRA attack on Thatcher feared

By Jim Wilkes Toronto Star

Security forces fear that two top IRA gunmen sought in a bloody European bombing last month are in Toronto.

Canadian authorities have sought the help of Interpol and other security networks around the world in a desperate hunt for Tony McAllister and Kevin Arti, suspected in machine-gun and car bomb killings of three British servicemen in Holland May 1.

Officials are worried that the Irish Republican Army may try to assassinate British Prime Minister Margaret Thatcher while she is in Toronto for the three-day Economic Summit of world leaders.

Intelligence forces are also working around the clock checking out reports the IRA has smuggled a Stinger anti-aircraft missile into Canada to attack Thatcher.

Although some reports indicate that the sophisticated shoulder-mounted missile was brought to Canada last fall aboard a ship from Lebanon that also carried illicit drugs, security officials in Toronto have played down the missile theory.

Streets barricaded

The Central Intelligence Agency warned Canadian officials that a "sleeper squad" of IRA agents from New York, San Francisco, Vancouver and Toronto may have been activated in a bid to pull off a spectacular attack at the summit.

Security was beefed up around Thatcher's downtown hotel after the arrest of a third suspected IRA man.

Side streets around the King Edward Hotel were barricaded and patrolled by uniformed police and members of the Joint Forces Tactical Group, an elite squad of heavily armed anti-terrorist officers from the Royal Canadian Mounted Police, Metro police and the Ontario Provincial Police.

Police were issued pictures of several key IRA fugitives, including McAllister and Arti.

Winos and bag ladies in the downtown core were stopped and had their plastic and paper bags searched yesterday as tension mounted.

The security alert intensified Saturday when Michael Derek Collins was arrested after a 10-day undercover operation by Canadian and British officers at a Toronto tavern.

Collins, a 31-year-old Irishman

See SECURITY/page A20

Today's vote in Quebec now big gamble for PM

By Ed Bantey
Special to The Star

MONTREAL — Once the votes have been tallied tonight in Quebec's Lac-Saint-Jean by-election, Prime Minister Brian Mulroney may find himself like the gambler who has bet his last chip — and lost.

Quebecers are born gamblers and, in his way, the Prime Minister is no exception.

One has visions of Mulroney seated at a blackjack table with a king as his only card, hoping that the dealer, the Lac-Saint-Jean electorate, will hand him the ace he desperately needs for a winning 21.

Some pros who have been looking over his shoulder are convinced that the lucky chip — his long-time friend and right-hand man, Secretary of State Lucien Bouchard — won't pull it off.

Mulroney's by-election gamble, which was to have been a sure thing, appears to have gone sour. A Bouchard defeat could mean game over — in Quebec and, inevitably,

See QUEBEC/page A2

Police search fields, woods for boy believed victim of random kidnapping

By Tracey Tyler Toronto Star

Christopher Stephenson is the victim of a random kidnapping by a stranger who grabbed the boy and disappeared, Peel Region police say.

"He was the nicest kid in the world. I wish this never happened," Christopher's friend, Garry Kober, 11, said yesterday as police expanded their search through fields and woodlands for the Brampton boy who was abducted Friday night.

Christopher, 11, was waiting outside a store in Brampton's Shoppers World mall when he was snatched by a man, said Detective Sergeant Tom Trevelyan.

Christopher's mother and younger sister were buying some sewing supplies a few metres away.

Nearly three dozen police officers and tracking dogs yesterday combed grassy areas off Steeles Ave. across from the mall, but turned up nothing.

Trevelyan said police are questioning a shopper who found a plastic Bi-Way bag at the mall Friday night, similar to one being guarded by Christopher just before he vanished at about 9.15 p.m.

Christopher's mother, Anna Marie Ste-

See POLICE/page A2

MISSING: Christopher Stephenson was a "nice kid."

EXPLORING IDEAS

1. ***(a)*** Discuss differences between the tabloid (page 72) and broadsheet (page 73) front page. Consider colour, typeface, photographs, captions, and the amount of written copy in proportion to visual material.
   (b) Generally, to what type of audience is each format designed to appeal?
   (c) What are the strengths and weaknesses of each format?
2. Traditionally, the front page of a newspaper presents the news in "hierarchical" order — that is, from the most important news to the least. Do you agree with the editors' decisions? Are there any other stories on the front pages of these newspapers you would highlight, change, or delete if you were editor?
3. The term "juxtaposition" refers to the placement together on the page of certain items: stories, photographs, advertisements. The juxtaposition may be accidental or it may be done for reasons of space.

   Study the juxtaposition of material on the two front pages. What is the initial effect on the reader? What effect might the editor be trying to create?

INVESTIGATING THE MEDIA

1. ***(a)*** Compare two newspapers' front pages for the same day — if possible, a broadsheet page and a tabloid page. Consider each newspaper's use of the following decisions:
   - number and choice of news stories
   - coverage of similar news stories
   - use of headlines
   - use of colour, typeface, photographs

   What differences do you note in the treatment of similar material? Summarize your findings and present them in a written or oral report to your class.

   (b) After examining the front page of several newspapers, share your opinions on the following statement:
   "*More and more today, we don't* read *newspapers. We* view *them.*"
2. Form groups to examine the juxtaposition of news reports, photographs, and advertisements in newspapers for one week. Collect examples of unusual juxtapositions. Report to the class on the possible associations created — momentarily — in the minds of the reader.

YOUR TURN

1. Using headlines, photographs, etc., gathered from other papers, compose a front page designed to attract the reader's attention.
   or
   Prepare a front page of a newspaper you would like to see in your city or community. (First you may wish to prepare an audiotape of the morning's news from radio, then rewrite the stories for the newspaper.)

   In composing the front page, you will have to make some key decisions:
   (a) selection and rejection of stories
   (b) emphasis given to selected stories
   (c) style of reporting: word choice, sentence structure
   (d) headlines
   (e) photographs
   (f) advertisements
   (g) juxtaposition

   Present the front pages to the class and evaluate the editorial decisions made. Which front page, in the class's view, seems to be the most "balanced and fair" in its reports of the day's news? Which front page is the most sensationalized? Which is the most interesting to the readers?
2. Take a story in a broadsheet newspaper and rewrite it as a tabloid story. Before writing, consider the changes the new format and target audience will require.

Media Facts & Techniques

The Newspaper Report

The standard news report is written in the "inverted pyramid" fashion. This means that the typical short-story structure of introduction, development, climax, and conclusion is turned upside down in newspapers:

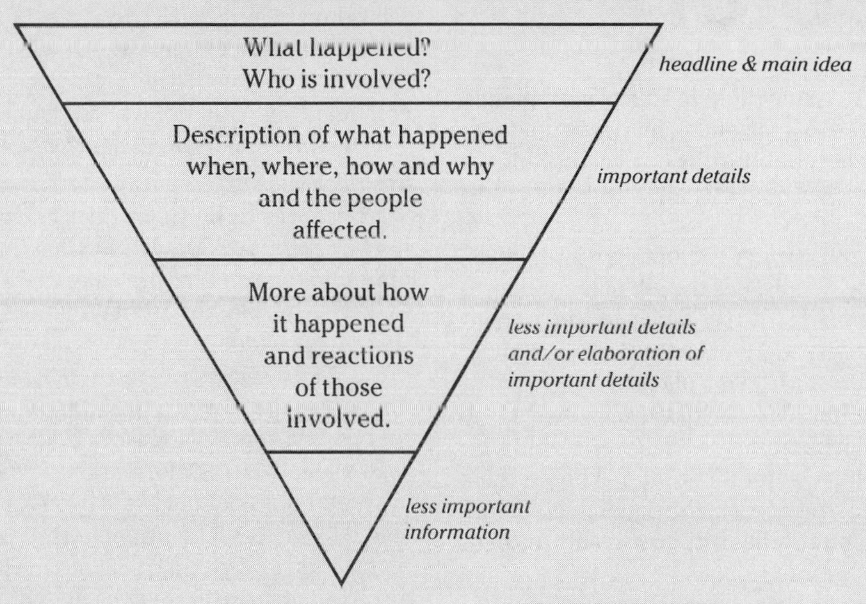

Thus the newspaper story presents the most important information first. In a sense, the reporter begins with the climax of the story. Then as the story unfolds, she or he discloses the less-important information.

Essential facts about the story are generally presented in the summary lead. The most common lead is the well-known "W5": Who? What? When? Where? and Why? (The extra "W" is often the final important question: How?)

The body is the development of the report as it follows the summary lead. Ordinarily, each paragraph flows naturally from the information in the lead. And the final element of the report is the headline. What are the purposes of the headline?

Of course, it is not only through format and design that the modern newspaper creates its effects. It uses the oldest, the most respected and sophisticated invention: the word. Below, two veteran journalists give advice on the use of "color" in words and details.

Color

Real things happen to real people in real places, people who bleed and sweat in Victorian hospitals or run-down courthouses, who wear double knits or tweeds, Rolexes or Timexes, and who, under stress, say wonderful or terrible things.

It is said that genius lies in the details. Good newswriting also lies in the details. It is the job of the writer to weave these threads of life into the story, to add authenticity and character to the bones of fact and circumstance.

That is called color, and it has a place in every kind of newswriting, from editorials to obituaries.

News is not fiction, but it can be exciting. People who make news usually have something interesting in their character. The reason stories get in the paper or on the air is that they describe out-of-the-ordinary events, or people, or both.

It's up to the writer to point up the extraordinary elements that take a story out of the so-what category.

Color comes in all shapes and forms. It is sometimes a small fact, such as what someone ate or wore. It is sometimes the writer's own observation of the weather, or the landscape, or the look on the face of the accused when the sentence is passed. It can be, and often is, a single word....

Color is best produced with details, not with adjectives. If the mural is painted in bright greens and reds, write that instead of "brightly colored." If the house is luxurious, try to estimate its price. If the fur coat dazzles, say if it's mink or sable. A fat man is a fat man, but a 285-pound man is better. Work at it.

Detail is the heart of color. When Henry Luce started TIME magazine, he searched for a way to make its stories appear more authentic than the competition's. He began what might be called the what-did-the-President-have-for-breakfast school of newswriting. Luce was after authenticity, and he sought it in the lives of the newsmakers. Food, wardrobe, private habits, favorite colors or books — all ended up in the magazine, adding what he believed was verisimilitude to the reporting. What Mr. Roosevelt ate in the morning didn't have anything to do with what he did during the day, but many a TIME reporter had to stand up at press briefings on serious matters to ask what the President had for breakfast.

Relevance is the key to skillful use of adjectives and adverbs. The modifiers must help define the noun or the verb.

Here, too, details can do it. If a speech is an hour and ten minutes long, write that. Or better, write seventy minutes. Don't call it lengthy. It will take time to find the specific, but it is worth doing. If something happened several years ago, find out when it happened. Use the date. Touches like that tell a reader that you know what you're talking about.

Luce was right. Color does add authenticity. It may not be essential to know that when medals were handed out for valor, some of the wounded recipients had to be helped to the platform. But it makes the story. A fact like that can be added in a phrase, a sentence, or a few words in the lead. It's best if not too much is made of it. Color that dominates the story is superimposed. Descriptive detail that flows as part of the story adds to the writing, to the reading, and to the information.

Color does not necessarily mean colorful words. It is stilted to write: "A courageous fireman risked death last night when he drove a truck into the blazing holocaust of an oil refinery fire to save the lives of 16 workers trapped in a sea of burning gasoline."

Better to write: "Sixteen workers trapped in a burning oil refinery were rescued last night by a lone fireman who drove a truck across a sea of flaming gasoline to bring them to safety."

"Less is more" has been used as advice to architects. It's a good rule for all writers. If you've got a good yarn, you can drop in the color sparingly, only where it helps. If you don't have a good story, all the color in the world won't dress it up.

— John Chancellor & Walter R. Mears
from *The News Business*

EXPLORING IDEAS

1. Evaluate the ways the author suggests in which "color" improves a news report.
2. *"The reason stories get in the paper or on the air is that they describe out-of-the-ordinary events, or people, or both."*

   Do you agree that this is why stories "make it" in the media? What do you think should happen to a story that is important but just plain dull?

INVESTIGATING THE MEDIA

1. Select several news reports and examine them in small groups:
   (a) Choose three details the writer uses in an effort to achieve drama and color.
   (b) What use does the writer make of adjectives? Does she or he follow the advice on adjectives given by Mears and Chancellor?
   (c) If possible, compare the way different newspapers write the same story. Locate specific differences and similarities in the use of details. In both cases, judge the impact of color on news reporting. Does it improve the news or does it actually color the truth?
2. Study the structure of the same news reports and discuss:
   (a) To what extent has the reporter followed the inverted pyramid pattern?
   (b) What information does the summary lead provide? Would it have attracted *your* attention?
   (c) Does the body of the report flow naturally from the information in the lead? Is there any new matter that the reader hasn't been prepared for?
   (d) Does the headline of the story fit the whole story as the reporter wrote it? Would it attract your attention?

YOUR TURN

1. Select one writing tip the authors suggest for using color. As a cub reporter, write a one-sentence lead following the authors' advice.
2. Following the advice of Chancellor and Mears and the standard news report structure, report on some event of interest in your school or community.

   As a class, compare different reports of the same event. Discuss which reports you would choose to publish and why.

THE POPULAR MAGAZINE

The magazine is a hybrid, some analysts say, a form somewhere between a book and a newspaper. Despite recent changes, it's still a form that goes back to the 19th century. Following are some facts about magazines today:

- The word *magazine* is derived from the Arabic *makhzan*, meaning "storehouse or granary."
- Canadians spend 90% of total reading time on paid-circulation magazines.
- Readers read magazines differently from the way they read, for example, newspapers. Many magazine readers do not read from the beginning of the magazine, but may flip backwards from the end.

General-interest magazines such as Life, Vanity Fair, Esquire, *or* Saturday Night *— magazines that appeal to as many different readers as possible — are becoming rare. We are seeing instead a growth of special-interest magazines — directed to boaters, movie fans, and so on. The following article offers an explanation for this trend.*

Readers for Sale

Canadian magazines aren't selling information to readers, they're selling readers to advertisers.

Sick of magazines? Tired of insipid, uninspiring articles? Frustrated with chasing a story through a jungle of ads? Curious why newspaper magazines like *Today* gave up the ghost? Or why so many glossy lifestyle magazines slide through the mail slot free? The answer, in a word, is advertising, and its wide-ranging effects are changing the profile of the consumer magazine industry.

Virtually every Canadian magazine generates some advertising revenue. For consumer magazines, the ratio of advertising revenue to other revenues can be used to distinguish three broad categories. At one extreme is the magazine which generates little ad revenue. These magazines could be broadly classified as "cultural." In addition to newsstand sales, subscriptions, and private fund-raising, such magazines also receive grants from various levels of government. At the opposite end of the ad spectrum are controlled-circulation magazines which come free in the mail in certain urban neighbourhoods: all of their revenue comes from advertising. In between are the general-interest paid-circulation magazines ranging from *Chatelaine* to *Saturday Night* where ads may contribute from forty to sixty per cent of the total revenue.

Unlike books, most magazines have gone the way of newspapers in regard to advertising and cannot be considered pure cultural objects. As a *Globe and Mail* op-ed piece on July 28, 1983, pointed out: "The definition of the product of a modern newspaper...appears to be news information, but in actuality the product is not information that is sold to readers; it is readers who are 'sold' to the advertisers.... The industry should be defined as carriers of advertising."

The effect of advertising on editorial content has to be placed in the context of a major shift in advertising philosophy over the past two decades. Traditionally, advertising in North America has operated on a quantitative principle: if an ad reaches enough consumers, sales will rise to provide an acceptable level of profit. In a large market like the United States with many advertising forums, this may still be true. In a small market like Canada, however, with few available forums, advertisers realized some time ago that they had to adopt more accurate methods of targeting potential consumers.

From that perspective, controlled-circulation magazines, which first appeared in Canada in 1969, are ideal. After exhaustive analysis of reader demographics, they are delivered on postal walks carefully selected to serve up a high percentage of potential consumers for their advertisers' products. This shift away from mass-marketing to specific targeting in the magazine medium was graphically illustrated by the demise of weekend newspaper inserts like *Today*. They were in fact precursors of controlled-circulation magazines since they were, in a sense, "free." But advertisers abandoned them for other forums, including full-fledged controlled-circulation magazines, once it became clear that the wide readership net cast by newspapers was not catching enough hardcore consumers.

One obvious result of such a shift for the public at large is reduced access to information and opinion. Many articles which would have been available at low cost in a newspaper supplement are now read only by those affluent households deemed demographically suitable for controlled-circulation magazines. This amounts to a selective restriction on freedom of the press in response to market forces.

Controlled-circulation magazines are not an isolated phenomenon: they are in fact bellwethers for the entire industry. "The expertise they have achieved in satisfying the advertiser forced other magazines to compete on the same ground," says Dawn MacDonald, former editor of the controlled-circulation magazine *City Woman*. "No matter what is said about needing to satisfy the reader to get the advertiser, the real trend is to satisfy the advertiser first."

This trend has been amply illustrated by the new magazines included "free" with *The Globe and Mail*. At first glance it might seem that the general-interest magazine inserts like *Today* have returned. But in fact what has happened is that *The Globe and Mail* is no longer a general-interest newspaper. Instead, it has targeted a high-income readership of managers and professionals. The editorial content of the newspaper — and the magazines it encloses — is now selected with that income bracket in mind. All Canadian consumer magazines — whether paid or controlled circulation — now rely heavily on reader demographics, and the battle for the advertising dollar is intense. Consumer magazines are Canada's fastest-growing ad medium with a 467 per cent growth rate in the last decade and total revenues of over $200 million annually; of that amount, controlled-circulation magazines now absorb one dollar in six.

Although a major distinction between controlled and paid circulation seems to be that one is free and the other isn't, even that difference is now blurry. Paid-circulation magazines often deal with subscribers as if their product was in fact controlled circulation, again because of advertising. For example, readers who cancel their subscriptions to a paid-circulation magazine may be puzzled when they keep receiving it for months afterward. One reason is evidently that the magazines keep hoping they will change their minds. But whether or not the magazine receives that subscription revenue, from the advertisers' viewpoint the net result is the same; the magazine still enters the house — just like a controlled-circulation magazine — and the ads may be read. Such non-paying "subscriptions" cannot legally be included in an audit. But they will still attract ad revenue if the magazine lets it be known that it will absorb the overrun and mailing costs in order to deliver potential consumers to its advertisers.

Given these similarities between controlled-circulation and other magazines, it is not surprising that, at first glance, they might be indistinguishable editorially. The trend-setting by controlled-circulation magazines becomes clearer, however, if editorial content is examined in light of what an advertiser might ideally expect from a story. From this perspective, one concern is obvious: advertisers do not want stories which downgrade their products. Often they object to negative articles, threatening to withdraw ads and applying pressure on editors to censor copy.

Far subtler, however, and potentially far more damaging to good journalism, are the unspecified ways in which editorial form and content can adapt to serve advertisers. Received wisdom has it that the better the journalism, the better the advertiser's prospects. However, it could be argued that exactly the opposite is true: if the text is too absorbing, the reader may not notice the ads at all. Gary Zivot, publisher of the controlled-circulation magazine *Goodlife*, is quite clear on what *Goodlife* does and does not do: "We're in the business of matching media markets to advertising needs. If I were selling this product to consumers, I wouldn't call it journalism." Zivot does call it "highest denominator publishing," however, aimed at "busy people who have little time for ruminating about what's happening in this world."

Goodlife-styled journalism is no longer confined to controlled-circulation magazines. Often it appears as advertising supplements in paid-circulation consumer magazines; in such an insert, the accompanying editorial content's only function is to focus reader attention on the ads.

This awkward hybrid is appropriately called "advertorial" content. Unfortunately, in many paid-circulation magazines, it is increasingly difficult to distinguish genuine editorial from advertorial content.

Whatever the quality of the piece, the length of an advertiser's "ideal" story would also be a prime consideration. Long stories which keep the reader's eyes searching for text are anathema — the shorter the story, the better. Instead of quickly leafing through and overlooking ads in pursuit of a story continuation, the reader of brief articles disengages attention from the text more frequently and is receptive to the surrounding ads. By the same token, if a story must be long, any sustained argument should be flattened out and broken up: disjointed stories bore readers into giving up and relaxing into the ads.

Obviously, a reader persistently confronted with such journalism would reject the magazine entirely and a balance must be struck. The ideal compromise, therefore — and one perfectly reflecting the dynamics of a consumer society — is to constantly tantalize the reader on the cover, the table of contents, and the opening page of a story with the promise of satisfaction and then not deliver.

But the advertiser's ideal story can be made even more precise. As far as the treatment of subject is concerned, "issue" stories of any kind–layered, insightful analysis of a significant theme — are dropped in favour of "profiles." Well-written issue pieces propel readers past the ads; profiles of institutions, communities, or personalities have minimal linear thrust. No matter how sensitive or unusual, they can be picked up here and dropped there with no danger of losing the narrative or thematic thread — because there isn't one. The end result is soft journalism for the reader and hard cash for the advertiser.

So much for the advertiser's ideal. Clearly they do not in reality demand short, disjointed, marginally interesting journalism from editors. What is astonishing, however, is that so many editors deliver it anyway on the misguided assumption that they are "giving readers what they want." This is patently untrue: editors are giving *advertisers* what they want and conning readers into believing they want that too. In Canada today it is easy to forget what good journalism is really like.

Arguments about the quality of *Saturday Night* apart, it may well be true that the Canadian market is too small to sustain a serious, general-interest magazine of that kind.... With most general interest magazines dedicated to business objectives, only government has the power to divert the course of magazine journalism towards cultural ends.

If the government truly wants the print media to reflect the country's broadest cultural concerns, values other than those of free-market enterprise must regulate their activities. Certainly government interference in freedom of the press is abhorrent. But why should the only alternative be *business* interference in freedom of the press? Is there no way to break the industry's bondage to advertising without impairing its right to speak freely?

A sign of the times can be read in the misfortunes of *Atlantic Insight*, whose top editorial staff resigned. Started in the late 1970s to provide a voice for the Atlantic provinces, this general-interest magazine nearly went bankrupt in 1982. In an effort to insure profits, the newly appointed publisher approved advertising supplements without consulting the editor, prompting her resignation. At the 1984 Atlantic journalism awards dinner, *Insight* contributor and former editor Harry Bruce publicly suggested that an award be established for resigned editors who stood up for editorial integrity. His speech drew a huge round of applause.... The moral for magazines is clear: when advertisers not readers are the buyers, let the public beware.

— Mark Czarnecki
This Magazine

EXPLORING IDEAS

1. Evaluate the factors the writer presents in accounting for the fall of the general-purpose magazine. What advantages and disadvantages did this type of magazine offer?
2. **(a)** As a customer, how do *you* feel about ads in magazines? Do they affect you the same way they do on TV or radio?
   (b) How has advertising been an important factor in changing the content and design of the magazine today? Share your observations.
3. What are the reasons the magazine has become the fastest-growing medium in Canada today? What *do* people receive from magazines that they can't possibly receive from other media? Discuss in small groups; then choose one member to present a written or oral report to the class.

INVESTIGATING THE MEDIA

1. Bring to school one of your favourite magazines. Form groups to discuss your reasons for purchasing the magazine. Consider factors such as:
   (a) the content: reports, feature articles, and so forth. (Which items would you read first? Which items would you pass over?)
   (b) the writing style: word choice, sentence structure
   (c) the use of photographs and artwork
   (d) the placement of advertisements
   (e) the general layout and design of the magazine: ads, features, graphics
   (f) the cover
2. Bring to class special-interest magazines targeted at different groups. Examine carefully one magazine. Using the criteria above, make notes on this magazine. Write a "Reader Profile" describing the target audience of this particular magazine.
3. Examine carefully the contents of one of your favourite magazines. What kinds of topics do the feature articles deal with? How long, generally, are the articles? Do they follow a general pattern of organization? Is the writing style formal? informal? What sources do the writers cite for their information?

   Assume you are one of the editors of this magazine. Draft a set of writer's guidelines for prospective writers.

YOUR TURN

1. Using the guidelines you developed in the previous activity, write a short article for a magazine of your choice. Working in groups, edit and revise the articles. You may wish to submit some of the articles to appropriate magazines.
2. In groups, plan a special-interest magazine that will appeal to a specific group of readers. Consider, for example, a magazine specific to sports or rock music. Brainstorm strategies related to the following areas:
   (a) readership — who will be the target audience, and what are their interests?
   (b) possible advertisers
   (c) marketing strategies — title, advertising, distribution
   (d) content and layout
   Design the cover and table of contents for your first issue.

One exception to the trend to special-interest magazines is the newsmagazine: TIME, Newsweek, U.S. News and World Report, Maclean's. *Most are weekly or bi-monthly publications that provide background on the stories the other media (newspapers, television, radio) headline first.*

Maclean's at 80

In 1905, a wonderfully vivid if irrepressibly ambitious 43-year-old Toronto entrepreneur named Lt.-Col. John Bayne Maclean realized a burning ambition.

Maclean decided that prosperity lay in publishing his own periodicals for tradesmen. But he yearned for a general-interest magazine, a public platform that would offer something beyond the dry and dogmatic contents of the most popular Canadian magazines of the day, *The Presbyterian Record* and *The Christian Guardian*. And in October of 1905, *Maclean's* appeared: a 20-cent digest of extracts and reprints taken, with permission but without payment, from other magazines.

From the beginning, and with gathering speed, the magazine documented the building of a nation. Now commissioning original material, it portrayed the significant men and women, painted the land in all its moods, and described the currents of history that made Canada what it is. *Maclean's* was also a prism for a century that, it became increasingly clear, was born under an evil star — crowded with war and hard times and domestic and international tensions. And it served as the training ground for an astonishingly varied number of Canada's best writers, artists, and photographers.

The country that *Maclean's* began to chronicle more than 80 years ago, according to Peter C. Newman, an employee of *Maclean's* for 22 years — editor for 11 — was "a spiritually narrow and bigoted land" where Canadians, 87 per cent of them born in Canada, were only newly adjusting to waves of immigrants settling the empty West. Canadians' lives revolved around life on the farm and in the small towns where three-fifths of them lived and around their church (the 1911 census reported that there were only 11 000 "pagans" in the country). In their free time they paid formal calls on each other, and even their most adventurous pleasures rarely exceeded the gentle arts of vaudeville or Swiss bell-ringing.

The 1920s saw a time when Canadian women enjoyed a social freedom they had never had before and the national climate was abuzz with the fresh breeze of jazz, which *Maclean's* termed "a moral smallpox." Associate editor W. Arthur Irwin, a dour but hugely intelligent man whom Newman calls "the inventor of *Maclean's*," saw it as his mission to "Canadianize" the magazine. He set out to convince his superior, editor-in-chief Napier Moore, that *Maclean's* "should be a mirror for Canadians to see themselves, to see their national identity and soul." And that, said Irwin, who was to stay with *Maclean's* for 25 years, "with extensions, aberrations, enlargements, fumblings, and occasional glaring backsliding," became *Maclean's* reason for being.

Both Canada and *Maclean's* — which *Time* magazine described in 1932 as a 10-cent fortnightly with a circulation of 160 000 that "is Canada's *Saturday Evening Post*" favoring "native authors" — struggled toward adulthood with the country it mirrored. The magazine's concerns still centred on the home and family, their belongings and the arcana of modern medicine. But the best-read features of the magazine were "Parade," a potpourri of humorous slices of life from across Canada, and the musings of its British correspondent, a former Toronto piano salesman and contributor to

October, 1905

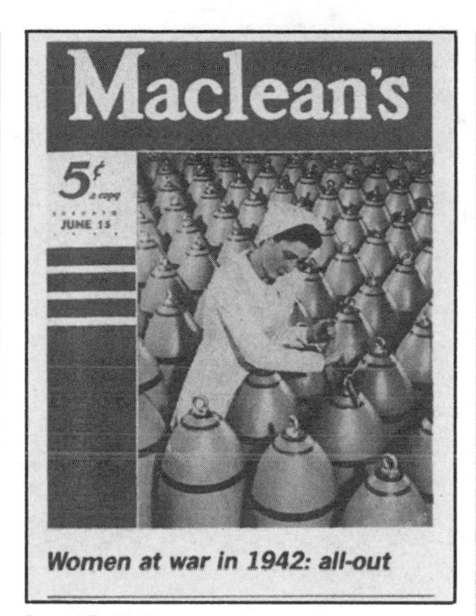

June 15, 1942

INSIDE: Harvesting a plague of plenty
Maclean's
THE BOSS
The summer of rock idol Bruce Springsteen

September 3, 1985

Maclean's named Beverley Baxter.

Other articles, serious and crammed with facts, were by Irwin himself and such other writers as historians Arnold Toynbee and Arthur Lower, philosopher Bertrand Russell, and political journalist Grattan O'Leary. They outlined a world that had taken on a complexity never known before and rarely even imagined. A four-part series in 1927 chronicled the exodus to the United States. An article in the Aug. 15, 1930, issue proposed an unemployment insurance scheme. There were continuing debates in *Maclean's* pages on the need for Senate reform and a distinctive Canadian flag.

Beginning in 1939 *Maclean's*, like all Canadian publications operating under the restrictions of the War Measures Act, went to war, painting in only uncritical strokes the lives of the soldiers abroad and the civilians they left at home.

But the gloss of enthusiasm for the war effort was often scarred by hard reality, most notably the bloody and futile 1942 invasion on the beaches at Dieppe.

The magazine continually exhibited its boundless interest in all things Canadian, its nervousness about coming disasters, the looming presence of discontent in Quebec and an increasingly urban society filled with unsettling evidence of social alienation and distress. There were portraits of the new horrors of drug addiction and a society meeting problems it had not seen before, including the life awaiting returning soldiers.

Indeed, the times were increasingly violent; there were seven murders in Toronto in 1947 — more, reported *Maclean's*, than in any year since 1918. Stress had tightened the fibre of the nation.

Maclean's wrote about the new plagues of urban loneliness and troubled children. Another enticing topic was the relatively new phenomenon of teenage courting. A 1950 article on "going steady" said that "it has really little to offer. It brings none of the responsibilities that teach something of life. It has none of the give and take found between husband and wife." That dissuaded few teenagers, most of them far more independent and affluent than those in the previous generation.

The Atomic Age pervaded many aspects of life in the 1950s. By 1950 the bombs dropped on Japan five years earlier had spawned a 15-cent model A-Bomb, a best-selling toy in Canada that year. The A-Bomb was only one of the Big Questions in the air. In the popular *Maclean's* feature "For the Sake of Argument," McGill University scholar Norman J. Berrill speculated that if the whole race did not disappear in some calamity, then half of it — the male half, soon to be biologically unnecessary — might vanish through nature's own design.

But there was fun to be had. *Maclean's* had always been full of light-hearted cultural notes like the 1948 story about a mammalogist who said in Toronto that he had learned the language of porcupines. Gordon Sinclair had written about raising goldfish, the life of a nightclub drummer, and dieting ("Fat is like a black eye — it comes fast and feels awkward").

Maclean's, with boldly illustrated articles on the rivers, prairies, small towns, and teeming cities of Canada, was forever asking the

Decade of change—In the trend-conscious 1960s, *Maclean's* documented such movements as the so-called counterculture.

questions: who are we? What is our soul?

As the cozy and placid 1950s turned the corner into the yeasty 1960s, *Maclean's* began to document a once-complacent nation in a state of self-doubt, if not disarray.

The most popular features in the 1960s' *Maclean's* remained the ones that appeared on a regular basis, like family friends in an otherwise strange house whose design, price and even size often changed. Those mainstays included the potpourri "Parade," "Wit and Wisdom," and cartoonist James Simpkins' "Jasper" the bear. "For the Sake of Argument" endured, and in it, in 1960, novelist Hugh Garner stung many readers when he argued that "we Canadians today aren't mad at anything or anybody. We are sitting on our custom-built lethargy, waiting for our pensions to begin and our mortgages to mature. As a people we are dead and we died of self-inflicted ennui."

While trend-conscious Canadians began to practise organic farming and transcendental meditation, writer Ken Lefolii reported that air travel accidents, which had taken 390 lives in the first three months of 1960, represented an "epidemic of destruction." Editor Blair Fraser boldly declared that Canada should open its doors to oppressed South African refugees. Wrote Fraser: "We are hypocrites on this subject of racial equality. No matter what we may say, we do not in fact give all races equal treatment in this country." Peter Gzowski, *Maclean's* new and prescient Quebec editor, wrote in 1962 about an "unflinchingly honest" Liberal cabinet minister named René Lévesque, who, Gzowski predicted, "could lead to the formation of a new provincial party of the left."

As well as writing about Canada, and writing about the outside world from their snug, cluttered Canadian offices, *Maclean's* writers travelled a world that was fast closing in on them. Blair Fraser reported from Israel, India, and China. Ralph Allen, still active as a contributing editor, went to Cuba, the seething Congo, and war-torn Cyprus. Mordecai Richler visited Israel and wrote a tart three-part profile of that much-promised land which, like most of his contributions before and since, left few readers unmoved either by anger or approval.

It was also a decade marked by the ascension of Pierre Trudeau, subject of hundreds of articles in *Maclean's* since Peter Gzowski first discovered him in 1962. There was the high promise of Centennial Year and Expo 67, which, *Maclean's* reported, inspired Canadians to discover a long-lost sense of self.

But whatever the merits, in the same decade general-appeal magazines like *Maclean's* had been losing ground to special-interest and leisure magazines and were folding all over North America. Between 1960 and 1970 *Maclean's* had been losing an average of $600 000 a year. In 1971, the Maclean Hunter management placed it in the hands of Lloyd Hodgkinson, a creative publisher who had remodelled Maclean Hunter's *Chatelaine*. MH executives told Hodgkinson to make *Maclean's* successful or close it.

Hodgkinson, a great admirer of Peter Newman, who had become editor-in-chief of *The Toronto Star*, the country's largest and richest newspaper, asked him to return to *Maclean's*. Newman, like *Maclean's* other editors, was fully aware of Canada and its possibilities. But he was a man who loved the country in a way that perhaps only a child arriving here from war-torn Europe could. And he began, once again, rediscovering and measuring Canada's dimensions, asking the country's foremost writers — among them Irving Layton, Jack Ludwig, Alden Nowlan, and Margaret Laurence — to describe the Canadian

U.S. geodesic dome at Expo 67 in Montreal—The high promise of Canada's Centennial Year inspired a new sense of self.

"Trudeaumania"—Former Prime Minister Pierre Elliott Trudeau came to symbolize a new, revitalized era in Canadian politics.

experience. Many readers welcomed the rapturous nationalism.

But Newman and Hodgkinson say that they could see major dangers ahead unless there was a radical change in the magazine's format. Newman wrote a memo saying, "We can keep this up for three or four more years." But the editor went on to argue that the time for the old *Maclean's* had passed. In *Maclean's* future they both saw a newsmagazine.

In 1978 the publisher and editors launched a weekly newsmagazine similar to the archetypal newsmagazines in the United States. Newman had set up the operation after studying *Newsweek* in New York. The change was more than just a commercial necessity. It was demanded by the times — times of worldwide regional warfare, economic complexity, dizzyingly swift changes in government, the arts, and society.

The magazine that used to take as long as three months to produce is written and prepared for printing by an editorial staff of 88 in six days. In the *Maclean's* of today, any news event that occurs on a Sunday morning can be chronicled and analysed in the same issue of the magazine that appears on newsstands 24 hours later. Every week 2 399 000 Canadians, 55 per cent of them male and 45 per cent of them female, spend an average of 64 minutes reading the latest metamorphosis of the modest little blue book that Maclean offered to the public just after the turn of the century. It is the way we were, and it is the way we are.

— Glen Allen
Maclean's
December 30, 1985

EXPLORING IDEAS

1. What information do newsmagazines provide that the other media cannot? How do they make their information interesting to the reader?
2. List some of the important changes that *Maclean's* has gone through in the history of its publication. Judge how successful these changes have been in "keeping up with" the magazine's readers.
3. What would you say is distinctively Canadian about the way *Maclean's* has delivered the news each week? If there were no Canadian publication like *Maclean's*, would it really matter?

INVESTIGATING THE MEDIA

1. Compare the way in which *Maclean's* and an American publication such as TIME treat the same news story. Examine details in
   (a) selection and organization of content
   (b) writing style
   (c) use of photographs and captions
   (d) evidence of slanting or bias
2. Study an entire issue of each magazine for the same week. Compare the two magazines by examining details in
   (a) the cover and cover stories
   (b) editorials and letters-to-the-editor
   (c) content: stories selected and length of the corresponding stories
   (d) number and type of news departments
   (e) the ordering of the news: most important to least important
   (f) importance of photographs and photojournalism

   Prepare a report based on your observations and conclusions.

Based on your interests, choose two or more activities to investigate further topics you have explored in this unit. Or choose other aspects of the print media you would like to research in depth.

1. ***(a)*** Create your own school or community newspaper. Working in groups, decide who will investigate newsworthy stories, who will work on the copy editing, who will do layout, and so on. The following is a partial list of newspaper jobs — your specific needs may require changes in the assigned tasks. Before beginning, you may wish to discuss the skills, time needed, and outcome required in each job.
   - editors — assign stories, read and revise them
   - reporters — interview, write articles
   - columnists — compose longer feature articles and opinion pieces
   - photographers/illustrators — photograph news scenes, acquire "file" photos
   - layout artists — design and assemble the actual pages
   - advertising salespersons — acquire advertising revenues and copy

   (b) Brainstorm a list of possible news items to cover, and then decide *how* to cover each item. For example: How much background information will readers need? Where will you go to get the information? What people should be interviewed? Will interviews be conducted on tape, or will notes be taken instead? What photographs/illustrations should accompany the reports?

   (c) Once the news has been collected and brought back to your "newspaper office," it must be written down and edited. After the first draft has started taking shape, the "real" work of the newspaper begins:
   - selecting appropriate stories
   - editing and rewriting
   - laying out stories in combination with headlines, photographs, captions, cartoons, and other artwork
   - deciding on placement of suitable advertising
   - inserting other features: editorials, let editor, and so on
   - printing
   - distributing the newspaper

   Don't forget to give your newspaper a men name.

   (d) Following publication, acquire feedback from your audience. What changes, additions, deletions, and so on should be made for any future editions of your newspaper?

   As a group, evaluate how successfully you took your newspaper through all the steps of planning, composing, revising, editing, and publishing.

2. Investigate another popular print form, such as comic books. How have they changed over the years in content, format, marketing, and so on to remain competitive with other forms of media? Present an oral or written report, describing the changes that have taken place.

3. How has the concept of literacy changed since printing began? Research and report on the influence that *one* of the following events has had on literacy:
   (a) the invention of the printing press
   (b) the industrial revolution
   (c) universal education
   (d) the paperback revolution
   (e) the information age

   Prepare a time line of major events in print literacy to accompany your report.

4. Find out about the type of popular reading that people in your community prefer. Prepare a readership survey of popular reading forms (newspapers, magazines, romance novels, "how-to" books, etc.). What is selling well and why? Analyze the aspects of content, format, price, and marketing/packaging that help account for popularity.

   Assemble your information and draw some conclusions about the future of print. What types of reading matter do people in your community prefer? Based on this information, what trends do you see for the future? Write up or tape your findings and conclusions.

UNIT THREE: CHANGIN FOCUS: PHOTO FILMS

G
GRAPHY &
CCCP
CCCP

In discussing a televised political debate, one analyst commented that over 80 per cent of the information influencing the viewer would be visual. She recognized that a gesture or facial expression is often more influential than words. Visual images have a special power to capture our attention and influence how we think and feel.

One reason for the special impact of visual images may be the common belief that "the camera doesn't lie." Does the camera tell the whole truth? Visual communication is, above all, selective. It records only a portion of the total event. Still photography especially is a medium of the moment: the photographer freezes only a moment of time on film. The moving image extends the power of the still photograph; movement — action — brings life to the image and heightens its reality. Still, the moving image cannot record the whole event, only what happens within the camera's range.

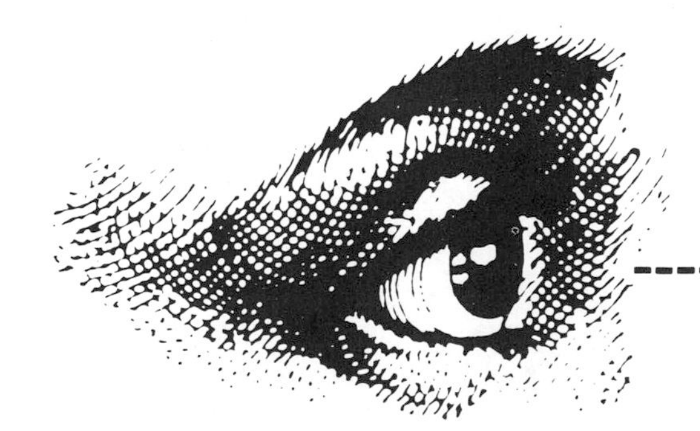

YOU & THE MEDIA

1. Do you have a personal collection of pictures in your wallet, pasted on your locker door, or in a photo album at home?
   (a) What kinds of pictures do you keep? Why do you keep them?
   (b) What do you think the pictures tell others about you? (You may wish to respond in your journal to this question.)
   (c) Why, do you think, are we fascinated by pictures of ourselves and others?

2 As an ongoing project for this unit, begin to build a file of photos that have captured your attention. Share your collection with others in the class and talk about why you chose particular photos for your file. The kind of picture you are looking for probably won't appear every day, so be patient.

3 Bring to school a picture or photograph that has special meaning for you. Use it as a basis for a poem or story titled "This Is a Photograph of ________."

THE IMPACT OF PICTURES

It has been said that words make us think and pictures make us feel. Certainly, the best photographs do more than simply convey information or tell a story. Our response to such pictures will likely be intensely personal, subjective. Successful photographers realize the emotional potential in their visual images and use their skills to communicate an attitude towards, or an impression about, their subjects ... whether those subjects are news events, the geographical landscape, or the human landscape.

"If there is any single characteristic that can be said to distinguish photojournalism from all other forms of photography it is its sense of the moment. No studio photograph can match a truly superior news photograph for immediacy and impact, nor can it establish place, time, and circumstance with such conviction."

— The Editors, Newsweek Books
The Best of Photojournalism 3

The Mission of the Camera

To me, photography is a means to an end — the picture with purpose and meaning.

The purpose. Any photograph is a means of communication. A photographer takes pictures for other people to see. Every photograph is a message from photographer to observer. The purpose of such a message is to tell, in visual form, something that the photographer feels worth communicating to others. A picture that does not "say" anything is pointless. Of course, sometimes the "message" may not be of interest to others, or may not be "understood." This is particularly true of "experimental" photographs — the usually grainy, blurred, distorted, or zoomed pictures that seem to be in vogue today. In this respect, photographers share the fate of many other artists whose work is too "advanced" for their time, whose public is not "ready" for what they have to say. Such artists are ridiculed by their contemporaries, yet their work, once labelled "radical" and worse, sets the style one generation later. It would be well for those who automatically condemn anything they don't understand, anything they consider too "modern" and too "far out," to remember this. Even if such pictures don't always "come off" — a hazard that, incidentally, they share with any kind of pioneer work — to me they are still more stimulating than most "conventional" photographs. Of course, photographers who merely imitate the work of others, who indulge in "fads" for the sake of "being different," and who have nothing worthwhile to say produce pictures that serve no purpose and justly invite criticism. But a photographer who is sincere in his work should always be respected. Sincerity and purpose go hand in hand, and a sincere photograph is always a purposeful and valid one.

The meaning. Any message has content. This content is its "meaning." The content of a photograph can be almost anything; it can be educational, informative, satirical, entertaining. Even a picture taken merely for record's sake has a meaning — to provide a record for future reference. The majority of amateur pictures fall into this category — all the photographs of babies, children, and sweethearts; of birthdays and picnics; of happy vacation times and strange lands — they are "records for future reference," to be taken out,

Photographer Feininger's Opel automobile — Dessau, Germany 1931

looked at, and enjoyed in times to come. Compare those photographs, which many a "serious" amateur derides as "snapshots," to the types of pictures so often seen in photographic salons. The snapshots at least mean something to the photographer and his family; the "salon pictures" are often completely meaningless.

Any meaningful photograph begins with an idea. The more original the idea, the more likely it is that the picture will convey something new to the observer, and the new and original are always stimulating. This automatically makes an *original* photograph an *interesting* photograph. And vice versa: A photograph based on a trite idea can never be anything but trite. All pictures that are imitations of other photographs are trite because they are repetitious. To me, imitating is equivalent to duplicating, repeating something that somebody else has already done, a pointless waste of time and energy; but many photographers still seem to disagree. Otherwise, how can we explain the continuous production of such photographic clichés as pattern shots of rows of empty chairs, coils of heavy rope, bums with beards and battered hats, spectacles on open books, and gnarled hands folded in simulated prayer? Aside from the hope of winning a prize at the local photo-club contest, what is the purpose of such pictures? What do they mean?

The first step on the road to original work is the realization that a camera is no more than an instrument for making pictures. Forget its glamor and value as a status symbol, its precision workmanship, its chromium trim, its shiny lens; look at it in the way you would look, for example, at a typewriter. What a typewriter is to the novelist, a camera is to the photographer — a machine for recording ideas. And as anyone can learn to type, so anyone can learn to photograph. Nobody cares what make of typewriter a novelist uses. Similarly, why should anybody care what brand of camera a photographer uses in making his pictures? The only thing that matters is whether his work is interesting and good or pointless and bad.

A camera is an instrument potentially as versatile in the realm of exploration as a microscope or a telescope. Similar to these, it can be used to present in picture form far more than merely images of things seen before. Imaginatively used, a camera becomes an instrument for making discoveries in the realm of vision. Many of us have seen such photographs. But few amateurs seem to realize how many such opportunities are within the scope of their cameras.

— Andreas Feininger
from *Successful Photography*

The article that follows features a Canadian, Dilip Mehta, who ranks among the best photojournalists. Mr. Mehta explains what he looks for when covering his beat, the world.

Dilip Mehta The Journey of a Photojournalist

A picture may tell a thousand words, but a good photograph tells the complete story. That conclusion can be drawn from even the quickest glance at Dilip Mehta's work.

Mehta is a gifted Canadian photojournalist. Some say one of the 10 best in the world.

When you talk with Mehta it is clear that he sees himself as more than a professional shutterbug. He is a journalist or storyteller who just happens to work with images — powerful images — rather than words.

The youthful looking Mehta insists photography has a purpose and that purpose is to capture an enduring yet accurate image of the pain, sorrow, joy, triumph, and everyday happenings that make up the world.

Sometimes subtle, sometimes overpowering, Mehta's photographs are much more than snapshots.

"I don't believe in taking a picture for the sake of taking a picture," he says during an interview at Sunrise Films Ltd. in Toronto after a press screening of the company's one-hour documentary on Mehta.

The 33-year-old Mehta was born in Northern India and is a Canadian citizen who travels the world to find photographs to grace some of the biggest and most influential publications.

He explains that he wants to create photographs that will make a statement, "something that will sustain itself for a number of years, not just the moment."

Mehta has done just that with photo essays and covers for TIME, *National Geographic*, *Fortune*, *Newsweek*, *Geo*, New York *Times*, *Equinox*, and *Paris-Match*.

Mehta, quick with a smile or a gesture as he emphasizes a point during the interview, also has photos in the popular books *A Day in the Life of America*, *A Day in the Life of Australia*, *A Day in the Life of Canada*, and *A Day in the Life of Japan*.

He explains his life as a photojournalist is lonely and involves a lot of travel. In one year he has travelled to 17 countries and five times around the world.

There is glamor, but as often danger. Mehta says it is tough mentally.

"How do you understand a bag lady...and the next day the splendor of a huge conglomerate?"

In 1985, Mehta won a special citation for excellence in photojournalism from the Overseas Press Club of America and two World Press Gold Awards. One was for a photo essay on the transition of prime ministerial power in India to Rajiv Gandhi after Indira Gandhi's assassination, and the other for his coverage of the Union Carbide tragedy in Bhopal, India.

The Bhopal tragedy is an event that Mehta speaks of with emotion. His stunning pictures of the victims of Bhopal convey much more than the written story.

"You don't have to weep, you don't have to wring your hands, you don't have to tear your hair out to show you care. It is all in the mind, it's in the heart."

He says the camera can act as a temporary shield, but mustn't be allowed to remove the photographer too far from the situation being shot.

In the case of Bhopal he says he used his photography to convey the horror of the catastrophe.

Although Mehta sometimes finds himself in situations where, as he puts it, he wants to "throw up," he also says there are things he would not photograph. Sensationalism for its own sake is against Mehta's personal code.

He is self-taught. When he first arrived in Canada Mehta worked as a graphic designer, but soon realized it was not for him. He travelled across Canada taking pictures and returned with what he admits were some lousy photographs.

But he learned by trial and error and 13 years later finds himself one of a select group of photojournalists working for the prestigious N.Y. agency Contact Press Images Inc.

News photography is fine, but Mehta says he enjoys photo essay work the most.

While Mehta sees a potential photo wherever he goes, he also knows when he'll finally hang up the bag that carries his five cameras and 13 lenses.

He wants to end his photojournalism career one week before he loses the analytical part of his mind.

— John McClyment
The Sunday Sun
January 11, 1987

A victim of Bhopal, India, tragedy

A woman finds her home repossessed by a bailiff.

Rajiv Gandhi campaigning

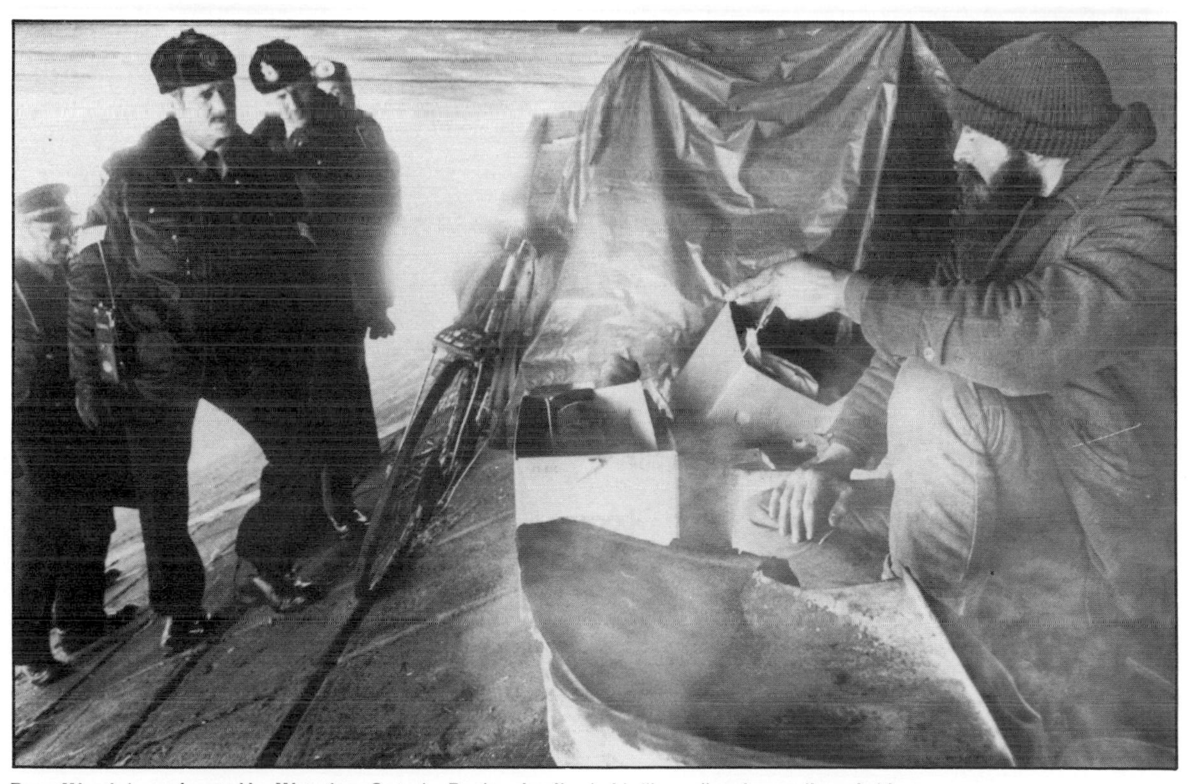

Doug Woods is confronted by Waterloo, Ontario, Regional police in his "home" under a railway bridge.

EXPLORING IDEAS

1. *"The whole point of taking pictures is so that you don't have to explain things with words."*

   (a) What, in your opinion, is the point of taking pictures? What can pictures do that words cannot?
   (b) Why, do you think, do pictures have such a strong emotional impact?
2. Some media analysts refer to "image fatigue." They say that if individuals see too much of the same thing, they become tired or bored with that visual image. Thus photographs can lose their power to arouse a response; for example, if people are overexposed to pictures of the suffering caused by war they tune out and turn off.

   Discuss "image fatigue" in small groups. Can you identify any types of photos that have lost their power because of overexposure? How did you respond the *first* time you viewed such an image? the *tenth*? Select one group member to present your ideas to the class.
3. The writer of the second article quotes Dilip Mehta as saying that as a photojournalist "there are things he would not photograph." What types of photographs do you feel should *not* be taken or printed by photojournalists? What, in your opinion, are the responsibilities of the photojournalist?

   Share your views as a class. Following the discussion, develop a set of "Guidelines for News Photographers."
4. The last sentence in the article suggests that Mr. Mehta believes a photojournalist must remain *analytical*. Do you agree? What might happen if a photojournalist "loses the analytical part of his mind"?

INVESTIGATING THE MEDIA

1. *"Different people can look at the same photograph and see different things."* Examine the photographs on pages 91-97. In small groups, share your opinions on the following:
   (a) Which of the pictures attract you? Why?
   (b) What emotions are aroused by the photos? What elements in the pictures trigger these emotions?
   (c) What "story" do the photos tell; what message do they send? Write a comment or story in your response journal.
   (d) Do you agree that "a good photograph tells the complete story"? What questions might you ask about the events depicted in the photographs? What information is not given? What could words or language convey that these photographs do not?
2. Discuss differences in your reactions to the photographs on pages 91-97. How might you account for these differences?
3. On April 11, 1987, a police officer was shot and killed. The *Toronto Star* published this photograph taken by a photojournalist covering the slain officer's funeral.

Last Salute — Milford, Connecticut, police officer Melissa Piscitelli salutes at the funeral of her fiancé, police officer Daniel Scott Wasson.

Form small groups to discuss the following issues. Select one person to report your group's conclusions to the class. Your "Guidelines for News Photographers" may be useful reference points in the group discussions.

(a) What is your initial reaction to the photo? Is it an effective news photograph? Explain why or why not.

(b) Does the photo represent an invasion of privacy? A reader criticised the *Star's* decision to publish the photo. In response, the newspaper's ombudsperson, Ron Goodman, wrote:

> *The* Star *does not routinely cover funerals or publish pictures of them.... The exceptions involve funerals of public figures and funerals of public interest, and the full-dress funeral of a policeman killed on duty is an event of public interest.*
>
> *A newspaper photo of Melissa Piscitelli's sad farewell offended the sensitivity of some, but struck me more as a commentary on society's ills than as an intrusion of privacy.*
>
> — *The Toronto Star*
> April 16, 1987

Assess the validity of Mr. Goodman's justifications.

(c) If *you* were the photo editor of the *Star*, would you have published this photo? Can you suggest additional reasons either for or against publishing "Last Salute"?

As a result of your discussion, is there anything you would like to change in your guidelines for news photographers?

YOUR TURN

1. *"...even though we may not know the subject personally, we seem to comprehend who he or she is — and what the person is like."*

Choose a photograph from pages 91-97 and write a brief description or biography of one of the persons depicted.

or

Using news photographs from the media, create a photo collage entitled "This Was the Week of __________ 19______."

2. Use a visual format — a self-portrait, a photograph, a photo essay, or a collage of magazine pictures, for example — to make a statement about yourself.

Present your statement to a small group. Have the students comment on what the presentation tells them about you, *before* you tell them why you have selected the various images.

or

Select one of the photos in your file, or from this book. What story do the relationships between the objects in the picture suggest to you? Use the photograph as the starting point for a short story or narrative poem.

3. *"The role of a news photograph is to illustrate the drama, humour, or import of an event that in some way touches our daily lives."*

— Ron Goodman

(a) Create a collage or slide show of news photos entitled "The Drama and Humour in World Events."

or

(b) Try your hand at news photography. Take photographs of events occurring in your school and community. Present your photos as a series of slides or as a poster display entitled "The Drama and Humour of Life in __________."

or

(c) Create a display of news photos that illustrate a single theme such as "a commentary on society's ills" or "the ever-present risk faced by police officers everywhere."

4. *"Editors are regularly called upon to decide whether a photo approaches the line between good and bad taste."*

— Ron Goodman

(a) Write a letter-to-the-editor of a newspaper or news magazine in in which you have found a photo that crosses the line, in your view. Explain your reasons for being critical of the photo.

or

(b) Develop a portfolio of news photos you believe are in bad taste. Prepare a presentation either for the class or a small group. After outlining your criticisms of the photographs, invite comments from your audience.

There are times when a single photographic image has such power that the attitudes and values of an entire society can seem to be swayed by it. John Filo, who today works mainly as a sports photographer, talks about one photograph he took in 1970. First, examine the picture.

Kent State

A traumatic event recreated with unflinching fidelity

Mary Vecchio kneels over a dead Kent State University student in John Filo's famous 1970 photograph.

On the night of May 4, 1970, John T. Filo was driving at top speed along the Pennsylvania Turnpike, racing home to Pittsburgh.

His palms were sweaty, he hadn't eaten all day, and rolled up inside his pant leg was a series of pictures he'd taken that morning on the campus of Kent State University in Ohio. He was scared. Very scared.

He didn't know then that one of those pictures of the Kent State shootings would win him the Pulitzer Prize.

Nor had he known a week earlier, as he sat down with his fellow university photojournalism students to watch Richard Nixon on television announcing the invasion of Cambodia, that he would be swept up in events which would take four lives, change his own forever, and alter the course of American history.

His photo of Mary Vecchio, kneeling over the slain body of student Jeff Miller, is an image imbedded in the consciousness of a nation as the ultimate comment on the domestic pain America experienced during the Vietnam War years.

Filo is now a photographer with the Associated Press Kansas City bureau.

As he sits talking to me in a Hollywood hotel suite, his voice still breaks with emotion as he remembers those events of nearly 11 years ago.

"Kent State still gets to me," he says. A tall quiet man who still wears his celebrity status uncomfortably, he looks away over the L.A. skyline. "It's not that I tire of talking of it — I don't, but it gets to me.

"I had a borrowed camera and a borrowed lens and I was just out making pictures of what I thought would be another demonstration. I wasn't with the students but I could sympathize because I was a student too. Cambodia was just one more lie from the leaders and they were hurt and angry.

"I knew I had to get between the students and the National Guard to get the best pictures, but I couldn't take refuge with either group. The Guardsmen thought I was out to get shots of police brutality, and the students...you have to remember these fears were real and founded in those days...they thought I was taking pictures for the CIA.

"As far as I knew the Guard was using blanks, as a scare tactic. I thought it was pretty funny really, the dumbest thing I'd seen. Blanks. There was a concrete embankment and when the students started running away from the Guards, I was afraid they'd get hurt jumping over it, so I laughed and yelled at them to slow down and be careful."

It was then, as Filo pointed his camera at the Guards, that he noticed a Guardsman's rifle discharge up in the corner of his viewfinder.

"All of a sudden this metal sculpture right beside me just erupted into a cloud of dust. Disintegrated. Then I actually heard the bullet go through it and saw the bark fly off a tree behind me."

Filo says he's never felt terror like that moment when he realized the ammunition was live.

"I was walking back when I noticed this body lying in the street and I stopped in my tracks, thinking, 'Wait a minute, I've got to record this.'"

Walking toward it, taking pictures all the time, Filo noticed a girl run to the body. She was 14-year-old Mary Vecchio, a runaway who happened to be on campus.

"She was crying, she knelt down beside the body to see if there was any life left, if anything could be done. And she was just sobbing and looking down at the body, when she screamed and threw her arms in the air."

At that point the campus was thrown into chaos. The university was closed, police and federal agents swarmed everywhere.

"I hid the film in my sock," says Filo. "I didn't know what I had but I knew a lot of people would like to get their hands on it and I wanted to develop it first."

He rushed to a darkroom, made prints, then determined to get out of town. "The first reports said two students and two guardsmen had been killed. The townspeople already had it in for the students and I was afraid they'd come out to the campus looking for trouble. So I drove to the first place I thought of — home in Pennsylvania — I was still hiding the film, I guess I was paranoid."

Not too paranoid though. When Filo woke up the next morning, there were FBI agents at the door ready to guard him for the rest of the day. But Filo's pictures were already on their way around the world.

Upon arriving in Pittsburgh, he found the major papers had had photographers at Kent State, so he went to The Associated Press. When they saw what he had, they made a deal then and there. Suddenly Filo became famous.

Filo's pictures had a tremendous impact on America. Ordinary Americans who were ambivalent about the anti-war movement suddenly turned against the war when it occurred to them that their own sons and daughters might be killed at home by their government.

"It was an ironic thing. Kent State was both the peak and the end of organized protest against the war,

Eddy Adams's controversial photograph — South Vietnamese National Police Chief Brig. General Nguyen Ngoc Loan executes a Viet Cong suspect on Feb. 1, 1968, in Saigon.

a black page in our country's history."

"The Pulitzer Prize photo really wasn't that great a picture, but I know that no matter what I do for the rest of my career, I won't be able to top it. In that sense I guess it's a handicap."

Filo now takes mostly sports pictures in Kansas City, though he is proud of a photo essay he did on the Kickapoo Indians. He says he has no desire to be a war photographer. Kent State gave him enough of that to last a lifetime.

He testified at numerous hearings, but says it's not the incident itself that bothers him, but the impact it's had on others.

"I became famous over someone else's misfortune, and that still haunts me. Mary Vecchio was picked up for prostitution in Miami a while back. She says my picture ruined her life. Now she's trying to forget it all and put herself together, but I keep thinking about that.

"I knew Eddy Adams. He was the cameraman who filmed that Viet Cong suspect being executed; shot in the head at close range in the streets of Saigon. That clip ruined him. He was working for the army then and took all sorts of footage of Viet Cong atrocities the same day, but it was that film everyone saw. His army career was ruined. Now he's running some short-order restaurant in Washington State, trying to forget it all, too."

Again, Filo looks away, out the window. "There are still all sorts of pressures. People don't realize how much one picture can change lives."

— Charlene Potter
Hamilton Spectator

EXPLORING IDEAS

1. *"People don't realize how much one picture can change lives."*

Assess the impact the Kent State photograph had on individuals and on the American people as a whole. How do you explain the tremendous influence it had on people?

2. In the article, John Filo mentioned Eddy Adams, who was a war photographer in Vietnam. Skim the last two paragraphs in the article to recall what happened to Adams, and why.

   Reprinted on page 102 is the photograph mentioned by Filo — the picture that made Adams famous.

   (a) Why do you think the photographer took this picture?

   (b) Now consider this: The man holding the gun was on the side supported by the United States. He was interrogating a prisoner and this photograph captures a moment just before the gun was fired. How, do you think, did the American public react when this photo was published? How would the audience's image of the world be affected by this photograph?

3. Often photographs such as the ones discussed in this article become so strongly associated with an event that they come to represent that event.

   (a) What images are strongly associated in your mind with a particular event?

   (b) In what way do these images *not* tell the complete story?

INVESTIGATING THE MEDIA

1. Contact a photographer who works for a newspaper or television station in your community. Invite her or him to speak to your class. Working with a partner or in a small group, prepare in advance some questions you would like your guest to answer about photography in the news media.

YOUR TURN

1. Pictures of the war in Vietnam are for many North Americans symbols of the 1960s. What images will symbolize the current decade for your generation? Create a collage, slide show, or video entitled "Images of the 19__s." Write or tape a brief commentary to explain *why* you chose these photos as symbols of the decade.

Media Facts & Techniques

Basic Photographic Techniques

"In deciding how a picture should look, in preferring one exposure to another, photographers are always imposing standards on their subjects. Although there is a sense in which the camera does indeed capture reality, not just interpret it, photographs are as much an interpretation of the world as paintings and drawings are."

— Susan Sontag, *On Photography*

Deciding *what* to shoot is just the beginning of a photographer's job. The photographer must then decide *how* to treat it — how to present the subject to the audience. In much the same manner as a writer composes a story, a photographer often composes a picture with a specific audience and purpose in mind. The mood suggested by the subject as well as the statement the photographer wants to make influence how the photo is composed. All of these factors combine to affect our responses to the picture.

Following are some of the elements a photographer may vary to achieve a certain effect:

Distance: A photographer can move in on the subject to take a *close-up*, or stand back in the distance and present a *long shot*. The apparent distance between camera and subject contributes to the overall impression or message conveyed by the picture. Generally speaking, close-ups invite a sense of shared feeling and intimacy, because the subject is isolated. If the close-up is of an individual, the viewer's attention is focused on the body language and facial expression.

On the other hand, long shots or *wide-angle* shots can create a sense of objectivity: there may be more detail to look at, the objects in the picture may be small, and the apparent distance between subject and camera can create a less-intimate feeling. In advertising, a photographer may choose a long shot to link the product with a certain lifestyle; the long shot allows the photographer to place the product in a particular setting and to show you, the consumer, the details of that setting.

As you might expect, there is a middle position: the *medium shot*. The medium shot is popular in sports photography and advertising because it allows the viewer to see all of the main subject and to recognize at least some of the background detail. News photography and television are usually restricted to close and medium shots — their image size is too small to do justice to the long shot. In contrast, cinema can do justice to the grand vistas that look unimpressive on television.

Close-up shot

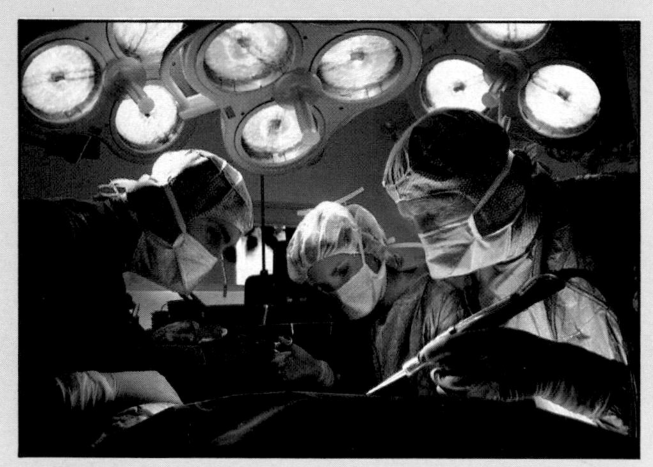

Medium shot

Long shot

Camera angle: When a photographer places the camera at *eye level* with the subject, we the viewers see the shape and proportions of the subject as we normally would. There are other options however. The camera can be placed below the subject, so the viewer will have a sense of looking up at it. This is called the *low-angle shot*: it makes the subject seem "larger than life." In some extreme examples the subject is so distorted that it appears to loom over its surroundings.

Low-angle shot

The opposite of the low-angle shot is the *high-angle shot*. The photograph is taken from above the subject, so the image we see seems to be smaller than its surroundings. High-angle photography can be used to emphasize space and distance.

High-angle shot

Lighting: Creative use of lighting can be a photographer's most important asset. Manipulating the amount of light and shadow in a picture can suggest a specific mood — light and airy or heavy with threat or drama. Placing the subject in front of the light source can create a silhouette, emphasizing general shapes rather than detail. When the subject is *behind* the light source, the viewer sees fine colour and detail. Sometimes it is possible to "paint with light," to highlight the subject's shape by using light to outline its edges.

Natural lighting: Midday

Same subject: Evening, subject in front of light source

Composition: Sometimes the photographer can design a shot: arrange, or *compose*, the elements in a picture to create certain effects. In choosing which elements to place in front — in the *foreground* — and which to put in the *background*, the photographer influences what we notice and how we respond. This arrangement of elements — the *composition* — can create a sense of a relationship between the things within the photographic "frame."

"Framed" composition: Subject off-centre

"Centered" composition

"Diagonal" composition: Strong diagonal lines are often used in news photos.

"Framed" composition: Subject in background

Focus: We tend to think the best pictures are those with everything in clear, sharp focus. This is not always the case; a photographer may deliberately blur details and outlines in a picture, using special filters or manipulating the camera lens itself. Such a picture has a *soft focus*. Soft focus is often used to suggest a romantic, ideal, or dreamlike quality. Sharp and soft focus can be used in combination to emphasize one element in a picture while merely hinting at less-important details.

Selective soft focus

Composition and lighting create a striking image.

INVESTIGATING THE MEDIA

1. Analyze the photos you have placed in your file. Look at them with a critical eye, and apply what you have learned about basic photographic techniques.
   (a) What emotions do the photographs evoke in you? What statement is the photographer making?
   (b) What specific techniques help the photographer convey her or his attitude and statement about the subject? *How* do these techniques convey the "message"?
   Select two of your favourite file pictures and share your analysis of them in a small-group discussion.
2. Select a photograph and make it the subject of a poster project. Paste your picture in the centre of the poster, then draw a line down the middle of the poster. On the left side of the poster comment on techniques used in creating the photo: camera angle, lighting, composition, etc. On the right side write about your personal reactions to the photo — the thoughts and feelings it inspires.

YOUR TURN

1. Create a "technique collage." Photograph/videotape, or collect, pictures that illustrate *one* of the basic photographic techniques. For example, all the photos may be low-angle shots
   or
   Create a collage of contrasting techniques featuring the *same* subject. Photograph/videotape your subject from a number of different angles and distances. Shoot it at different times of the day and in different types of lighting. If Polaroid cameras are available, use them so that you can see the products of your experiments immediately. Before creating your collage, evaluate your photos informally in small-group discussion. Present your work to the class and discuss the different effects achieved.
2. Develop a photographer's eye. Working in small groups, choose a theme that can be interpreted through a broad range of visual images. Decide on a statement you wish to make or an emotional effect you wish to create and outline the photographic techniques you could use. Take the photographs, decide which you will use and in what order, then present your finished product to the class as a slide program, a video, or a bulletin-board display.

In the article that follows two sports photographers outline the impressions and images they're after when capturing the action and beauty of sports on film.

People in Action

The dedication of man involved in sport has always endured. It is the freest expression of his existence. Over the years the record of this world of action has never been explored. It has been touched on often by the painter and by the sculptor but only as a gesture — a peripheral glance — a Degas horse, a Lautrec jockey, a Bellows fighter, or an Eakins boatsman. The pictures were often passive and somewhat distant. They were reflections of memory rather than experience. They were faithful to the laws of art, not necessarily to the forces of sport. In the first half of the century black-and-white photographs began to search out and find the beginnings of this intimate world of dedication. In the last two decades this world of sport and the sporting life has been recorded magnificently in photography. . . .

The athlete's dedication everywhere in the world is the same. A long-distance runner from Kenya or a marathon runner from Ethiopia flies by jet aircraft to compete in California or Japan; a ski jumper from north of the Arctic circle jumps at Lake Placid and a Russian high-jumper is the main attraction in Madison Square Garden in New York; an Austrian farm girl wins a championship ski race in the Andes; a Brazilian soccer player commutes to Europe to play and an Australian tennis team travels the globe to retain a trophy; race horses and motor cars are flown across oceans for Derbies and Grand Prix.

There is a holy alliance in sports that brings forth the maximum skill and strength and striving, the classic greatness and dignity in man. The paradox of sport is that in the contest and clashing, in the struggle and the race there is almost a divine accord of beauty and grace, a poetry in the harmony of all peoples together. If sport is a microcosm of life — pictures hold the significance of a lifetime and are a tribute to man.

Photographs are not frozen moments in time. There is no such thing as a still picture, any more than there is such a thing as a still person.

• • •

The world is a great picture. The texture of each land, of each day, of all people moving through a moment of their lives is a great picture — if you see it just right. Photography is a miracle, a phenomenon, a delight. Photographing the drama of sports is fascinating.

It seems most of us are suspended on the tedious hook of indifference. Nothing happens. There is little time, little chance, little energy, little reason, little *feeling*. There is no room for us to maneuver into the one day of adventure that would change our lives. There is a numbness, and against the soft edges of inaction we make no crucial decisions because there are none exciting enough to make. For many of us, most things in a day just happen.

The athlete is blessed. His line is clear cut. The time of decision for him is absolute. He faces it again and again and his feelings are real. There is a total awareness to the full scale of emotions all the time. No one tells

him what he should feel. *He experiences it!* This experience, this feeling is worth all of his brutal effort and dedication.

It is this tonal reverence for the athlete that has driven me to portray him in a particular way. I was trained as an artist and as a draftsman I discovered the beauty of movement in the human figure and the endless variety of its form in changing light. As I began to sketch athletes I began to photograph them to study and analyze various men involved in sports I knew little about. One day I found I had 10 000 football negatives in a closet. Since I had approached my subjects directly and honestly I found the photographs were strong, pure expressions of man in sport and not incidental fragments.

Sports photography is simply a matter of marksmanship and intelligence. It demands an inordinate amount of energy and imagination. You cannot possibly photograph a sport unless you understand it completely and understand and know the men who play it. The indefinable aspect is devotion or caring. The same intensity they have to play the game you must have to record it. Not stop it but suspend it forever in time. This is the whole art.

— Robert Riger

• • •

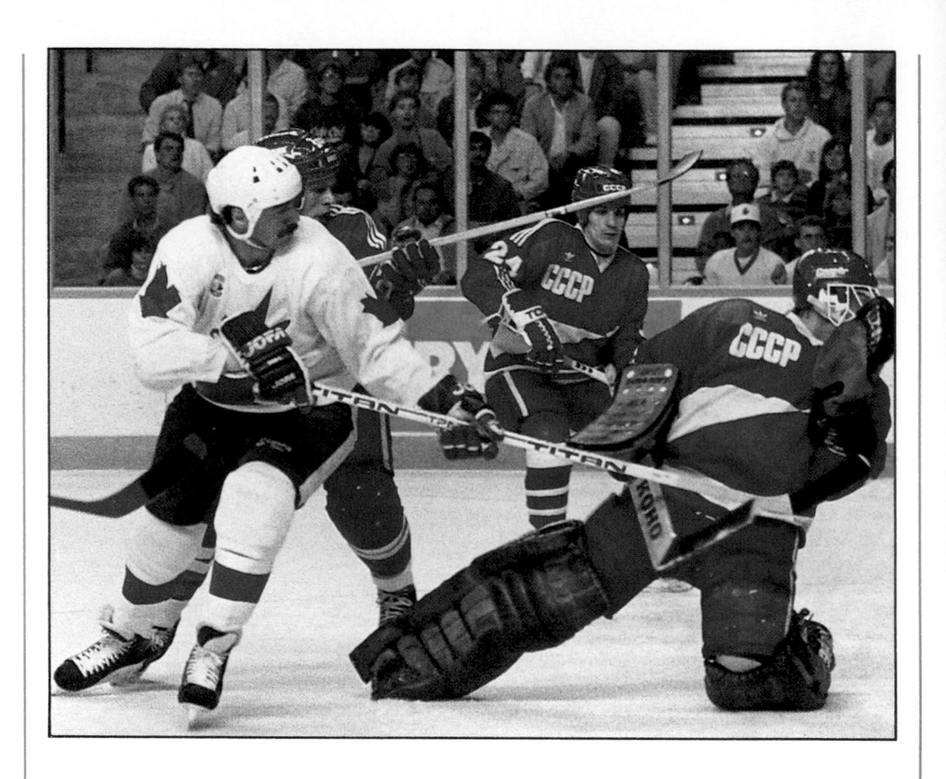

My own experiences in the sporting life have helped me enormously. I shoot and ski — skiing is my favorite sport — so I knew what I was trying to get. My pictures of powdered snow show the ultimate in a skier's wish to get the best out of an untracked slope. In fox hunting, someone who has cubbed and fox hunted will have known the mist that rises up as the Master takes the hounds out.

When you are photographing, nothing else counts at all. Every picture is the most important one. Sports photography is the top *sport* today: to try to catch someone unaware and get a picture of it is far more exciting than *shooting* a bird. I would rather *shoot* a person's expression when they've shot down a bird or won a cup at a field trial. Or a photograph of a skier ... no, I'd rather ski myself, that's the trouble. Photography is a sport as we do it. It's really a game to stalk people and catch them or to talk them into it so they'll forget they are being photographed. The best photographs are something you just suddenly see and catch quickly.

The scrapbooks I keep bring back to me the flavor of the places I've been to. I'm recording a way of life that may vanish and I want to record it accurately. A photographer keeps a biographical record with every new assignment and a set of pictures. The photographer's subjects help to shape his destiny. I try to get the flavor of a scene so that when people look, they'll smell the flower on that hillside or they'll feel the wind and sense the freedom. Technically, you must take what Kodak says you can't possibly take. It may be your best picture.

The public's appreciation of the general spectator sports has changed enormously. We are all glued to a golf match or football game on television and the stadiums are filled, but the world of the sportsman in field trials, fox hunting, duck hunting, and fishing generally speaking hasn't changed as much except for skiing, alas, to my regret.

— Toni Frissell

EXPLORING IDEAS

1. Evaluate the differences Robert Riger points out between sports paintings and sports photography. Do you agree or disagree with his views? Explain.
2. How is television coverage changing the public's perception of sport? What can a single photograph of an athlete or event capture that live coverage of the action cannot?
3. *"There is no such thing as a still picture, any more than there is such a thing as a still person."* What does this statement imply about the kinds of images sports photographers should try to capture?
4. Based on statements by Mr. Riger and Ms. Frissell and ideas of your own, develop a profile of a successful sports photographer.

INVESTIGATING THE MEDIA

1. With a partner, develop a list of criteria for great sports photography. Then, examine the pictures on pages 108-111. Decide which, in your opinion, best demonstrate these criteria. Discuss and compare conclusions with other students in your class.

YOUR TURN

1. Choose a topic related to the general theme of "People in Action" — for example, children at play, people at work. Find or take your own series of photographs or video images that capture the variety of human emotion and activity. Present or display the pictures you collect. Seek feedback from your audience to help you evaluate how effectively you represented your topic.

As compelling and dramatic as a single photograph can be, there are subjects and themes that benefit from a series of pictures in vividly portraying their story. Photographers sometimes combine visuals and written text to create a "photo essay." In the best of these, text and images work in tandem to re-create for the audience the photographer's experience.

The Jail — *A Photo Essay*

Toronto's Old Don Jail — Classic architecture of the period, but how can one imagine the impact of life within the walls?

The main cell blocks — Row on row of eight foot square cells, with windows just beyond the line of sight.

The stairway to confinement. No glory, no freedom.

Caged. I walked into a cell measuring three by eight feet. The heavy metal gate closed behind me with an ominous, eerie thud. I sat down on the cold concrete floor at the far end of the cell, contemplating the bars in the door, and looking through them to the blank wall on the other side of the corridor. I don't know how long I sat there ... time takes on a very different meaning in the heavy brick walled environment of a jail cell. I do know one thing, though, for the first time in my life I fully understood the meaning of the word *caged*, and I didn't like the feeling.

I found only a small degree of comfort in the knowledge that I had walked into the cell of my own free will.

I don't know how much more of an effect the experience would have had if the massive iron locks had still been on the doors. I could feel the accumulation of a century of loneliness within these walls...even the knowledge that I could walk out of the cell whenever I chose to couldn't diminish the impact of the fact that I was there, alone, on the wrong side of the bars in Toronto's Don Jail.

When I was offered the opportunity to photograph the Old Don Jail in the spring of 1978, I grabbed it with both hands — a camera in each, of course. The jail had been closed down for some time, and while it had been cleaned up and the cells were no longer capable of imprisoning anyone, they still held the memories of their occupants captive.

The cell I put myself into was part of a block of cells, all measuring the same three by eight feet. Think of the space. It is the width of the door, with a wall on the right and a wall on the left, and a cold concrete floor eight feet long.

I don't know what these particular cells were used for, but I have a great need to believe that they would only have been used for a

Once through this door, there is no return.
On the other side — the gallows.

The main rotunda. A hub between twelve cell blocks. Olympus OMI, 28mm Zuiko.

short period of detention. I saw other cells measuring eight by eight, rows and rows of them. I would hope that these larger cells were the ones used for inmates who had longer sentences.

The cells which chilled my blood the most were found in a separate corridor, closed in at both ends by a metal door. The door at one end leads into Death Row; the door at the other end, to the gallows.

Walking through the old jail should have been a rather simple matter of looking for the right composition, reflecting on the scene as it must have appeared to inmates through the last 120 years, and making the photographs. It all seems so obvious ... yet once you are on the inside, you quickly realize that the issue of human detention is a very complicated one. I was alone in the jail, yet I was not alone. I was dealing with my own raw emotion. The jail does that to you ... it is as if every nerve in your body is exposed.

Looking at the photographs I made on this assignment produces yet another conscious dilemma: which pictures should I show, and which should I hold back for another time, another place. The decision is an agonizing one. The images I have

One chair, three walls, and a door. Solitary confinement for an inmate at the Old Don Jail.

selected for this feature could only show how inhuman the punishment of isolation can be — they can never show how inhuman the crimes have been for their victims.

In all fairness to the system, I must say that the Old Don Jail was constructed in a time between 1859 and 1864. When Architect William Thomas designed the facility, the attitudes of society toward the rehabilitation of criminals were very different from the standards of today. The Old Don Jail has been closed down for a number of years now; I hope it will stay closed forever.

I spent only a couple of days there while I was photographing the facilities. I was all alone in the cell blocks during that time, except for the occasional visit from an official to see how I was doing. During those two days I learned the meaning of another word ... *spooky.*

When I decided to exhibit this body of work, and write about it, I had to first see for myself what was happening to the Old Don Jail. A few years ago, there had been quite a controversy surrounding the facility, but I hadn't heard very much about it recently. I called a friend who I thought might know something about the current status of the Old Don Jail, and he told me that the place was in use again!

This news was enough to make my stomach turn. I called the jail, and spoke with the superintendent. He was very courteous, and assured me that the only way the space was being used was for the storage of some old materials. He invited me to come down for a visit, and I accepted.

I returned to the Old Don Jail in the spring of 1987. The place looks about the same, only *spookier*. It just gets older and shabbier. I saw some junk stored in the corridors, and I noticed that many of the old metal doors had been replaced by fake wooden ones — it seems that the place is sometimes used by film companies as a movie location.

Four cells make up the Death Row area of the jail. All that remains, once you are here, is to wait.

It is interesting that the person who first suggested that I photograph the Old Don Jail did so after having seen my pictures of Ellis Island. This famous New York location, the *Isle of Tears*, as it had been known by many who landed there and were denied admission to the United States, has been stabilized so that it will not deteriorate any more, and is now a tourist attraction. Ellis Island has been preserved as a public reminder of one of the major eras in the evolution of the American nation...the Old Don Jail was built more than 120 years ago, long before Ellis Island. I would treat the Toronto landmark in much the same way, as a reminder of how society has dealt with its problems, and a deterrent for those who may not realize what the dark side of life is like.

— Nir Bareket
Toronto Photo Life
May 1987

Noon, in a large cell, at the Old Don Jail. Olympus OMI, 35mm Zuiko, Tri-X.

EXPLORING IDEAS

1. First, consider only the photographic images in "The Jail." What emotions and thoughts do the photos re-create in your, the audience's, mind? Brainstorm words and phrases that summarize your impressions. Now read the accompanying article.
2. Next, form small groups to analyze the photo essay and discuss the following:
   (a) Develop a list of words and phrases that summarize *the photographer's* feelings and attitudes as he approached the photo-essay assignment.
   (b) How closely do these feelings and attitudes mirror your own first impressions of the photo essay? Which photos best convey the photographer's message? Be prepared to support your choices.
   (c) What photographic elements and techniques contribute to re-creating Nir Bareket's experience? Why, do you think, did he choose to use black and white for this photo essay?
   (d) *"The images I have selected...could only show how inhuman the punishment of isolation can be — they can never show how inhuman the crimes have been for their victims."*

   Evaluate this statement. Does Nir Bareket's photo essay present a balanced, fair representation of "crime and punishment"? How might *your* representation of this subject have differed from that of Bareket?

YOUR TURN

1. Create your own photo essay. Choose a subject or theme that interests *you*. Tape or record a written text to accompany photographs you either shoot or collect from newspapers or magazines. You may wish to present your photo essay as a slide show with taped or "live" commentary.

   Gather responses from your audience to help evaluate how successfully you re-created your experience of the subject. Did any of your audience's emotional reactions and ideas surprise you? In what ways?

OUR WORLD ON FILM

When the first, silent, motion pictures were exhibited, audiences were spellbound. The later addition of sound increased the magic. The novelty of movement and sound have long since worn off, but the power of film to capture and hold our attention has persisted. Today, musicians, journalists, and the makers of documentaries — to mention just a few — recognize the potential of the moving image to touch our emotions, to entertain and keep us informed.

Documentaries — informational films that usually deal with social issues — use both narration and visual effects to tell their story. When it comes to documentaries, Canadian filmmakers rank with the world's best. The next article features Terri Nash, whose work for Canada's National Film Board won an Oscar in 1983.

Filmmaker isn't spoiled by an Oscar

An Academy Award hasn't changed 37-year-old Canadian filmmaker Terri Nash. She's spontaneous, refreshingly unpretentious, and disarmingly honest.

But I find it astounding that winning an Oscar hasn't changed her professional life.

This seems to have everything to do with the kind of films she makes and whom she makes them for. Nash makes social-issue films for Studio D of the National Film Board, the studio created to encourage women to become filmmakers.

Nash won the Oscar in 1983 in the category of best documentary short subject for her first major film, *If You Love This Planet*. The 26-minute film featured Dr. Helen Caldicott, who outlined in stark human terms the horror of a nuclear holocaust.

Interspersed with this footage were clips of the Hiroshima victims of the first atom bomb. Nash also used footage of Ronald Reagan playing a bomber pilot in a movie — a propaganda film made by the U.S. government.

In an ironic turn, the U.S. Justice Department immediately labelled *If You Love This Planet* "political propaganda." This meant that before the film could be shown in the United States, it had to be preceded by a declaration that the contents hadn't been approved by the U.S. government.

It also meant that the name of every organization and individual to whom the film was distributed had to be filed with the government.

What's doubly ironic is that things wouldn't necessarily have come to this had some NFB officials had their way in the first place.

Nash says that when the film was in its final cut stage, she showed it to a meeting of film board distributors. One distributor maintained that he wouldn't allow the film to be shown in the United States. He questioned the

The first hydrogen bomb dropped from an American plane spreads its fireball into the Pacific sky over Bikini Atoll, May 23, 1956.

ethics of using Reagan ("out of context" as he wrote in a memo), implying it might offend Americans. The distributor asked Nash to remove the clips of Ronald Reagan. She refused.

Nash argued that the Reagan clips depicted a certain "macho" mentality that continued to influence U.S. foreign policy. In a three-page memo, widely circulated in the NFB, she maintained that "it is not criticizing the American people, but rather an 'I'm bigger than you' foreign policy, which could lead to the end of civilization as we know it."

She did, however, cut the Reagan clips back to only 27 seconds.

Winning an Oscar gave the film bureaucratic credibility, but Nash says she isn't getting any more work because of it. And the criticism of her brand of filmmaking continues.

In 1986, for example, she collaborated with Bonnie Klein in the making of *Speaking Our Peace*, a film about women and the peace movement.

"We were criticized for excluding men," she says. "But the film board made a seven-hour film series about war and didn't use one woman. Nobody noticed."

While only 2 per cent of the National Film Board's budget goes to Studio D, the returns are remarkable.

As part of a masters thesis, one student compared the distribution of all Studio D titles with a random sample of English films. She discovered that Studio D films are booked twice as frequently — with films like *If You Love This Planet* booked more than five times as often.

People obviously hunger to see films that speak to their experience or that challenge social presumptions. It'll be interesting to see how Nash's next film — about women in the Soviet Union — is received.

— Lois Sweet
The Toronto Star
March 9, 1987

EXPLORING IDEAS

1. How would you define the term "propaganda"? What techniques are associated with propaganda? What, if any, are the differences between "social-issues films," or documentaries, and propaganda?

INVESTIGATING THE MEDIA

1. If possible, view *If You Love This Planet* or another documentary film. As you view, note:
   - the style of the narration or dialogue (often less formal than that in the print media). Is the narration spoken off-screen, by a commentator, or on-screen?
   - the message or emotional effect of the visuals. (You might wish to take notes in your response journal on the visuals and their effect during your viewing.)

YOUR TURN

1. Make a documentary film or video *or* create a photo essay on a topic such as the following:
   (a) a place of interest in your community or school. (You may want to plan a travelogue designed to promote tourism in your area or attract students to your school.)
   (b) an issue of common concern, such as pollution or the effects of second-hand smoke
   (c) an event occurring in your school or community
   (d) a process or activity: how to apply for a job, how to select your first car, how to meet a member of the opposite sex. (Your approach can be serious or humorous.)

   If you have access to video equipment, you may want to work in groups to film your documentary.

Media Facts & Techniques

Camera Movement in Film/Video

"First and foremost, a film is visual rather than verbal. Thus, the feelings and ideas communicated by words must be changed to feelings and ideas communicated by visual symbols."

— Dr. F. Marcus, *How Does a Movie Mean?*

Whether considering documentaries or other films, there are two fundamental rules of filmmaking. The first is LET THE CAMERA DO THE TALKING. If possible, let the camera *show* the audience what they need to know; don't use words unless it's necessary.

A skilled movie director composes each shot using the basic photographic techniques you examined in the previous "MEDIA FACTS AND TECHNIQUES" section. A film is more than simply a series of still pictures, however. Another fundamental rule of filmmaking is THE MOVIE MUST MOVE.

In any film, there are two categories of movement:
1) movement created by the actors or objects in the film
2) movement created by the camera as it films a scene and as the film moves from scene to scene.

The following are the basic types of camera movement:

BASIC CAMERA MOVEMENTS

Panning: The word *pan* is a contraction of the word *panoramic* and is used to describe the movement of the camera from side to side to follow the action in a scene. Pan shots are often used to establish the setting for the audience. A *subjective pan* is used when the movie camera "becomes" the eyes of one of the characters.

Tilting: The camera can move vertically up or down to record a person climbing a flight of stairs, for example, or follow an object falling from a height.

Dollying or tracking: The camera is mounted on a cart or some other vehicle so that it can move alongside the subject, and keep pace with it. The camera can also dolly or track in towards the subject or away from the

Movement created by actors — A stationary camera (*at left*) captures the action "on location" at a Canadian TV shoot.

subject. In car chase scenes the camera is sometimes mounted in a car that travels alongside the car that is the subject of the action.

Zoom (in or out): Through use of a special lens, the camera can appear to move towards or away from a subject quite quickly. The sense of movement is usually more rapid with a zoom than with a dolly in or out.

Reaction shot: This shot is usually employed to show the effect that someone's words or actions have on another individual, or to show how a character reacts generally to a particular scene. A reaction shot may be a close-up to catch a look of surprise or fear, or a medium shot to show a person's body language.

Quick cut: This label is used to describe what happens when the film seems to "jump" from one scene to another. Technically, this effect is not created by the camera at all, but by splicing (joining) pieces of film together.

TRANSITIONS BETWEEN SCENES

The most commonly used techniques when a change of scene is required are the following:

Dissolve: A visual effect created by the gradual disappearance of one shot while another shot gradually appears and comes into clear focus.

Fade out/in: Ending a scene by underexposing to black or overexposing to white; beginning a scene in the same manner, moving from black or white to clear focus.

Freeze frame: As a way of ending a scene, the film appears to stop and the image is "frozen" or held for a few seconds. Used for a dramatic effect.

INVESTIGATING THE MEDIA

Form small groups for the following activities.

1. Examine a movie on television. For any two-minute sequence, record:
   (a) the number of times the camera moves
   (b) the type(s) of movement

   Analyze and comment on the purpose or the effect created by the camera movement. If possible, note the methods used to end a scene.
2. Compare various group records for different types of movies: comedies, mysteries, action/adventures, dramas, romances, and so on. Are there differences in the dominant types of movement for different film genres? Which genre showed the greatest variety in camera movement?

OUR LIVES AT THE MOVIES

Many people maintain that "fictional" cinema is as much a record of our lives as non-fictional accounts of events in history books and documentaries. Virtually all aspects of our experience have been dramatized on film — our fantasies and dreams, our fears and frustrations, our tears and laughter. Movie comedies and dramas offer a glimpse into the styles and values of times past, the turmoil that has characterized different eras, and human triumphs through the years.

The writers of the two selections that follow discuss the place movies have had in their lives. As you read, think about your own "magic moments" with film and compare them with the writers'.

Spellbound in Darkness

As an adolescent, I went to the movies as often as I could, and for the same reasons as young people do today: I needed images I could emulate in forming my personality. And I was eager to learn about those aspects of life and adulthood which were still hidden from me. Moving pictures, more than any other art, give the illusion that it is permitted to spy upon the life of others, which is exactly what children and adolescents love to do, in order to find out how these adults manage their lives and, even more important, how they manage to satisfy their desires.

Also, I wished to escape from reality to daydreams, and the movies provided content for these. Waiting for the next installment of *The Perils of Pauline* gave us all something exciting to look forward to and fantasize about in class instead of listening to our teachers. The moviehouses to which I went as a youth were true pleasure domes, very different from those of today, which are characterized by their spareness and cold functionality. As soon as one entered these old dream palaces, one felt transposed to another world. Inside, there were nooks and crannies and boxes with heavy curtains which suggested privacy and intimacy. Here one could escape the watchful scrutiny of one's parents and all other adults, and do nothing constructive whatsoever — but daydream.

The moviehouses also provided unique opportunities for letting down one's defenses and experimenting with being in love. The unreality of the setting, and its attractiveness, encouraged uninhibited reaction to what was seen on the screen. I do not recall having ever laughed as heartily and unrestrainedly as I did when watching funny scenes in these pleasure palaces. In fact, watching the movies thus carried me away so that I was no longer quite myself. Instead, we were part of the world of the moving picture. I was lifted out of my shell into a world where what I felt and did no longer had any relation to the real me and to reality.

— Bruno Bettelheim

Magic Moments

One thing has become apparent to me ... and that is that my magic moments are growing fewer with each decade since the peak forties. Part of the reason is the fact that the major studios and independent filmmakers have turned out fewer and fewer pictures each decade. Perhaps another reason is that I am myself a good deal older now than when I discoverd movies for myself in the early thirties, have seen an awful lot of them, and have become somewhat jaded. Certainly I perceive a good deal of repetition, not only in a growing number of remakes, but in ideas and techniques. One of the hallmarks of a true magic moment in films must surely be a sense of freshness, newness, uniqueness. Due to the sheer preponderance of movies released in Canada and the United States in the last fifty years alone, there are bound to be repetitions of an enormous order and possibly this sheer quantity is at last beginning to exert a numbing effect on my psyche.

But I fear that the main reason might be that the magic is really going out of the movies. The late Henri Langlois, curator of the French Cinémathèque in Paris, suggested a few years ago that we may be in the process of experiencing the "death of cinema" — that movies as we have known them might not outlast the next decade. I have no notion of what M. Langlois believed would succeed the movies. I expect home TV screens will increase in size and much of what we see in the cinema today will be transferred to the family set....

A final explanation is more difficult for me to write about because it probes into areas I would much rather leave in the dark. Perhaps, on the whole, movies have really grown up, become more mature, more sophisticated, while I haven't changed, haven't grown up. Perhaps the things I have always loved most in movies — things I call magic moments — were mainly fanciful and naive clusters of film frames, odd bits of editing, ingenious camera angles and movements, freakish flights of a director's, a writer's imagination that were really capricious and cute and not too far removed from the sawdust and circus sideshows that the movies grew up with in their beginnings.

Perhaps I am still looking for my childhood in motion pictures, a childhood that is no longer there.

The truth, if there is one, is probably a mixture of all the foregoing explanations. One thing we do know is that distance *does* lend enchantment. Conceivably in thirty years the seventies will mysteriously seem to contain far more magic moments than I can remotely imagine at present.

— Elwy Yost
from *Magic Moments from the Movies*

EXPLORING IDEAS

Discuss the following in small groups. Appoint one member to record your group's ideas and present them to the class.

1. Bruno Bettelheim believes going to movies is an important part of growing up. Evaluate the reasons he presents. Which of the reasons, if any, do you identify with? What can you add, from your own experiences, to the discussion of the role of movies in the life of a young person?
2. Consider the movies you have seen in the last four or five years, or movies that are presently popular:
   (a) What do they offer in terms of role models — "images to emulate"?
   (b) What glimpses of adult life are presented?
   (c) What "magic moments" have there been in recent films for you?
3. Why, do you think, have movies been "a favourite scapegoat for moralists"? What might critics find to complain about in terms of the models and lessons presented in popular films today?
4. How is the experience of viewing a movie at home on videotape different from going to the theatre to see a film? Which is the better environment for viewing a movie? Why?

INVESTIGATING THE MEDIA

Respond to the following questions individually, then share your answers in a class discussion:

1. What are the five most popular movies of the year? What, do you think, are the reasons for their popularity?
2. What kinds of movies do you make a special effort to see? Why?
3. What are some of the best films you have seen? Why? Were they current pictures or film "classics"?

4. What are some of the worst films you have seen? What made them bad, in your opinion?
5. Be a movie critic or reviewer. What criteria would you use to judge a film? Work as a class to develop a list of questions or criteria.
6. *"Perhaps, on the whole, movies have really grown up, become more mature, more sophisticated...."*

   — Elwy Yost

   How valid is the judgment expressed in this statement? Form small groups and arrange to view movies produced in past decades. (Check movie listings in TV guides or borrow or rent "classic" movies on videocassette.)

   Present a group report based on your observations and conclusions.

YOUR TURN

1. Write about one of the "magic moments" in film for you, describing a particular scene and what it meant to you.
2. Using the criteria developed in class discussion, review a movie that you have recently seen.

One spellbinding moment in movies for the following reviewer is an eight-minute sequence from The Untouchables, *in which a runaway baby carriage bounces towards disaster on the steps of Chicago's Union Station. The scene is not new. It was first used in the 1925 film classic* Battleship Potemkin*; the sequence has come to be known as "the Odessa Steps sequence."*

Jesse Kornbluth describes how this compelling device was used in The Untouchables.

The Untouchables: Shot by Shot

The line on Brian De Palma has it that he's one sick puppy. *Carrie, Dressed to Kill, Blow Out, Body Double, Scarface* — face it, this isn't the resumé of a director they're going to ask to make *Splash II*. Nor is De Palma like Joel and Ethan Coen, who distance themselves from the mayhem they create with lighthearted banter. Just the opposite. When De Palma's choreographing one of his signature murders, he's focused, emotionless.

The line on Brian De Palma will need considerable revision after *The Untouchables*. For De Palma has — at least for now — banished the ghost of Alfred Hitchcock. "The humanity of this film will surprise a lot of people," he says.

For much of the film, the credit for that goes to David Mamet, the Chicago-born playwright and screenwriter who went to high school across the street from the site of the St. Valentine's Day Massacre. There was, however, one sequence in *The Untouchables* that Mamet didn't write — and if reaction to the film is any indication, it's the eight-minute sequence in Chicago's Union Station that audiences will never forget. It has everything we might want from a suspense scene: brilliant point-of-view shots, sudden violence, and one great device.

This device is not new. Eisenstein invented it in 1925, and the "Odessa Steps" sequence — with a runaway baby carriage bouncing toward disaster in the midst of carnage — has become the best-remembered moment in *The Battleship Potemkin*.

What first attracted director Brian De Palma to *The Untouchables* wasn't the idea of bloody shoot-'em-ups and gory corpses. It was the script that David Mamet had written. Mamet's script wasn't about blood — its subject was values. Not for this film the tough-guy Eliot Ness of the old TV series; instead, Kevin Costner plays Ness as a prototypical John Ford hero, a straightforward and decent man who comes to Chicago to do a job for which he's not really suited.

How can Ness build the case against Al Capone? Not easily. Maybe not at all. But because he quickly realizes that Chicago is so corrupt he can't trust the police, he does one smart thing: He recruits his own crew--a grizzled beat cop (Sean Connery), a rookie (Andy Garcia), and a bespectacled government tax accountant (Charles Martin Smith).

"He sends one of yours to the hospital, you send one of his to the morgue," Connery tells Costner. "That's the Chicago way." This injunction frames the conflict of the movie: a fraternity of good men who must bend their ethics and lose their innocence — along with several of their brethren — to enforce the law. It's a contemporary, realistic conflict, and one that presents an unfamiliar challenge to a director who's generally considered the greatest visual thrill-maker since Hitchcock. "The problem of a movie like this is that these were real people," De Palma says. "You want to see Capone killed, and yet you just can't have Ness shoot Capone."

On the other hand, if you want to make a movie for the studio that likes its summer pictures to have a visual punch, you've got to have big action scenes. *The Untouchables* has them aplenty: shoot-outs on the Canadian border with Ness and his Untouchables on horseback, Capone's machine-gunners enforcing Mob law in Chicago, a supercharged confrontation between Ness and Capone.

But the story that binds De Palma to historical fact also ties him to a great irony: Eliot Ness couldn't connect Al Capone to his larger crimes — murder, corruption, bootlegging. All Ness could prove was that Capone evaded taxes. And to do all that, he needed testimony from the wimpiest member of any crime family: the bookkeeper.

In the script, the capture of the bookkeeper occurs about twenty minutes before the end of the movie. It's a good place for an action scene. Mamet has Walter Payne, the Capone ledger-man (played by Jack Kehoe), try to leave town by train. Naturally, Ness and George Stone (the Untouchable played by Andy Garcia) are caught in traffic counting off the seconds as the scene begins.

But why paraphrase? Here is the scene as Mamet wrote it:

INTERIOR (INT.) — THE CAR

Ness and Stone. Ness driving. Stone looks down at the train schedule in his hand.

ANGLE POV (POINT-OF-VIEW)

The schedule, the entry circled reads: "Departs Northwestern Station 6:04."

ANGLE

Stone looking up.

NESS
What time is it?

ANGLE

Stone looking at his watch.

STONE
We can just make it.

ANGLE: THE WATCH

It reads 5:58.

NESS
(off screen)
NO!!

Ness looking out the window as the car slows. The drawbridge across the Chicago River is up, and the car can progress no further.

Mamet now cuts inside the station, where an "old man" in a wheelchair—he's really the youngish bookkeeper — is being rolled toward the train by a priest and two elderly ladies. As the priest's cassock blows open, it reveals a submachine gun held under the arm. No one notices. The "old man" safely boards the train, and Mamet cuts back to:

EXTERIOR (EXT.) — BRIDGE OVER THE CHICAGO RIVER

A large boat has just passed under the bridge, and the bridge is being lowered the last few feet. The car with Ness and Stone speeds up on the bridge and reaches the other side before the two halves of the bridge have met.

INT. — STATION

The Brakeman at the end of the train looks down at his watch, signals ahead to the Conductor. The train starts to pull out of the station.

EXT. — LAKESHORE DRIVE

The car with Stone and Ness.

INT. — CAR

Stone looking at his watch.

ANGLE POV

The watch reads 6:06.

ANGLE

Stone looks up.

NESS
Where's the next station?

INT. — TRAIN COMPARTMENT

Payne and the bodyguards. One hands Payne some sheets of paper.

BODYGUARD
The big fellow needs these sheets before we get to Florida.

INT. — NESS'S CAR

Ness speeding through a small residential community, scattering pedestrians, makes a screaming turn. We see the sleepy suburban station. The car stops beside the tracks. Ness jumps out, runs toward the station. He turns back to Stone.

NESS
Put the car on the tracks!

Stone hesitates.

NESS
PUT THE CAR ON THE TRACKS.

Stone follows orders. The train has to slow down. Stone moves the car, and then, as the train eases past the car, he and Ness swing onboard. Ness is spotted by a bodyguard. A gunfight begins. Another bodyguard, submachine gun blazing, leads Payne back to the suburban train station. Ness and Stone shoot their way in — only to find the bodyguard holding a gun to Payne's head.

"I'm coming out with the bookkeeper, and we are driving away," the bodyguard shouts. "Or else he dies. He dies and you got *nothing*. You got five seconds to make up your mind."

Ness looks over at his partner. Stone, without looking up, nods imperceptibly. "Stone raises his gun and fires," Mamet writes, "and the bodyguard's head disappears."

This unadorned action writing delighted De Palma. And it pleased Paramount — until mid-production anyway. Then, with only a month of shooting left and the chase a few weeks from filming, the studio noticed that *The Untouchables* was becoming one seriously pricey movie. This wasn't De Palma's fault. When De Niro decided he'd like to play Capone (at an estimated $1.5 million for eighteen days of filming), the studio had to pay off the already-hired Bob Hoskins (an estimated $200 000 for zero days of filming). And that salary bulge wasn't the only reason the movie's budget was swelling from its original $18 million to over $20 million and change. Period movies eat money — the 1930s train alone, the studio people said, would cost $200 000. So out it went.

Brian De Palma is a director who meticulously draws (okay, doodles) every shot in his movie long before the equipment is rented. He is also a seasoned professional who's been making films for 22 of his 46 years; if improvising on short notice were beyond him, he would have been out of this business long ago. On the other hand, when you're working with David Mamet — and hewing to his script — you want to involve him.

This turned out to be the one thing De Palma couldn't do: Mamet was off in Seattle directing his own movie, *House of Games*. So De Palma sat in his hotel room. Listened to the ticking clock in his head. And, suddenly, he was writing a two-page scene. He'd had an Idea.

"I thought a gangster should try to shoot Ness," De Palma recalls. "And the best time — the most unexpected time — was as Ness comes out of the hospital after his wife has given birth. He'd be coming down the steps, a woman would be bringing her baby out in a carriage at the same time. And then, as the ambush began, something would happen to jostle the carriage, and it would start to bounce down the stairs."

This was, De Palma realized, "a very good idea — good enough for Eisenstein, after all. But the sequence floors you," he says. "It's a pure cinematic sequence, and halfway through the script, you're not prepared for that. Leave it there, and you've got nowhere to go."

On the other hand, why not move the bouncing carriage to the train station nearer the end of the movie? Why not use it to divide Ness's focus (and the audience's attention) during the Untouchables' attempt to capture Walter Payne? Here, at the action climax of the film, you've not only got somewhere to go — the courtroom, in the very next shot — but you've also got something great, a scene that moviegoers will be talking about as they leave the theater.

De Palma had no time to plan this sequence in advance. Or to screen *The Battleship Potemkin*, which he hadn't seen in 30 years. Indeed, he was so busy by then that he wasn't even able to write the scene. In the final script, it's practically a footnote: "Ness and Stone go into action. This action will take place on the steps, to be outlined later."

There are *very* few directors who can, without notes, shoot as many as 50 setups a night for six days straight and, a week later, have a flawless sequence in the can. Not surprisingly, this directorial tour de force became a Hollywood legend even as it was happening. "Spielberg told me the stuff was great," De Palma notes.

In a theater, as these nail-biting minutes whiz by, even the most diligent cineast will have difficulty deconstructing this sequence. So, on a rainy afternoon, I sat with De Palma in his office near Washington Square. On his desk were hundreds of stills from the Union Station shootout — we were going to take the scene apart, beat by beat.

"Here's the setting," De Palma begins. "Union Station has 35 steps, with one landing. The waiting room's at the bottom of the steps. I started wide, as Ness and Stone enter the station. Using a camera set on a crane at the bottom of the steps, Ness goes to the balcony and Stone comes down the stairs. Ness stands at the corner of the balcony, looking in Stone's direction. He watches Stone cross the floor of the station and exit."

1. "The camera cranes up. We pick up Ness. He's looking out.

"It's midnight. The train for Miami leaves at 12:05 a.m. A big clock in the station tells us exactly how much time there is before it leaves. We can build the tension by showing Ness looking around for several minutes.

"All this time, a woman with a baby is struggling. She can't afford a porter, she's got a big baby carriage and two suitcases, and her baby is crying. She lifts him out, holds him, puts him back, and starts up the stairs. Step by step, she pulls the baby carriage then the suitcases. It's an arduous process. No one helps her."

2. "Now the tension builds. Ness knows that Payne — and Capone's bodyguards — have got to be coming in. And he can't have that mother and child on the steps. So he goes to the bottom of the steps and starts to help the mother up.

"At just this moment, the gangsters arrive. Because he looks like a man with a family, the gangsters don't recognize him. Two of them — there are six — come down to the bottom of the steps."

3. "Ness gets the baby carriage to the top of the steps — and who does he see coming in but Walter Payne. Payne's with a goon named Bowtie. As they cross in front of Ness, he turns back. Another bodyguard enters the station, a man with a bandage on his nose. We go into slow motion as he stops and looks suspiciously at Ness. This is very bad for Ness. Earlier that day, he punched this guy in the nose. Now this guy can get his revenge — he's the only bodyguard who can identify Ness."

4. "Ness turns, pulls his gun from his trenchcoat with his right hand. He's still holding onto the carriage with his left. But as he rotates to shoot, he bumps the carriage. It starts to roll. Very slowly. And it is fifteen feet to the steps."

5. "As the gunfight develops, Ness throws down his shotgun and pulls out a revolver. At the bottom of the steps, a gangster with a machine gun prepares to fire at Ness. Ness is unprotected. Suddenly, the gangster's throat explodes. We cut to the balcony at the far side of the station and see Stone with a smoking revolver. Stone starts to run. The baby carriage keeps rolling. It starts down the steps. What will Ness do?"

6. "He decides to go after the baby — even though there's a guy at the bottom shooting up and a goon at the side shooting across. The sailors are on the steps because I realized the stairway was too narrow. In a real shoot-out, it would have been over in seconds. So I put bodies in the middle and had the gangster on the steps get wounded in the shoulder."

7. "Stone's been running back, and now he's finally here. He shoots the guy at the bottom of the steps. Then he flips a gun to Ness and slides across the floor to stop the carriage as Ness reaches out to catch the gun. And Ness blows the bodyguard on the steps away."

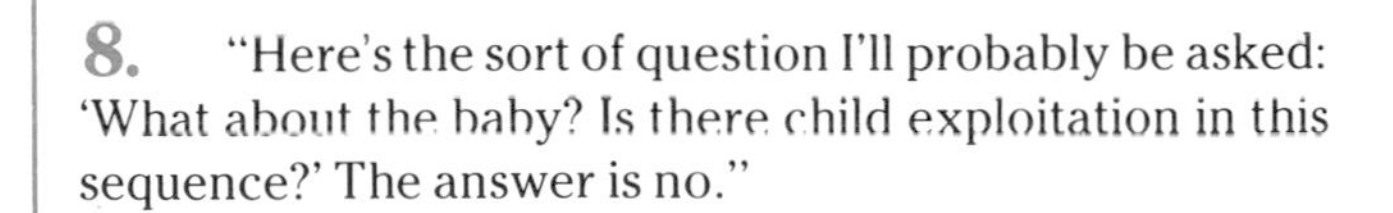

8. "Here's the sort of question I'll probably be asked: 'What about the baby? Is there child exploitation in this sequence?' The answer is no."

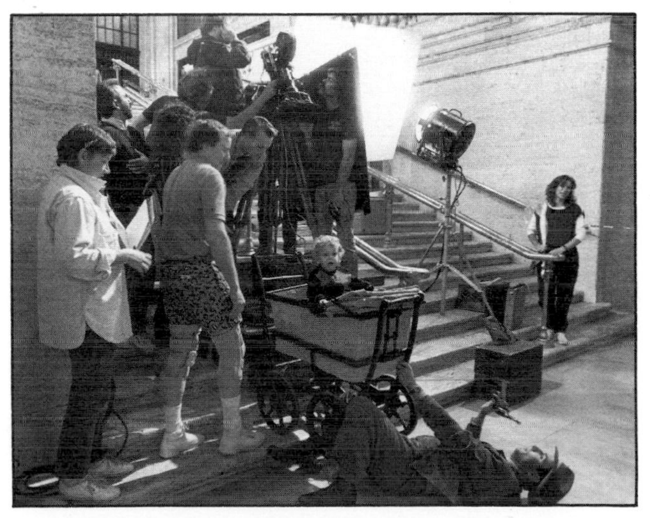

9. "The kid — Colin Hymes, the sixteen-month-old son of Gary Hymes, our stunt coordinator — loved being in that carriage. The bouncing relaxed him.

"The only difficult moment with him was the final shot of the baby in the carriage. After a scene that's required several hundred cuts — some nights, we went through double alphabets — you want to break the tension with one shot showing the kid laughing. But how do you make him laugh? We had Kevin Costner wave a rattle. No go. Then Colin's father — up in the top of the frame — fired off a gun. And the baby gave us a beautiful laugh."

— Jesse Kornbluth
Premiere
July/August 1987

EXPLORING IDEAS

1. Review the action scene written by David Mamet that leads up to the final confrontation in the train station. How has he used the camera to build tension?

2. Examine the sequence of stills from the movie. Notice there is virtually no dialogue in this sequence. How has the camera been used to
(a) suggest personality and character?
(b) communicate information about the conflict?
(c) build tension?

3. ***(a)*** The written text beside each still indicates, in very general terms, camera movement for this sequence. The final version has much more camera movement. Reread the text and choose *one* place in the action where the following could be used:
- a reaction shot
- zoom in
- panning
- tilt up
- zoom out
- tilt down

(b) Compare your suggestions in a small-group discussion.

Media Facts & Techniques

Planning a Film

When planning any type of film presentation, remember the basic rule LET THE CAMERA DO THE TALKING. If the camera can *show* the audience what they need to know, words will not be necessary.

There are two basic methods you can use in planning the visuals and dialogue in a film. The first is called a *shooting script*. The excerpt from David Mamet's script for *The Untouchables*, page 125, is a good example of this type of plan. Basically, a shooting script contains the following kinds of information for each scene or segment in a film:

(a) *Information about the setting and action:*

INTERIOR (INT) — THE CAR
Ness and Stone. Ness Driving. Stone looks down at the train schedule in his hand.

(b) *Information about camera placement and/or movement:*

ANGLE POV (POINT-OF-VIEW)
The schedule, the entry circled reads: "Departs Northwestern Station 6:04."

(c) *Dialogue:*

Stone looking up.
NESS
What time is it?

The second planning method is called a *storyboard*. A storyboard is a series of sketches representing the image that will appear on the screen, plus a brief written description of the action and information about camera movement and technique. Together, the drawings and notations act as a blueprint for the final version. A storyboard resembles the sequence of stills included in the article on *The Untouchables*, pages 127-130.

Either method will help you visualize your film before you start shooting. Your shooting script or storyboard does not have to contain detailed information about every aspect of each scene. However, the more carefully you have planned the action, photographic techniques, camera placement, and dialogue, the less time you will waste "on location."

YOUR TURN

1. Select a favourite scene from a short story, novel, or narrative poem you think might be turned into a magic moment on film. Create a shooting script or storyboard for the scene.

Working in groups, study the print excerpt; then discuss how a film version of the scene might look. Consider questions such as the following:

- What mood, feeling, or general impression do you want to communicate in your film adaptation? How can filming techniques, costumes, props, and so on contribute to this overall impression?
- Sometimes several pages of descriptive details in printed text can be conveyed very quickly on film. How would you go about establishing the setting for your audience? Will you need to subtract any details in the text to give the scene a strong, visual focus?
- If your excerpt is *not* very descriptive, will you need to add any details, costumes, props, etc., to set the scene?
- Should you delete minor characters or add characters to portray the scene effectively?
- What will you use as your opening shot?
- What camera movements would be effective?
- What sounds/dialogue/music will your soundtrack require? Will you use a narrator's "voice-over" to portray characters' emotions and thoughts, or let the camera do all the talking?
- What techniques will sustain drama, suspense, comedy, and so on, as is appropriate to the mood?
- How will you end the scene?

Remember, you need not portray *everything* in the printed text. Film is a different medium from print; your aim should be to maintain the main spirit, mood, or message of the story in your film adaptation.

Present your storyboard or shooting script to the class. Lead a discussion on the decisions your group has made. Audience feedback may provide suggestions for improving the impact of your adaptation.

“It's been the most trustworthy genre. It's always been there. The first motion picture ever made was a horror film. It was Edison's Frankenstein, *where a guy put baking powder all over his face and played the creature. It's successful for the reason it has always been successful — people are scared.”*

— Stephen King

“If you're dealing with horror, it must be human centred.... Horror is a representation of the idea that you carry the seeds of your own destruction around with you always — they can erupt at any time. There is no escape from the destruction.”

— David Cronenberg,
Canadian filmmaker

“The central structure of the horror film has, at least until recently, been the struggle between the forces of normality and the monster.... The monster traditionally becomes the real hero of the horror film, the centre of sympathy, although this can never quite be acknowledged because the monster also has the designated evil. This is a basic given of the genre.”

— Robin Wood
from *Long Live the New Flesh: The Films of David Cronenberg*
June 6, 1987, on CBC

Whether or not we agree with these observers of the genre, we must admit that horror remains a popular film theme. The writer of the next article explores some reasons for this continued ability of horror to thrill and chill audiences.

A Taste for Terror

Something very weird has happened to horror films. These days when we see Vincent Price, he's cute, he's lovable, he sells 35-mm cameras. But even 30 years ago, he wasn't that scary. Neither were Peter Cushing and Christopher Lee, who were awfully well mannered. In fact, in retrospect, one could almost conceive of the Creature from the Black Lagoon as being cuddly.

But we accepted them as our movie villains, so we hissed at them and endured their collective droolings and the cranking of their torture wheels. Nevertheless, we were confident that they would soon crumble under the righteous, square-jawed forces of Good. The climax of a horror film once stood as convincing proof of the morality of our universe, according to the Judeo-Christian ethic, the Hollywood Production Code, and Bruno Bettelheim.

Let loose in today's horror films, however, Vincent, Peter, or Creature wouldn't last through the credits. They're simply no match for their antecedents in terror — Michael, Jason, and Freddy. Contemporary practitioners of the genre have found there is no longer any reason to make do with mere villains, when Pure Evil — nonverbal, relentless, merciless, and really ugly — is far more effective.

They're not witty or charming, and their tactics are far from ingenious, but nothing can stop The Three Dusketeers of modern mayhem: Michael, a mental-institution escapee, whose frequent returns to his hometown on *Halloween* to hack up all the available babysitters are becoming as commonplace an annual event as bobbing for apples; Jason, who has frolicked at Camp Crystal Lake on *Friday the 13th* for no less than *six* almost consecutive seasons, carving his initials into the new counselors, then slipping back

Pure Evil — "Dusketeer" Freddy from the popular *Nightmare on Elm Street* series of horror films

into his bog; and Freddy, a grinning spirit with a face like a meat loaf and fingers the envy of a Benihana chef, who has had such good times slicing open sleeping adolescents in the midst of their *Nightmare on Elm Street* he's coming back again. The forces of Good don't seem to frighten The Three Dusketeers much. And if Mr. Bettelheim ever met them face to face, he'd probably wind up with an ax in his.

But something ever weirder is happening to horror-film fans.

Instead of recoiling with indignation, audiences, while buried in each other's armpits, are actually *rooting* for Michael, Jason, and Freddy. They think they're cute! They wear T-shirts silk-screened with their likenesses. And they don't seem to care if the good guys ever turn up.

Strange as it may seem, the shift in loyalty is really just logic over morality: your average screen hero can bump off a villain or two, maybe even a whole dungeonful with the proper ammunition, but his odds drop drastically against Total Rottenness. Evil Incarnate, like a diamond, is forever, and at six dollars a ticket, the audience has the right to want to go with a winner.

It's a new, insatiable taste for terror that is being served up in movie theaters; what it lacks in universal appeal it makes up for in fanatical devotion. Younger audiences began in 1976 to spend their Saturdays at the movies at midnight. A slapstick, freak-filled musical called *The Rocky Horror Picture Show* began appearing at the stroke of 12 (it had failed in its initial run a year earlier, and then went on to earn over $60 million when it found these fans after hours), and reminded a generation of TV babies of the magic of movies as a collective experience.

After seeing *Rocky Horror* 10, 50, 300 times, this eager core audience became hungry for more communal thrills. Enterprising exhibitors, sensing easy acceptance of weirdness, fed them George Romero's cult classic *Night of the Living Dead*, Tobe Hooper's gleesome *Texas Chainsaw Massacre*, and a haunting fantasy called *Eraserhead* by a young unknown named David Lynch (who later made *The Elephant Man*, *Blue Velvet*). And the lines got longer.

But it took John Carpenter's brutally elegant night of slaughter, *Halloween*, in 1978, to show the motion-picture industry demographers that the midnight crowd was no longer a noisy fringe group with blatantly neurotic tastes. This independent low-budget thriller earned over $50 million.

Halloween's plot was neither clever nor fresh; Carpenter used a simple, primal fear — the bogeyman. Then he gave it a twist. No one, not Daddy, or anyone else, makes the bogeyman go away. He just leaves. But you know he's coming back. No matter what you do. We screamed our heads off.

Halloween is, in another way, this generation's *Psycho*. Hitchcock's cinematic joke was that we never actually see Tony Perkins' knife stabbing Janet Leigh's body in *Psycho*. Our minds do all the dirty work. Many of the violent scenes in *Halloween* are set up the same way. Both films also establish the evil character so fully that just his appearance is enough to generate apoplexy.

Unfortunately, not all of today's terror fests are this accomplished or subtle. For every *Halloween*, there are five movies like *Chopping Mall* ("Where shopping costs an arm and a leg") and *The Mutilator* ("By sword, by pick, by ax, bye bye") that owe everything to the wonders of latex.

But John Carpenter tapped the right vein by returning to childhood lore to find something to scare us. He correctly assumes that an audience sensorially overloaded by tabloid journalism, television violence, and the graphic horrors of daily living doesn't scare easily. Childhood is the last time we have no defenses. Our fears are completely open and unguarded.

Because we now live in a world that is too much with us, young people have a surprisingly lousy sense of fantasy. Consequently, they don't find castles slipping into the mists, mad epigrammatic Englishmen, or the secret tribal rites of Haitian witch doctors particularly scary.

Our own world has become frightening enough. When, as Stephen King cites, "We've got enough explosives to turn Planet Earth into the second asteroid belt, [while] the largest weekly magazine in the country is talking about where celebrities shop," who needs Transylvania? The loonies are here and they are us. So horror films are now firmly set in the present; more often than not, in ordinary shopping-mall suburbia. And in affectionate homage to the audience, they consistently star people just like them; depicted either as upwardly mobile couples or coeds and their boyfriends.

Often horror movies are also funny. No, it isn't funny when the young writer in Steve Miner's *House* accidently shoots a creature he believes is his wife. It is funny that she/the creature is transformed into an enormous ticked-off Cabbage Patch Doll and that when he starts chopping it up "Dedicated to the One I Love" by the Shirelles comes over the soundtrack. And when the Dee Wallace character and her child find themselves trapped in their car by a rabid dog in Lewis Teague's *Cujo*, the audience can't help but register that they've been forced to take refuge in a (notoriously recallable) Ford Pinto.

None of these things seems as funny if you are alone. The VCR has its limits. Meryl Streep is a welcome addition to anyone's living room, but Freddy is not as easy to explain to the relatives. "But a good horror film," Sean Cunningham (producer-director, *Friday the 13th: Part I* through *Part VI*) believes, "*should* be a social event. You can't scream at a VCR while your mother is in the kitchen cooking. We're all too cool for that. But in a full house, a horror film becomes a roller-coaster ride, with people laughing, screaming and scratching, covering their eyes. It's part of why we love movies." Especially weird ones.

— Hal Rubenstein
Elle
March 1987

EXPLORING IDEAS

1. What is your opinion of horror films? Why, do you think, have they been so successful in recent years?
2. Discuss the following in small groups. Appoint one member to record your group's ideas and present them to the class.
   (a) The writer suggests that in the best horror movies "our minds do all of the dirty work." Do you agree? Discuss this in relation to specific movies you have seen.
   (b) Do you agree that movies set in the present and in very "ordinary" locations are scarier than those set in distant times and places?
   (c) *"...John Carpenter tapped the right vein by returning to childhood lore to find something to scare us."* Describe some horror films you feel are good illustrations of this concept.
   (d) *"The trouble with most horror films made now is that there is no serious content."*
   — Maureen Gaffney, producer of educational films
   Do you agree or disagree with this assessment? Support your opinion by referring to some of today's popular films.
3. If you were going to film a takeoff on the typical horror movie, what elements common to most horror movies would you be compelled to use in your satire? Make a list and brief description of typical elements and compare it with those of your classmates.

YOUR TURN

1. Write a brief essay entitled "Horrifying Moments in Film" in which you describe your favourite scary scenes in movies. Explain why you found the scenes so frightening. Consider films you have seen from childhood to the present.
2. Write a brief essay about your favourite horror-movie creature.
   or
   Write a short story that could be the basis of a horror film.
3. Working with a partner or in a small group, script and present a scene that is a takeoff on what audiences might see in a typical horror movie.

Star Wars, *first released in 1977, had a profound impact on the movie-going public's attitudes and tastes. In the views of the writers of the next two articles, it not only established science fiction as a popular art form — it "changed the look of movies forever."*

Bringing Sci-Fi Down to Earth

A long time ago (May, 1977, to be exact) in a galaxy far, far away (where people watched movies on huge screens instead of tiny video tubes), a spectacular film called *Star Wars* gave science fiction a quantum boost into mainstream culture.

And now, having past the 10th anniversary of our first eye-popping encounter with Luke Skywalker, Princess Leia, Han Solo, R2-D2, C-3PO, and Darth Vader, science fiction in all its forms has finally become as homey and comfortable as the ultra-logical murder mystery, the down-to-earth Western, and the no-nonsense espionage tale.

No one would argue that *Star Wars* was the first science fiction milestone to capture the public's imagination. That distinction has been spread over dozens of books (*From the Earth to the Moon, The Time Machine, 1984*), movies (*Metropolis, The Day the Earth Stood Still, 2001: A Space Odyssey*), and TV shows (*The Twilight Zone, The Outer Limits, Star Trek*).

But, in their day, many of these works were considered oddities — imaginative and gripping, perhaps, but not quite important enough to raise science fiction to the level of artistic respectability.

In fact, only recently has the genre come to be viewed by society as something more than the amateurish attempts of a few starry-eyed dreamers to amuse an indiscriminating audience of juvenile minds.

And for that we can thank *Star Wars* — and its sequels

The Empire Strikes Back and *Return Of The Jedi* — and their enormous economic clout.

The stunning box-office success of George Lucas' trilogy — $4 billion in theatre tickets, cassette sales, and screenings on free and pay TV, plus $2.6 billion in licenced merchandise — confirmed the existence of a market of all ages for grand epics in an interplanetary context.

At the same time, it became proper, even for adults, to wonder aloud and without embarrassment about faster-than-light travel, robotic technology, the dark consequences of scientific research, and a whole galaxy of themes that science fiction fans have cherished for decades.

The long-term effect has *not* been to turn science fiction into the hottest artistic trend of the late 20th century. Something even better has happened. Science fiction has become an accepted fact of life whose presence is now felt in a great many everyday ways.

Some examples:

- Top-grossing movies about extraterrestrial life (*Close Encounters of the Third Kind, E.T.*), the horrors of a soulless society (*Brazil, Blade Runner*), changes in us as individuals (*Back to the Future, Cocoon, The Fly*), and out-and-out adventure yarns (*Alien, Aliens*).

- Controversial TV specials and mini-series about terrifying, possible futures (*The Day After, Amerika, V*) and series about inspiring and troubling societies (*Star Trek, Max Headroom*).

- The regular appearance on best-seller lists of authors such as Isaac Asimov, Arthur C. Clarke, Robert A. Heinlein, Ursula K. LeGuin, and Frank Hebert, plus critically acclaimed crossover novels by mainstream writers such as Canada's Margaret Atwood (*The Handmaid's Tale*) and Doris Lessing (the *Canopus in Argos* series that includes *Shikasta* and *The Sentimental Agents*).

- Presence of a strong science fiction element in the popular CBC radio series *Vanishing Point*.

- Futuristic, other-worldly toys such as Charan's Lazer Tag, Tonka's Supernaturals and Go-Bots, Hasbro's Transformers, and Mattel's Masters of the Universe.

Within the science fiction community, reaction to *Star Wars'* influence has ranged from grudging praise to outright condemnation. Chief among the problems, say the critics, is the public's tendency to believe *Star Wars* is pure science fiction instead of space fantasy populated by cartoonish stereotypes.

Vancouver's William Gibson, winner of the genre's top writing awards for his novel *Neuromancer*, dismisses Lucas' creations as "a pattycake Zen world view, with nothing new in it other than superior special-effects technology."

Real science fiction, he says, changes only one or two basic social or scientific premises and then, in a consistent and logical manner, measures the results on a group of people.

Anthologist Judith Merril, founder of Toronto's Spaced Out Library (one of the world's largest repositories of science fiction books and magazines), concedes that *Star Wars* "may actually have moved someone to consider his or her relationship with the universe. But its main effect is to get people to think, 'Kill, kill, kill.'

"The first half of the movie delighted old science fiction fans, because it was like watching home movies of scenes we'd had in our heads for so long. Old images and characters were spread all over the landscape. But as soon as we came to the interplanetary tavern scene, it all changed, and *Star Wars* began turning into a funny cross between a Western and a war movie."

The irony, adds director David Cronenberg (*The Fly, Videodrome, The Dead Zone*), is that "George Lucas has done a wonderful job of humanizing technology for children and creating a complete overwhelming victory of the imagination."

But, he says, even though producers now are much more receptive to science fiction proposals, they're reluctant to invest in serious projects that don't contain dazzling special effects.

Not only do these visual tricks turn the project into a greater budgetary risk — thereby placing it beyond the involvement of fledgling filmmakers — but they often threaten to distort or obscure a sensible plot and an intelligent script.

Still, even writers such as Isaac Asimov, while recognizing *Star Wars'* weaknesses, acknowledge its importance as a catalyst among members of the public who have actually seen science fictional dreams — the atomic bomb, micro-computers, and rockets to the moon — come true.

"Admittedly, only a small percentage of the people who saw *Star Wars* began to read science fiction," says Asimov. "But even that small percentage is a large number in the world of publishing, and it's been increasing considerably.

Bringing extraterrestrials down to Earth — Steven Spielberg's *Close Encounters of the Third Kind* paved the way for his "pro-alien" E.T.

"Now it's relatively easy for science fiction writers to make the best-seller lists, and from that standpoint, *Star Wars* has done a noble job."

Halifax's Spider Robinson, who with his wife Jean picked up top international honors for the novelette *Stardance*, says *Star Wars* has raised "a curious problem for science fiction writers who are reluctant to disassociate themselves from a multi-million dollar phenomenon.

"Even though the science fiction publishing boom of the late 1970s has slowed down, science fiction still sells well. And a science fiction writer is still a hip and sexy and popular thing to be. When I got into the field and people asked what I did, I usually changed the subject. Or I said I wrote speculative fiction and I hoped nobody knew what I was talking about."

Robinson, too, criticizes *Star Wars* for "playing fast and loose with the laws of physics — things like spaceships making U-turns or noisy explosions in the vacuum of space. But I like to think the movie has also made society more receptive to science fiction and less intimidated by it.

"It's slowly becoming apparent to more and more people that we're going to be living in the future any minute now, and if we look ahead at some possible futures, maybe the real thing won't scare us when it arrives. If *Star Wars* has somehow helped ease that process, all the better."

— Henry Mietkiewicz
The Toronto Star
May 24, 1987

ILM magic — The Rancor Pit monster from 1983's *Return of the Jedi* was born in George Lucas' "creature shop."

Lights! Camera! Special Effects!

Hollywood's magic moments used to be mostly quiet ones: Rick telling Sam to play it again in *Casablanca*, Charles Foster Kane muttering his dying "Rosebud" in *Citizen Kane*. The memorable screen moments of recent years are more, well, eye-catching. A fleet of rebel spaceships enters the Death Star for a climactic battle against the Empire's forces in *Return of the Jedi*. The shards of a stained-glass window are transformed into a sword-wielding knight in *Young Sherlock Holmes*. Runaway mine cars career at breakneck pace through hair-breadth twists and turns in *Indiana Jones and the Temple of Doom*.

It might be called the "wow" school of filmmaking, and no one has mastered it better than Industrial Light & Magic, the special-effects division of George Lucas' Lucasfilm Ltd. Some moviegoers may miss the old days, when subtleties of character and story seemed to matter more. Indeed, American movies can no longer claim undisputed pre-eminence in the world of filmic art, as they could during the 1930s and '40s. But for sheer technical dazzle, U.S. filmmakers are clearly setting the international standard, with Industrial Light & Magic at the forefront.

Special effects are hardly new to movies, nor are they an exclusively American invention. The groundbreaking special-effects movie *A Trip to the Moon* was made in 1902 by a French filmmaker named Georges Melies. Techniques were improved over the years in such landmark films as *King Kong* (1933) and Stanley Kubrick's *2001: A Space Odyssey* (1968). But most Hollywood studios had closed down their special-effects units by the mid-1970s, when Director Lucas set out to make a space adventure called *Star Wars*. To create the futuristic world he envisioned, Lucas set up his own shop in a Los Angeles warehouse, hired a crew of eager young technicians — and proceeded to change the look of movies forever.

"It was a big adventure at the time," says Lucas. "We really took a plunge into the unknown." After the astounding success of *Star Wars*, his special-effects group, dubbed Industrial Light & Magic, relocated in San Rafael, Calif., just north of San Francisco, and became a permanent operation. ILM devised the special effects not just for Lucas' three *Star Wars* epics, but for such Steven Spielberg hits as *E.T.*, *Poltergeist*, and *Raiders of the Lost Ark*. Now ILM's handiwork seems to be everywhere. The company created the effects for six releases in 1985, among them *Cocoon* (for which ILM technicians won their seventh visual-effects Oscar), *Back to the Future*, *Young Sherlock Holmes*, and *Explorers*. And that does not count smaller jobs on films like *Out of Africa*. (The train that wends its way through the African landscape in the opening credit sequence is actually a miniature built by ILM and inserted into the scenic footage.)

Flying DeLorean — In this still from 1985's *Back to the Future*, it's hard to believe the airborne auto is actually a detailed miniature.

Computer wizardry — The stained-glass man from Lucasfilm's *Young Sherlock Holmes* took four people four months to create.

In one room, artists work on mat paintings that provide the fake backgrounds for many scenes (the outer-space vistas in *Star Wars*, for example, or the cavernous warehouse at the end of *Raiders of the Lost Ark*). In the model shop, workers craft detailed miniatures of such objects as the spaceship from *Cocoon* and the DeLorean car that flew through time in *Back to the Future*. The creature shop is the birthplace for most of the monsters and other grotesques that populate Lucas' fantasyland, from the Rancor Pit monster in *Return of the Jedi* to Howard the Duck.

Much of ILM's trickery is aimed at making these inanimate figures appear to move and act. In some cases, movement is simulated by stop-motion photography (the same technique that gave life to the original King Kong). The object is photographed one frame at a time and moved manually a tiny bit for each shot; when the film is projected at normal speed, the figure appears to be in action. Today, however, creatures can also be manipulated by computer-controlled motors in an ILM innovation known as "go-motion," which produces more realistic movement.

Creatures, spaceships, and other objects are inserted into the action of the film by means of the blue-screen process. The figure is photographed against a blue background and then combined in an optical printer with the scene into which it will be placed. This procedure must be repeated each time a new element is added to the scene. The pastry creatures that came to life in *Young Sherlock Holmes*, for example, were hand-manipulated rod puppets, each shot individually and added one by one in as many as twelve layers. For a brief shot of a space battle in *Return of the Jedi*, 63 layers were required. This and other complex scenes are made possible by a computer-driven camera developed by ILM that can repeat the same motion over and over so that new elements can be added with great precision.

Computers are also being used to create entire images from scratch. For effects like the stained-glass man in *Young Sherlock Holmes*, all the visual elements of the figure — size, shape, and surface characteristics — are fed into a computer, along with such data as camera angles and light sources. The computer then uses this information to construct an image. Simple geometrical shapes are relatively easy to create, but the process is far more difficult for complicated figures. The stained-glass man, for instance, took four people some four months to create.

ILM technicians are accustomed to seeing months of effort speed by in just a few minutes of screen time. Kenneth Smith, who operates the optical printer, estimates that he and his co-workers spent eight months creating just 3 1/2 minutes of special effects for *E.T.* like the bicycles that flew through the air at the film's end. "I compare it to working on a cathedral," he says. "I'm just a stone mason working on a gargoyle in a corner. I want to make the best one I can, of course. But I wish they'd use more gargoyles."

Despite its high-tech tools, ILM uses homey techniques as well. Clouds might be simulated by wads of cotton, the dirt on a remote planet by a pile of cork. The walls of the mine in *Indiana Jones* were made of scrunched-up aluminum foil, spray-painted to look like rocks. "We have no commitment to using the most sophisticated techniques," says Warren Franklin, ILM's general manager. "We go with what works."

Yet some contend that hardware too often takes center stage in ILM films and that the familiar "ILM look" is too cold and technology-driven. Others claim that the spirit of innovation is waning.

But to critics who fear that ILM-style effects are driving out more traditional movie values, like characters and plots, Lucas is unsympathetic. "Special effects are just a way of visualizing something on screen," he asserts. "They have expanded the limits of storytelling enormously. ILM is a wonderful tool that allows the imagination to run wild."

— Richard Zoglin
TIME
June 16, 1986

EXPLORING IDEAS

1. The first article points out a distinction between pure science fiction and space fantasy. Give examples of movies you have seen that fall into both these categories.
2. Form groups to share views on the following:
   (a) "(Star Wars) *main effect is to get people to think, 'Kill, kill, kill.'* " Do you agree or disagree with this opinion?
   (b) "Star Wars *began turning into a funny cross between a Western and a war movie.*" What elements do the *Star Wars* movies have in common with both Westerns and war movies?
   (c) In your opinion, what, if anything, have the *Star Wars* movies contributed towards easing the public into the future?
3. *"Some moviegoers may miss the old days, when subtleties of character and story seemed to matter more."*

   Form small groups and evaluate some of the sci-fi movies the members of the group have seen. To what extent do you feel that plot and character development has become of secondary importance — behind that of visual effects — in these movies? Prepare a group report based on your discussions.

INVESTIGATING THE MEDIA

1. Evaluate some films you have seen recently in which special effects played a major role. Do you agree or disagree that these movies are becoming "too cold and technology-driven"?

YOUR TURN

1. *"It might be called the 'wow' school of filmmaking. . . ."*
   Write a poem entitled "Wow!" in which you describe some stunning visual effects that have been memorable for you.
2. Experiment with creating special effects. Develop your own "F/X," or try one of the following:
   (a) If you have access to video equipment, use stop-motion photography to create a brief video. For example, you may wish to select an inanimate object for your subject. Shoot the object briefly, stop the tape, move the object, tape it again, and so on.
   (b) *Or*, you might choose a human subject. Your subject could place an egg in his or her mouth. Stop the tape, remove the egg; then start the tape as the subject places the egg in his or her mouth again. If you continue this sequence, when played back the video will show the subject placing a series of eggs in his or her mouth.
3. Create a collage to advertise a sci-fi movie of your own invention. Experiment with pasting pictures of objects or people into unusual settings to create an unusual effect.
4. Create a series of drawings for the setting, costumes, and vehicles in a science-fiction movie.
   or
   Create a series of drawings, models, or written descriptions of "creatures" for a science-fantasy movie.
5. Take a scene from a science-fiction novel or story and use it to develop either a shooting script or a storyboard for a movie.

How much realism and soul-searching do audiences want when they go to the movies? Brian D. Johnson explores a trend towards "a new realism" in movies that began in the late 1980s.

Hollywood's new vision

David Denby, *New York* magazine's influential film critic, sent a shock wave through Hollywood in the summer of 1986 with a damning indictment of American cinema headlined "Can the movies be saved?" Denby lamented that marquees across North America were offering an increasingly bleak range of options — violent revenge pictures in the *Rambo* mould, crass comedies about spoiled teenagers, and special-effects extravaganzas. Denby's attack voiced a common concern. But, less than a year later, the state of the screen visibly changed: once again, Hollywood was getting serious.

Mature movies focusing on America's troubled conscience — especially the indelible stain left by Vietnam — were suddenly fashionable. The most obvious example: *Platoon*, a grunt's-eye view of Vietnam that won four Oscars and grossed more than $160 million at the box office. *Platoon* supplanted director Francis Coppola's 1979 epic *Apocalypse Now* as the war movie to end war movies. But then Coppola released *Gardens of Stone*, which explored the Vietnam trauma from yet another angle, that of the ceremonial soldiers back home who must bury America's Vietnam dead. The battle-scarred jungles of *Platoon* and the manicured graveyards of *Gardens* form symmetrical halves of the same nightmare.

Getting serious — Tom Berenger in *Platoon*

Movies with a social conscience are not new to Hollywood. From the working-class politics of 1954's *On the Waterfront* to the antinuclear intrigue of 1983's *Silkwood*, filmmakers have often forged drama from the furnace of social conflict. But the industry's political mood swings closely mirror those of the country. And when scandals weakened the conservative Reagan administration, Hollywood's basic liberal instincts revived. A new generation of independent producers stretched the frontiers of what is commercially viable onscreen. Impressed by their success, studio executives have learned that social vision can be a marketable commodity. Says *Gardens of Stone* producer Michael Levy: "The people who finance and distribute films are getting a sense of America's conscience. They're aware that today's audience wants to deal with real subjects."

An element of social advocacy has even begun to creep into Hollywood's more escapist fare. 1986's box-office champion, *Top Gun*, was a jingoistic tribute to the school that trains the U.S. navy's fighter-pilot elite. One of 1987's most popular movies, *Project X*, also deals with a young airman (Matthew Broderick) whose father is a military hero. But Broderick's character becomes a savior for a squadron of chimpanzees subjected to lethal doses of radiation. *Project X* coproducer Walter Parkes did not set out to make "a message movie" about animal rights. "But if it brings about a residual raising of consciousness," said Parkes, "so much the better." Meanwhile, executives at TriStar Pictures released a new antinuclear movie, *Amazing Grace and Chuck*. Starring

Gregory Peck, it is a fable about a young boy who is so horrified by a visit to a missile silo that he gives up playing baseball to protest against nuclear weapons and triggers a global disarmament movement.

The makers of *Amazing Grace* had to build a mock missile silo after the U.S. defence department refused their request to film a real one. But the U.S. army gave full co-operation to *Gardens of Stone*, its first large-scale collaboration with Hollywood since helping John Wayne romanticize Vietnam involvement in 1968's *The Green Berets*. The army generals were so pleased with Coppola's movie that they awarded him a citizen's medal. "It's a pro-army antiwar film," said Anjelica Huston, who portrays a peace activist in love with a military veteran. "Attitudes in Hollywood are changing, but so is the public consciousness."

One clear sign of change is that Ed Asner is working again. In 1982 CBS killed Asner's *Lou Grant* series after its sponsor complained about the actor's public stance against U.S. policy in El Salvador. An unofficial blacklist hampered Asner's career for four years. But Asner says Hollywood is more tolerant of U.S. foreign policy critics. And the acceptance of *Platoon*, he adds, is "a great step forward to offset the *Rambo* mentality."

Hollywood and the U.S. military share a common trait: they are two of the most powerful sources of American influence abroad. As the military makes history, Hollywood's rearguard draws up a big-screen balance sheet of heroes and villains, aggressors and victims. Hollywood magic may not cure America of its traumatic ills. But it is creating ever-more adventurous forms of treatment.

— Brian D. Johnson
Maclean's
May 11, 1987

EXPLORING IDEAS

1. Some films are labelled "escapist" while others are identified as having a "social conscience." In your experience, what are the characteristics that differentiate one type from the other? Which of the two types do *you* prefer watching, and why?
2. Discuss reasons for the apparent revival in the '80s of films with a social conscience. What factors other than those noted by the writer would influence such films' audience acceptance?
3. Do *you* believe that today's audience wants more movies that deal with "real" subjects? What do audiences want *less* of? What evidence do you see that indicates filmmakers are responding to audiences' changing attitudes and tastes?

INVESTIGATING THE MEDIA

1. In small groups, share your observations and opinions on the following issue. One member should record and present your group's ideas to the class.

   Identify films produced in the past few years that could be said to have a social conscience. What are the messages contained in these films? Taken all together, what do these films indicate about the attitudes and values of our society? Develop a "Profile of Us" as it has been presented in films.

YOUR TURN

1. Form groups to brainstorm a list of concerns you think people will have over the next five or ten years. Select one issue that could be the basis for an effective film. Develop a story outline for the film.

The writer of the next article sees "something new and conspicuously un-Canadian" happening in this country's fiction film industry. Do you sense a trend in Canadian movies towards a depiction of characters who are "beginning to hit back and even winning"?

New Canadian character — Polly (Sheila McCarthy) wears her goofiness proudly in Patricia Rozema's *I've Heard the Mermaids Singing*.

Canadian films slowly shucking their loser image

Canadians just don't make heroes of themselves. We're pretty keen on heroes from other countries, but that's another story.

As Margaret Atwood noted about Canadian poetry and literature in *Survival*, and as American journalist Andrew Malcolm pointed out about Canadian politics and economics in *The Canadians*, there are no more reluctant horn-blowers for Canuck accomplishment than Canucks themselves. Whether it's due to weather, insect bites, or antiquated booze laws, given the choice between telling a story of triumph or tragedy, Canadians always go for gloom before glory.

Nowhere has this dark cloud of chilly fatalism loomed heavier than in our movies. While its history has been spotty, its success sporadic, and its activities interrupted by both historical and geographical distances, the Canadian fiction film tradition has been bound by a single, all-consuming characteristic: it's in love with losers.

Limping toward victory — Marcel (Gilles Mahu) and Julie (Lynne Adams) in Jean-Claude Lauzon's *UN ZOO LA NUIT ("NIGHT ZOO")*

If this seems unfair, consider a few titles from the roster of Canadian classics: *Nobody Waved Goodbye, Goin' Down the Road, Mon Oncle Antoine, Le Vrai Nature De Bernadette, Wedding in White, Paperback Hero, The Rowdyman*, and *Shivers*. With startling consistency, each of these deals with crushed ambition, shattered dreams, fatal miscalculations, and the absolute hopelessness of hope.

But something new and conspicuously un-Canadian is happening. Many Canadian movies opened in 1987 have shuffled off that damp and dingy cloak of terminal Canadian loserdom.

What's most significant about some of the newer Canadian films is that while many (including *I've Heard the Mermaids Singing, Life Classes, Night Zoo, Family Viewing*, and *The Kid Brother*) deal with characters displaying all the necessary characteristics of classical Canadian losers, they show us losers in the act of gaining ground, limping — in their modest, Canadian way — toward victory. Call it the triumph of the wimp.

While it's premature to suggest this new sense of worth represents the excavation of Canada's culturally entrenched inferiority complex, it's clearly a start. There's no single reason why, but maybe it's because some of the new directors see a rosier future for Canada than did their predecessors or maybe just learned from the loser negativism that was portrayed so often.

With their determination and modest go-for-it-ness, these new Canadian characters constitute a new notion: instead of people that life hits in the face, these characters are beginning to hit back and even winning.

Polly (Sheila McCarthy), the endearingly daffy "person Friday" heroine of Patricia Rozema's *I've Heard the Mermaids Singing*, is not only prototypical, she's one of a remarkable number of vibrant female characters in today's Canadian movies. Ostensibly however, she displays all the earmarks of classic Canuck loserdom: she's lonely, introverted, prone to daydreamy fits, and firmly convinced of her own social inferiority.

Mermaids' radical departure from tradition lies in its unequivocal endorsement of Polly's eccentricities. Where 10 years ago, Polly probably might have ended up pregnant and abandoned, like Carol Kane in *Wedding in White* or Jayne Eastwood in *Goin' Down the Road*, writer-director Rozema lets her heroine brandish her goofiness proudly, as a badge of distinction in a conformist world.

Further proof of the new positivism resides in the unprecedented title of Phillip Borsos's Canadian-Chinese historical epic, *Bethune: The Making of a Hero*: Until recently it would've been unthinkable for his Canadian countrymen to deem the fervently pro-Communist, hard-drinking Bethune a *hero* — though " The Making of a Loser" would hardly have made a sexy seductive advertising campaign.

But then again, until recently, Canadian movies had a hard time calling *anyone* a hero.

— Geoff Pevere
The Toronto Star
December 12, 1987

EXPLORING IDEAS

1. ***(a)*** What Canadian films have you seen? Do you make a point of going to see movies produced in this country? Why or why not?
   (b) How closely do the writer's comments match your own impressions of Canadian films?
2. In your opinion, *does* the average Canadian go for "gloom before glory"? Why, do you think, do so many of our movies emphasize this attitude? Is the same Canadian attitude evident in other media — Canadian-produced television programs and popular novels, for example? Discuss this as a class.

INVESTIGATING THE MEDIA

1. Arrange to view one of the films from the group of Canadian classics mentioned in the article or from among other Canadian movies currently playing or available on videocassette. Write a review of the film, focusing especially on the image of Canada and Canadians it presents.

YOUR TURN

1. Working in small groups, select a Canadian short story or a current news story that would make a good film. Your main objective is to present a Canadian character who is definitely a "winner." Draft a story outline for the film. Select a group of students to act as potential financial backers for the film. Present your outline to your "clients" for their approval.

Inquiry

Based on your interests and abilities, choose two or more of the following activities and research projects to investigate further topics you have explored in this unit. Alternatively, choose other aspects of photography and film *you* would like to investigate further.

1. For a period of several weeks resolve to watch only *movies* on TV. Look through the weekly listings and select only 3- or 4-star movies. Try to see films from various decades. If possible, view the movies in their complete versions (on public stations, without commercials). Keep a personal-response journal over the complete viewing period. Conclude your journal with summary comments on what the weeks' experience has helped you understand about movies and about your own tastes and perception of movies.

2. Make a study of a film category, or genre, of your choosing — for example, Westerns, comedy, horror, fantasy, science fiction. Prepare a report or presentation on the topic of "The Evolution of __________." How do changes in these types of films reflect changes in society and movie audiences over the years?

3. Review your file of photographs that have captured your attention. Prepare a "live," taped, or written commentary to accompany your "final selection" of meaningful photos. Investigate and report on the techniques and processes that help make such photos effective.

or

Research and present an oral or written profile of a photographer whose work you admire. This person might be currently working in the photographic medium (such as the photographer you may have invited to speak to your class), or a famous photographer from the past, such as Edward Steichen (1879-1973). Your school or local public library/resource centre can supply you with examples of the work of well-known photographers. In your analysis, focus especially on how this photographer's work has helped shape our image of the world.

4. *"In general, it can be said that the public no longer discovers movies, the public no longer makes a picture a hit. If the advertising for a movie doesn't build up an overwhelming desire to be part of the event, people just don't go. They don't listen to their own instincts, they don't listen to the critics — they listen to the advertising."*

— Pauline Kael, *The New Yorker*

(a) Investigate the promotional techniques used for a recent or current film. How did people involved with the film (directors, actors, public relations people) create the sense of "an event" for this film? Consider publicity created through

- talk shows
- television advertising
- newspaper and magazine advertising
- songs from the film (or albums of the soundtrack)
- "spin-off" toys, clothing, and other items
- movie magazine articles and profiles
- reviews in newspapers and magazines
- entertainment programs on television

(b) Present a report to the class based on your findings. As part of your report, view the movie and comment on whether or not you believe it lived up to its advertising. Include your personal reactions to the opinion expressed by Pauline Kael.

5. ***(a)*** Below is a partial list of films based on Canadian short stories and poems. Many of these films will be available through your schoolboard or the public library. Arrange to view some titles from the list and compare the film and print versions of the story.

Short Story or Poem	***Film***
One's a Heifer	same
The Painted Door	same
A Cap for Steve	The Cap
All the Years of Her Life	All the Years
Boys and Girls	same
David	same
Morning on the Lièvre	same

or

(b) Read a novel that has been made into a film, then see the film. Compare the two versions.

The following questions may help to guide your thinking as you prepare your comparison:

- What has been added to or left out of the film version? Is the emphasis in the film different from

that in the original print version? What explanations can you propose for these changes? Are some of the changes necessary because of the nature of film as a medium?
- Which version is more complex? Why?
- Which version do you prefer? Why?

6. If possible, make a short silent film or video based on one of the storyboards or shooting scripts you developed earlier in this unit. Your challenge is to communicate ideas and emotions in purely visual terms.

Arrange a screening for your classmates or family members. Lead a discussion to help you evaluate how successfully your film met this challenge.

7. Although standards have relaxed considerably during the 1970s and 1980s, the issues of censorship and film classification continue to be hotly debated. Do research into these issues and present a report based on the information you collect. The following questions will help you focus your research:
- What is the difference between censoring and classifying films?
- How do the criteria, classification categories, and the preview processes differ from province to province?
- Who previews movies in each province and makes the determination? How are these individuals selected?
- Where do *you* stand on these issues? Do you agree with the principles of censorship and film classification? Why or why not?

8. So-called "cult" films such as *The Rocky Horror Picture Show* have maintained a dedicated following of fans who often see them time and time again. Do research into cult films and cult stars. What conditions create a cult movie or star? If possible, arrange to view a cult film. Prepare a report in which you analyze the film and present your conclusions about why it has such a powerful appeal. The following titles and names will help get you started:

Harold and Maude
James Dean
Marilyn Monroe
2001: A Space Odyssey
Eraserhead
Purple Rose of Cairo

UNIT FOUR:

GETTING THE MES
ADVERT

Giorgio
I just hired a new assistant.
I just met him. Will he work overtime?
SAGE:
ISING

Many of us feel we are immune to the appeals of advertising; ads can seem merely distractions — at times interesting, at times annoying.

Advertisement *itself is an old word, derived from the Latin* ad, *meaning "towards" and* vertere, *"to turn." Thus the literal meaning implies that ads catch our attention, turn us away from other matters and* towards *their message. Even if we notice advertising, does the brief time we spend reading or viewing ads actually seduce us into trying new products or switching brands? Advertisers answer "Yes!" For although many people regard advertising as a pervasive, almost invisible part of the "landscape," advertisers continue to spend billions each year in search of the most-effective way of getting their message across.*

In this unit we will examine the techniques and processes on which those dollars are spent, as well as the role of advertising in North American society.

1. How strongly do members of your class feel they are influenced by advertising? Conduct a survey in your class. How many people believe advertising influences them
   (a) a great deal?
   (b) some?
   (c) very little?
   (d) not at all?

2 As a class, discuss the following:

(a) What ads, if any, do you have taped to your locker door or in your room at home? Why have you collected these particular ads? Organize teams for a "walkaround" in your school. What ads do other students tape on their lockers? Do students of different ages and in different grades select *different* types of advertisements? Discuss the findings of your walkaround.

(b) Are you a walking advertisement for certain products? Which brand names or logos are prominent on the clothes you wear? Does the presence or absence of a logo influence whether or not you buy a particular item of clothing?

(c) What expressions or phrases you have picked up from ads have become part of your personal language?

(d) What new products have advertisements influenced you to try? What made the ads so persuasive?

(e) Which of the following advertising media has the *most* influence on you as a consumer? Why?

- radio
- television
- newspapers
- magazines
- billboards
- *other* (Specify.)

3 Consider whether you agree or disagree with these statements about advertising. Then discuss them as a class or in small groups:

(a) *"Advertising nourishes the consuming power of men. It sets up before a man the goal of a better home, better clothing, better food for himself and his family. It spurs individual exertion and greater production."*

— Winston Churchill (quoted by David Ogilvy in *Confessions of an Advertising Man*)

(b) *"The purpose of advertising in our capitalistic system is to educate and inform people so they can make a choice."*

— Sue Feldman, Research Director for American Express Canada, Inc.

(c) *"You don't spend millions in this business* not *to affect people."*

— Tony Schwartz, advertising designer and analyst

(d) *"Advertising and marketing are not primarily interested in creating needs but in detecting consumer needs in order to fit the product...to the consumers' self-designed desires."*

— Michael Schudson, researcher

(e) *"Advertising sells ourselves to ourselves."*

— Judith Williamson, advertising analyst

(f) *"The trouble with most advertising is that it insults the intelligence of the public and bores you to death."*

— David Ogilvy

(g) *"A* TV *ad can be offensive, silly, annoying and exaggerated, yet it can still accomplish its ultimate goal of making people buy."*

— Erich Fromm

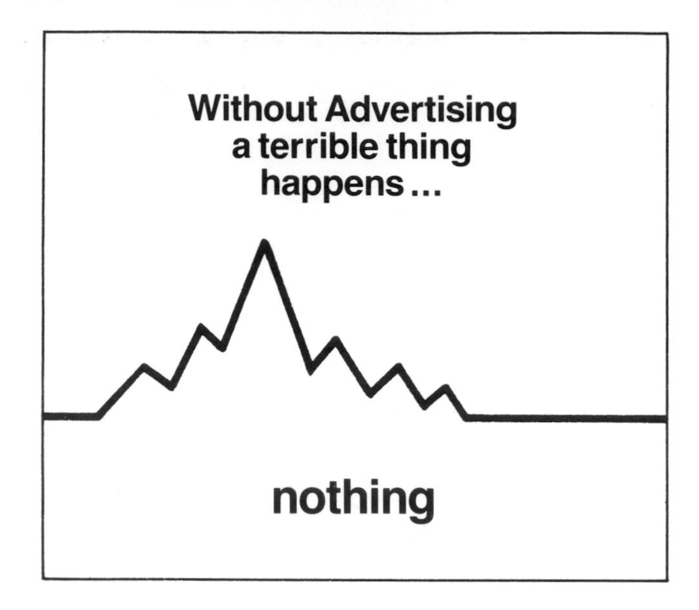
Without Advertising
a terrible thing
happens...
nothing

4 Assess this point of view from the perspective of
(a) the manufacturer
(b) the communications industry
(c) the public
(d) the family

5 Working in groups, brainstorm a list of the pros and cons of advertising. Compare your list with that of other groups. In general, do most students see advertising as a beneficial or harmful influence in our society?

6 Begin a file of print ads that *you* find effective. You will be drawing on this file throughout your examination of advertising.

WHAT MAKES AN EFFECTIVE AD?

Like any other major force in our society, advertising doesn't simply happen casually or accidentally. Today most ads are the result of research, discussion, planning, and design undertaken by teams of advertising experts. Even advertisements that are failures are studied by advertisers. *Why* one extensively thought-out ad failed can be just as important as why another succeeded.

Advertisements in print media and on television have two basic elements: the *verbal* content (in print, the text or copy) and the *visual* content. Newspaper ads generally rely less on visual content. And, of course, radio ads rely on verbal content exclusively — with songs, jingles, and slogans to enhance the effect.

When you examine a number of advertisements, you will notice certain patterns in the way language and pictures are used. Understanding these patterns will help you become a wiser consumer.

David Ogilvy's theories and techniques, outlined in Confessions of an Advertising Man, *had a profound effect on print advertising in the 1950s and '60s. Basically, Ogilvy outlined two "laws" for a good ad: it should create a look or an image; it should be intelligent in its use of copy, typeface, and layout. Above all, an ad should give the potential buyer some solid information about the product.*

Here are some of Ogilvy's "rules" for effective ad design.

Confessions of an Advertising Man

Advertisements are twice as memorable, on the average, when they are illustrated in *color*.

Avoid historical subjects. They may be useful for advertising whiskey, but for nothing else.

Don't show enlarged close-ups of the human face; they seem to repel readers.

Keep your illustrations as *simple* as possible, with the focus of interest on one person. Crowd scenes don't pull.

Avoid stereotyped situations like grinning housewives pointing fatuously into open refrigerators.

Always design your layout for the publication in which it will appear.

Magazine editors have discovered that people read the explanatory captions under photographs more than they read the text of articles; and the same thing is true of advertisements. When we analyzed Starch data on advertisements in *Life*, we found that on the average *twice* as many people read the captions as read the body copy. Thus captions offer you twice the audience you get for body copy. It follows that you should never use a photograph without putting a caption under it, and each caption should be a miniature advertisement, complete with brand name and promise.

If you can keep your body copy down to 170 words, you should set it in the form of a caption under your photograph, as we have done in our magazine advertisements for Tetley Tea.

If you need very long copy, there are several devices which are known to increase its readership:

1. A display subhead of two or three lines, between your headline and your body copy, will heighten the reader's appetite for the feast to come.

2. If you start your body copy with a large initial letter, you will increase readership by an average of 13 per cent.

3. Keep your opening paragraph down to a maximum of eleven words. A long first paragraph frightens readers away. All your paragraphs should be as short as possible; long paragraphs are fatiguing.

4. After two or three inches of copy, insert your first cross-head, and thereafter pepper cross-heads throughout. They keep the reader marching forward. Make some of them interrogative, to excite curiosity in the next run of copy. An ingenious sequence of boldly displayed cross-heads can deliver the substance of your entire pitch to glancers who are too lazy to wade through the text.

5. Set your copy in columns not more than forty characters wide. Most people acquire their reading habits from newspapers, which use columns of about twenty-six characters. The wider the measure, the fewer the readers.

6. Type smaller than 9-point (this is 9-point type) is difficult for most people to read.

7. Serif type like this is easier to read than sans serif type like this.

8. When I was a boy it was fashionable to make copywriters square up every paragraph. Since then it has been discovered that "widows" increase readership, except at the bottom of a column, where they make it too easy for the reader to quit.

9. Break up the monotony of long copy by setting key paragraphs in **boldface** or *italic.*

10. Insert illustrations from time to time.

11. Help the reader into your paragraphs with arrowheads, bullets, asterisks, and marginal marks.

12. If you have a lot of unrelated facts to recite, don't try to relate them with cumbersome connectives; simply *number* them, as I am doing here.

13. Never set your copy in reverse (white type on a black background), and never set it over a gray or colored tint. The old school of art directors believed that these devices *forced* people to read the copy; we now know that they make reading physically impossible.

14. If you use leading between paragraphs, you increase readership by an average of 12 per cent.

The more typographical changes you make in your headline, the fewer people will read it. Run straight through headlines in the same type face, in the same size, and in the same weight.

Set your headline, and indeed your whole advertisement, in lower case. CAPITAL LETTERS ARE MUCH HARDER TO READ, PROBABLY BECAUSE WE LEARN TO READ in lower case. People read all their books, newspapers, and magazines in lower case.

Never deface your illustration by printing your headline over it. Old-fashioned art directors love doing this, but it reduces the attention value of the advertisement by an average of 19 per cent.

— David Ogilvy
from *Confessions of an Advertising Man*

A HASSELBLAD IS UNDENIABLY EXPENSIVE. SO IS A RE-SHOOT.

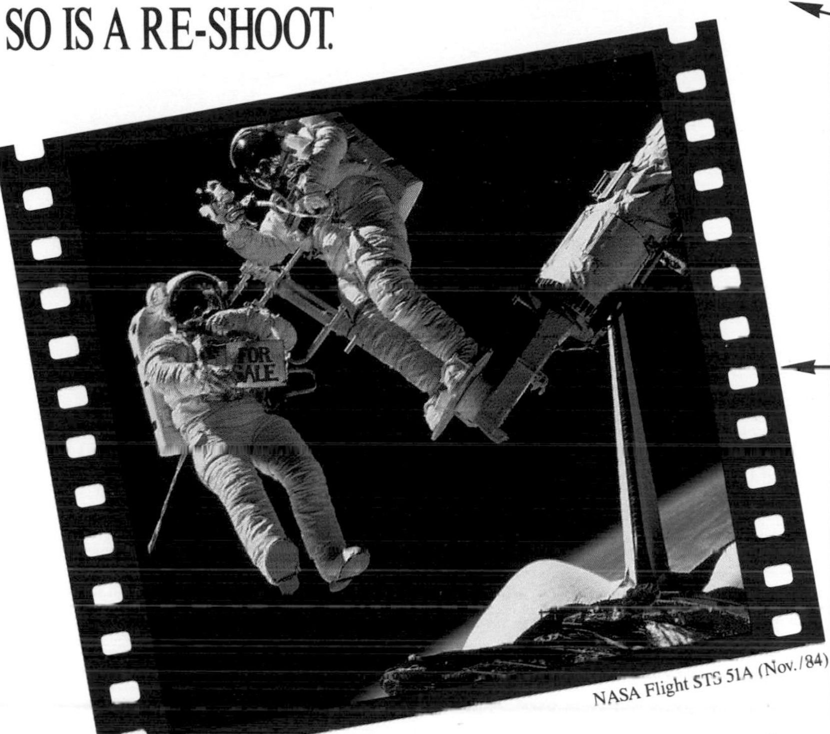

NASA Flight STS 51A (Nov./84)

Inside or outside the studio – inside or outside the atmosphere, or anytime when you must capture that memorable moment – the last thing you want on a shoot is a camera that lets you down.
Every Hasselblad camera starts with a rugged aluminum shell and ends with a Carl Zeiss lens.
Everything in between receives thousands of checks.
The time we spend making a Hasselblad naturally affects the money you spend buying one.
In exchange, you get a camera that takes beautiful pictures, time and time again.
No doubt that's why Hasselblads are the only cameras to have been on every one of NASA's manned space flights since 1962.
Of course, the Hasselblads used by NASA have been specially adapted and cost a bit more.
But when it costs billions of dollars to get to the location, you're hardly going to skimp on the camera.

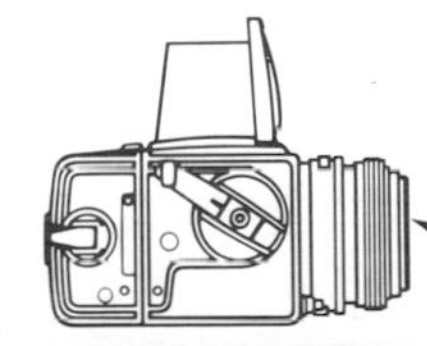

HASSELBLAD

When you shoot for perfection

For more information visit a Hasselblad dealer or contact
Lisle•Kelco Limited, 6799 Steeles Avenue West, Rexdale, Ontario M9V 4R9

THE HEADLINE
Usually

- promises a benefit or makes a claim
- mentions the brand name
- uses short, simple words
- arouses interest

THE VISUALS

- present appealing images to attract the eye
- work with the text to get across the ad's message

THE BODY COPY
Usually

- explains or backs up claims made in the headline
- points out the major benefits of the product and/or delivers the ad's "story" or message
- encourages the reader to contact the retailer or manufacturer to find out more about the product

THE BRAND NAME, LOGO, AND SLOGAN

- help consumers identify the product in stores

Viyella robe by State o' Maine; breakfast-set by Wedgwood.

See The Conquering Hero Comes—in a Viyella® Robe!

Sound the trumpets, beat the drums, see the conquering hero comes—dressed to the nines in a Viyella robe, and armed with Sunday breakfast for his deserving bride. The superb thing about a Viyella bathrobe is that you can *wash* it. If it shrinks, we replace. Lamby-soft Viyella (rhymes with hi-fella) wears for *years*. A customer who bought a Viyella shirt eleven years ago tells us that he has had it washed and cleaned more than sixty times. "The colors are just as bright and distinct as when it was new . . . the only casualty throughout the years has been the loss of two buttons." Viyella robes (like the one our hero is wearing) come in authentic tartans, tattersalls, checks, stripes and plain colors. They weigh only 21 ounces and can be packed in your brief case next time you travel. $28.50 at fine stores everywhere. For the name of your nearest retailer write William Hollins & Company, Inc., 347 Madison Avenue, New York 17, New York. MU 4-7330.

I just hired
a new
assistant.
I just met him.
Will he
work overtime?
Just two of the nice little ladylike dresses from Leslie Fay.
White or black two-piece dress, about $90. Safari print dress, in shades of black, taupe and white, or navy, maroon and white, about $80. Each, sizes 6 to 16.
At Lord & Taylor, Macy's, New York; A&S, Brooklyn; Jordan Marsh, Boston; Marshall Field's, Chicago; Burdine's, Miami; Maas Bros., Florida;
Bamberger's, New Jersey; Woodward & Lothrop, Washington, D.C.; Rich's, Atlanta; G. Fox, Hartford.
For other stores nearest you, dial toll-free 1-800-LF DRESS. Leslie Fay, 1400 Broadway, New York, New York 10018.

I return to days gone by as if I'd never left.
Technics
Moments like these are why we make hi-fi the way we do. Designed and engineered for the love of music. There is no better reason to choose Technics.

YAMAHA

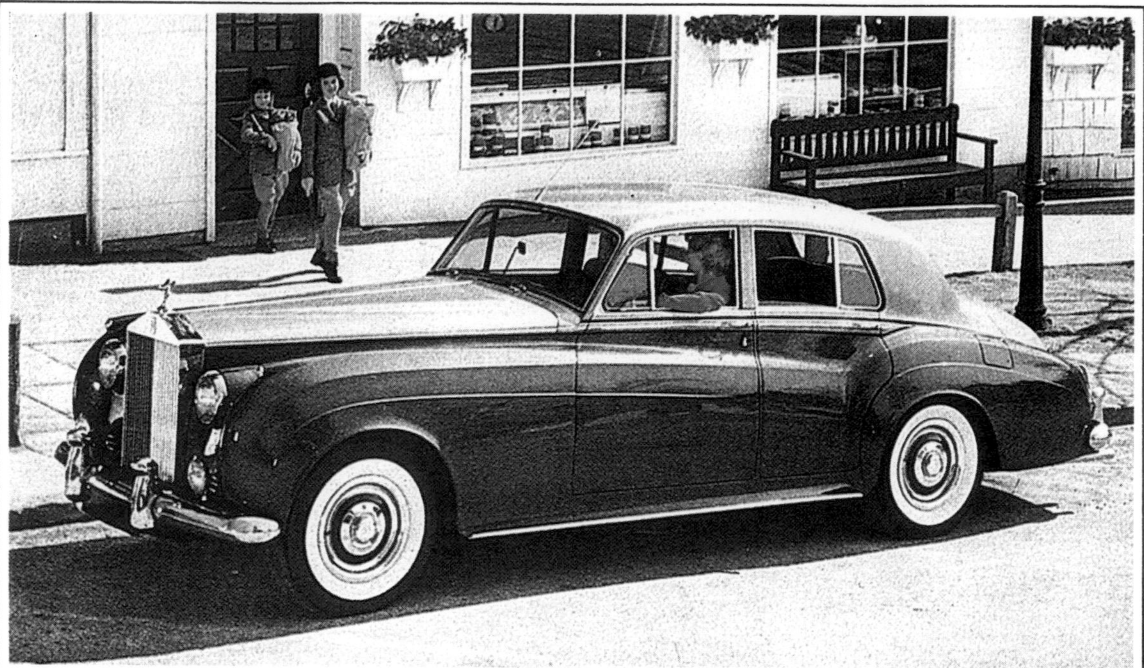

The Rolls-Royce Silver Cloud—$13,995

"At 60 miles an hour the loudest noise in this new Rolls-Royce comes from the electric clock"

What makes Rolls-Royce the best car in the world? "There is really no magic about it—it is merely patient attention to detail," says an eminent Rolls-Royce engineer.

1. "At 60 miles an hour the loudest noise comes from the electric clock," reports the Technical Editor of THE MOTOR. Three mufflers tune out sound frequencies—acoustically.

2. Every Rolls-Royce engine is run for seven hours at full throttle before installation, and each car is test-driven for hundreds of miles over varying road surfaces.

3. The Rolls-Royce is designed as an *owner-driven* car. It is eighteen inches shorter than the largest domestic cars.

4. The car has power steering, power brakes and automatic gear-shift. It is very easy to drive and to park. No chauffeur required.

5. The finished car spends a week in the final test-shop, being fine-tuned. Here it is subjected to 98 separate ordeals. For example, the engineers use a *stethoscope* to listen for axle-whine.

6. The Rolls-Royce is guaranteed for *three years*. With a new network of dealers and parts-depots from Coast to Coast, service is no problem.

7. The Rolls-Royce radiator has never changed, except that when Sir Henry Royce died in 1933 the monogram RR was changed from red to black.

8. The coachwork is given five coats of primer paint, and hand rubbed between each coat, before *nine* coats of finishing paint go on.

9. By moving a switch on the steering column, you can adjust the shock-absorbers to suit road conditions.

10. A picnic table, veneered in French walnut, slides out from under the dash. Two more swing out behind the front seats.

11. You can get such optional extras as an Espresso coffee-making machine, a dictating machine, a bed, hot and cold water for washing, an electric razor or a telephone.

12. There are three separate systems of power brakes, two hydraulic and one mechanical. Damage to one will not affect the others. The Rolls-Royce is a very *safe* car—and also a very *lively* car. It cruises serenely at eighty-five. Top speed is in excess of 100 m.p.h.

13. The Bentley is made by Rolls-Royce. Except for the radiators, they are identical motor cars, manufactured by the same engineers in the same works. People who feel diffident about driving a Rolls-Royce can buy a Bentley.

PRICE. The Rolls-Royce illustrated in this advertisement—f.o.b. principal ports of entry—costs **$13,995.**

If you would like the rewarding experience of driving a Rolls-Royce or Bentley, write or telephone to one of the dealers listed on opposite page. Rolls-Royce Inc., 10 Rockefeller Plaza, New York 20, N. Y. CIrcle 5-1144.

The sound this magazine makes when you turn a page is louder than the Accord LXi moving at 55 miles per hour.
HONDA

EXPLORING IDEAS

1. One of Ogilvy's "rules" is that factual advertising always sells better than empty advertising. Examine the ads in your file. How many of these illustrate Ogilvy's rule? Generally speaking, what sells best in advertising, in your view?
2. Discuss the following in small groups. Appoint one member to report back to the class.
   (a) Should advertisers give the facts and only the facts in order to educate and inform consumers? Or is some emotional appeal necessary for an ad to be effective?
   (b) In the 1960s a variety of people were asked if advertisers should give consumers "only the facts."

Following were the results:

	Yes
Religious leaders	76%
Editors of "highbrow" publications	74%
High-school administrators	74%
Economists	73%
Sociologists	62%
Government officials	45%
Deans of colleges	33%
Business leaders	23%

— statistics reported by David Ogilvy in *Confessions of an Advertising Man*

- How might you account for the differences in the responses?
- Do you think the results would be different if a similar survey were taken today? Why or why not?

INVESTIGATING THE MEDIA

1. Study the ad on page 156 for Viyella robes, which was created by Ogilvy's agency.
   (a) What facts about the product are included in this ad?
   (b) Ogilvy believed that ads also had to have "a strong story appeal that would make readers stop and take notice." What details in this ad create a story appeal? What image or look is created?
   (c) What products today use similar devices in their ads? What image or look, do you think, are advertisers hoping to create?
2. Choose an ad from your file or from those printed in this book. Study the ad for two minutes. Now write down five questions you would like to ask the design team regarding the decisions they made in designing the advertisement.
3. Compare the ad for Rolls-Royce, one of Ogilvy's most successful, with the more-recent Honda ad.
   (a) In a chart, list categories for comparison and comment on how the two ads are similar, how they are different.
   (b) Discuss which of the two ads, in your view, is the more memorable and why.
4. *"Always design your layout for the publication in which it will appear."*
   Form small groups for the task of reviewing ads in different types of publications, for example:
   - newsmagazines (*Maclean's*, TIME, *Newsweek*)
   - fashion magazines (*Vogue, Taxi, GQ*)
   - specialty magazines (*Sports Illustrated, Car & Driver, Photo Life*, etc.)
   - entertainment magazines (*People, Us*)
   - music magazines (*Rolling Stone, Spin*)

   (a) Make a list of the general features or characteristics of the ads in the magazine.
   (b) Report to the class on how the content and design of the ads suit the image of the magazine and its target audience.
5. Examine the ads on pages 157-159 and several from your file. Select two or three you like best and test them against David Ogilvy's guidelines.
   (a) Do they follow the guidelines? If not, in what ways do they differ?
   (b) Why, in your opinion, are the ads effective? Based on your observations, develop your own guidelines for effective print advertisement.

YOUR TURN

1. You are working at an advertising agency that follows Ogilvy's guidelines. Your job is to develop an ad campaign that adheres to these guidelines.
   (a) Create an Ogilvy-influenced ad selling a new product that would appeal to teenagers.
   (b) Present your ad to a small group or the whole class, who will act as your "clients." Explain why the ad will be effective. Be prepared to respond to your clients' questions and comments.
2. Assume that you believe Ogilvy's guidelines need to be adapted to suit the times. What changes in advertising strategies would you make? For example, how should Viyella robes be sold today to
   (a) yuppies?
   (b) women?
   (c) teenagers?

   Design your own ad series to reflect this modern look and approach. Seek audience feedback in evaluating how successfully your ads appeal to today's consumer.

Media Facts & Techniques

Claims and Appeals — The Language of Advertising

Creators of advertising campaigns use two basic strategies in trying to motivate you, the consumer, to buy a product. The first involves making CLAIMS for a product. Claims provide information. They direct your attention to the product itself by describing how it is made, by explaining its features and benefits, by reporting test results from experiments with the product, and so on. The second strategy may be called APPEALS. The emotional side of your personality is the target for appeals. Appeals stir your desires, dreams, beliefs, and fears. They work through *association*, which simply means that people link certain products with certain desires or needs. For example, a car provides transportation — but it may also be associated with social status. The associations formed are seldom logical ones — which is precisely why appeals work!

Following are some commonly used claims and appeals.

CLAIMS

Product Superiority

Advertisers may suggest that their product is better than the one you're using by claiming, for example, that theirs has a unique ingredient not found in similar products. If consumers believe that one brand is truly different from all the others, they may be tempted to try it. Thus, words such as "new" or "improved" are often used.

Weasel Words

As a result of recent consumer-advocacy concerns and court actions regarding false advertising, many advertisers are very careful *not* to make bold claims they may find difficult to substantiate. Instead, their ads may contain *"weasel words"*: vague words or statements that avoid potentially unverifiable claims. For example:

- "*May* contain . . . ." — Does it or doesn't it? The product may or may not actually contain certain ingredients.
- "*Helps fight* wrinkles. . . ." — The advertiser doesn't promise the product will prevent or correct wrinkles, only "*help* fight" them.

Watch out for weasel words. Their presence implies advertisers are unable or unwilling to state that their products are superior.

Test Results

Today's consumers are often skeptical of advertisers' claims. They demand facts that prove a product works before they'll invest. For this reason, you'll often read statements such as: *"Independent tests show that aluminum shingles are 70% more effective in reducing home heating bills. . . ."* (The word "independent" is key. It reassures consumers that the "tests" were unbiased.)

Product Benefit

Most people lead busy, complex lives. If consumers believe a product can ease the burden — even a little — they may be persuaded to try it. Ads will state that a product helps save money, or time, or both. Other benefits frequently promised in ads are better health, prompt relief, safer living, and so on.

Product Reliability

You are likely to buy a product you have confidence in. Advertisers recognize this and do their best to win your trust. A slogan such as: *"Serving customers for three generations. . ."* is often used. A long track record implies a quality product.

Product endorsements are often used to develop confidence in a product. There are several types of endorsements. The *candid interview* uses "just plain folks" to tell how a product has made their lives better. The *celebrity testimonial* can be successful because consumers tend to accept advice from those they like and admire. The *expert testimonial* is a variation which recognizes that the average person respects professional people, so ads often use physicians, dentists, engineers, scientists — or actors posing as these people — to sell their products. Finally, there is the *employee testimonial*. Friendly, proud workers who enjoy their work promote a sense of confidence in both the product and the company.

A *product endorsement* using celebrities: authors

Giorgio
BEVERLY HILLS
EXTRAORDINARY
PERFUME
Giorgio
BEVERLY HILLS
LIVE THE LIFE.
GIORGIO BEVERLY HILLS.
Giorgio, Rodeo Drive, Beverly Hills; 47 East 57th Street, New York.
Or call our Fragrance Specialists at 1-800-GIORGIO anytime.

This appeal combines the *successful* and *person of distinction* images.

APPEALS

You Deserve It!

"You're a good person . . . you've worked hard today. . . . you owe it to yourself to relax, to pamper yourself, to treat yourself to a little luxury. . . ."

Many advertisers appeal to our feelings that we have a right to a reward at times.

Love

The desire to be loved, wanted, and needed is a powerful motivation for humans. Many advertisers play on this by suggesting — directly or indirectly — that by using their product you'll be more attractive to the opposite sex. A visual variation of this strategy is the *gaze* or *the look*. This can be seen in ads featuring a close-up of a model looking out from the page or the screen at you. The "look" may be seductive, innocent, mysterious, or mischievous — but it is designed to attract your attention.

Image

How do you see yourself? How do you want others to see you? What would you like to be like? Answers to these questions are related to your self image. Advertisers project a variety of images in an effort to reach different consumer groups:

- *youthful*: Many products imply they will make you look and feel younger — or keep you feeling young.
- *successful*: Some ads suggest that using certain products will help you on that long, hard climb to the top. And even if you don't quite make it, there's a whole range of products to help you look and feel as if you have.
- *one of the crowd*: There's security and comfort in numbers. The suggestion that thousands of others are already using the product acts as an incentive for *you* to try it. "Crowd scenes" as part of the visual element of an ad strengthen this appeal.

We still think there's a lot to be said for small talk.

You get more out of every long distance call on AT&T.

Whether you're just checking in with the folks back home, or checking up on a business deal, AT&T helps you make the most of every long distance call.

The unmatched capacity of the AT&T Worldwide Intelligent Network helps put your calls through twice as fast as any other company. And on the first try.

What's more, AT&T has lowered its long distance prices overall by more than 35% since 1984 (based on direct-dial, state-to-state calls).

So if you value every call, let AT&T's network and lower prices come through for you.

We're reaching further to bring your world closer.

AT&T
The right choice.

An appeal to the sense of *family* and *belonging*

• *a person of distinction*: On the other hand, there are times when people like to feel *different* — and perhaps just a little superior. Some ads compliment you on your unique good taste, your desire to stand apart from the crowd and be exclusive.

Lifestyle Advertising

A variation on the image-based theme is "*lifestyle advertising*." In this technique advertisers strive to identify their product or service with a certain lifestyle, one consumers generally regard as successful, healthy, or otherwise desirable. The validity of this approach has been questioned when the product being identified with an enviable lifestyle may, in fact, be harmful to consumers' health and well-being. Consumer groups and government agencies have attacked lifestyle ads that promote such items as alcoholic beverages and tobacco products.

Security

Advertisers may play on your fears as a method of persuading you to buy. The strategy behind this appeal is simple: when your fears are forced out into the open, you'll be eager to buy or do something to ease your stress and anxiety.

The Family

Any product that is presented as strengthening the family unit is often seen as "good." This appeal is often aimed at parents.

Patriotism

Your country is, in a sense, an extension of family, and some advertisements will appeal to this aspect of *belonging*. Ads that urge you to *"Buy Canadian to keep Canadians working. . . ."* appeal to your sense of responsibility to your fellow citizens as well as your sense of patriotic duty.

EXPLORING IDEAS

1. *"Lifestyle advertising is generally defined as the portrayal of activities rather than products."*

— Barbara Land
Media Magazine
January 1986

"In this technique advertisers strive to identify their product or service with a certain lifestyle, one consumers generally regard as successful, healthy, or otherwise desirable. The validity of this approach has been questioned when the product being identified with an enviable lifestyle may, in fact, be harmful to consumers' health and well-being."

Do you agree or disagree with the argument that alcoholic beverages should be treated like any other product? That is, should lifestyle advertising be banned for one product but be allowed for others?

2. In what ways might the content of television programs and films — outside of the commercials — also be considered "lifestyle advertising"? Consider several specific television programs. What type of lifestyle and products do these programs promote?

3. Discuss the following in small groups. Select one person to record your group's ideas and present them to the class.

(a) Spokespeople for the industry claim that their ads don't encourage people to start drinking, but are only effective in persuading customers to switch brands. What is your response to this claim?

(b) Is advertising becoming a scapegoat for other problems in society that lead, for example, to alcohol abuse?

INVESTIGATING THE MEDIA

1. Form small groups to examine and discuss ads you have collected in your files, or use the ads that appear on pages 155-165. Fill in a chart like the one below:

Product	Claims	Appeals

Discuss:

(a) Who is the likely target group for each ad? Judging by the claims and appeals used in the ad, what are some of the characteristics of that group?

(b) If claims are used, what exactly is claimed? Watch especially for "weasel words."

If "miraculous" ingredients or "scientific" terms are used, what do you think the terms mean and what exactly do the ingredients do for the consumer? If possible, investigate what these ingredients actually are and what, if anything, they really do. You may wish to invite a science teacher or other expert to discuss the validity of claims for various ingredients.

(c) If emotional appeals are used, how reasonable are they? Is it likely the product will help satisfy the emotional need that is appealed to?

(d) In your opinion, which is the most effective ad? Does it rely mainly on claims, appeals, or a combination?

2. *"...recent U.S. surveys have produced doubts about the potency of the 'celebrity sell' because many famous faces soon wear out their welcome. A new study....revealed that only five of the ten Hollywood celebrities deemed 'most convincing' in a 1982 survey had retained their popularity with viewers three years later."*

— Cy Jameson, *Maclean's*, March 11, 1985

(a) List ten celebrities used to pitch products today. What products do they promote? What images are projected in their commercials?

(b) Discuss the following: To what extent are advertisers using the associations viewers form with a TV character to help sell their products?

3. Form teams to survey TV commercials and print ads.

(a) Approximately what percentage of advertisements have a lifestyle emphasis as opposed to a product emphasis?

(b) What products tend to be advertised by identifying the product with a certain lifestyle?

(c) What associations do the ads suggest between the product and the lifestyle?

(d) Do you believe that lifestyle advertising is any more- or less-persuasive than product advertising? Has your point of view regarding lifestyle advertising changed as a result of your investigation?

4. The *Clio* awards are TV advertising's equivalent of the Oscars. Below is a list of 1986 winners:

(a) Best non-alcoholic beverage: *Pepsi-Cola* featuring Michael J. Fox taking a cooling sip from a photocopy reproduction of a Pepsi can.

(b) Best overall food, Best animation, Best new adaptation of music: *The California Raisin Advisory Board* won in all three categories for their commercials featuring clay-animated raisins singing "I Heard It Through the Grapevine."

(c) Best apparel: *Nike* basketball shoes using NBA superstar Michael Jordan to endorse the product.

(d) Best automotive: *Subaru* for a commercial showing the U.S. ski team beating all competitors to the next race driving their Subaru.

(e) Best retail food: *Pizza Hut* for a commercial emphasizing their chain's salad bar for dieters and luscious pizza for those who don't have to count calories.

Other award categories include

- Best male performance
- Best female performance
- Best home-product commercial
- Best editing
- Best cinematography
- Best public-service commercial
- Best home-furnishings commercial

Imagine you are a judge on the panel deciding this year's Clio awards. Submit a list of your nominations for two or more categories. Include a *brief* description of each commercial and the reason you think it deserves to be this year's winner. Compare your choices with those of your classmates.

YOUR TURN

1. Collect promises and claims in ads on radio, TV, and in print media. Use your list to create a poem entitled "It's a Miracle!"
or
Write a short personal essay in which you state your ideas and opinions on this question: *Are endorsements convincing?* Use concrete examples to support and explain your point of view.
or
Write a letter-to-the-editor in which you express your personal views on lifestyle advertising. Assume you are writing as one of the following:
(a) a manufacturer
(b) a consumer
(c) an advertising executive

2. Working on your own or with a partner, design an ad for an imaginary or existing product to be sold to a group of students similar to yourselves. Work through the following steps:
(a) Develop a profile (description) of people in your target group. What are their lifestyles? needs? interests?
(b) Brainstorm a list of the types of claims and appeals that would likely work for this group. What could this product do for them?
(c) Brainstorm possibilities for the visual content of the ad.
(d) Decide on the magazine in which the ad will be featured.
(e) Prepare a print ad for your product and present the finished ad to a small group of your classmates. Have them comment on the effectiveness of your claims and appeals.
or
Working in groups, select a product commonly promoted through lifestyle advertising. Design an advertisement for a magazine, television, or radio campaign intended to counteract whatever potentially harmful influence lifestyle advertising might have.
or
Select a product that seems to have *no* potential for mass-marketing (for example, shoelaces, nail files, fish food, rubber bands). Design a lifestyle advertising campaign designed to turn the product into one of life's most-desirable objects.

3. Working with a partner, script an "on-the-street" interview about a product of your choice. If possible, tape the interview for presentation to the class — or, present it "live."

4. *"Ad writers tell us more about our culture than historians do."*

— Morton M. Hunt, *Horizon*, November 1959

Working in a small group, create a visual presentation that uses advertisements as the basis for an examination of our culture. Script and tape a commentary to accompany the visuals.

or

In the 1920s the first cigarette ads aimed at women appeared and *"cigarettes came to be a personal and social marker for 'the new woman,' a sign of divorce from the past and inclusion in the group of the new, young, and liberated."* (Michael Schudson, *Advertising, The Uneasy Persuasion*, 1985)

What products are used to symbolize the "modern" man or woman today? Create a collage *or* compose a poem or short essay on the topic "If You Want to Be Modern."

In this tongue-in-cheek article Jennifer Fisher suggests that in times of personal crisis "we tend to go to all the wrong people for help." Instead, we should be following the advice of TV's "experts" — the commercials.

Crisis time? Don't touch that dial!

Ever have a life crisis and don't know where to turn? Trouble is, we tend to go to all the wrong people for help: psychiatrists, clergymen, concerned health-care professionals; these people all want to know how you really feel, to shower you with concerned encouragement, and help you live your life to the fullest. Who has time for that? In the fast-moving '80s, the average overachiever has, say, about 30 seconds to deal with emotional dilemmas. Luckily, there is a solution — something, in fact, you can do while watching TV. Think of it as "How to Enrich your Life Through Commercials," or "30 Seconds to Happiness."

Haven't commercials been telling us how to live for decades? Here, gleaned from years of ad advice, are just a few trouble-saving tips to get you started.

How to find a job: Contrary to what politicians tell us about solving unemployment (elect them), finding a job is easy, according to commercials. Just use the right deodorant soap in the morning. Sure, you may wake up a somnambulant slob, but after a few minutes in the shower, you'll emerge humming — and imminently employable.

Keeping your job: Evidently, this has a lot to do with finding the right courier service. You may come in to work late, punch out your supervisor, and embezzle millions, but if you can get a parcel to Whitehorse by 9 the next morning, your boss will never cause it to rain in your office.

How to cure persistent headaches: Next time you're in a shopping mall, put your hand to your head and look as if you've just suffered through an episode of *Pet Peeves*.

Soon, some headache researchers will sit you at a desk in front of a TV camera and discuss the throbbing. As soon as you discover how many milligrams of relief can be yours, you'll start to feel better.

How to find the perfect man: First, wash your hair in a shampoo that contains enough organic ingredients to feed a family of five. Next, give in to that irresistible urge to lope through a trendy restaurant and swing your head from side to side as if you're trying to dislodge a small insect from your nose (this move is particularly effective in slow motion). Soon, at least 10 Ted Danson lookalikes will flock to your side, handing you flowers and glasses of expensive wine. Throw your head back, laugh uproariously at nothing at all, and toss the wine playfully into one of the men's faces. He'll be yours for life.

How to find the perfect woman: Always carry the correct change for flowers. You never know when a woman who's found the right shampoo may pass by, and if you're stuck fumbling with your chequebook at the florist, she may disappear up an escalator.

How to have a perfect honeymoon: Marital bliss inevitably starts with knowing exactly the right way to let your spouse know he or she has morning breath. Usually a stern but perky approach, along with a strategically raised palm works. And using the word "honey" seems to make even "Stand back, buffalo breath" an OK thing to say.

How to live with young children: Buy quality fabric softener. As we all know, kids are particularly sensitive to whether or not their tiny togs smell April fresh. And having softer than soft clothing distracts them from melting crayons on the rug or setting the au pair on fire. Your child will say, "This sweater is as soft as my bunny," then fall into a delicate sleep in a meadow full of white, fuzzy kittens.

How to live with adolescents: Never buy mints — they always lead to the inevitable quarrel of whether or not it's a breath mint or a candy mint, one of the most baffling issues of our time.

How to explain death to your kids: Though ads haven't spoken at length about that big commercial break in the sky, when they do, they are definitive. Take the famous dog food ad allegory: One day your child asks how long his dog will live. You just say, "Oh, Rusty [or Grandma, Grandpa, etc.] will be with us for a long, long time." Evidently this works.

How to get rid of unsightly stains: There's only one solution: If you're a woman, never do the wash. After thousands of commercials, it's clear that women still can't get the hang of making wash whiter than white, or deal with the static-cling crisis. Only men should do the laundry. After all, wasn't it a man who solved ring around the collar? So it's all yours, fellas. Good luck shouting that dirt out. And if you have any questions, ask that guy in the washing machine — he seems to know everything.

— Jennifer Fisher
TV Guide
August 15, 1987

YOUR TURN

1. **(a)** Working with a partner, brainstorm a list of "life's little problems" that concern almost all of us.
   (b) Identify products advertised on TV that offer us a solution to these problems. Then write brief notes on the content and message of the commercials.
   (c) Compose your own piece entitled "Do You Have a Problem?"
   or
   Use your notes to compose and perform a satiric skit about television commercials that suggest "How to Enrich Your Life."

In Amusing Ourselves to Death, *Neil Postman called the television commercial "the most peculiar and pervasive form of communication to issue forth from the electric plug. An American who has reached the age of forty will have seen well over one million commercials in his or her lifetime."*

In the following article Joyce Nelson discusses the hows and whys of television advertising techniques that have revolutionized the advertising industry.

As the brain tunes out, the TV admen tune in

After a long day at the office, the unsuspecting viewer flicks on the television set for a little enjoyment and relaxation in the comfort of his living room.

What he doesn't know is that half of his brain will relax *a lot*. Staring at the screen, the viewer drifts into the twilight world of the Alpha state, the term that describes the unfocused realm of daydreaming. It is a state in which the mind's analytical functions slow to a crawl and emotional response works overtime. The viewer is now putty for the television adman, who is only too willing to mold the subject's thoughts.

Herbert Krugman, who is now manager of public-opinion research at General Electric Headquarters in Connecticut, is credited with discovering what goes on in the mind of a person placed in front of a TV set. In 1969, Mr. Krugman taped a single electrode to the back of his subject's head and turned on the television. What the brain monitoring showed was that the left hemisphere, which processes information logically and analytically, tuned out. The brain's right hemisphere, which processes information emotionally and holistically, stayed alert and fully functioning. It was a discovery which revolutionized television advertising.

Verifying through their subsequent research with electroencephalographs that television is the special province of the right brain, advertisers have significantly changed their concept of what makes an effective (and affective) TV ad.

Today's products are promoted on TV mainly by striking an emotional cord within the viewer rather than through specific claims. Most recently, politicians have been added to this type of commercial packaging.

An ad used to be considered effective if it made claims about a product which were easy to remember. Ads were designed to spell out the logical advantages of buying a product. During the 1970s, advertisers began to realize that this approach appealed largely to the left hemisphere of the brain and began to change tactics.

Consequently, the singing commercial, the use of jingles, and the carefully selected slogan emerged, based on the fact that melody and lyrics are easily retained for years, much longer than rhetorical claims. One adman in the forefront of the change was Tony Schwartz, who has masterminded hundreds of ad campaigns, not only for commercial products but also for several hundred political candidates, including two presidents.

In 1973, he announced his "resonance theory" of communication. According to this theory, "certain stimuli, in the proper context, can recall experiences that we could never remember at will," Mr.

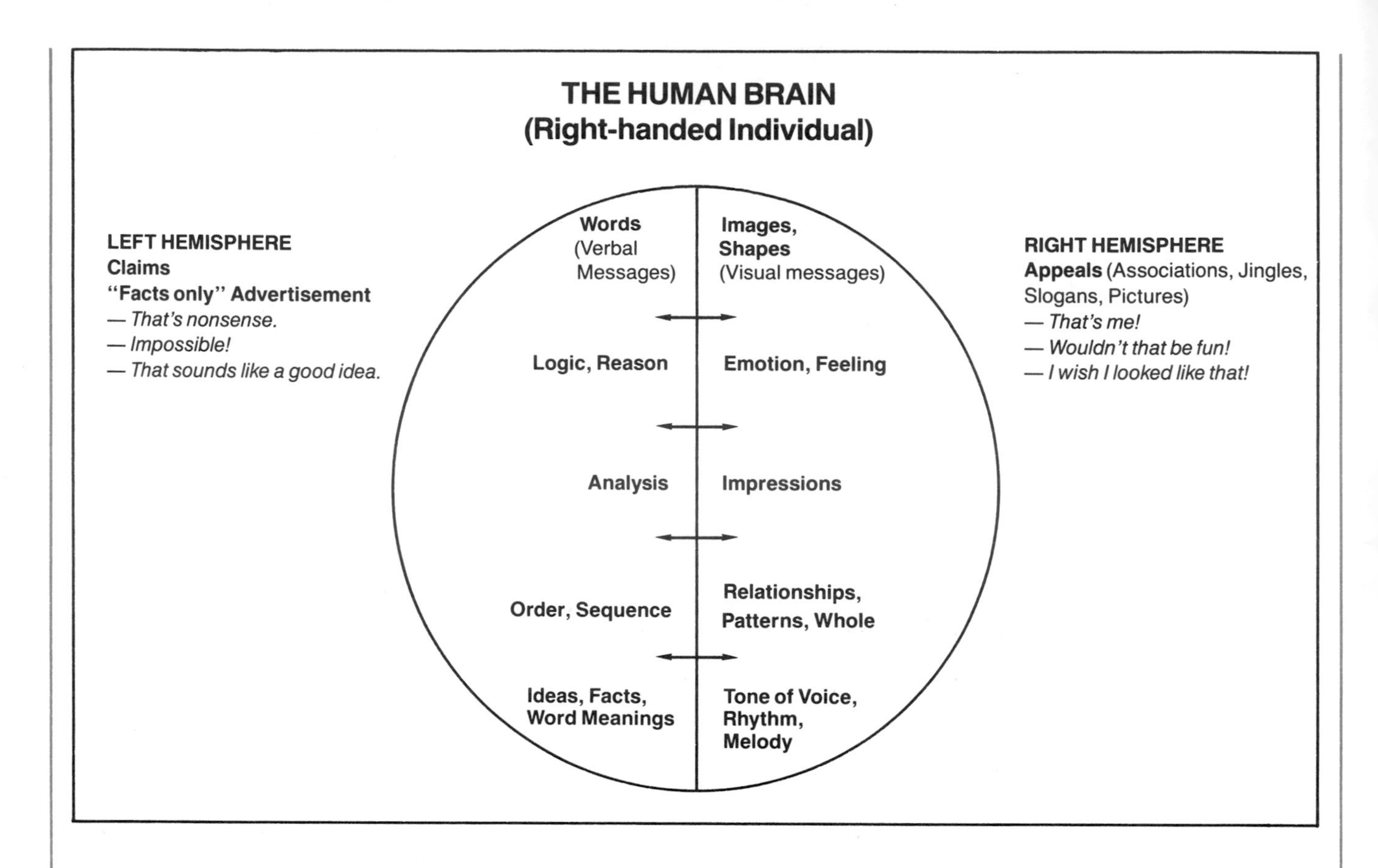

Schwartz wrote in a magazine article. "I do not care what number of people remember or get the message. I am concerned with how people are affected by the stimuli."

Admen work for products and politicians alike. Jerry Goodis has sold us Speedy Muffler, Wonder Bra, and the Liberal Party; Gerald Rafshoon sold the Americans Sears Roebuck and Jimmy Carter; Peter Dailey Sr. took a leave from his Los Angeles ad agency to be media director of Ronald Reagan's campaign. It is common sense that what they know about selling in one field will be applied to another.

Back in the sixties, ad agencies used techniques such as measuring heart rate, pupil dilation, and galvanic skin response to test audience response to specific ads. Says U.S. political consultant David Haskell Sawyer: "Frankly, 1968 was still the dark ages of political communication. It was a beginning, but techniques weren't very advanced."

Then Mr. Krugman and his electrode appeared. The results of his initial tests surprised him and everybody else who heard about them. By 1971, NW Ayers-ABH International, one of the largest ad agencies in the world, was using EEGs in order to evaluate its TV commercials for several clients, including AT&T. The agency's subsequent ads for Bell Telephone (Reach Out and Touch Someone...) are now considered classics of applied brain research. During the mid-1970s, other agencies began following suit. In 1977, a Toronto agency unveiled its own brain research to the Association of Canadian Advertisers.

In order to grasp the TV-brain interaction that has so fascinated advertisers and political media advisers, it is necessary to know some basic facts about two specific areas: the hemispheric division of the brain and the process of television transmission.

The human brain is divided into the left and right hemispheres, which are connected by nerve pathways. In right-handed people, the left hemisphere (which controls the right side of the body) tends to deal with sequential logic or rational thinking. The mode of approach of the right hemisphere (which controls the left side of the body) is in terms of recognizing spatial relationships and grasping whole contexts. It excels at tasks like the recognition of faces and places, and the completion of patterns.

While the left hemisphere seems to have a coldly analytical style of processing information, the right hemisphere is more emotionally involved and tends to perceive the world in terms of past emotional experiences. (In left-handed people the functions of the hemispheres and the sides of the body which they control are reversed.)

In the healthy adult, logic and emotion combine forces to process information. Through the nerve pathways, the right and left hemispheres pool their relative strengths. According to Mr. Krugman and later researchers, this bond is broken in response to television transmission. When Mr. Krugman's subject switched to leafing through the pages of a magazine, the left hemisphere functions speeded up again.

The Alpha state emerges largely in the right hemisphere, since it is from this hemisphere that our dreams take shape. Researcher Thomas Budzynski says of Alpha state. "The dominant (left) hemisphere stops functioning efficiently, while the other (right) side keeps plugging along. Without the normal censorship of the dominant hemisphere, the other is free to accept and act upon suggestions or commands made under these conditions. Less critical by design, the non-dominant (right) side is more likely to attempt to implement the command even though it may be nonsensical."

As viewers of television, it is certainly possible to watch in analytical-critical frame of mind: noticing the use of specific camera angles, camera distances, sound-image relationships, composition and framing, and relating such techniques to the creation of over-all meaning. But the typical viewing situation is one which discourages such attentiveness. Most of us watch TV when we are already tired from a day's work. We are not intent on focused analysis.

As brain reaction to the TV came to be known, ad agencies began testing to see just what stimuli would most appeal to the right hemisphere. Agencies found that the right hemisphere is engaged by tone of voice, rhythm and melody, rhyme and harmony, pictorial emotional triggers. It is primarily involved in the recall of information that has not been deliberately memorized. And the right hemisphere has its own language skills: it responds to simple commands and emotion-laden words.

Probably the best-designed ads based on the TV-brain interaction are the Bell Telephone ads. The first series (Reach Out and Touch Someone...) truly struck a responsive chord and set long-distance lines humming. Later ads simply combined the lyrics and melody of a familiar, nostalgic and sentimental song with images of togetherness, loved ones, caring. Such ads, which make no mention of a product being sold, clearly bypass any logical appeals and simply use audio and visual triggers. As one Toronto adman puts it, "In a sense, what we're doing is wrapping up your emotions and selling them back to you."

Jerry Goodis says, "Advertising doesn't always mirror how people are acting, but how they're dreaming." "The key," Pepsi adman Norman Sylvester says, "is that the emotions are already there, the ads just trigger them."

— Joyce Nelson
The Globe and Mail
April 19, 1983

EXPLORING IDEAS

1. *"...the typical viewing situation is one which discourages attentiveness."* Describe *your* typical viewing situation. What is there about the environment in which you watch television — particularly the commercials — that discourages close attention?
2. As a class, make a list of TV ads you have found memorable. For each ad list the images or techniques that made it so effective. Which would you classify as "logical" appeals, and which emotional?
3. In *Amusing Ourselves to Death* Neil Postman commented *"by substituting images for claims, the pictorial commercial made emotional appeal, not tests of truth, the basis of consumer decisions."*

   To what extent do you agree with Mr. Postman's conclusions? Discuss commercials that support or disprove his statement.

INVESTIGATING THE MEDIA

1. *"Carefully selected slogans...are easily retained for years."* How many products or companies can you identify from the following list of slogans? (Answers on page 174.)
   (a) *Any way you look at it, _______ is photography.*
   (b) *Have you driven a _______ lately?*
   (c) *Only in Canada you say?...Pity.*
   (d) *Oh, what a fun bunch of guys!*

(e) *The choice of a new generation.*
(f) *Make it _______ tonight!*

Work in groups to develop a list of slogans that are popular today. See if your classmates can identify the product that goes with each slogan.

2. For the next few evenings, when you watch television, concentrate on the commercials. Keep a record of the commercials you see and bring your viewing notes to class as a reference for class discussion.

Product	Slogan	Melody or Jingles	Visual Content	Emotions Appealed to

(a) To what extent do your observations support or challenge the description of TV commercials in the article?
(b) Is there a difference in the type of commercial shown in different time slots? on different nights?

3. Many print ads now follow the lead of television. Copy is kept to a minimum and the ads rely almost totally on visual content and emotional appeal.
(a) From your file, select at least one example of an ad that appeals primarily to the "right hemisphere."
(b) What feelings, associations, and suggestions are elicited by the ad? What techniques — visual images, language — create this effect?

YOUR TURN

1. Prepare two television commercials for a product that is already on the market, or one that you invent yourselves. One of your commercials should appeal to the viewers' sense of logic and reason, while the other should work on feelings, associations, and suggestions. Prepare a script or storyboard for each of the commercials.

Present your TV commercials to the class. Discuss the different effect of each. Which is more effective?

2. *"Music has become much more popular in the last two years. There's a tremendous amount of contemporary music in commercials."*

— John Leffler,
Gray Advertising

(a) Make a list of contemporary songs that have been your personal favourites. What associations or memories do you connect with these songs? What products could be linked with the song? What "statement" about the product could you make by using the song?

Song Title and Artist	Memories/ Associations	Product	Advertising Statement

(b) Design a radio or television commercial for one of the products on your list. If possible, tape or film your commercial and present it to the class.

Answers for "Investigating" no. 1:

(a) Blacks *(b)* Ford *(c)* Red Rose Tea *(d)* Toyota *(e)* Pepsi *(f)* Mac (McDonald's)

KEEPING THE MESSAGE CURRENT

Styles and tastes in popular culture are constantly changing. While new consumer demands spring up, important issues remain, testing the conscience and accountability of the advertising industry and the clients it represents.

Does advertising tempt us into buying—and eating—products we don't need? Should young children be exposed to TV commercials prepared specifically for these little consumers? Do advertisers have a responsibility to speak out on social issues; and when they do speak out, how effective is their approach? Should advertising techniques be used to sell an image of a corporation — an *idea* rather than a product?

The advertising industry works diligently in self-regulating its standards and practices, but sometimes that self-policing seems insufficient to consumers and government agencies. *When* and *how* should "outside" groups and agencies step in?

"...surveys show that only 3 per cent of new food comes from consumer demand surveys. Advertising creates the need."

What advertisers pitch we rush to gobble up

Around the turn of the century, two American brothers, John and William, operated a health sanatorium for the Seventh-Day Adventists, whose brethren they were. The brothers worried away at the problem of coming up with palatable meat substitutes for the sanatorium's menu, since Seventh-Day Adventists avoided meat at all costs.

Fiddling around with corn cut from the cob, John and William found that if the corn was soaked in water and then baked, it flattened, inflated, and toasted rather nicely. The new breakfast cereal worked well for the two Kellogg brothers. Everybody at the sanatorium liked it.

But soon William, a doctor (physician heal thyself?), got bigger ideas than catering to the brethren. He wanted to add sugar to the new cereal and sell it to the masses. John was adamant: he wanted it kept a health food. So they split up. John kept the sanatorium and continued to run it and William went commercial with Kellogg's Corn Flakes.

Some would say the rest is history. But it isn't. The rest is advertising. Would you eat a cereal called E.T. if left to your own culinary devices? Or Mr. T? Are Corn Pops different from Sugar Pops from Rice Krispies from Puffed Rice from Sugared Wheat?

According to George Armelagos, who teaches anthropology at the University of Massachusetts, "surveys show that only 3 per cent of new food comes from consumer demand surveys. Advertising creates the need.

"How long is the cereal Mr. T going to last? Till the TV series is cancelled. Are you inherently going to buy E.T. cereal? The company has to create the need, and the TV program is a 30-minute commercial for the new cereal. But these products have a short life, so the companies have to constantly develop new products. Take tostadas: they went from zero to $160 million in sales in one year in the United States. How? They spent $10 million to advertise it."

Fibre cereals—"Good for you" is in.

Tostadas promise LIGHT. Like Lite (sic) beer and wine and the host of low-calorie meals on the market, *lite* (sic) products play to the current mass paranoia about being overweight. Thinness is next to godliness. To many people, given the declining popularity of houses of worship compared with fitness parlors, thinness has supplanted godliness. So smart food companies develop products that play lite.

Fibre has also found its spot on centre stage in mass food culture. Helped along by doctors who have promoted fibre to the media (a bran muffin a day keeps the chemotherapist away), *fibre* has become the new password for food that's good for you. Food that's good for you is in style. Ergo, fibre is in.

Unless you make a bran muffin at home using whole wheat flour and no white sugar, it's not vastly different from a chocolate bar.

Its virtue is precisely its lack of same, a midday sugar hit to be enjoyed, guiltlessly, with one's coffee. The same could be said of most of the cereals and breads that are capitalizing on the health food/fibre craze. Read the labels. Then read the labels on products that offer themselves up as healthy.

Take the mass-produced bottled salad dressings that sell their yogurt content as if yogurt were the precursor of the Second Coming. Ask yourself whether all the preservatives that come with the yogurt are really so very healthy. It's like tofu, a previously unadulterated product, which is now appearing on supermarket shelves with a new additive — calcium sulphate — and a new (higher) price. Thus goes the mass marketing of "health."

George Armelagos, who teaches a course called Food and Culture, says his students believe they have "an inordinate number of food choices. They point out the rows of cereal on the shelves, and I say yes, but your choices are essentially wheat, corn, and oats, with or without sugar. The ads say we can have anything we want, they can get us a tomato any time, all winter. But the tomato they get us from California, you can drop from four feet and its skin won't break, it's so thick. We don't have much choice in the tomatoes we eat."

Reading between the lines of both TV and print ads for food makes the message clear: Freedom is good. Freedom comes from choosing whatever food is being sold.

Some companies make it crystal clear: one convenience store chain in the United States prints the word *Freedom* on its disposable drinking cups. The sad thing is that it works. The real ingredients of the package don't seem to count.

Fibre, lite, and *freedom* are this year's buzzwords.

George Armelagos predicts calcium will be the next mini-trend because "osteoporosis is getting sexy now." He says: "Advertisers will soon be talking about getting enough calcium — in their product, of course — to keep your bones from thinning." Are you listening, O aging baby boomers?

— Joanne Kates
The Globe and Mail
March 1, 1985

EXPLORING IDEAS

1. Advertising has been accused of manipulating the consumer by creating "false needs."
   (a) Assess the evidence Ms. Kates provides to support this complaint.
   (b) To what extent do you agree with the writer's opinion? What products, if any, have you recently bought you don't really need? What role did advertising play in your decision to purchase?
2. Why do advertisers link the concept of "freedom" with advertising? How much freedom to choose do consumers get in our society? Do we have too many choices — too many brands, too many products — or little significant choice, in your opinion?
3. According to the writer, "*fibre, lite*, and *freedom*" were the buzzwords of the mid-1980s. What are this year's buzzwords? How might current trends create new products, new packages, and new ads?

Discuss these issues in small groups. Select one member to record your group's ideas and present them to the class.

INVESTIGATING THE MEDIA

1. How does advertising affect *your* purchasing habits. To find out, choose one of the following two research activities.

   Conduct your own personal survey in an effort to link the commercials you see or the ads you read with what you buy. List the commercials or ads you come across in a one-day or one-week period.
   (a) What types of ads seem to attract your attention the most?
   (b) What types seem to by-pass you?
   (c) Describe *one* product you purchased recently. How did you find out about the product? Were you trying something new or switching brands? What was it, exactly, that caused you to buy one particular brand over another?
   (d) Note a product you tried recently as a result of an advertisement. Detail your satisfaction or disappointment with the product.
   (e) What conclusions do you reach about your own buying habits? About the effect of advertisements on you personally, in the long and short term?
   or
   Take an inventory of all the items in one room of your home — your bedroom, for example, or your living room. Which of the items in the room do you believe were purchased as the result of advertising? Which particular brands were purchased as the result of advertising?
2. Bring to class empty containers of different brands of similar products: detergents, cereals, shampoo, soft drinks, chocolate bars, and so on. If possible, also collect ads promoting these products.
   (a) Working in groups, compare the ingredients of different brands of similar types of products. Do different brands generally offer a significant choice? Report back to the class.
   (b) How are similar brands of products promoted? What techniques are used in ads to sell a particular brand to the consumer?

YOUR TURN

1. **(a)** Based on recent trends, create a new or improved product that reflects perceived consumer demands. This might be a reflection of a new lifestyle or a new media hero. Explain your reasons for developing this product.
   (b) Design the advertisement for your new product. You may wish to use the "celebrity-endorsement" technique, or you may decide to cash in on the popularity of a recent movie or a figure from popular culture. Your advertisement may be in the form of a print ad in a popular magazine, the tape for a radio commercial, or the storyboard for a TV ad.
2. Form a group and debate the following issue. *Resolved*: "Advertising doesn't lead society, it follows."
   — John Farrell, Young and Rubicam Advertising Agency
3. Survey shelves in a supermarket. List brands or products that are relatively new. How long do you think these products will last? Write a poem or a satiric article entitled "Shelf Life."
   or
   Make a list of products you were familiar with as a child that are no longer available. What trends were these "extinct" products linked with? Use your list as the basis for an article or poem called "When I Was a Child."

In the mid-1970s "advocacy advertising" started assuming a major role in the media. Using this approach, businesses — and governments — buy advertising not to sell products or services but to advocate, or plead a cause for, a specific point of view. Morris Wolfe sees this "selling of ideas" as a vehicle for propaganda rather than a valid presentation of public concerns and worthy causes. He wants government and the media to ban advocacy advertising. After evaluating the arguments, consider where you stand.

The Case Against Advocacy Advertising

Those who own the media have always had more freedom of speech than those who don't, but in recent years the balance has shifted slightly toward the traditional underdog. The enormous growth of media — more magazines, more TV stations, more everything except daily papers — means that more alternative views are reaching the public. Naturally, a favourite target of the new voices has been big business. It's widely and often argued in the media that excessive profits are being earned by the big oil and insurance companies, and that other companies are polluting the environment.

Now many of the businesses under attack are fighting back. And who's encouraging them to do so? The very media that permitted the anti-business voices to be heard in the first place. The media have promoted something called "advocacy advertising" for this purpose. Businesses are encouraged to buy print space and broadcasting time to answer their critics. It's good for business, the media insist. Certainly it's good for the media business.

Advocacy advertising has been around for at least a decade in the U.S. By now many of us are familiar with Mobil Oil's ads in support of free enterprise. Thirty per cent of *The Wall Street Journal*'s ad lineage now consists of advocacy advertising. In Canada it's been much slower to catch on. (I suspect that's because our deference to authority means we're not so quick to criticize.) But the Insurance Bureau of Canada's "Let's free enterprise" commercials began in the mid-70s, and around the same time Imperial Oil began running ads that said the company was making only six per cent profit and needed more money to help Canada become less dependent on foreign oil.

But advocacy advertising didn't *really* arrive here until 1980. That year the Toronto *Globe and Mail* ran Dale Carnegie-style full-page advertisements offering to tell business leaders "How to win acceptance in a world full of critics." One result of the information explosion, says the *Globe*, "was a corresponding growth in the number of society's self-appointed critics." What's needed, Canada's national newspaper advised in a follow-up brochure, was more "corporate vocality." Businesses should buy space in the *Globe* and tell their side of the story. In case the business world has any doubt whose side the *Globe* is on, its publisher, A. Roy Megarry, asserts, "We are enthusiastic supporters of the free-enterprise system — sometimes more so than some segments of the business community."

If I were a corporate businessman, I wouldn't hesitate to use advocacy advertising. I have no doubt it would be in my interests. (And I could deduct all of what I spent as a business expense.) But I have considerable doubt about whether it's in the public interest that I be allowed to do so. Advocacy advertising, it seems to me, represents a step backwards; it reaffirms the old notion that those who have money are entitled to more freedom of speech than those who don't. The fact is, consumer and other critics usually can't afford to reply in kind. They can only hope that whatever they say in response to advocacy advertising will be sufficiently newsworthy to make it into print or onto the air.

A couple of years ago, one might have argued that the whole sticky question of advocacy advertising should be examined by governments, especially since the media themselves didn't seem too concerned with the problem. At that time governments hadn't yet gone into the business of advocacy advertising themselves. Government advertising consisted of consumer information about services we were entitled to as citizens. It promoted tourism, or encouraged us to wear our seat belts, or suggested we not drink too much. Most of us could agree these were reasonable ways to spend taxpayers' money.

The 1980 referendum in Quebec changed all that. A tidal wave of federal advertising inundated Quebec in the days preceding the referendum. Ads urging Quebec drinkers to say "Non, merci." Ads reminding Quebec tourists that the Rocky Mountains provided "so much to stay for." During one hour of a widely viewed tennis championship on CFTM, a private French-language station in Montreal, federal ads appeared nine times: at 2:04, the Department of Energy, Mines and Resources; at 2:08, Customs; at 2:15, an ad urging people to buy Canadian; at 2:17, the Department of Regional Economic Expansion; at 2:37, Health and Welfare; at 2:41, Energy, Mines and Resources (again); at 2:51, Public Works; at 2:53, Energy, Mines and Resources (yet a third time); at 2:58, a tourism ad. The Quebec government tried to stop the federal campaign, but a superior court judge in Montreal ruled in favour of Ottawa.

Because all good federalists approved of Ottawa's campaign, no one I know of — except, or course, outraged *indépendantistes* — questioned the implications of what the government had done. But for the Trudeau Liberals it was a short step from the Quebec campaign to the slick, subliminal advertisements all of us were subjected to in 1979 (prepared under the supervision of something called the Canadian Unity Information Office, with a total budget of $35 million). Billboards that looked like Canadian flags proclaimed: "Let's Work Together to Build a Better Country. Now." Radio spots on which an announcer intoned, to a soothing background of strings and flutes, "The wind that blows across our land is a free wind. A spirited wind. A wind that carries our hopes and dreams. And makes distances and differences disappear. Let's harness that wind and, working together, make those hopes and dreams come true. For all Canadians. This message is brought to you by the government of Canada." TV commercials, with gorgeous shots of geese in flight, announced: "Freedom is an important part of our heritage as Canadians. The right of each and every one of us is to strive, to rise, to be free, riding the winds of freedom, working together to make our hopes and dreams come true for all Canadians."

The purpose of the federal campaign as outlined in a confidential cabinet memorandum was twofold: "First...to keep the issue of constitutional reform before the public at a time when there was no other means for doing so since Parliament was not sitting. Second...to persuade the provinces that the federal government was not bluffing; that it really did intend to take action this fall — unilaterally if necessary; and that to achieve this goal it was prepared to treat this round of constitutional negotiations more like a street-fight than a diplomatic negotiation." According to the memorandum, "*The fundamental question to be addressed* [by cabinet] *concerns the legitimacy of spending taxpayers' dollars to promote what will be deemed by many to be a politically partisan postion.*" (The emphasis belongs to the memo.) The cabinet treated the question as essentially political rather than moral.

Meanwhile, not to be outdone, some provinces got into the act. The B.C. government distributed a million copies of an eight-page tabloid stating that if the federal government got its way, it would take "real control of any province away from the people who live and work in it, and hand it over to a government that is mainly elected by, and regrettably too often solely represents the wishes of, central Canadians." Thus citizens of British Columbia could choose between the advertising campaigns by two ad agencies for two governments, both of which were using B.C. taxpayers' money. The Quebec government announced it, too, would spend tax money to tell *its* story. But the CBC, which was running the federal government's TV commercials, refused to run those from Quebec because they didn't conform to the corporation's advertising policy. (The CBC's commercial acceptance code requires that government advertising be "factual, informative, and non-controversial, and free of political persuasion and comments or opinion.") Most of the federal government's ads were sufficiently flabby to satisfy the CBC code.

Because Ontario supported the federal government's postion on the constitution, it didn't feel the need to become involved in constitutional advertising of its own. But it's found other ways to use advocacy advertising. A public-opinion survey commissioned by the Ontario government revealed that people in Ontario were concerned about the environment and felt the provincial government wasn't doing enough to protect it. So the government simply hired an ad agency to change the public's perception. (It's cheaper to change the way people think than to change reality.) One TV ad offered some vignettes of beautiful Ontario (deer lapping water, etc.) while an actor said, "I'm an engineer. I work all over the world and Ontario is the cleanest place I know."

There's a clear difference between ads selling products and ads selling ideas. The first are part of our mixed economy; the latter shouldn't be. As Leonard Brockington, the first chairman of the CBC, put it in 1939: "Above all there should be no preference for wealth. Freedom of speech is not for sale." Of course, freedom of speech has always been for sale, as anyone who has checked the price of a printing press or a TV transmitter knows. But advocacy advertising, which puts the manipulative techniques of product selling in the hands of propagandists, increases the *extent* to which it is for sale. Governments and the media have it in their power to put a stop to advocacy advertising. It's in the public interest that they do so.

— Morris Wolfe

Saturday Night/December 1980

EXPLORING IDEAS

1. *"There's a clear difference between ads selling products and ads selling ideas."*

   Assess the dangers Morris Wolfe points out in the use of advocacy advertising. To what extent do you agree with his views?

2. *"...when an advocacy ad gets on the air, it can be one of the most effective techniques used."*

   — Lynda Hurst, *"The New Ad Pitch"*

   Can you suggest reasons for the success of this type of advertising? In what ways might advocacy advertising *not* be effective? Share your views in a class discussion.

INVESTIGATING THE MEDIA

1. As a small group, examine and discuss the ads on pages 181-185. Some were placed by corporations, others by government departments or agencies. For each ad, consider:

   (a) Can the ad be termed a form of advocacy advertising? Why or why not?

   (b) Who has sponsored the ad? For what purpose?

   (c) What image, idea, or message is it trying to sell? To whom?

   (d) Is the ad effective? What factors contribute to its success or failure?

   (e) For each ad you find effective, briefly describe the techniques that contribute to its success. Examine copy, visuals, design, and layout.

   (f) Which ads, if any, do you consider controversial? Why?

   Have one member report your comments and conclusions to the class. Compare and discuss your views.

YOUR TURN

1. Working in a small group, brainstorm a list of social issues or causes about which you feel strongly. Select one issue or cause from your list and suggest some techniques or approaches that could be used in an advertising campaign. Design a print ad or poster intended to change people's minds or promote your point of view.
2. Your new agency has just opened for business. Your first client, the federal government, is planning a campaign of national ads to coincide with new legislation. It wants to inform the public and possibly change some deep-seated prejudices. Your job: to produce ads for a national campaign selling legislation presently in place or that you would like to see enacted. The "product" you sell might be Free Trade, Immigration, The Young Offenders Act, Universal Daycare.
3. Research one of the issues presented in the ads on pages 181-185. Prepare an ad or write an editorial presenting another, differing point of view.

For Lois Cowan Jones, juggling a variety of jobs comes easy when you've got McDonald's experience behind you.

At 27 years of age, Lois (née Cowan) Jones is a woman who knows how to take charge. Blessed with a quick mind, and a bubbly sense of humour, Jones has a voracious appetite for business and a solid commitment to a job well done.

Jones at 15 years of age: Full of promise.

"McDonald's was my Alma Mater."

As Manager of Commercial Production for CJOH TV in Ottawa, Lois Jones is responsible for the writing, direction and production of TV commercials for local clients, as well as the supervision of a small department. She unhesitatingly attributes her ability to juggle a variety of jobs to her three years at McDonald's. McDonald's, she says sportingly, was her 'Alma Mater'.

"Working at McDonald's taught me a great deal. I came away with the feeling that customers were everything. Without them, you wouldn't have a job. It's the same here. Without my clients, where would I be?"

"At McDonald's, it was 'Time to Lean, Time to Clean'."

"At McDonald's, they have a motto: 'Time to Lean, Time to Clean'. It really sunk in. Even if I have only 5 minutes, I want to use that 5 minutes productively. At McDonald's, if you saw something that needed doing, management would encourage you to do it, they'd expect you to do it. They hired bright people for a reason."

"Just like at McDonald's, I'm always on the go here. I love it!"

From McDonald's to a Fine Arts degree and a short stint in graphic design, Jones moved into television. Hired as a receptionist for a summer at CKNY in North Bay, she quickly saw the need for a promotions person. Creating the position herself by writing simple, informative copy like 'Coming Up Next…' and 'Tonight on the Late Show…', she then walked into a copywriting job when the lone writer went on vacation then stayed on after his return. After that it was off to CJOH in 1979 where she's been ever since.

"I'm always on the go here and I love it. I'm constantly meeting new people, gathering new information, learning about new businesses. It's exciting. The people part of my job at CJOH is very similar to my work at McDonald's. At McDonald's I worked the 'window' which was the cash and counter area and later I was promoted to hostess.

I was dealing with new people all the time. The enthusiasm and the 'smile for everyone' I required then, I require now. McDonald's gave me basic training in public relations.

"Thinking back, the place still amazes me. People didn't come to

Jones with daughter, Arden.
An appetite for McDonald's runs in the family.

McDonald's just to buy hamburgers. They came *for* McDonald's for the character of the place, for the place itself. People still go for that. My daughter, Arden, is two years old. And she loves it there.

Working at McDonald's wasn't just a job. It was an event."

People. Our most important ingredient.

The solution to Canada's tragic 4,000 traffic deaths a year isn't just better cars. It's better drivers.

Accident Photo: Globe and Mail

Here's how professional driver training of young people can cut the toll by almost a third over the next five years. And what Texaco is doing to help.

If it was a disease that was killing Canadians at the rate we do on our highways, it would be an epidemic.

We would rally, organize, and work to stamp it out. But over the years the newspaper images of crushed metal have taken a numbing toll on our minds.

Did the picture on the opposite page shock you?

Likely not.

And that should tell you just how de-sensitized we've become to the carnage.

The statistics *should* shock us: more than 4,000 killed on our roads last year; almost 250,000 injured.

Traffic accidents are now the leading cause of death for Canadians under 34. A terrible, useless waste of our young; our future.

Texaco believes, as grim as the facts are, that there is hope. And it starts with the most shocking statistic of all:

85% of all traffic accidents are due to human error. Drivers who make mistakes. Deadly mistakes.

But this also means that 85% of traffic accidents are *preventable.*

Drive to survive.

Of the people who get their drivers' licences in Ontario each year, 60% don't have formal training.

If we can put more new drivers on our roads who are more highly trained in the demanding skill of driving a car, we can save lives.

If every new driver was a graduate of a professional driver training program; calm, alert, and well-versed in defensive driving techniques, we could cut our death toll dramatically. Perhaps by as much as a third in the next five years.

Teaching your teenager to drive could be dangerous—because you may unknowingly pass on deadly habits. (Many people who have been driving for years could use re-training courses.)

Good driver? Bad teacher.

Test yourself right now on how good a driver you are:

When a traffic light turns green you step on the gas and proceed with caution. Right?

Wrong.

You should always look left, centre, right and left again before proceeding to be certain all traffic has cleared an intersection. (Nearly half of all accidents happen right here.)

If you failed this test, let a professional teach your teenager to drive. And survive.

Texaco is making the reduction of traffic deaths and injuries our cause.

And we're not going to just talk about it, we're going to do something about it.

A 10% reduction in the cost of professional driver training.

Starting now, we'll arrange for a 10% reduction in the cost of sending your teenager to **Young Drivers of Canada,** one of the best driver training programs available.

We'll do the same for older drivers, too.

Our 'Drive to Survive' information kit contains full details on our cost-reduction program, as well as the application that qualifies you for this reduction.

The kit is available by calling toll-free:
1-800-268-4520

Or drop by a nearby Texaco service station and pick one up.

Proper driver training is costly—but there's no comparison with the cost of human lives. That's priceless.

This folder could save a life.

Course fees are federally tax deductible by the student, and there may be substantial insurance reductions which could easily save the initial expense in a very short time.

(You're a driver for life remember, and accident-free drivers tend to pay less for insurance.)

Just the beginning.

Texaco will also be taking steps to raise public concern about traffic fatalities and the vital importance of professional driver training in many other ways too.

We want to stop the carnage. And better drivers mean fewer accidents.

It may not stop all the traffic deaths and injuries, but it's a start.

Because the way we see it, our job isn't just to help get your car safely from one place to another, but to help get you and your family there safely, too.

Let a professional teach them to drive. And survive.

"People won't give my dad a chance"

"All my dad wants is a fair shot. I mean he got sick and then he got better. Why would anyone hold it against him that he was sick once? Haven't they ever been sick? I just don't get it."

A fair shot. Isn't that what we all want out of life. A chance to be productive, contributing members of society. To earn enough to be independent. To be judged on what we do, not what we are. To take part.

Yet there are those among us who are being denied that chance, that fundamental way of life. People who are being denied an opportunity to participate in our community not because of something they've done, but because of who they are.

People recovering from mental illness have shown time and time again they can succeed if given a chance. They've shown that with the help of community and government agencies and enlightened employers, they can participate and contribute.

Just as importantly, they've shown that much of the stigma of mental illness in the workplace is based on fear and ignorance.

We've produced a brochure that provides straightforward answers to questions you might have about hiring or working with people recovering from emotional disorders or psychiatric backgrounds. It explodes myths. And deals with facts. It'll show you that hiring them should be no different than hiring anyone else.

You'll find that, like all of us, all they want is a fair shot.

Canadian Mental Health Association
ONTARIO DIVISION

Ministry of Health
Ontario

A CARING COMMUNITY IS THE ANSWER.

For more information please complete and mail this coupon or call **1-800-268-1121.**

I would like to:

☐ Receive your brochure "An Equal Chance"
☐ Find out how I can become a volunteer in my community.
☐ Know more about the activities of the CMHA, and how I can show my support.

Name ________________________

Address ________________________

____

Postal Code __________ Telephone __________

Canadian Mental Health Association,
Ontario Division
56 Wellesley St. W., Suite 410
Toronto, Ontario
M5S 2S3

"Dad, you've got to help me."

"Sandy, what's wrong? Are you hurt?"
"No, Dad, I'm fine."
"Where are you?"
"At Pat's. We all came over here to celebrate after the game."
"It's almost 12:30. Isn't it time you called it a night?"
"That's just it. Remember you always told me if I was out never to drive with anyone who's had too much to drink? And not to be afraid to call you if I had no other way of getting home? Well, tonight I'm taking you at your word."
"Stay right there. I'm coming to pick you up."
"Thanks, Dad. Oh, and something else."
"Shoot."
"Are you angry with me?"
"Angry? No, Sandy. Not on your life."

Seagram

We believe in moderation and we've been saying so since 1934

For a free chart on responsible drinking limits, write to us P.O. Box 847, Station H, Montreal, Quebec. H3G 2M8

We don't advertise to children.

Who are you kidding?

The newspapers and magazines and billboards are filled with cigarette ads. Kids can't help but see them.

How can you expect us to believe you're not trying to reach and influence our children?

We're not surprised if many people feel this way—especially when years of negative publicity have made them totally cynical about our industry.

Nevertheless, we'd like to set the record straight.

First of all, we don't want young people to smoke. And we're running ads aimed specifically at young people advising them that we think smoking is strictly for adults.

Second, research shows that among all the factors that can influence a young person to start smoking, advertising is insignificant. Kids just don't pay attention to cigarette ads, and that's exactly as it should be.

Finally—and this is sometimes hard for people outside the marketing field to understand—all of our cigarette ads are what we call "brand advertising." Its purpose is to get smokers of competitive products to switch to one of our brands, and to build the loyalty of those who already smoke one of our brands.

At the present there are some 200 different cigarette brands for sale in the U.S. Many of them have only a very small fraction of the total cigarette market. Getting smokers to switch is virtually the only way a cigarette brand can meaningfully increase its business.

That's why we don't advertise to young people.

Of course, if you'd like to share *this* ad with your children, that would be just fine with us.

R.J. Reynolds Tobacco Company

"In the past, children's knowledge of the outside world, which includes the issue of what to buy and consume, was filtered through parents. Children now tend to be very much plugged into one of the major marketing devices in society, which is the TV set."

"In the United States, advertising to children under 13 is a $500-million-a-year business."

Child-directed advertising has been compared to "shooting ducks in a barrel." The following articles explore some of the issues in advertising aimed at the "little consumer" and attempts to regulate such advertising.

'Born to shop' electronic age kids are spending billions on themselves

They usually hang in clusters: preteen girls with a precocious and similar sense of fashion — long T-shirts, acid-wash jeans — giggling and tugging at price tags in clothing stores.

In North America today, "born to shop" is becoming more than a bumper-sticker expression of material self-indulgence.

At surprisingly early stages in their development, children are making decisions about what to buy, say parents and other observers of children's behavior.

"Children are now major consumers," says Joshua Meyrowitz, a U.S. academic who has studied the impact of electronic media, including advertising, on social behavior.

In the United States, advertising to children under 13 is a $500 million-a-year business. The U.S. toy industry alone accounts for $13 billion in yearly revenues. In Canada it's about $1.2 billion.

On average, U.S. children aged 2 to 11 are exposed to an amazing 20 000 commercials a year.

Cereal marketed for children accounts for 40 per cent of all cereals sold, according to Cy Schneider, a California ad executive who specializes in children's products.

Those products have gone beyond the traditional areas of toys and candy, into consumer items that used to be reserved for adults. For instance:

- There is a line of perfume for 10- to 12-year-olds.
- Some restaurants cater specifically to children.
- In August, 1987, an afternoon talk show on television featured a line of children's clothing that included lingerie.

"If she's looking for things to wear, she has very definite preferences," says Suzann Shear, a North Toronto mother whose 6-year-old daughter Kady is given considerable choice in selecting a wardrobe.

Kady likes dresses "of a certain kind," a range of tastes that extends to a pricey gold lamé outfit she spotted during a back-to-school shopping trip last month.

In the past few years, clothing for children has become more varied and style-conscious. It has also become more adult-like. There is less of a distinction between older and juvenile styles, says Toronto clothier David Margolis.

"Kids want to look like their big brothers and sisters or even their mothers and fathers," says Margolis, whose Winners chain of clothing stores attracts large numbers of back-to-school shoppers.

Margolis says many children as young as 10 have their own clothing allowance.

Why children are making shopping decisions sooner and how those decisions are formed are questions open to debate. But it's clear that the socialization of children into consumers owes a lot to the influence of the media, particularly television, and is a symptom of a larger cultural phenomenon.

Social scientists like Joshua Meyrowitz and Neil Postman argue that television has blurred the distinctions between children and adults. Before television, adults could control the flow of information to children — in effect maintaining "secrets of adulthood."

"In the past, children's knowledge of the outside world, which includes the issue of what to buy and con-

Born to shop—Six-year-old Kady Shear models a dress she picked out herself.

sume, was filtered through parents," says Meyrowitz. "Children now tend to be very much plugged into one of the major marketing devices in society, which is the TV set."

They are, as a result, "much more aware of the spectrum of available behavior and products." And "once any one of them knows about a certain option of clothing, then everyone has some potential access to it."

Consequently, even children shielded from television are subject to the effect it has on their peers.

They can exert pressure even on 5-year-olds. When many of the kids in Kady Shear's class got their ears pierced, she asked as well, but her mother said no. Nor did Kady get the gold lamé dress.

Child psychologist David Elkind, whose 1981 book *The Hurried Child* is considered a pre-eminent work in the field, says children are under enormous pressure to grow up fast. Parents encourage them to make more decisions at an earlier age.

To stimulate their child's budding intellect, some parents employ flash cards and send them to camps that specialize in music, foreign languages, or computers.

Airlines, including Air Canada, have regulations for unaccompanied minors, a response to the large number of children travelling alone, many visiting divorced parents.

"We're seeing a lot more during the years, and not just divorced parents but situations where one parent is working in a different city and commuting," said airline spokesperson Maureen Curow.

Indeed, the socialization of many children now includes watching their single parents date and act romantic, a phase of traditional relationships usually long passed by the time children were old enough to notice it.

In the past decade, more latchkey children have taken on greater responsibilities. They shop for working parents, and make a lot of decisions about brand names.

Advertising directly to children is not a new concern. In the Babylonian Code of Hammurabi, one of civilization's earliest rules of legal and social behavior, selling to children was considered a crime.

Not so in North America where children usually start to watch television at 18 months to 2 years. Between 2 and 3 they become aware of brand names.

A report published in the summer of 1987 by the U.S. advertising agency Bozell, Jacobs, Kenyon & Eckhardt provided an insight into how marketers target children.

Excerpted from a book by ad exec Cy Schneider, the article provides 17 tips on how to "communicate" with children. It says advertisers should "try to make children feel more grown-up." A sample quote:

"The success of many products has been based on a positioning that allows children to pretend they are more grown-up in their sex-role identification.

"Boys are concerned with power and strength. Girls are concerned with looks and cuteness."

In an interview from his California office, Cy Schneider maintained that advertisers have no choice but to practise what works.

"Advertising reflects society as it is, not as it should be," he said. If an ad doesn't "ring true," it doesn't work.

Schneider argues that parents are the gatekeepers and advertising merely the stimulus to children's desires.

After providing 16 tips on how best to manipulate children, including the fact that for children under 5, the commercial, oftentimes *is* the product, the 17th and final suggestion in his article urges marketers to "above all, be honest."

By age 6, more than 90 per cent of American children are watching television as a regular habit, says John Condry, a professor of human development and family studies at Cornell University in Ithaca, N.Y.

A lot of research has shown that conflicts are introduced into the family by television. "If parents are not wealthy, children react with great stress" when they can't have something all their friends own, says Condry.

Children are most susceptible to pressure of this sort from ages 3 to 7, he says.

Condry is no friend of advertisers who target children. In the early 1970s he testified before the U.S. Federal Communications Commission, urging them to ban all advertising to children under 7 years.

"American capitalists think I'm a vicious Communist swine for suggesting that," he says. But businessmen have no right, Condry maintains, to manipulate the minds of 3-year-olds.

"I just think it's not a proper business practice. The business of selling and buying should be for people who have a minimal understanding of what they're engaging in."

Condry is particularly incensed by increasing commercialization of children's programming, particularly Saturday morning shows, which have virtually become half-hour long advertisements for products like GI Joe, Smurfs, Strawberry Shortcake, and other dolls that particularly blossomed in the period between 1983 and 1985.

Canadian regulations tend to be more stringent. Many U.S. ads aired by private Canadian broadcasters are altered before they appear.

"Young children don't understand the selling intent of commercials," said Dr. Tannis MacBeth Williams, an associate professor of psychology at the University of British Columbia. Williams has studied both the content and effects of television and says research shows that young children have, not surprisingly, an unsophisticated concept of economics.

"In the early grades, they believe the teacher's salary is the money kids bring for lunch," she said.

Schools have been slow to acknowledge the enormous effect of media on children. Recently in Ontario, the Ministry of Education mandated "media literacy" programs for junior high and senior grades.

But Meyrowitz and others say such programs make more sense earlier in the curriculum — when children are most susceptible to television manipulation.

"The current difficulty of maintaining school discipline and of teaching students reading and other subjects may lie more in the antiquated structure of the school than in a sudden change in children's basic abilities or willingness to learn," says Meyrowitz.

Schools can no longer pretend that they are where real learning about our culture begins. For one thing, they could address the enormous impact of television and, at least in early grades, get rid of traditional grade structures.

— John Ferri
The Toronto Star
September 6, 1987

Do you know what your tots watch?

The average American child, aged from two to 11 years old, sees about 20 000 television commercials every year. This adds up to perhaps 200 hours-worth of TV advertisements, annually.

The figures are no less astounding when rendered on a daily basis: Something like 55 commercials, as much as 33 solid minutes of sheer promotion.

While these numbers — from a recent publication by agency Bozell, Jacobs, Kenyon & Eckhardt — are for the United States, it is safe to assume that Canadian kids are subjected to almost as many ads for sweetened cereals and the like.

Parents can be forgiven if they feel vaguely nauseous about the whole business. It is, after all, a nasty intrusion of adult commercialism into what we should like to consider the idyllic world of childhood.

Yet it could be much worse. Our kids could be exposed, not just to the same quantity of ads as the Americans, but to precisely the same content all of the time — not just when they tune in to U.S. stations.

"If every U.S. ad directed at kids was submitted to us unchanged, we'd reject a good 95 per cent of them," says Susan Burke, director of the standards division at the Canadian Advertising Foundation.

All children's advertising must first be approved by an eight-member committee before it can be broadcast on any Canadian station. And, as Burke points out "most of the commercials that come to us are produced in the U.S."

To a large extent, the unaltered American ads are rejected because of relatively minor violations of the Broadcast Code for Advertising to Children, first introduced in 1971.

Under the Canadian code, for example, the fact that a toy isn't sold with batteries included must be both stated in the voice-over and printed on the bottom of the screen. This is not required in the U.S., where "self-policing" means that every network has its own guidelines on children's advertising.

But some of the violations are more glaring.

Burke says that a recent U.S. ad — which showed kids, dressed in khaki outfits, playing with war toys — was summarily rejected for broadcast in Canada. The American spot, she says, fell afoul of the "social values" clause of the code.

Stars—That's how Canadian ad watchdogs view the Smurfs. They cannot be shown *with* a product.

And the committee — made up of representatives from the Consumers' Association of Canada, broadcasters, advertisers, agencies, and the Canadian Radio television and Telecommunications Commission — would also reject most U.S. ads which feature a real-life or cartoon "celebrity."

Here, however, some strange anomalies creep into the code.

If the ad is directed at children (or aired during a TV show directed at kids), then the celebrity can appear only as background entertainment. In the words of the code, such celebrities can be used only for "mood or theme-setting."

The Smurfs, for instance, can frolic about for a few frames, but they cannot be shown *with* a product. Nor can a Wayne Gretzky expressly tell the kids to eat Pro*Stars cereal. He can tell them a balanced breakfast is a good way to start the day; he can even say that Pro*Stars is a good source of vitamins X,Y, and Z. But no more.

Yet Ronald McDonald is in quite a different league, at least according to the code, because he is a creation of the advertiser. It is not a case of the restaurant chain trying to gain extra legitimacy by associating with a celebrity from the outside world.

Among other things, the code also stipulates that any "premiums" — like the plastic toy in "specially marked boxes" of cereal — can be shown or talked about for no more than half of a 30-second commercial.

Nor can an advertiser use such words as "only," "just," or "bargain price" to minimize the cost of his product. Comparison claims — "longer hair than any other doll on the market" — are strictly forbidden.

For the most part, advertisers alter or re-edit their American ads to conform with the Canadian code before submitting them for pre-clearance. But a good many violations still occur.

In 1986, 581 commercials were submitted for pre-clearance. Of that number, 446 were accepted and 135 rejected. (Ads that were quickly re-submitted after minor changes are still entered in the "accepted" category.)

In 1985, only 496 ads were submitted, of which 400 were accepted.

"It's been growing every year," Burke says of the number of ads her group must handle.

But, largely because of pre-clearance, consumer complaints about individual ads are few and far between.

In 1973, the year such pre-clearance became mandatory, Burke's group received 97 complaints. That compares with an annual rate of 6 or fewer in the 1980s.

— Kenneth Kidd
The Toronto Star
August 2, 1987

Commercial Dos and Don'ts

Highlights of the Broadcast Code for Advertising to Children

DO

- Clearly establish the relative size of a product, showing it in relation to a child or something from a child's world
- Give products as much air time, at least, as any premiums being promoted along with them
- Give clear and complete pricing and purchasing information
- When a product needs assembly or additional parts or accessories (e.g., batteries), explain so in easily understood terms
- If a range of toys is shown, make it clear that each is sold separately and, if one toy in particular is featured, show it by itself in the closing shots

DON'T

- Exaggerate service, product, or premium characteristics
- Use words like "new," "introducing," etc. for more than one year for the same product or service
- Advertise drugs, proprietary medicine, or vitamins
- *Directly* urge children to purchase or ask their parents to do so
- Schedule commercials for any single product, premium, or service more than once during a half-hour period, except when there is full program sponsorship
- Use puppets, characters, or persons well known to children or featured on children's programs to personally endorse products
- Minimize costs by using terms such as "just," "only," "bargain," etc.
- Make direct comparisons with previous year's model or with competitive makes
- Portray adults or children in unsafe acts or situations (except for safety messages) or show products being put to unsafe or dangerous use
- Encourage values inconsistent with the moral, ethical, or legal standards of the community
- Imply that ownership or use of the product confers superiority in any way

— Taken from the TVO Publication
Television & Children

EXPLORING IDEAS

1. When you were a child, did you ever badger your parents to buy you something you had seen on television? Why did you want it? What effect do you think television commercials had on you?
2. To what extent do you agree with each of the following statements:
   (a) *Children are more susceptible to advertising than adults.*
   (b) *There is now considerable evidence that child-directed advertising has harmful effects.*

   Support your views using information from the articles and from your own experience, past and present.
3. Form groups to discuss the following points of view:
   (a) *We cannot shield children from advertising. It is up to parents to teach their children to be skeptical and to refuse to buy products they can't afford.*
   (b) *Parents should not be put in the position of having to say no to their children.*
   (c) *Without the support of advertising, children's TV programming would decline in quality and quantity.*
   (d) *All child-directed advertising is basically unfair.*

   Report back to the class on your group's views on child-directed advertising.

INVESTIGATING THE MEDIA

1. Some highlights from Canada's Broadcasting Code for children appear on page 190. Watch children's Saturday morning programs on a variety of networks. Take notes on the content, techniques used, and the social values implied in the commercials you watch.
   (a) Do most ads follow the *Dos* and *Don'ts* of Canada's Broadcasting Code? Make note of any that, in your opinion, violate these rules.
   (b) In your opinion, does the Code adequately protect children? What other provisions, do you feel, should be added?
2. Draft a congratulatory letter to one of the companies who you think produces responsible commercials for children, *or* a letter of complaint regarding one you believe violates the code.

YOUR TURN

1. What specific advice or training would you give small children to help them deal with children's advertising? Prepare a brochure for parents to help them educate their children about commercials.
2. Write a poem or article, or prepare a visual display, entitled "The Commercialization of Childhood."
3. You are part of a team that is developing a commercial for a new children's product. Keeping in mind the rules in Canada's Code for Advertising to Children, design an ad or commercial.
4. Talk to some children to find out how they are affected by TV ads:
   - What toys do they play with most? Are they advertised on TV?
   - What toys do they want to have? Where did they learn about them?
   - What foods/snacks/treats are their favourites?
   - What TV programs do they watch on weekends when their parents aren't around?

   Prepare a written or oral report on your findings.

Investigate further the various aspects of advertising which interest you or which you would like to learn more about. Develop your own activities and research projects or choose from the list of suggestions that follows.

1. Research and report on the various agencies that regulate advertising in Canada:

Canadian Advertising Foundation —
Standards Division
350 Bloor Street East
Suite 402
Toronto, Ontario
Canada M4W 1H5

or

Le Conseil des normes de la publicité
4823 ouest, rue Sherbrooke
suite 130
Montréal, Québec
Canada H3Z 1G7

Regional Councils:

Advertising Standards Council — B.C. Region
P.O. Box 3005
Vancouver, B.C.
Canada V6B 3X5

Alberta Advertising Standards Council —
Edmonton
Box 2421
Edmonton, Alberta
Canada T5J 2S6

Alberta Advertising Standards Council — Calgary
P.O. Box 6630, Station "D"
Calgary, Alberta
Canada T2P 2E4

Advertising Standards Council —
Saskatchewan
P.O. Box 1322
Regina, Saskatchewan
Canada S4P 3B8

Advertising Standards Council —
Manitoba
Box 1001
Winnipeg, Manitoba
Canada R3C 2W3

Advertising Standards Council — Atlantic Region
P.O. Box 394, Station "M"
Halifax, Nova Scotia
Canada B3J 2P8

What are their areas of responsibility? What regulations exist regarding advertising in Canada?

2. An excerpt from The Code of Standards, developed by the Advertising Standards Council, appears on pages 194-195.
(a) Working in groups, examine television commercials, radio commercials, or print ads for adherence to the Code.
(b) Write a letter of complaint regarding any advertisements that violate the Code, in your opinion, explaining why.

3. Research and write a report on the history of advertising. At what point in history would you begin? What important breakthroughs or changes have occurred in advertising?

4. Read and review one of the following books on advertising:
Michael J. Arlen, *Thirty Seconds*, Penguin, 1981
Stuart Bay and William Thorn, *Visual Persuasion*, Harcourt, Brace, Jovanovich, 1974
Larry Dobrow, *When Advertising Tried Harder*, Friendly Press, 1984
Robert Glatzer, *The New Advertising: Twenty-One Successful Campaigns from Schweppes to the Sierra Club*, The Citadel Press, 1970
Jerry Goodis, *Have I Ever Lied to You Before?*, Toronto, 1972
David Ogilvy, *Confessions of an Advertising Man*, Dell, 1964 *Ogilvy on Advertising*, John Wiley & Sons, 1983
Rosser Reeves, *Reality in Advertising*, New York, 1961

5. Working with a partner, create your own advertisement that makes a statement reflecting *your* feelings and thoughts about advertising. For example:

The advertising industry works to standards and guidelines. However the idea of what's acceptable or not will vary with the times and the people you talk to. If you've got something to say about advertising, we'd like to hear it.

Advertising. Talk to us about it.
P.O. Box 2150, Station A,
Toronto, Ontario M5W 1H1

6. Which medium carries the most effective advertising? Which medium do people trust the most? Conduct a poll to find answers to these questions. Encourage the people you interview to explain the reasons for their responses. Record both the answers to the two specific questions and the explanations. Prepare and present a report on your findings.

7. Can advertising be considered an art? Do some ads rise above the mechanical use of persuasion and attention-grabbing techniques?

Find a number of ads that will illustrate your point of view on this issue.

8. How is an ad created? Contact an ad agency to inquire about arranging a visit to talk to people who can help answer this question. If you are a photographer yourself, you could ask for permission to take some slides to use in your presentation to the class.
9. Who are the experts in the field of advertising?
   (a) Prepare a short bibliography on some of the following media critics and analysts: Marshall McLuhan, David Ogilvy, Tony Schwartz, Jerry Goodis, Benjamin Singer.
   (b) Read and review one book written by these analysts. What contribution has this particular thinker made in this particular field?
   or
   Study the contribution made by Canadian ad agencies and designers. Is there anything distinctive about the Canadian market and Canadian advertisements?
   (a) Make a list of Canadian ad agencies and write them to get their views on the above question.
   (b) Compare print ads from Canadian sources with those from American and European sources. Is there a significant difference? Make a display with a commentary that outlines your conclusion based on the information you have found.

Authority and Scope of the Code

The Code deals with how products or services may be advertised, not with what may be advertised. Thus, the authority of the Code and the jurisdiction of the Council are over the content of advertisements and do not include, in any way, the right to prohibit the promotion of legal products or services or their portrayal in circumstances of normal use.

The Code

This Code of Standards, which has been approved by all participating organizations, is designed to help set and maintain standards of honesty, truth, accuracy, and fairness in the marketplace.

No advertisement shall be prepared or knowingly accepted which contravenes this Code of Standards.

The clauses should be adhered to in letter and in spirit.

1. Accuracy, Clarity

(a) Advertisements may not contain inaccurate or deceptive claims or statements, either direct or implied, with regard to price, availability, or performance of a product or service. Advertisers and advertising agencies must be prepared to substantiate their claims promptly to the Council. Note that, in assessing the truthfulness of a message, the Council's concern is not with the intent of the sender or the precise legality of the phrasing. Rather the focus is on the message as received or perceived, that is, the general impression conveyed by the advertisement.

(b) Advertisements may be deceptive by omission of relevant information.

(c) All pertinent details of advertised offers should be clearly stated.

(d) Disclaimers or asterisked information should be so located and large enough as to be clearly visible.

2. Disguised Advertising Techniques

No advertisement shall be presented in a format which conceals its commercial intent. Advertising content, for example, should be clearly distinguished from editorial or program content. Similarly, advertisements are not acceptable if they attempt to use images or sounds of very brief duration or physically weak visual or oral techniques to convey messages below the threshold of normal human awareness. (Such messages are sometimes referred to as subliminal.)

3. Price Claims

(a) No advertisement shall include deceptive price claims or discounts, unrealistic price comparisons, or exaggerated claims as to worth or value. "Regular price," "suggested retail price," "manufacturer's list price," and "fair market value" are misleading terms when used by an individual advertiser to indicate a savings — unless they represent prices at which a reasonable number of the item was actually sold within the preceding six months in the market where the advertisement appears.

(b) Where price discounts are offered, qualifying statements such as "up to," "xx off," etc., should be in easily readable type, in close proximity to the prices quoted, and, where practical, regular prices should be included.

(c) Prices quoted in Canadian media in other than Canadian funds should be so identified.

4. Testimonials

Testimonials must reflect the genuine, reasonably current opinion of the endorser and should be based upon adequate information about or experience with the product or service advertised. This is not meant to preclude, however, an actor or actress presenting the true experience of an actual number of users or presenting technical information about the manufacture or testing of the product.

5. Bait and Switch

The consumer must be given a fair opportunity to purchase the goods or services offered at the terms presented. If supply of the sale item is limited, this should be mentioned in the advertisement. Refusal to show or demonstrate the product, disparagement of the advertised product by sales personnel, or demonstration of a product of superior quality are all illustrations of the "bait and switch" technique which is a contravention of the Code.

6. Comparative Advertising

Advertisements must not discredit or attack unfairly other products, services or advertisements, or exaggerate the nature or importance of competitive differences. When comparisons are made with competing products or services, the advertiser must make substantiation available promptly upon the request from the Council.

7. Professional or Scientific Claims

Advertisements must not distort the true meaning of statements made by professionals or scientific authorities. Advertising claims must not imply they have a scientific basis they do not truly possess. Scientific terms, technical terms, etc., should be used in general advertising only with a full sense of responsibility to the lay public.

8. Slimming, Weight Loss

Advertisements shall not state or imply that foods, food substitutes, meal replacements, appetite suppressants, creams, lotions, or special devices will enable a person to lose weight or girth except in conjunction with a balanced, calorie-controlled diet; and reference to the part played by such a diet shall be so located and large enough to be clearly visible.

9. Guarantees

No advertisement shall offer a guarantee or warranty, unless the guarantee or warranty is fully explained as to conditions and limits and the name of the guarantor or warrantor, or it is indicated where such information may be obtained.

10. Imitation

No advertiser shall deliberately imitate the copy, slogans, or illustrations of another advertiser in such a manner as to mislead the consumer. The accidental or unintentional use of similar or like general slogans or themes shall not be considered a contravention of this Code, but advertisers, media, and advertising agencies should be alert to the confusion that can result from such coincidences and should seek to eliminate them when discovered.

11. Safety

Advertisements shall not display a disregard for public safety or depict situations which might encourage unsafe or dangerous practices, particularly when portraying products in normal use.

12. Exploitation of Human Misery

Advertisements may not hold out false hope in the form of a cure or relief for the mental or physically handicapped, either on a temporary or permanent basis.

13. Superstition and Fears

Advertisements must not exploit the superstitious, or play upon fears to mislead the consumer into purchasing the advertised product or service.

14. Advertising to Children

Advertisements to children impose a special responsibility upon the advertiser and the media. Such advertisements should not exploit their credulity, lack of experience, or their sense of loyalty, and should not present information or illustrations which might result in their physical, mental, or moral harm. (See also Broadcast Code for Advertising to Children and the Quebec Consumer Protection Act, Bill 72.)

15. Advertising to Minors

Products prohibited from sale to minors must not be advertised in such a way as to appeal particularly to persons under legal age and people featured in advertisements for such products must be, and clearly seen to be, adults under the law.

16. Taste, Opinion, Public Decency

As a public communication process, advertising should not present demeaning or derogatory portrayals of individuals or groups and should not contain anything likely, in the light of generally prevailing standards, to cause deep or widespread offence. It is recognized, of course, that standards of taste are subjective and vary widely from person to person and community to community, and are, indeed, subject to constant change.

UNIT FIVE: THE PUBLIC'S RIGHT TO REPORT THE

KNOW:
ING
NEWS

The news is an important part of our daily lives; routines are often established around reading the morning or evening paper, or watching news on television. In the age of the "information explosion" we increasingly look to the media not only to keep us informed but also to help us interpret the information reported.

We expect that members of the press will act responsibly and fairly when they bring us the news. Is this a reasonable expectation? In this unit we will examine some fundamental questions about our news systems and the manner in which they operate. What is news? What should and should not be reported? How accurate is the information we read or view; and how can we obtain the most accurate information to base important decisions on? How can we become more wise, discriminating, and unbiased as consumers of the news?

YOU & THE MEDIA

1. What is the most popular source of news for the students in your class? How many
   - watch news on television?
   - listen to news on radio?
   - read newsmagazines (*Maclean's*, TIME, *Newsweek*, etc.)?
   - read newspapers?
   - watch in-depth news programs on television, such as *W5*, *the fifth estate*, or *60 Minutes*?

(a) What are the strengths and weaknesses of each of these media in accurately reporting the news?
(b) Which medium do you trust the most? Why, do you think, is this medium more reliable than the others?

2 Following is a card from a game called *Psychologizer*. Take a class poll to find out which choices best express students' attitudes. Discuss reasons for your choices.

Politics & Current Events 48

Going home and reading the newspaper is an automatic routine for many people. Is this routine an extremely important one? Which of the following statements best describes your attitude about the press?

a) More than anything else, the press is the guardian of society's freedom.
b) The press is big business and is interested mainly in selling its product through advertising and sensationalism.
c) One cannot generalize about the press — it ranges from extremely good to extremely bad.
d) One can generalize about the press — it is almost always the voice of criticism, cynicism, and skepticism.

— from the board game *Psychologizer*
used with permission of Managhan Game & Toy Corporation

3 As a class, rate the following professionals in terms of your view of their "trustworthiness."
(a) educators
(b) politicians
(c) bankers
(d) doctors
(e) journalists
(f) scientists
(g) lawyers
Where did journalists place on your list? What does the ranking suggest about the degree of confidence you have in journalists?

How would *you* define "quality" journalism? Working in groups, outline what you see as the responsibilities of the journalist and the news systems.

THE NEWS BEAT

“. . . if you think about what you're doing, you understand the information you're giving is important to people, and that imbues a sense of responsibility.”

— Lloyd Robertson

“. . . our job, first and last, is to get the story.”

— Linda Ellerbee

As these and other journalists have pointed out, we the public want news information that is accurate and reported with integrity — we rely on “quality journalism” to help us make sense of an increasingly complex world. In addition, both the public and the journalist's employer demand instant information: the news “as it happens.” In the next articles news people discuss what quality journalism is — the responsibilities and challenges of their highly competitive profession.

Knowlton Nash is renowned as a journalist and television news anchor. In the following article he takes a hard look at how his profession is doing its job.

Cleopatra and the Messenger

In our increasingly complex society, the news media constitute the only way the mass of the people can find out what's going on, the only way they can communicate with their government and their government can communicate with them. We stake everything on a rational dialogue between an informed public and a political leadership aware of public concerns. But today two factors challenge the effectiveness of that journalistic role.

If you remember your Shakespeare, when the Messenger arrives and advises Cleopatra that Mark Antony has married Octavia, Cleopatra calls the bearer of the news an “infectious pestilence” and suggests he be “whipp'd with wire,” “stew'd in brine,” scalped, and finally be killed.

That's the essence of the Cleopatra Syndrome: If you don't like the message, blame the Messenger. And that's exactly what many of society's leaders do today. When they don't like the message, they blame the media and try to change the message.

The wise old Saskatchewanian Graham Spry, reporter, author, and winner of the John Drainie Award for distinguished contribution to broadcasting, once said: “Information is the prime, integrating factor nourishing, adjusting, and sustaining a society.”

Political parties alternately woo and castigate the media. They want to shape our reporting to their objective. And their objective, of course, is to win elections, not necessarily to be fair or honest or even accurate in what they say and do. Once in power, they view managing the media as a vital condition of their domination of legislatures and the public. It's the same manipulating story in business, labor, or any field where someone is trying to persuade the public that their ideas or products are the best.

But, stripped of the glowing protective coloration of public relations, what politicians, business, labor, and social activists of all kinds really want is to have the media reflect their own self-image. They prefer a sympathetic and sometimes sycophantic media, not an asser-

Knowlton Nash — For many years, CBC Television's chief correspondent and anchor of *The National*

tively independent media.

In a recent speech, John Craig Eaton, chairman of Eaton's and one of the most powerful advertisers in Canada, suggested that newspapers must provide a more positive content, or advertisers would stop putting ads in the papers. Although Mr. Eaton agreed newspapers should report gloomy economic news, fires and crimes, the newspaper environment itself, he said, should find new ways to project what he called "good vibes."

I can appreciate his desire, but for journalists his perspective is a prescription for disaster. Freedom for an assertively independent media, which reports good vibes or bad as reality demands, is the price of democracy, and a necessity for a mature, well-informed electorate. Those in authority must be able to cope with sometimes cantankerous, sometimes obstinate media, so the country can preserve the greater values of freedom of expression and the right of people to know.

That freedom, incidentally, doesn't exist very widely. According to the International Press Institute in London, only about 20 countries currently have what we know as a free press. Dictatorships, communist or fascist, view the media as instruments of the state.

It should be understood that as long as we in journalism are doing our proper job as agents for the public, there will be a continuing love-hate relationship — often tempestuous, sometimes ferocious — a never-ending conflict between the media and the news makers. The news makers are trying to sell something, while the media are trying to reflect reality.

There is, however, another side to this. There are those who feel the most formidable threat to consistently responsible journalism comes not so much from external pressures as from the media themselves. And I share some of that apprehension.

Certainly our job must be to enlarge public understanding of uncomfortable problems, and I quite understand how that riles some people. But, in doing our job, our effectiveness boils down to one word: credibility. Without credibility we have nothing. It is the heart and soul of our business.

Reporters, editors, producers, and all of us in journalism have power — it is only through us that the public at large knows what's happening, how, where, when, and why. So the public as well as the news makers has a right to expect a proper journalistic job.

In some ways journalists must have the same attitude to news as a bank employee has to money — it isn't ours. We're handling it on behalf of other people, so it cannot be converted to our own use.

Reporters cannot try to change people's minds or confirm their beliefs. We must give untainted news so the public can make up its own mind. We can report apparent abuse, but not crusade for its abolition; report a demonstration, but not take sides. Reporters simply report;

we do not approve or disapprove.

There are, of course, those journalists who do comment, who do advocate, but they are opinion columnists, commentators, and editorial writers. That's a separate journalistic function, quite different from news reporting. What is critical is never to confuse or contaminate fact with opinion within news stories — always to separate news and opinion.

Perhaps the most worrying cancer in journalism today is the idea that the news business is show business. Too often some news organizations give priority to theatricality over substance. That's a particular danger for television and tabloids in their frantic search for greater ratings and readership. But when "show business" takes over news, the emphasis is on entertaining, not on informing and enlightening.

Journalism today is a "hot profession." It has graduated from the rafish irresponsibility of the fedora-and-trenchcoat days of *The Front Page* to the zealous crusading of the post-Watergate era. But the over-glamorizing of investigative reportage has often led to its own kind of journalistic irresponsibility.

Investigative reportage can be journalism at its finest when done with thoroughness, accuracy, and fairness. But too many try quickie investigative journalism on the cheap. Because of pressure from editors for a scoop, or under their own pressures for instant fame, promotion, and money, some reporters commit journalistic felony. In their self-indulgence, they embezzle from the bank of journalistic credibility by unscrupulous or careless or lazy reporting.

Take, as an example, Janet Cooke of the Washington *Post*, a talented young reporter who fabricated a story brilliant enough to win, temporarily, a Pulitzer Prize. Apologies cannot make up the harm such incidents have done to the credibility of journalism as a whole.

Too many ambitious young reporters are attracted to the "new journalism" that seems to put more weight on assertion than on evidence, and puts a premium on impressionistic and cynical reporting rather than on the plodding, detailed work of true investigation.

There is a great deal of talk about the need for objectivity in journalism. I happen to think objectivity is impossible to achieve because we all are products of our various backgrounds and environments.

But what must be done is to strive continually for it, to put aside, as much as possible, our prejudices, our most passionate likes and dislikes. In other words, I suppose, simply to be fair.

I also believe news people must develop a healthy skepticism, but must stop short of cynicism. Skepticism is necessary for an inquiring mind; cynicism is a malign prejudgment.

Finally, there is the major ethical problem for reporters: When does the public's right to know conflict with the equally fundamental right in a democracy to privacy and a fair trial? Conflict it certainly does, and unhappily there is not a clear-cut formula for when the right to know overrides the right to privacy. In my own judgment, however, it does so rarely.

Every time the conflict arises, reporters and editors should ask themselves if the story is important, relevant, and fair. It's a judgment call, but one based on the highest sense of professionalism, not on prurient curiosity intended to titillate.

The media hold a mirror up to society, but do so selectively. We have to recognize that the very raising of the mirror will change the character of the event or issue, by intensifying it, glamorizing it, or denigrating it. We're not giving truth a fair chance if we are adversaries, if we sensationalize, if we're shallow. Too many of us do not look deeply enough for the nuances and subtleties of complex situations.

I've spent a good many years in radio, television, wire-services, and newspaper newsrooms, and I know practice does not always measure up to good intentions. It likely never will, given the constraints of time, space, and human frailty. But what is important is that we have those good intentions and strive to achieve them. I can think of no occupation that performs a higher public service than serving the public's need to know. The very survival of democracy itself depends on how well the journalist performs that service.

— Knowlton Nash
Reader's Digest
February 1982

EXPLORING IDEAS

1. Comment on the following statement:
"I can think of no occupation that performs a higher public service than serving the public's need to know. The very survival of democracy itself depends on how well the journalist performs that service."
2. Evaluate Mr. Nash's "code of ethics" for journalists. Rank each item in his code in order of its importance to you personally. Explain and support your priority list in a class discussion.
3. Share your views on the following statement:
"Those in authority must be able to cope with sometimes cantankerous, sometimes obstinate media, so the country can preserve the greater values of freedom of expression and the right of people to know."
4. ***(a)*** To what extent do you agree with Mr. Nash that it is impossible for journalists to be objective?
(b) In your judgment, is the goal he suggests journalists strive for an acceptable compromise? Explain your opinions.

INVESTIGATING THE MEDIA

1. Do we need more "good vibe" news stories? Survey a variety of news media. What is the ratio of "good vibe" to "bad vibe" stories? Is there a balance? Are both types of story given equal prominence in the news? Prepare a visual presentation in which you outline your observations and conclusions on this issue.
2. *"The 'new journalism'... seems to put more weight on assertion than on evidence, and puts a premium on impressionistic and cynical reporting...."*

   How valid is this claim? Survey a variety of news media. In the news stories you evaluate, how much hard, factual evidence have journalists used to substantiate general statements? How do they use language to create a specific tone or impression? Prepare a report based on your findings.
3. Create a portfolio of news stories that are controversial, in your view. Prepare an oral presentation explaining why you think the stories are controversial. Include your own ideas about how the stories should have been handled.

YOUR TURN

1. *"Without credibility we have nothing."* Write an article or an editorial in which you explore the issue of the public's — and your personal — trust in the press.
2. Use cut-and-paste techniques to create both an "all good news" and an "all bad news" newspaper. Test market your two products; which newspaper did people prefer, and why? Write a report based on your findings.
3. What implications lie behind the suggestion made by Mr. Eaton that *"newspapers must provide a more positive content, or advertisers [will] stop putting ads in the papers"*? Present your ideas in the form of an editorial or article.
4. Script and present a segment of a news program prepared by a news team that obviously wants to inject more "good vibes" into the news. Use items from newspapers and magazines as sources for the items used in your telecast.
5. *"...viewers have a responsibility to hold the media to account."* Write your views on a story which you think was not properly presented.

Ann Medina is one of Canada's leading TV journalists, having worked as both a foreign correspondent and news anchor. Writer Robert Collison explains what makes her tick.

Ann Medina TV Foreign Correspondent

When CTV journalist Clark Todd and two American network crews were reported missing in Lebanon in 1983, Ann Medina was also on assignment in Beirut. She is arguably the finest example in the country of a new breed of journalists who have become heirs to a glorious if gory tradition — the war correspondent. She covers wars and revolutions, coups d'état, and states of siege. Whereas in the past there were only a handful of female war reporters, today there is a legion of women dodging bullets in combat zones around the world. Journalistically, women like Ann Medina are on the cutting edge of world politics, and she recognizes it. "Doing this job, you're bearing witness to history in the truest sense."

She has reported on the plight of the Palestinians on the West Bank, the blood feud between the Druze Moslems and the Christian Phalange in Lebanon, the civil war between the Sandinista regime and the U.S.-backed Contra counterrevolutionaries in Nicaragua, and the Marcos regime in the Philippines. In all these documentaries, she has demonstrated a talent for making today's great geopolitical conflicts understandable in human terms. Caught in the crossfire between warring ideologies and religions are average women, men, and children, and Medina's reportage seems particularly committed to telling their stories: "I try to get out of the capitals and avoid just seeing officials. I want to see how fighting affects the people."

As with many good journalists, Medina's reporting possesses a studied dispassion. "I believe that you present information to the viewers so they can draw their own conclusions." But good journalists always carefully monitor their own sympathies. And often, this depends on the "filters" through which they perceive the world. This is especially important for foreign correspondents, who frequently find themselves reporting political conflicts that pit the privileged against the dispossessed. When asked, Medina quickly admits that she is a member of the Establishment. ("Anybody who makes a certain amount of money is, I suppose. You can't get any more 'Establishment' than the CBC.") But she rejects the idea that she is powerful. "I live off the government."

The temptation to be outraged by the insanity of politics in such places as Lebanon or Manila is as much a hazard of the trade as a sniper's bullet. "Of course, I get *personally* angry sometimes," says Medina. "But if it ever gets into my work, it's time to quit. I've been accused of being pro-Palestinian by the Israelis and pro-Israeli by the Palestinians." Moreover, she is rather proud of the accusations; they seem, to her, to be a testament to her objectivity.

Unlike most of her Canadian colleagues, Ann Medina's career began with the American networks, which, she believes, explains the common perception of her as intensely competitive. "The big difference between the U.S. and Canada is that people here aren't always looking over their shoulders. In the U.S., if you come back without a story or you miss something another network has, then you're in trouble."

Stamina is an important asset in the field, and her own physical resilience surprises Medina as much as anybody. "I don't exercise. I smoke too much. I'm over 40. Most of the guys at least jog. Not me. But on the road, whatever energy you have goes into the story."

All of Ann Medina's colleagues agree that she has a great talent for acquiring information in volatile situations. According to producer John Scully, "Ann has a way of making people feel relaxed. They trust her."

To Ann Medina, it's just a question of making human contact. "You exchange confidences. You tell them something about yourself; they tell you something about themselves." Humor is a key weapon in her "people skills" arsenal.

— Robert Collison
Chatelaine
February 1984

Volatile situation — Ann Medina on assignment during Israeli pullback from Lebanon, September 1983

EXPLORING IDEAS

1. ***(a)*** Working with a partner, use the information in the article to develop a profile of a truly professional journalist.
   (b) Discuss which points in the profile matter to you most as a consumer of news. Compare your conclusions with those of other students.
2. *"I believe that you present information to the viewers so they can draw their own conclusions. But good journalists always carefully monitor their own sympathies. And often, this depends on the filters through which they perceive the world."* What types of "filters" might affect the objectivity of journalists?
3. *"Of course I get personally angry sometimes. But if it ever gets into my work, it's time to quit."* What is your reaction to this statement? How much personal emotion, if any, should news reporters convey in their reports?

YOUR TURN

1. Would *you* want to be a war correspondent? As a foreign correspondent, what aspects of war would you concentrate on in your reports? How, do you think, would you be affected personally over the years? Respond to some or all of these questions in your journal.

TELE-VISION JOURNAL-ISM

"The news, like everything else on television, is packaged like a show and therefore the first principle is not to have anything on the news that is not instantly interesting. Television does open a window to the world, but it is a very peculiar world. It is a world in which there are no connections between one thing and another. Each story has nothing to do with any other. Everything is very fragmented and discontinuous. As a result, Americans know of many things but they know about very little."

— Neil Postman

The medium of television presents some unique challenges in presenting the news. The following selections examine how this medium "massages" the news message.

A 1986 survey reported some interesting facts concerning how the public views each of the mass media as a source of news and other information.

Canadians favor TV for news, poll says

Reliance on television as a source of information and news has increased among Canadians in the past 15 years, according to a poll by Environics Research Group Ltd.

In the 1986 poll, 69 per cent of those responding said they relied on TV for national news, up from 48 per cent reported in a 1969 Senate report on the mass media.

For international news, 66 per cent said they relied on TV compared with 56 per cent in 1969, and for local news, the figures were 41 per cent compared with 25 per cent.

Nineteen per cent said they relied on newspapers for national news, down from 29 per cent in 1969; 20 per cent for international news, down from 24 per cent; and 34 per cent for local news, compared with 39 per cent.

The Environics study found that Canadians see newspapers as the most serious medium, television as the most entertaining and exciting, and radio as the most soothing and relaxing.

Although TV had a slight edge over newspapers as "open and frank, informative, believable and honest" in reporting news, both were seen equally as helpful and useful.

But television was clearly considered the most provocative, with 51 per cent saying that TV was more upsetting. Only 19 per cent regarded newspapers as more upsetting.

— Rudy Platiel
The Globe and Mail
January 30, 1987

EXPLORING IDEAS

1. ***(a)*** How did the results of your class survey of news sources ("You and the Media") compare with the findings of the Environics poll? Suggest reasons for any differences.
   (b) What are the advantages and disadvantages of television in comparison with the other media as a news source?
2. Why, do you think, do Canadians consider TV the most "provocative" or "upsetting" form? To what extent do *you* see TV news as provocative? Explain.
3. What reasons might account for the decline in popularity of newspapers as more consumers come to rely on TV for their daily news diet?

Morris Wolfe declares that "anyone who relies on both print and the electronic media for information can have little doubt about the very real limitations of TV news."

Can TV "tell the truth"? If you're undecided, Mr. Wolfe's article may help you judge the credibility of the "electronic news gatherers."

Can TV Tell the Truth?

According to polls, people believe what they see on TV newscasts far more than what they read in the papers. That's an astonishing statistic. What it reveals is that the majority of people don't read much, certainly not much news. Because anyone who relies on both print *and* the electronic media for information can have little doubt about the very real limitations of TV news.

First, there are severe limitations of space. The entire text of *The National*, for example, which runs twenty-two minutes, fills only about half a page of *The Globe and Mail*. Individual items are rarely longer than two or three minutes or perhaps 300 to 400 words. Try to say something substantial on a subject you know something about in so little space. Usually, items are much shorter, particularly if it's a story — however important — that's not inherently visual. Anyone interested in the details of the Reichmann brothers' takeover of Gulf Canada wouldn't find them on TV. Television still hasn't learned how to do business and economic stories well. For most stories, TV provides little more than a headline service.

Then there are the structural limitations of the medium. Watching the news on TV is different from reading a newspaper. A good newspaper contains several hundred items. ("All the news that's fit to print," says *The New York Times*.) One can choose to read, skim, or ignore as many or as few items as one wishes. The same freedom isn't there on TV. The viewer is locked into the dozen or so items that have been selected by a lineup editor and the order he or she has chosen to put them in. The first story on almost all newscasts as I write is the major league baseball strike. South Africa has temporarily been relegated to second place. There's no way the TV viewer can skip the baseball story as the newspaper reader can. Ultimately, we're told, television will offer viewers the same kind of freedom that newspaper readers have. We'll be able to plug into only the items we want, but that is still a long way off.

And there's another important structural difference between TV news stories and newspaper stories. A newspaper story is not only longer and contains more facts, it's also more untidy than a TV story and in that sense it's more true-to-life. A good newspaper story starts with the most important facts and observations and trails off into less important details. The assumption of the writer and the editor is that most people aren't going to read the whole piece. A TV news story, on the other hand, is a neat, dramatically structured package with a clear introduction, body, and conclusion and few, if any, loose ends. If there's something a bit inconclusive about the typical newspaper story, there's something too certain about the TV news story.

Because of brevity, structure, and the large numbers of people involved in putting a story together, TV news demands of us an even greater suspension of disbelief than do newspapers. The print story, as *Toronto Life* publisher and former CBC executive Peter Herrndorf suggests, "has a built-in detector." One can go back and reread portions of the text to make sure that a point has been clearly made. Unless one's using a videocassette player, it's impossible to do that with television. What it all comes down to on TV is the credibility of the reporter — we have to trust that he or she has *fairly* (after all, only objects can be objective) reduced a story to its essentials.

The good TV reporter has to be able, as reporter and anchorman for *The Journal* Bill Cameron says, "to tell us quickly what the point is." And that, adds Herrndorf, makes the television reporter's job more difficult than that of the print reporter. It requires *more* expertise, not less. Obviously we can't know what footage the TV reporter hasn't used any more than we can know what material the print journalist has chosen to omit. "*All* editing processes," argues former *National* anchorman Knowlton Nash, "are susceptible to manipulation."

But it's not just the editing process we have to worry about with TV. Part of the reason we trust television more than print is that we've been taught to believe that "the camera doesn't lie," that "one picture is worth a thousand words." There's no doubt that pictures *are* far more powerful and direct than words. "It's much easier," Herrndorf points out, "to make a six-hankie TV movie than it is to write a three-hankie magazine article." In that sense, TV is inherently more manipulative than print. Writer and broadcaster Warner Troyer has written that "Unless directed by an incompetent, a close-up lens is a truth machine." Knowlton Nash reminds me that TV destroyed Joseph McCarthy; it did what print couldn't do. At the same time, we know that we don't always see what we're told we're seeing on TV.

Television can manipulate us in other ways. We know that events are stage managed by the various interest groups who compete with one another for snippets of air time. Governments stage press conferences for the camera; people demonstrate or riot for the camera. The IRA holds terrorist funerals — "all berets and gear," says *The Economist* designed

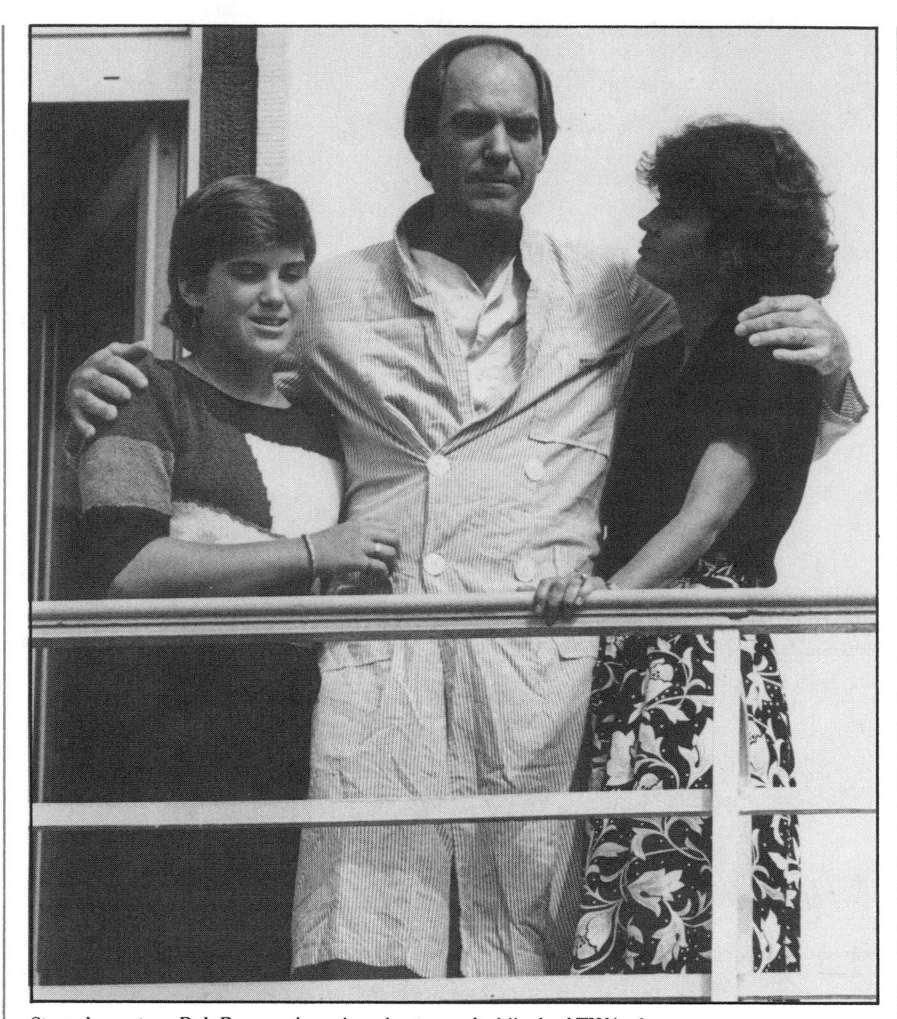

Staged events — Bob Braum, American hostage of a hijacked TWA plane, poses on a hospital balcony with his wife and daughter, who were flown to Frankfurt by NBC.

"to convey the impression of a legitimate army for a legitimate cause." No one can doubt the potential propaganda value of the visual image.

The TV networks, of course, do their own staging of events. In the summer of 1985, NBC flew some hostage families to Frankfurt so they could be taped being reunited with loved ones who'd been on a hijacked TWA plane.

TV news also manipulates us in the sense that it makes us feel that we know more than we do. Its certainty encourages ours. One of the results is that we've become infomaniacs because TV news is oddly reassuring. We're terrified of war, convinced that the world around us is out of control. And with good reason. Serious newspapers and magazines reinforce those fears. But TV news makes us feel we've got a handle on things. So like ravenous Pac-Men we consume more and more TV news and current affairs shows. They become addictive. And the amount of such material available is increasing. I know people who have CNN, the Cable News Network, on in the background all the time. It provides them with Newzak.

Does all the above mean that we shouldn't believe TV? Not at all. Only that we have to be realistic about what TV can and can't do. None of the media has a monopoly on truth. The "truth" comes to us in dribs and drabs from a variety of sources. We need to get whatever we can from as many sources as we can.

There's no doubt that governments are afraid of the power television has to tell the truth. On a number of occasions in the past twenty years they have intervened to prevent material from being seen. In 1965, for instance, the Liberal Party stopped *Mr. Pearson*, a *cinéma vérité* documentary about the prime minister, from being shown on the CBC. Shots of Pearson with his feet up, watching the World Series on television during a crisis, embarrassed his advisors.

On October 15, 1970, a day *before* the War Measures Act was brought in, Peter Trueman, then executive producer of the CBC's national news, was called into his superior's office. In *Smoke & Mirrors*, Trueman recalls: "We were to avoid commentary and speculation of all kinds. We were not to use man-on-the-street interviews or shoot film of any public demonstration. We were to air no panel discussions on the October Crisis and were to avoid reporting speculation, particularly speculation about what the government was doing."

The National, despite its limitations, is the best front page in English Canada. There is no better place to go for a fast overview of the day's news. It would be foolish not to go further — to newspapers, magazines, and other radio and TV programs — and equally foolish not to be skeptical, but *The National* is a useful starting point. Print addict though I am, I wouldn't want to be without it. I want to be able to see the people in the news — the visual component helps fill in the spaces around the words they speak.

Obviously, one needs more than a front page. The best current affairs shows on television — programs such as *Canada AM* and *Question Period* on CTV, the *MacNeil/Lehrer Newshour* on PBS, and *Meet the Press* on NBC — help provide that something more. *The Journal*, which follows *The National* Monday to Friday, reminds us that most stories in the news are far more complicated than TV news alone can tell us.

A documentary item, which is put together over a much longer period of time (the TV news interviewer, after all, has only a few hours to prepare) allows us to see and weigh a multiplicity of points of view. On *The Journal*, a documentary item can run as long as half an hour. On *the fifth estate*, a story can be explored in even more detail; it can run an hour, or occasionally ninety minutes as in the case of the award-winning *Just Another Missing Kid*. And television is slowly becoming better at handling ideas. David Suzuki's *A Planet for the Taking* is an eight-hour TV essay whose point is essentially nonvisual.

So, can TV tell the truth? Yes, but not the whole truth, and it takes sophisticated, vigilant viewers to ensure that it tells as much as it can. The informed citizen clearly needs as much information as possible from as many diverse sources as possible. Schools teach children a little — although not nearly enough — about how to deal with the credibility of print sources. It's time they began teaching about the content and structure of television.

— Morris Wolfe
Toronto Life/ November 1985

EXPLORING IDEAS

1. In your opinion, how can the public ensure that they get "the truth" on important issues?
2. One expert states that *"the television reporter's job is more difficult than that of the print reporter."* Do you agree or disagree? What evidence can you find to support your opinion?
3. *"Even on a slow day, it's the anchor's job to sell the news. If they're lousy pitchmen, the ratings inevitably drop. To some critics, this close identification of the news with those who deliver it smacks of celebrity journalism, with all its sins of speciousness and superficiality. News purists venerate England's old BBC overseas service, where plummy-voiced 'announcers' read the news that 'journalists' wrote. As in so many other things, Canadians have tended to be a hybrid of the American contemporary and classic English styles."*

— Robert Collison
Chatelaine
May 1986

Form small groups to discuss the following issues. Have one member report your group's conclusions to the class.

(a) How would *you* define the term "celebrity journalism"?

(b) Name some TV news anchors who have

become "stars." Examine some of the characteristics that make these women and men so successful.
(c) What are the consequences, both positive and negative, of celebrity journalism? In your view, which better serves the needs of news consumers, the announcer of the "classic English style" or the "American style" of star anchor?

4. As a class, discuss the following:
(a) *"TV is inherently more manipulative than print."* Find evidence in the article and from your own experience of the media to support your views.
(b) *"...governments are afraid of the power television has to tell the truth."* To what extent is this an accurate statement?

5. What examples can you think of to either support or refute the claim that television *"can mobilize us into action in a way that print can't"*? Discuss this issue in a small group, then compare your views with those of other groups.

6. *"...most stories in the news are far more complicated than TV news alone can tell us."*
If this statement is correct, what are its implications for
(a) television journalists?
(b) the public?

INVESTIGATING THE MEDIA

1. How does the form of TV news dictate its content? View an evening newscast, making note of
- the length of time of the total newscast
- the length of each news item
- the subject of each news item
- the format of each news report: introduction by the anchor, on-site report, etc.

Share your observations and conclusions in a class discussion.

2. Conduct the following experiment in your class. Select a major news story that is just beginning to break. Divide the class into three sections; each section is to follow the story through a single source: TV, radio, *or* newspapers. Each member of a section follows the story for one week, and avoids exposure to any other source of news for that week.
At the end of the experiment, hold a class "debriefing" to compare and contrast how the sections experienced the same story in the three different media. Did different students end up with different impressions of the news story? If so, how would you account for this?

3. Is there a difference between Canadian and U.S. news anchors? To find out, form teams and survey news broadcasts on at least one Canadian and one U.S. television network. Prepare a group report in which you compare and evaluate the style, performance, and credibility of the TV news anchors.

4. *"There's no doubt that pictures* are *far more powerful and direct than words."* How important are visuals to television news? Survey a variety of TV newscasts, making note of
- the types of visuals used (still photograph or film clip)
- the frequency with which visuals are used to accompany news items
- the content of the visuals (on-the-spot interviews, action shots, and so on)

Share your observations and conclusions about the importance of visuals to TV news coverage. Discuss their emotional impact and their potential propaganda value.

YOUR TURN

1. Select a news item in a newspaper and adapt it for television news. Following this activity, discuss how the items were altered.

2. Select a short story or poem and adapt a "newsworthy" incident from it for television news. Consider the characters who could be interviewed and the film footage that could be part of the story. Script and tape
- the introduction by the TV anchor
- the reporter's voice-over for the visual footage
- the interviews to be included as part of the item

Media Facts & Techniques

Slanting the News

Whether intentional or not, the news we read, view, and listen to in the mass media is sometimes *slanted* so that a specific impression of an event, issue, or individual is created. In order to be aware of slanting, it is wise to examine some of the ways in which the news we rely on for important information about our world is slanted. The following are "techniques" that can result in slanted news:

Selection: Someone, usually the news editor, must decide which stories from all those available on a given day will be printed or broadcast. What is included — and what is left out — is one way in which news can become slanted. For example: A reporter files a story about a huge, enthusiastic crowd applauding a political leader at a rally. A second reporter files a similar story about a politician from a different political party. The editor selects the first story and chooses *not* to mention the second event. Thus the editor is slanting the news in favour of one individual or party.

The selection of news photos can also result in slanting. Several years ago photojournalists were snapping pictures of Robert Stanfield, then leader of the federal Progressive Conservative party, tossing and catching a football. He caught several passes, then dropped one. Newspapers ran the ball-dropping photo, not the pictures of the successful catches. Some observers claim that this slanted coverage contributed to the negative image the public formed of Mr. Stanfield.

The necessity of attracting audiences and advertisers may contribute to slant in our news. The news may be overloaded with stories of crime, corruption, and so on in an attempt to make it more interesting or exciting. Over-emphasizing "bad news" is a form of slanting because it creates an inaccurate impression of what is happening in the nation or the community.

Coverage: In a newspaper, the amount of space given to a story, the headline used to identify it, and the page it is printed on all affect the amount of attention people pay to it. A story printed on page one of the first section is likely to be read by more people than a story on page five. Therefore, the news may be slanted simply through the position it is assigned in the newspaper. The same is true on radio and television. Audiences are likely to pay more attention to the first two or three items in a broadcast or to those stories given the most air time.

Creating News: The minute someone decides to publish or broadcast a story it becomes news. An event that may not have attracted much attention suddenly becomes important. Journalists and editors are aware of the power they have to "create" news, and choose items carefully.

Today, this creating of news has gone one step further, resulting in the *media event*: a news event that is staged. Organizers of such events woo the press with the promise of a spectacle. Critics accuse politicians in particular of staging media events, but anyone can do it — with a little media know-how. Though many media events are relatively harmless, acts of terrorism such as hostage-taking and hijacking have been staged as a form of media event, complete with news conferences, letters to the media, and videotaped statements — all designed to draw attention to an issue or cause. Although such potentially tragic events may be seen as genuinely newsworthy, the media must consider to what extent their coverage *becomes* the story.

Language: The actual words journalists use in telling their stories can directly influence the public's perceptions of an individual or event. For example, if a journalist chooses to describe a group as "terrorists" as opposed to "freedom-fighters," or labels a gathering a "mob" rather than a "crowd," she or he can slant a story to create a very definite, negative image in the reader's mind.

By employing connotative adjectives such as "feisty," "fanatical," "helpless," "courageous," "loud-mouthed," "well-known," "futile," and so on, a writer can slant a story. Responsible journalists understand the distinction between adding words and detail for colour, and using words to sensationalize or distort a story.

Reprinted with permission: Tribune Media Services

CHARLIE

Reprinted with permission: Tribune Media Services

INVESTIGATING THE MEDIA

1. ***(a)*** Which of the following headlines do you consider slanted? Explain why.
   (b) Rewrite those headlines you think are slanted so that they appear more objective. Do the reverse with those you consider objective. Compare your versions with those of your classmates.

Bitter war of words erupts as PM fends off opposition

Teacher strike closes schools for 15 700

Grant cutback puts squeeze on medical science

PM accuses opposition of operating 'in gutter'

Better service top priority
Tory postal boss declares

A scorecard needed for PM's crises

Reagan plots response to Tower report

2. Collect examples of slanted news photos. In a class discussion, explain
   (a) why you consider the photo an example of slanting,
   (b) what impact the photo would likely have on public opinion.
3. Form small groups to investigate how news is reported.
   (a) Bring samples of a variety of newspapers to class:
   - Scan the first section of the papers and select one major story as your focus.
   - Compare the coverage of the story in different papers in terms of the headlines, amount of space devoted to the story, and the position given.
   - Read the different versions of the story and compare the details that are included.
   - Compare the news photos accompanying the story. What impressions are created by the pictures?

   (b) Check the editorial page. Are there any cartoons or written commentaries about the story you have chosen? Compare how editors and cartoonists in the different newspapers respond to the story.

   Evaluate the information collected by your group. Describe and explain any evidence of slanted news coverage you may have discovered. What impressions of the story are given in different newspapers? Did every paper present the same impression? Present your findings and conclusions to the class.

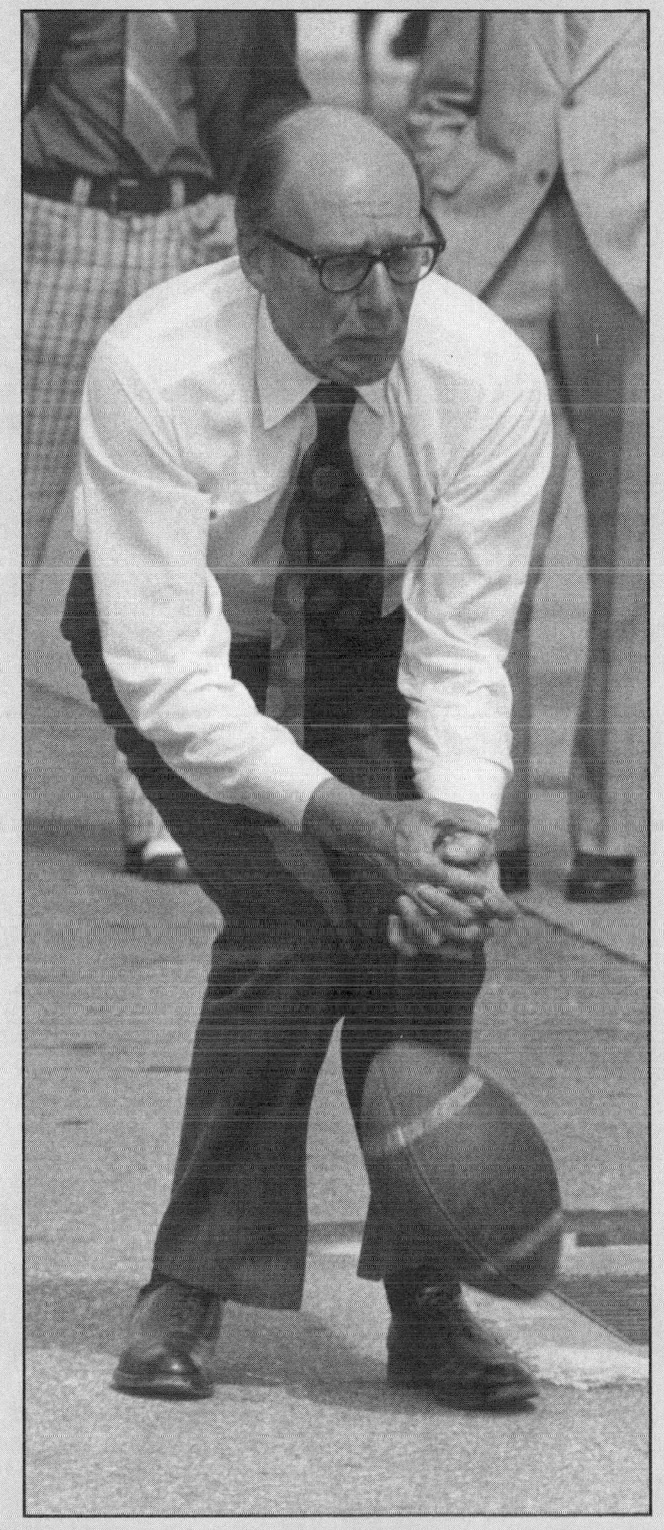

Former federal Progressive Conservative leader Robert Stanfield — Newspapers chose to run this photo, although Stanfield had also made several successful catches.

Federal Liberal leader John Turner in charge of the grill at a fund-raising picnic — How might this news photo affect Turner's image?

YOUR TURN

1. Use the poem "The Man Who Finds His Son Has Become a Thief" — or another literature selection — as the basis for creating *three* news stories. One story should have a slant favouring the father (or one character), another should favour the son (or another character). The third story should be as objective as you can make it. Describe the photograph you would use with each version.

The Man Who Finds
His Son Has Become a Thief

Coming into the store at first angry
at the accusation, believing
the word of his boy who has told him,
I didn't steal anything, honest...

Then becoming calmer, seeing that anger
won't help in the business, listening patiently
as the other's evidence unfolds, so painfully slow.

Then seeing gradually that evidence
almost as if slowly tightening around the neck
of his son, at first circumstantial, then gathering
 damage,
until there's present guilt's sure odour
seeping into the mind, laying its poison.

Suddenly feeling sick and alone and afraid, as if
an unseen hand had slapped him in the face
for no reason whatsoever; wanting to get out
into the street, the night, the darkness, anywhere to
 hide the pain that must show to these strangers,
 the fear.

It must be like this.
It could not be otherwise.

— *Raymond Souster*

2. Watch some investigative news programs such as *W5*, *60 Minutes*, *20/20*, and *the fifth estate*, making notes on how the issues are presented.

Using the style and format of one of these programs, prepare a report on an issue of concern to your school or community.

Following your presentation, have your classmates comment on the fairness and accuracy of the report. Discuss any problems you may have encountered in trying to accurately and fairly present all sides of the issue.

THE RIGHT TO KNOW

Freedom of the press to investigate and report is one of the most cherished values in our society. But should that freedom be unlimited? The articles in the next section examine instances when the public's "right to know" clashes with other rights — an individual's right to privacy, for example, or the right to a fair trial.

"The truth takes a little longer to come out."
—Ted Koppel, ABC News

"Questioning is an important part of what we do. It's really our function. The skepticism, the unwillingness to take things at face value. It's how the system works."
—Bill Plante, CBS News

In "Cleopatra and the Messenger," Knowlton Nash commented that "...the over-glamorizing of investigative reportage has often led to its own kind of journalistic irresponsibility." In the following interview, Bob Woodward defends the techniques of "in-depth journalism."

The honorable tradition of not naming names

The Watergate scandal of the early 1970s rocked the United States, ousted Richard Nixon from the presidency, and made heroes of two young reporters from *The Washington Post*, Bob Woodward and Carl Bernstein, who were credited with spearheading the investigation. Their books, *All the President's Men* and *The Final Days*, rode the best-seller lists for months and were followed by a popular movie with Robert Redford and Dustin Hoffman as the "Woodstein" team. But the journalistic technique of Woodward and Bernstein — where the identity of many key sources is not divulged — is the subject of some controversy. Toronto writer Terry Poulton spoke with Woodward about the ethics of not naming names.

Maclean's: What is the journalistic legacy of the Watergate investigation?
Woodward: Well, a lot of people think the legacy is tons of investigative reporting, reporters out of control, digging around looking for dirt on everyone. That has just not turned out to be the case. There's too little investigative reporting — I really don't like that term — too little in-depth reporting. People still do the quick and dirty, the press conference, instead of going around talking to everyone and getting a real sense of what's going on.

Maclean's: Why don't you like the term investigative reporting?
Woodward: Well, it sounds like you *have* to find wrongdoing. I don't think reporters should ever be sent out to find wrongdoing. I think they should be sent out to obtain a description of whatever is really happening.

Maclean's: How would you describe the style of journalism that you and Bernstein began?
Woodward: You mean not naming sources? We didn't begin it. It's got a long and honorable tradition. A lot of journalists in America in the 1930s were doing it. When Franklin Roosevelt tried to pack the Supreme Court, for example, Joe Alsop, who later became one of the best-known columnists in America, and Turner Catledge, who became editor of *The New York Times*, wrote a book together using exactly the same style we used in *The Final Days* and *The Brethren*. There's a fiction in journalism that if something's on the record, the journalist has really done a good job or gotten to the meat of the matter. But, in fact, if somebody's lying on the record, as so many public officials do, it's no good, it's invalid. It's actually much riskier to write something not naming the sources. If you go to people and say, "Listen, I'm not going to name you as the one telling the true story but I *am* going to check it and verify it and see if I can document it," you're serving the consumers of your product much better because you have a better chance of giving them the truth. But when your source's version turns out to be contrary to what people are saying on the official record, you're putting your professional reputation on the line. So it's not easy; it's much harder. The idea that there's something cavalier or that it's on the cheap to not name sources is totally backwards.

Bob Woodward — His reporting exposed corruption in the U.S. Presidency.

Maclean's: But isn't telling a source that he or she will not be named just giving them carte blanche to be slanderous?
Woodward: No, because you're going to go back and beat them over the head if what they say doesn't check out. You make that very clear. So it doesn't give them an opportunity to be slanderous — it gives them an opportunity to tell what's really going on.

Maclean's: How can you possibly verify information from these secret sources?
Woodward: The same way police reporters do every day. You find out who else is involved. If it's an allegation of wrongdoing or improper behavior against somebody, you go to that person and ask them to give their side. It's very easy, very basic, but it takes more time.

Maclean's: Have there ever been any real gems of information that you felt certain were true but could not verify?
Woodward: All sorts of things that one person saw — they saw this, they witnessed that — but others denied and we couldn't use. I'll give you one example because it didn't involve wrongdoing. It's a terrific story but I'm not sure it's true. The day before Nixon resigned, when he was obviously emotionally charged and distraught, he got up in the middle of the night and said he was going for a walk. He ordered the Secret Service not to follow him. He just walked out of the White House gate and they lost him. It was the night they lost the president of the United States! A couple of hours later, he walked back in and they never found out where he'd been. Now I don't know whether that's true or not. Somebody who was in a position to know, and whom I trust, said it happened. But we never used it in a book or article.

Maclean's: Are you ever going to reveal the identity of the key, secret source in the Watergate case?
Woodward: Traditionally, this kind of thing does not come out for a long time. I remember talking recently to Pierre Salinger, who was Jack Kennedy's press secretary. I asked him to name the six most devastating leaks during the Kennedy presidency and whether he knew the sources of any of them. And he said, "No, but even now, 15 or more years later, I'd give my right arm to know." This kind of information just does not come out. And as a journalist I protect it because confidential sources are really our lifeline to a better version of the truth than that provided by the normal public-relations apparatus of government.

Maclean's: Why are you still working in daily journalism?
Woodward: My feeling is that we don't find out what really happens that often. I remember listening to Senator Frank Church, who headed the investigation into intelligence

Reprinted with permission: Edd Uluschak

agencies in the U.S. a number of years ago. He was giving a speech and he said, "The truth always comes out. We can feel very confident that we will always learn what's at the bottom of the barrel." As a practising journalist, I think he's wrong. In fact, disclosure is rare, not something we can count on. There is no department of truth. Besides, I think being a journalist is the best job there is.

— Terry Poulton
Maclean's
June 9, 1980

EXPLORING IDEAS

1. How would you define "investigative journalism"? In your view, what would be the difference between this kind of reporting and a report on a robbery or the marriage of royalty?
2. Discuss the following issues in small groups: *"Investigative reporting costs money, makes enemies, and causes lawsuits. It may bring rewards in prestige, and it may make the news staff happy, but it is risky, costly, and unpopular with most newspaper proprietors."*

   — Walter Stewart
   Canadian Newspapers, the Inside Story

   (a) What are some of the drawbacks or problems with investigative journalism from the point of view of (i) the publisher, (ii) the editor, (iii) the reporter, (iv) the advertiser?

   (b) How much freedom should reporters have in "uncovering news"? How far should they be allowed to go as they search for the truth?

   (c) How do you react to information in a news report that is credited to an "unnamed source"? Why?

   Does the addition of "reliable source" change the way you view such information? Explain why or why not.

YOUR TURN

1. Are you satisfied with Bob Woodward's defense of a journalist's use of unnamed sources? On occasion, attempts have been made to force reporters to reveal their sources, and some have been threatened with jail for refusing to do so. Under what circumstances, if any, do *you* think journalists should have to name their sources?

   Respond to these questions in your journal and share what you write with a partner.

Over the years the media's reporting of incidents from the private lives of politicians has helped shape the electorate's perceptions of how fit these politicians are to carry out their public roles. Such reportage poses a fundamental problem: where do we draw the line between the public's right to know and the politician's right to privacy?

Canada's Crucible

Between 1959 and 1960 Pierre Sévigny, associate defence minister in John Diefenbaker's Conservative cabinet, had an affair with a woman identified privately by the RCMP as a prostitute and a security risk. When Diefenbaker found out, he reprimanded Sévigny, but kept him in the cabinet. The story did not surface for five years. On November 29, 1984, Robert Coates, defence minister in Brian Mulroney's Conservative cabinet, visited a cabaret in West Germany where he chatted with a stripper and bought her drinks. When Mulroney found out about the incident on January 22, 1985, he said he assured himself that there had been no security breach. But when the Ottawa *Citizen* broke the story on February 12, the Prime Minister accepted Coates's resignation.

Ethics: In the star-crossed political fortunes of Coates and Sévigny lies the measure of how unforgiving public life in Canada has become during the last quarter-century. Says Arnie Patterson, a former press secretary to Pierre Trudeau and now a Halifax broadcaster: "Things have changed dramatically in the past 20 years. Nothing is private. I don't think it's a bad thing."

In fact, whether the issue is sexual morality specifically or the broader question of ethics, Canadian public life has clearly become a high-temperature crucible. A more aggressive press — possibly becoming even more aggressive in the aftermath of the scandal surrounding former Senator Gary Hart — pursues perceived and imagined peccadillos, from the use of government aircraft for private purposes to the size of the Prime Minister's clothes closets. Among the media's favorite targets: former New Brunswick Premier Richard Hatfield, acquitted in 1985 on a charge of marijuana possession, whose free-wheeling private life has long been a subject of intense speculation.

In part, the media's sharper focus may be the result of the declining calibre of political candidates. Says Vancouver lawyer Alexander Macdonald, former attorney general of British Columbia: "There is a general lowering of standards today, in terms of truth-telling, pork-barrelling, and the financial side." But the more able, qualified candidates hesitate to join the political circus.

Gossip: Fifteen years ago, recalls Sinclair Stevens, the former Mulroney cabinet minister forced to resign amid conflict-of-interest allegations, "there used to be an understanding of decency. There were all kinds of stories about Trudeau's personal life, but newspapers chose not to print them. I am convinced today they would." According to Stevens, the media's appetite for gossip is larger now. And he says, "If you look hard enough, presumably you can find something on any politician."

Still, many observers contend that the Canadian press corps seldom looks hard enough — remaining a timid shadow of its American and British cousins. Indeed, despite constant rumors about marital strains between Pierre and Margaret Trudeau in the mid-1970s, Canadian newspapers largely avoided the subject and its possible influence on affairs of state — until British journalist Robin Leach broke the story in *People* magazine in March, 1977. One Canadian who did broach the subject, Vancouver *Sun* columnist Marjorie Nichols, wrote a column on how Margaret's behavior might affect the prime minister. When the *Sun*'s editors told her it was not, as she put it, an "acceptable topic for comment," Nichols threatened to resign. The piece was published — in the paper's back pages.

Ottawa, of course, has always been a town where politicians, their aides, and journalists worked hard, played late — and kept the hottest stories out of the news. In the 1970s one prominent Tory MP discovered his wife was having an affair with a caucus colleague. The wife of a prominent Liberal MP left town for a vacation with another man. With alcohol and ice readily available in MPs' offices, after-hours socializing often turned into ribald parties. On one occasion, an MP was seen running down a corridor near his office wearing nothing but a towel. From alcoholic binges to adultery, those stories and the names of their participants have seldom, if ever, been published.

Security: In terms of sexual scandal, no Canadian story rivals the Sévigny-Munsigner saga, which rocked Parliament Hill on March 4, 1966. That was the day Liberal Justice Minister Lucien Cardin, angered by Conservative needling in the Commons over security leaks, invited Diefenbaker to tell the House all he knew about "the Monsignor case." Subsequent disclosures made it clear that ministers in the previous Tory government had kept company with German-born Gerda Munsinger, an alleged prostitute and security risk. The Tories said that she had died, but six days later the *Toronto Daily Star*'s Robert Reguly found Munsinger, then 37, living in Munich. Her lurid revelations enthralled the nation and led to a royal commission that subsequently criticized Diefenbaker's leniency, but found no security breach.

Trial by media? — Former New Brunswick Premier Richard Hatfield answers questions about marijuana found in his luggage.

Nor, apparently, was there any breach of security involved in Robert Coates's brief visit to the Tiffany cabaret near the Canadian Forces base in Lahr, West Germany. There, in November, 1984, Coates bought several drinks for a stripper named Micki O'Neill. Within hours of the media's discovery of the event, Coates resigned as defence minister and retreated to the obscurity of the Tory backbench.

Even now, say some observers, the extracurricular habits of some Canadian politicians are routinely and discreetly ignored. Says the *Sun*'s Nichols: "We accord our political leaders incredible privacy. We do have a duty to report more than we do."

Other observers maintain that in the absence of conduct that may be illegal, the press and the public must carefully decide where to draw the line of due scrutiny. According to Richard Emberley, president of Omnifacts Research Ltd., a Halifax-based polling company, "The line comes at the point where exposure of the information is in the public good. The fact that Brian Mulroney is the proud possessor of 85 pairs of Gucci shoes, from where I sit, does not either inhibit or enhance his ability to do his job."

Truth: What matters most to the public, says Jack Davis, minister of energy, mines and petroleum resources in B.C. Premier William Vander Zalm's Socred government, is telling the truth. "Lying is the greatest sin. If you're discovered lying, you're dead." In 1978 Davis himself admitted to converting first-class government airline tickets to economy fare and pocketing the difference. Davis credits his subsequent comeback to the fact that he told the truth.

The question now is what impact the Hart affair will have on reporters — and politicians. For better or worse, many observers say that Canadian reporting will become more aggressive — despite more stringent Canadian libel laws. Says Nichols: "This is all evolutionary — the matter of standards and the matter of law. These things are set by precedent, and there is going to be a spin-off effect." Like Gary Hart, some Canadian politicians may find themselves caught in the spin.

— Michael Posner
Maclean's
May 8, 1987

EXPLORING IDEAS

Each of the following quotations deals with some aspect of the issue of political scandal, the media, and the public. Read the items, then form small groups to discuss the questions that accompany them.

1. *"The contemporary public wisdom is that anything goes. Personally, I question that. If the past or present life of a public figure has a direct bearing on the performance of his or her job, then it seems to me to be perfectly legitimate and even necessary to report it. If it has no bearing, however, and is only an interesting curiosity, then I think it becomes a judgment as to whether or not the public interest is served by its revelation, and a matter of good taste. With the seemingly insatiable public curiosity about the personal lives of public figures, I suspect I'm fighting a losing battle."*

   — Knowlton Nash
   History on the Run, 1984

   (a) Do you agree that the press should ignore the behaviour of politicians unless that behaviour has a direct bearing on their performance? Explain.
   (b) What factors might make it difficult for journalists to follow Mr. Nash's guidelines?

2. *"We do not inquire into the sex life of surgeons who operate on us, bankers who keep our money, or editors on whom we rely for our information needs. Surely some relevance to something must be established to say we should in the case of politicians.*

   The police do not routinely stake out homes on the basis of anonymous information from persons whose motives may be financial gain, personal notoriety, or political vengeance; they need reasonable and probable cause to believe something of a criminal nature may be occurring. An extramarital affair is not that; it does not lead to the criminal courts, although it may to the divorce courts, where it is a private matter between two persons. The picture of the media, in trenchcoats in the shadows, playing divorce detective on the hypocritical excuse of the public's right to know all, is unappetizing."

   — George Bain
   Maclean's
   May 25, 1987

   What is your opinion about the rights to privacy of politicians? Should politicians have the same right to personal privacy as bankers and surgeons? Support your views.

3. *"Regardless of where politicians run, they must realize that the press will seek to expose their blemishes, and the public wants to read about them. If they fail to understand that, then they likely lack the judgment – indeed, perhaps the desire – to be in politics at all."*

   — Bob Hepburn
   "Gary Hart and the private lives of politicians"
   Toronto Star, May 7, 1987

   (a) Do you agree? If so, what type of "blemishes" should be exposed by the press?
   (b) What effect might this approach have on good candidates running for office?

4. *"Using the private aspects of a politician's personal life as a standard for judging how well the individual will perform in government is not necessarily a healthy development."*

   Do you agree? If not, what standards should be used for judging a candidate's fitness for office?

INVESTIGATING THE MEDIA

1. *"The fact that Brian Mulroney is the proud possessor of 85 pairs of Gucci shoes, from where I sit, does not either inhibit or enhance his ability to do his job."*
   (a) Examine news reports about political figures for personal facts that do not relate to how he or she does the job. Discuss these facts in class and whether or not they should have been reported.
   (b) Compare reports in different newspapers. Do different papers use different standards in reporting on the private lives of politicians?

YOUR TURN

1. *"...the press and the public must carefully decide where to draw the line of scrutiny. The line comes at the point where exposure of the information is in the public good."*

   Respond to this statement in an editorial. How would *you* define information that is in "the public good"? In other words, what does the public have a right to know about their politicians?

> *"... militants have shown impressive TV savvy... they know the size of the U.S. prime-time audience and are masters at staging media events."*
>
> — Arlie Schardt et al., "T.V.: Held Hostage?" *Newsweek* December 24, 1979

> *"... when news media make deals to interview terrorist fugitives the news organizations become 'accomplices.'"*
>
> — Robert Oakley, Acting Ambassador-at-Large, U.S. State Department's counter-terrorism section

Does media coverage actually encourage terrorism? Are the media manipulated by terrorists? Should governments and media organizations work together to establish a set of guidelines for responsible reporting of acts of terrorism?

Terrorism & Television

As television technology fast-forwards to the year 2000, the most compelling form of drama on TV — live coverage of international news events, and terrorist attacks in particular — is escalating right along with it.

Thanks to advanced video technology, instantaneous satellite links, and the increasing attention international news is getting from the networks, viewers are literally able to watch terrorist attacks unfold, whether it's a hostage-taking incident in Tehran, a hijacked ocean liner in the Mediterranean, or a one-man embassy takeover attempt in our nation's capital. "Terrorist attacks are like big Hollywood productions," says Yoram Hamizrachi, a retired Israeli army colonel and counterterrorist who's now the director of Strategic Planning Associates, International Division, a Winnipeg firm that monitors international terrorism. "Look at the most popular shows on TV; many of them are based on violence, whether it's police or detective stories. In the case of TV coverage of terrorism, you have a situation where suddenly the *A-Team* is not a joke, it's a reality. You have good guys, bad guys, and innocent victims — except, this is for real."

Cases in point: 1985's TV coverage of the hijacking of TWA flight 847 en route to Beirut, or the takeover of the Italian cruise ship Achille Lauro in the Mediterranean. In the TWA affair, American networks came dangerously close to legitimizing the Shiite Moslem skyjackers by allowing them to be interviewed on live broadcasts: "It was a classic example of the media playing into the hands of terrorists," says Hamizrachi, "and it was deliberate. Terrorists know how to use television to their best advantage. For example, they'll take video footage of hostages and send the cassettes to local TV stations, knowing that they will immediately broadcast it. It has happened in Lebanon, Italy and West Germany, and in America, during the Patricia Hearst case."

Of course, terrorism's most sought-after venue is the international news scene. Unfortunately, the terrorist is fully cognizant of a sure-fire way to commandeer the 6 p.m. news: Involve innocent victims. In some cases, the terrorist attack, as a TV event, is able to grab and sustain global media attention for indefinite periods of time — as in the hostage-taking and murder of Israeli athletes at the '72 Munich Olympics, or the 1979 hostage crisis in Iran, which went on for 444 days. But terrorists have their TV flops as well, such as the botched takeover of the Achille Lauro. Because TV cameras were not on board the ship, communications between the terrorists and the news media were strictly limited.

Libyan leader Moammar Khadafy — He became upset when the media didn't give the kind of coverage he wanted.

Like television coverage, terrorism has made quantum leaps in recent years. These days, a successful terrorist is one who knows how to get the best possible media coverage for his particular plan of action. "Any sensible criminal knows, 'I want to get attention, I grab a hostage,' " says Joseph Scanlon, director of the Emergency Communications Research Unit at Carleton University in Ottawa. "Acts by criminals who call themselves terrorists are publicity stunts — that's what happened in Ottawa."

Scanlon is referring to an incident in which an armed individual took some hostages at the Bahamian High Commission in Ottawa. While the incident, which ended with the safe release of all hostages, may seem small potatoes in comparison with international terrorist attacks, the perpetrator still knew the value of good coverage: He phoned local TV and radio stations immediately after the takeover and almost instantly became the lead news item on early evening newscasts across the country. "Everybody got caught in that one," said David Nayman, a senior producer for CBC's *The National*. "It was a live situation where the man was asking for his message to be conveyed by the media, and he was therefore using the media as part of his overall negotiating tactics."

Meanwhile, south of the border, American networks are locked in a dogfight to get the best coverage of terrorist attacks for the evening news. "The TV news people are much more aggressive in the U.S. than in Canada," says Hamizrachi. "Many Canadian stations don't cover international terrorism on the spot; they rely on U.S. and international network feeds. Each station goes after the best coverage of the attacks, because that's what the people want to see."

Although Canadian networks are often relegated to using American footage of international news events, including terrorist attacks, they do their best to keep a watchful eye on creeping American sentiment. "The American networks report from a purely American perspective," says Nayman, "and when Americans are being held hostage, the focus of their coverage dramatically crystallizes around them. At *The National*, we don't necessarily care about a story about *Americans* being held hostage; we care about the fact that *people* are being held hostage."

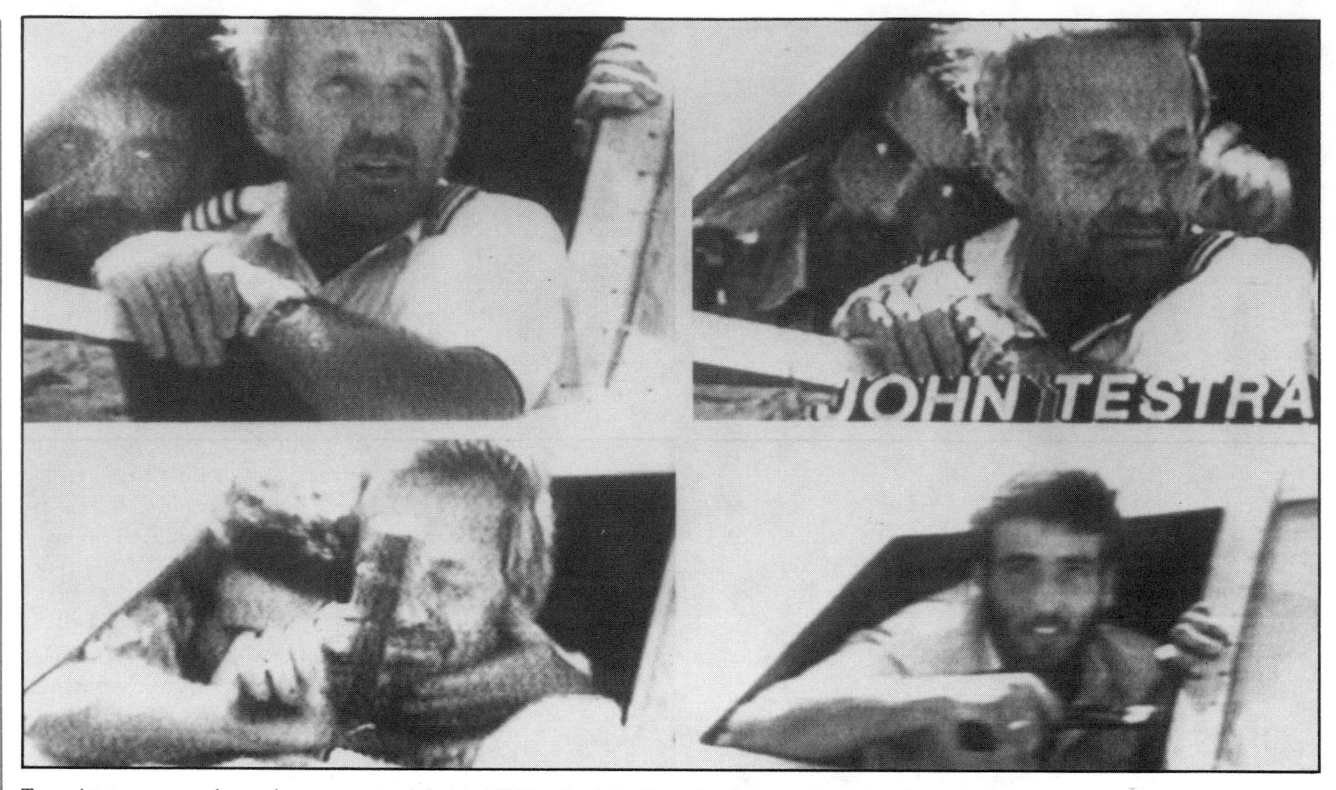

Terrorist stage managing — A gunman stands behind TWA pilot John Testrake during an interview from the hijacked plane (*top left*). The terrorist ends the interview (*top right*); he waves a gun in front of the pilot and grabs him (*bottom left*); then tells the ABC news crew to leave (*bottom right*).

In the U.S. networks' never-ending quest for higher ratings, though, they sometimes stretch the boundary between informing the public and giving terrorists free air time. NBC News drew public scorn for making a deal with Palestinian terrorist Abul Abbas for an interview on NBC *Nightly News.* (Abbas got a life sentence — in absentia — for his role in masterminding the Achille Lauro affair.) "It is essential that we know who our enemies are and what we are up against," said NBC News president Larry Grossman shortly after the affair came to light. "Ignorance and censorship that shield people from even the most distasteful information are no service to a democratic society." Robert B. Oakley, Acting Ambassador-at-Large for Counter-Terrorism at the U.S. State Department unit, called the deal — which allowed Abbas to maintain the secrecy of his whereabouts — "reprehensible," and charged NBC with acting as an "accomplice" to terrorism. Adds Nayman: "They [NBC] obviously got a lot of negative publicity for what they did, but I'd be willing to bet that the other networks were more upset about the fact that *they* weren't the ones to track down Abbas and get the interview."

A step toward more responsible coverage of terrorist attacks — at least in Canada — was taken recently when then-solicitor general Perrin Beatty announced that the federal government would be establishing guidelines for the media in covering terrorist attacks. At the press conference, in which Beatty also announced the creation of a 49-member Special Emergency Response Team (SERT) to deal with terrorist attacks, Beatty accused terrorists of using the media to spread their message: "In this context, terrorism becomes a tragic form of guerrilla theatre, in which the media audience and not the immediate victims are the ultimate target..." Beatty also announced that his department would be meeting with media heads "to reconcile the demands of a free press with the protection of public safety in times of crisis."

On occasion, though, the media will refuse to play the terrorists' game, such as during the military skirmish between Libya and the U.S. Libyan leader Moammar Khadafy, whom the U.S. suspects of backing terrorist activities in Europe and the Middle East, provided the international news media with stage-managed "guided tours" of damaged sites — only to kick them out two weeks later amid rumors of an impending coup. "They didn't give Khadafy the kind of coverage he wanted," says Hamizrachi. "The U.S. networks had learned from the 1979 hostage crisis in Iran, when the so-called revolutionary guards and the Khomcini regime used the Western media to the limit. This time, they were more cautious and professional. They knew they had to work very carefully, and not just to film whatever the Libyans wanted them to, so Khadafy was fed up with them and told them to leave the country. When the media decides not to play the game, the tyrants are angry."

Unfortunately, there's no easy solution to either the terrorist attacks or the media's vulnerability in covering such events. "If you don't cover it, research suggests an escalation," says Scanlon. "The so-called terrorists will just do something to the point where you can't ignore them. These are sick people who have figured out in a disturbed way that the best way to get attention is to do something brutal, and the media will be compelled to focus on it."

It's axiomatic, though, that the panting public *wants* to see coverage — live and as it happens — of terrorist activities. "People like to sit at home with a beer and watch the disasters of the world unfold on their little screen — where it's safe," says Hamizrachi. "If you have one minute on the news to cover the events in Lebanon, what do you show? A peaceful Lebanese village? Or fighting in Beirut? It's the dilemma of the media — but they know what the public wants to see."

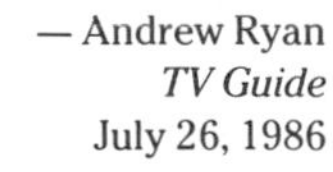

— Andrew Ryan
TV Guide
July 26, 1986

Five hostages of TWA hijacking are forced by their captors to give a "press conference."

TWA drama comes to a close—More media coverage as the liberated hostages return to the U.S.

New media guidelines urged for coverage of terrorist acts

The federal government and representatives of the media should negotiate national guidelines relating to news coverage of terrorist incidents, a Senate committee recommends.

The committee, in a 151-page report, says in the past there have been instances where television coverage of terrorist acts in Canada have endangered lives or hampered police activities.

Chairman Senator William Kelly said that during live coverage in 1985 of a takeover by three Armenian terrorists of the Turkish embassy, the deployment and location of emergency task force members was shown on TV.

"It didn't result in the death of the ambassador. It didn't result in the picking off of the members of the emergency response team," Kelly told a news conference. "But it could have."

The report says there have been other instances where the media have phoned terrorists involved in hostage-taking incidents. Still, the committee rejected calling for legislation to restrict media coverage of terrorist incidents.

"We think police and the media should think through how they act together," Kelly said. "It's foolish to think the media shouldn't be anywhere around. That is unreal, they are going to be."

The committee says to achieve its objectives the police have an obligation to take and enforce whatever steps they deem necessary within the law to secure the situation as quickly as possible.

"The most practical and effective way to minimize media intrusion or inadvertence is for police to take immediate action to restrict the media's physical access to the scene," the report says.

But the report also criticizes police and says they could help alleviate some of the difficulties by keeping the media informed.

— David Vienneau
Toronto Star
July 31, 1987

EXPLORING IDEAS

1. In small groups, evaluate the pros and cons of continued media coverage of terrorist acts.
2. As a class, develop a set of guidelines for how the police and the media should act together in handling terrorist activities.
3. Some analysts see a link between fictionalized violence in regular TV programs and media coverage of terrorist activity. Discuss this connection.

"I wouldn't print that," you may say if you see a newspaper item that seems to cause unnecessary injury or insult. But wouldn't you? The next article invites you to test your own judgment on these news stories.

You Be the Editor

Not long ago, *The Toronto Star* reported that a woman had been severely beaten and robbed leaving work one evening. It was another example of rising street crime and the *Star* printed it routinely, mentioning her name, her injuries, the street where she lived, and the fact that her assailant was still at large.

The article prompted her employer to write us. He said the woman lived in an apartment on a short street, and the information we published might enable her attacker to track her down, to ensure that she would not testify against him.

All newspaper editors agonize over what they publish. Is the story accurate? Is it fair? Does the public need to know this? Should newspapers manage the news for worthwhile social goals, or should we limit ourselves simply to telling readers what's going on?

The answers are not easy, but you judge us every day on what we decide. Almost certainly, at some time, you say to yourself: *If I were the editor, I wouldn't print that.*

But wouldn't you? After reviewing the information

available and weighing its importance, where would you draw the line between the public's need to know and possible harm to an individual?

We invite you to sit in the editor's chair and decide in each of the following hypothetical cases what you would do. Then compare your choices with those made by the *Star*'s readers and a panel of editors.

CASE 1

The 19-year-old son of a well-known politician who has taken a hard line against drugs is arrested for possession of a small amount of marijuana.

a) Would you run a story on the arrest?
b) Would you run the story if the arrest were for selling a pound of marijuana?
c) Would you run the story if the arrest were for using cocaine?

CASE 2

The newspaper has documentary evidence that a man regarded as a pillar of the community has stolen $50 000 from a charity he heads. You alone have the story and no charges have been laid. The man, contacted by the newspaper, promises to make full restitution and urges you not to print the story because his wife is in hospital after a serious heart attack. He says he is afraid public disclosure of what he has done could kill her.

a) Would you run the story now?
b) Wait until you've talked to the doctors and know that the woman is out of immediate danger, then run the story?
c) Give the man a chance to make restitution and, if he does, write nothing?

CASE 3

A businessman gives $10 million to a university to build a domed stadium. While checking his background for a profile, you learn the man was arrested at age 18 for armed robbery. He was given a suspended sentence, and his record has since been spotless.

The man refuses to talk about the incident and says that he never told even his closet friends. He threatens to withdraw his contribution to the university if you print the story. University officials urge you to write nothing.

a) Would you print a story containing details of the arrest as one element of the overall profile?
b) Hold off on the arrest information until the university has the money?
c) Decide the arrest information isn't relevant and discard it?

CASE 4

A woman teller thwarts a robber, but the robbers escape. The bank manager asks you not to identify the woman, fearing she might suffer reprisals.

a) Would you follow your usual style of carrying full name, age, and address?
b) Use only her name but no address?
c) Omit the name and describe her only as a teller?

CASE 5

A group of professional house burglars has moved into your city. Police say the burglars are reading your paper, particularly the obituaries and wedding announcements, to select their victims among people who will not be at home. Police ask you to discontinue these articles for several weeks, saying this will force the gang to move to another town.

a) Would you continue present practices?
b) Eliminate street addresses?
c) Comply with the police request and write a story explaining the purpose of the new policy?

• • •

After the *Star* published the questionnaire, it received 589 detailed responses from readers. It also had a panel of 21 editors answer the questions. There are, of course, no "right" or "wrong" answers, and sincere and thoughtful people can disagree on how they would handle each one. Here, in response to each question, are the percentages of readers and editors who said yes:

		Readers	Editors
Case 1	a)	54	71
	b)	78	90
	c)	67	81
Case 2	a)	22	62
	b)	45	33
	c)	30	0
Case 3	a)	4	10
	b)	3	0
	c)	93	90
Case 4	a)	1	5
	b)	6	38
	c)	92	57
Case 5	a)	15	52
	b)	41	29
	c)	40	19

John Miller, senior deputy managing editor of the *Star*, explained how he would handle each case:

Case 1: I don't print it. We wouldn't run a story about someone else arrested for possessing a small amount of marijuana, and the fact that the suspect's father is prominent doesn't justify it. How responsible is a father for the behavior of his 19-year-old son?

Questions b) and c) are more serious and we normally publish reports of this kind — trafficking, because it affects other people and is a graver crime in law; cocaine, because such offenses usually result in jail or fines.

Case 2: I run the story. The man is in a position of public trust and he violated it. I'd forewarn the doctors and let them protect his wife.

Case 3: The youthful arrest is irrelevant, and the light sentence indicates mitigating circumstances. I don't publish the information about the arrest, but I make sure the story I do print deals only with the businessman's current character. A detailed look at his rise to prominence would be misleading without mentioning how he rebounded from the arrest.

Case 4: I describe the woman only as a teller. She's probably the only witness to the identity of the suspects and I'd protect her. Lack of a name wouldn't detract from the credibility of the story if the details of her actions were described.

Case 5: Because they are important news, I continue to print wedding and death notices as before. Our announcements normally contain no addresses. But I'd also print a story about the burglars' method as a warning to readers.

— John Miller
Reader's Digest
February 1986

EXPLORING IDEAS

1. ***(a)*** Form small groups. Each group will select one of the five cases for discussion.
(b) Select one member of your group to act as Editor-in-Chief. This person will listen to all points of view raised at the meeting and make the final decision — one of the three choices listed below each case.
(c) Role-play the discussion that might take place at an editorial meeting. Consider the issues connected with your case and the consequences of each choice listed.
(d) Present your decision to the class. Then, take a class poll using the same three choices. Compare your class's responses with those of the readers who responded to the article.

INVESTIGATING THE MEDIA

1. The four news items on pages 229-232 describe situations that challenge the freedom of the press. Divide the class into groups. Each group should assume responsibility for reading one of the articles and presenting it to the class in the form of a panel discussion.

The following guidelines will help you organize a panel discussion:
- Select one member of the group to act as a panel moderator. This person will lead the panel discussion and direct questions to individual panel members.
- Identify the issue raised in the article.
- Summarize the arguments related to the issue that are presented in the article.
- Explore the issue as a group. What additional arguments can you think of that relate to the issue? Consider possibilities beyond the specific situation in the article by asking, "What would happen if...?"
- Be prepared to respond to questions from the rest of the class and to defend your point of view.

Trial by media

It's a dilemma news editors face every day.

Should they publish the names of people accused of crimes before innocence or guilt is established? Does the public's right to know jeopardize the accused's right to a fair trial?

"The toughest day in the life of my client is the day he's charged. It can never get worse after what the media does, with the picture on the front page," said Toronto lawyer Eddie Greenspan in an open forum on the subject of trial by media.

Greenspan's fellow panelist, Darlene Lawson, executive director of the Elizabeth Fry Society, agreed. But Alan Borovoy of the Canadian Civil Liberties Association, CITY-TV news director Gord Haines, and Toronto *Star* publisher Beland Honderich favored publication of an accused's name.

"It's a fact that anybody charged with a criminal offence, that when he's acquitted he lives with the damnation of acquittal because of what (the media) does," Greenspan argued.

He said it is not unusual to see a person accused of murder referred to as "the killer" in press reports before a trial has even begun.

The media can and does influence justice, Greenspan warned. "The common way juries are influenced is through the publication of highly damaging information which under the rules of our judicial system should never reach the minds of the jurors," he said.

Greenspan believes the solution is for the media to get together with lawyers and police to adopt voluntary restraints when covering a trial and to not name the person charged until the trial is over.

Honderich argued that any kind of muzzling of the press would inevitably lead to abuses of civil rights by governments and the police.

"Publicity is the very soul of justice and secrecy its most serious enemy," said Honderich.

If police were allowed to withhold the names of arrested people and the press was not allowed to print them, "Would this not open the door to a wide range of injustices including unlawful arrest or arbitrary search?" asked Honderich.

CITY-TV's Haines said publicity was the key to a free and democratic society. It gives the public access to enough information to allow them to make decisions involving their safety, he said.

"If you have a neighbor who is charged with committing an offence, be it child molesting, murder or whatever, it is a serious offence you have a right to know. That doesn't mean the person is guilty but it does mean you might want to keep an eye on your children until the matter is dealt with in court," said Haines.

Borovoy argued that most newspapers don't publish evidence that could be harmful to a person on trial.

Protecting someone from embarrassment is not nearly as important as "the right of the public to know who is charged at the time they're charged, which is at least one of a number of ways the public can monitor the integrity of the administration of justice," he said.

— John Paton
Toronto Sun
October 15, 1983

Star blasted for story of murderer

A Welland, Ontario, woman picked up *The Star* from her doorstep as usual one morning last week and received a shock that loosed a flood of bitter memories.

The first thing the Welland mother saw was a front-page picture of the woman convicted of helping to murder her father-in-law eight years ago.

Her anger rose as she read the story of Daryl Newstead Dollan and her studies in prison leading to a Queen's University arts degree in religion.

At the time of her capture with her boyfriend, Daryl Dollan, in 1978, was described as one half of a Bonnie and Clyde pair that had left behind a trail of abductions and shootings.

She was convicted of second-degree murder after her boyfriend shot a farmer in his Thessalon farm home. She is eligible for parole from her life sentence in 1988.

The story of the shootings and the trial was told at length in the news columns of *The Star*. The two were hastily married so neither could testify against the other in any appeal hearings and, when they were safely behind prison bars, their story lost its interest.

While in the Kingston Prison for Women, Daryl Newstead Dollan became interested in religion.

As it happens, Queen's University has an education program for inmates, and she enrolled in religion courses. This fall, she earned her arts degree.

A university official notified the newspapers that an inmate was about to graduate from a Queen's course — the first woman and possiby the first inmate to complete such a course in Canada while in custody.

Reporter Stan Josey went to Kingston for an interview with the "inmate." It was not until he and other reporters talked to her that they were aware of who she was. She brought the subject up herself.

Josey's story appeared on the front page along with a picture of the inmate-student. The headline read: *Murderer first to earn a degree in prison.*

The university official who runs the educational program for inmates was enthusiastic in his description of how Daryl Newstead Dollan worked on her degree while under a life sentence.

"It is really quite an accomplishment when you consider where she came from and where she has been," he told reporters.

Reading about this in her Welland home, the murder victim's daughter-in-law was incensed. She wrote a letter to the editor of *The Star* that morning.

It said in part: "This is the woman who helped murder my father-in-law. So she has found religion and earned herself a degree. Why didn't she do that eight years ago instead of destroying our family?

"She will walk the streets again; my father-in-law won't.

"She gets her education paid for by us. People on the outside who want an education have to work hard and pay for it. All she had to do was kill someone.

Daryl Newstead Dollan, the first woman to earn a university degree while in a Canadian federal penitentiary

"Is it fair now for *The Star* to make her out a hero? My mother-in-law and the family were put through hell eight years ago. That article will put her and all of us through it again."

An Etobicoke reader's letter to the editor criticized the "laudatory tone" of the story, saying the prisoner-graduate got a free ride to a degree and suggesting the sole newsworthy element was the Canadian taxpayers' "total support" to educating a convicted murderer.

I disagree. The story had a legitimate news angle. It did not play down the killing that led to Newstead Dollan's education; in fact, her criminal past was a major factor of the article.

It is not easy to address the complaint because she writes from a background of tragedy and no one who hasn't been there can claim to understand how she feels.

But the story must be placed in perspective. Newspapers rarely write about prisons except when someone either enters or escapes from one.

This was an example of what the system says it is trying to accomplish: Making a person better, not worse, for the stay behind bars.

— Rod Goodman
The Toronto Star
November 8, 1986

Reporter broke law to expose security flaws, Crosbie says

Justice Minister John Crosbie meets the press in 1986.

A CBC television reporter was "in clear breach of the law" when he exposed security flaws at Montreal's Mirabel and Dorval airports, Justice Minister John Crosbie says.

"A person went through security with a concealed weapon," he told reporters yesterday. "He brought along his own camera to make sure it had all the evidence and therefore they have to be responsible for the consequences."

Bertrand de la Grange was ordered to appear in court May 12, 1986, on a charge of causing mischief by delaying a flight earlier that April. The maximum penalty for the offence is five years in jail.

On April 4, 1986, de la Grange, accompanied by a camera crew, got a suitcase containing a starter's pistol through a metal detector at Dorval without arousing the suspicion of security personnel. He then carried the gun into the boarding area.

At Mirabel, de la Grange boarded a plane with a pistol and a package that resembled dynamite before he alerted authorities and got off the aircraft. His April 8 report on French and English television prompted the government to tighten airport security across the country.

Liberal justice critic Robert Kaplan suggested in the House of Commons that, because de la Grange had performed a public service that could lead to the saving of many lives, Crosbie should order the charges dropped.

Crosbie refused, and outside the Commons said reporters should be treated no differently than anyone else if they break the law.

He admitted, however, that he could change his mind if he receives a formal request from de la Grange to do so.

In September, Crosbie reversed himself and decided to order charges dropped against Richard Price, a former civil servant who leaked a secret federal report.

Kaplan told reporters that, because Price and de la Grange acted in the public interest, they should be treated the same.

"If it wasn't for de la Grange, the airport security system would be the same way it was," he told reporters. "His actions may have saved lives."

But Crosbie said security would have been tightened anyway because of the American attack on Libya.

— David Vienneau
The Toronto Star
April 22, 1986

Mounties question ethics of interview with B.C. escaper

VANCOUVER — When a television reporter was offered an interview with a prison escaper, should he have struck a deal and met the man or told the police where to find him?

That question was being asked yesterday as police continued hunting for eight men, all considered dangerous, who were among the 13 that escaped from the Lower Mainland Correctional Centre on New Year's Day.

At the same time, Attorney-General Brian Smith ordered a judicial inquiry into the escape from the jail, better known as Oakalla.

A judge, who was to be named today, "will have as his duties to find out the causes of the prison break, whether the staffing was adequate, whether the conditions and the safety and security were adequate, and to make recommendations so it won't happen again," Smith said.

The inquiry is expected to begin in a week or two.

Four of the inmates who overpowered two guards with homemade weapons were arrested quickly, three in a bar and another at his mother's house in Chilliwack.

Yesterday, Stephen John Gray, 23, charged with break and enter, was found crouching in a closet in a Burnaby apartment.

Among the eight who have eluded the police is 23-year-old Terry Hall, who was serving three years for armed robbery. He appeared on BCTV, British Columbia's largest television network, in interviews aired Saturday and Sunday.

Hall approached the provincial network through an intermediary and agreed to do an interview with reporter Alyn Edwards if the network promised not to call the police.

It kept the promise.

Royal Canadian Mounted Police called the action "morally wrong" but decided yesterday that they would not charge the network.

Hall had promised to give himself up yesterday, but by late in the day he was still on the loose.

I suppose you could say they were damned if they do or damned if they don't," RCMP Inspector Bob Bryam said. "You either want a story or you throw it away and in this case they wanted the story.

"But they could have done the interview and then called us. By not calling us we feel they could have been charged with aiding and abetting a fugitive. We feel they were morally obligated to call the police."

That accusation was dismissed by Cameron Bell, BCTV's news director, who said there never was any question of calling the police. He said the larger question was getting out information to his viewers from Hall, who spoke of deplorable conditions in the 76-year-old institution.

"The far greater good was served by getting that information out."

And if someone is injured or killed in the recapture of Hall?

"That's neither here nor there," Bell said. "We were not instrumental in getting him out, nor are we instrumental in getting him back in."

Bryam said police have been flooded by tips and have come within minutes of capturing some of the other escapers. But he acknowledged the longer they are at large, the more likely it is that they have fled the Vancouver area.

A Canada-wide police alert remains in effect.

— Tim Harper
The Toronto Star
January 5, 1988

Choose from the following or create your own activities and research projects to further investigate "The Public's Right to Know."

1. Investigate and report on the process of gathering and reporting news on television. How are the following decisions reached?
   - Where to send the reporters (that is, which stories will be covered?)
   - How to edit the footage reporters bring in?
   - Which stories will make it into the broadcast and in which order?
   - How much time will each story be allowed?
   - Who writes the script for the anchor?

   What influence does the audience have? the sponsor? the network? the station owner?

   Present your report in written form, or in the form of a photo essay (with text) or a documentary.

2. *"When does the public's right to know conflict with the equally fundamental right in a democracy to privacy and a fair trial?"*

   Research and report on a well-publicized court case that has focused attention on this issue: cases involving Donald Marshall, Susan Nelles, and Richard Hatfield are three examples. If possible, arrange to interview a lawyer and a reporter to ask their views on a specific case and on the general issue.

3. If possible, arrange to attend an event that will be covered by the media: a concert, a political event, a trial, and so on. Take notes during the event, then collect the media reports of the event the next day. In a brief report, compare your observations and impressions of the event with the media coverage. How accurate was it?

4. Arrange to spend a day with a reporter, following her or him on assignment. Take notes and, if possible, pictures. Prepare a report entitled "A Day in the Life of a Reporter."

5. *"The quality and substance of information has diminished. Performance and style take precedence over concept and issues."*

   Find out how valid this statement is. Survey a variety of news media; does the evidence you find support or refute this claim? Write an essay or present an oral report based on your observations, conclusions, and personal judgments.

6. *"Caught in a crossfire of deceit, red tape, censorship and logistics, truth is usually an early casualty in any war."*

   — John Borrell
   TIME
   February 16, 1987

   Investigate the coverage of wars during the last decade or so. Prepare and present a report, dealing especially with the following topics:
   - Should governments suppress facts during a war?
   - Should the press have free access to cover and report battles?
   - How have news correspondents reported on modern wars?

7. What does the public really want? Find out by reading the letters-to-the-editor section in newspapers and newsmagazines over several issues. Present a report that summarizes readers' "darts" and "laurels" — their dissatisfactions and satisfactions — relating to how the news is reported.

8. Arrange an interview with a prominent politician in your community, possibly your local provincial or federal Member of Parliament. What are her or his views on the treatment political issues and politicians receive in the mass media? Use your notes or tape from the interview as the basis for a presentation to your class.

UNIT SIX: IN WHOSE

IMAGE?
UNITED COLORS OF BENETTON.
SPOTS!
AND DAVE'S BOSS IS COMING FOR DINNER! HOW WILL I COPE?!

Each of us has a view of the world: an understanding of what life is all about, and what it should be. What we learn through personal experiences and experiences retold by others shapes and reshapes our world view. Since much of what we learn — consciously and unconsciously — is presented by the media, it is wise to examine carefully the messages the media send.

How much influence do the media have on our views, dreams, and expectations? Are they a major force, or simply one of many influences? For instance, should television be blamed when young people form unrealistic views of the future — or is TV becoming a scapegoat? We can better answer this, and other questions, by analyzing the images of ourselves and our society presented in the mass media.

YOU & THE MEDIA

1 (a) What are *your* expectations of the future? Consider your life in the following areas. In your response journal, briefly indicate what you believe your life will be like at age 30.

- employment
- marriage and family
- material possessions

(b) In your opinion, how are expectations different for males and females — or *are* they different?

(c) Media analysts use the term "media conditioning" to describe the way in which the media shape our behaviour so that we expect certain things from life. In what ways have your expectations been conditioned by the media?

2 What image do you have of major groups in society? Try this word-association activity:
(a) For each word listed in the left-hand column, write down whatever impressions come to mind.
(b) Review what you have written. Try to identify the source for the impressions you have recorded. Indicate whether, in your judgment, they have come primarily from personal experience, the media, or other sources.
(c) What are your conclusions about the influence the media have on the images you have formed of people and their roles in society? Is the influence basically positive or negative?

	Impressions	Source
teachers		
business executives		
police		
homemakers		
lawyers		
doctors		
media personalities		
parents		
secretaries		
senior citizens		

3 Begin a media file and categorize the articles, photos, and ads you collect according to the subject they deal with. For example:

- women
- men
- teenagers
- politicians
- musicians
- senior citizens
- minority groups

Throughout your work in this unit, add to your collection and categories. At some point in the unit, consider:

Is there a particular image that is presented of these groups? If so, what characteristics are often associated with them? Do you believe this is a realistic or fair presentation? How does this image compare with your "real-life" experience with members of these groups?

Share your observations with others in a small-group discussion.

Examine these ads that appeared in Maclean's *magazine in the 1930s, '40s, and '50s. Writer Glen Allen comments that the ads were "like the text they surrounded, an account of a nation in the making, a well-scrubbed, clean-shaven, mobile country all but beseiged by new and more beguiling ornaments...."*

EXPLORING IDEAS

1. In small groups, discuss the images of Canada and Canadians presented in these ads. Consider
   (a) the images of men and women
   (b) the lifestyle presented
   (c) the values presented
2. How do the images presented in the media today differ from those presented here? Discuss the design decisions that shaped the way in which these images are conveyed. What changes are reflected in today's advertisements?

A Canadian gasoline ad from the late 1940s

This Lifebuoy soap ad ran in 1935.

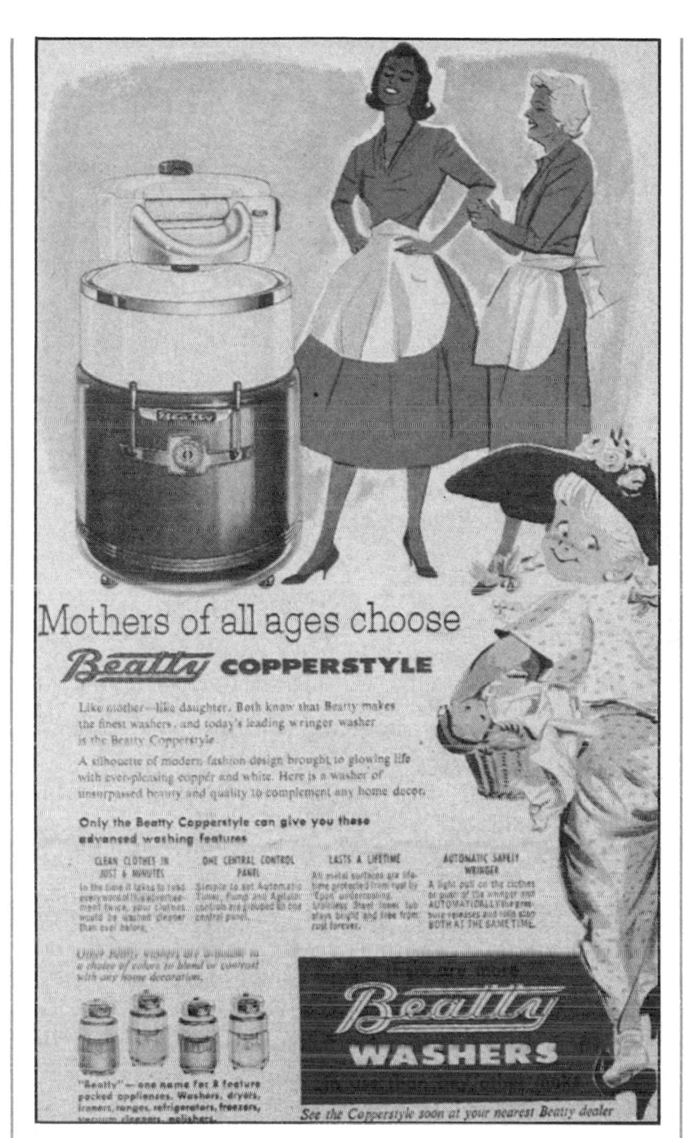

Ads such as 1958 Beatty washer (*above*), 1953 Oldsmobile (*top right*), and 1940 Kellogg's cereal (*bottom right*) reflected "a nation in the making."

THE IMAGE OF MEN & WOMEN

When people are exposed consistently to a single image of what is ideal, they may begin to accept that vision as being true. If we accept that our expectations and behaviour are shaped at least in part by the images presented through the media, then we can appreciate why government agencies and media executives are concerned about the issue of stereotyping in the media.

Advertising agencies are becoming increasingly sensitive to sexism and sex-role stereotyping in their ads. But as Tony Thompson reports, stereotyping is still there — though less pervasive as a result of efforts from all sides.

Advertising's not-so-subtle sexism

In the screening room of a Canadian advertising agency, a clutch of high-powered executives are sitting nervously watching a new TV commercial that will be the linchpin of a $10-million campaign to woo consumers into buying the product. It's the moment of truth; the culmination of months of endless meetings, script conferences, market research by the computerload, film production and editing — a 30-second *Gone With the Wind.*

The sticky hands are not sweating because the client might not like it. The agency team has been involved at every frustrating stage — even hanging around on the shoot, especially if it was at some exotic location. The group's worry is that a seemingly insignificant nuance, a phrase, a camera angle, may crack what they see as the eggshell skin of some women's groups. And if, as a result, the client gets egg in the face, the account would be put in jeopardy.

Over the past three or four years, agencies have become so jittery over the issue of sex-role stereotyping in advertising that they will reshoot a completed commercial — at their own expense. That is a complete turnaround from a decade ago when both advertisers and agencies would chauvinistically respond to complaints with: "It's just a bunch of uppity women. What do we care. As long as it sells the product it's OK. End of discussion."

The industry's concerns are real. Advertising has been on trial since 1979. In that year, a federally financed task force into sex-role stereotyping in advertising was begun by the Canadian Radio-television and Telecommunications Commission (CRTC). When the study was finished in 1982, the CRTC recommended that the industry be per-

1972

1983

1987

mitted to police itself through an industry watchdog, the Advertising Advisory Board (AAB).

As a result, viewers in Canada at least have not been assailed by commercials depicting dippy housewives, doting stay-at-home women, or near-nude females draped over the latest mobile plaything from Detroit. The change — and there is still some debate about whether it has gone far enough — was brought about not by the industry itself but by persistent pressure from women's groups. The early meetings of the task force in the fall of 1979, which brought together advertisers, agencies, the broadcast media, and the public, were described by one public member as acrimonious. The industry feigned shock at suggestions it was sexist and maintained it was not advertising's job to change society in the direction a vocal minority would like to see it changed. Advertising, they said, reflects society the way it is.

Eventually the activists made their point, helped by the threat of civil servants' censorious scissors snipping at advertising copy. But the transformation does not appear to have brought out any new creative genius from the industry. The form has changed, but not the content. "You can look at an ad for a household product that has an almost identical script to one done in the 1950s, but the behavior of the women is more intelligent and more feminine," says Suzanne Keeler, director of public affairs for the industry's AAB. "The presentation and style is different. Now you'll see a toothpaste commercial with two versions: one has the teenage son, the other has a daughter; the mother comes in and gives her approval of the purchase. It's probably all very realistic," says Keeler.

Women's groups generally agree that the worst excesses of the ads the industry called "slice-of-life" have gone. "There's no question there has been some improvement in terms of the dumb housewife stuff and there has been a certain cleaning up," says Judith Posner, a sociology professor at Toronto's York University and a board member of MediaWatch, a nationwide activist group. Still, Posner says that change has been insufficient. "No one expects the ad industry to be social workers, but if we look at the real world where, according to Statistics Canada, women make up 49.4% of the work force, in TV it's more like 13%." The thing that upsets Posner most is what she calls the superwoman. "She's got an attaché case and a Harry Rosen suit, but she's still headcocking at the boardroom table being blatantly seductive — or less blatantly seductive," says Posner. "Some of it (advertising) has gone underground, and that's even worse. It's gotten more insidious, with two or three hidden meanings."

Print and outdoor advertising, over which the CRTC has no jurisdiction, have become the latest target for the activists. After eight years of making "demerits" awards or "raspberry" awards, for what it considered the most sexist promotions, the Quebec Council for the Status of Women found no TV commercials offensive in 1985 but had no trouble in finding three print ads for their annual accolade. The first prize went to Birks Jewellers for a French-language color ad showing a complacent housewife who has just been rewarded by her spouse with a trinket. The text reads: "For all the evenings I spent at the office and she has waited patiently for me at home."

Posner agrees that print has become the main problem. "Women's magazines carry the worst stuff," she says. "Clearly you expect a certain amount of eroticism when it comes to personal products for women. That's OK. I don't mind when they sell a bum when they are selling jeans. But how far do you go?"

Canadian advertisers excuse some of the promotions by saying that "It wasn't our idea. Head office in the U.S. made us do it." Alan Rae, president of Lever Detergents in Canada, asks, "How do you explain to a shareholder in a third country (his parent company, Unilever, is headquartered in London and Rotterdam) that you want to change this because some raving feminists have complained? They turn round and say, 'Hey. This thing is selling. Don't you guys want to make a buck?' " Rae adds: "And whatever you may think about Ring Around the Collar, it happened to be a very successful campaign."

Even the best thing for Unilever's global treasury, though, has to come to an end somewhere, sometime. And it seems that Canada in the 1980s is that place and time. Rae, who spent an uncomfortable time as chairman of the AAB's subcommittee on sex-role stereotyping, says his peers in other countries are beginning to listen. "They are now saying, 'Maybe Canada's got a bit of a leading edge, and it's something we should be aware of in other areas where the company operates.' " Ironically, Rae quit his job as president of Unilever to become president of AAB — now called the Canadian Advertising Foundation — a case of poacher becoming gamekeeper.

The AAB is proud of its achievements, and believes the CRTC will see it the same way and let the industry regulate itself. "As far as I know, Canada is the only country in the world where there is active work with advertisers and agencies to help them change attitudes," says the industry board's Keeler. Indeed, without exception, the presidents of half-a-dozen major Canadian agencies conceded that their clients are extremely sensitive to the issue of sex-role stereotyping, taking the view that "you don't sell someone a product by insulting them." They also say they did not like making the demeaning "slice-of-life" commercials. Their clients say the same. In fact, their memories become a little foggy when they are asked to recall who exactly was responsible for those commercials.

Having cleaned up the act of major advertisers, the AAB's committee has regrouped and is directing its attention to the grassroots level. "Something like 80% of radio and 68% of TV advertising is local," notes Keeler, who adds that "We are finding local stations very responsive."

For the moment, advertisers seem to have eased off on women as stereotypes. Their creative genius has come up with a new target for their "slice-of-life" reflecting society as they believe it is: the Yuppies. "It seems to me," bemoans Ogilvy & Mather Canada Ltd.'s creative director, Tony Houghton, "that in nine out of 10 new commercials you see them (Yuppies). They leap up and down; go jogging; ride bicycles and spend their lives having a heck of a good time being wildly athletic."

Who will be the next group to receive the treatment? With women gradually making their way up the marketing ladder, both as clients and in the agencies, some think it could be men who will be the stock comics or sexual fantasy characters in commercials. "The interesting point is: Are women going to make the same mistake as men have? Are we becoming sexist?" asks Roxanne Labrie, president of the Toronto-based Dick & Labrie ad agency. "Or are men going to think we are?" Perhaps by the turn of the century the only thing that will have changed in ad stereotyping is the gender. As long as it sells the product, the script will not change.

— Tony Thompson
Report on Business Magazine
November 1985

As the baby-boom generation gets older, advertisers and the media will have to cater more to an ever-increasing sector in society: affluent senior citizens. Joan Irwin examines how successfully — and unsuccessfully — the media have employed older people in ads and on TV shows. Are the media ready to respond to "gray power"?

Gray power altering face of television

Credible TV senior — Wilford Brimley (*left*) in *Our House*

The creators of TV commercials sell us everything from political parties to mouthwash. They can persuade us to eat more eggs, drink milk, or get our bodies in shape. But when it comes to making ads aimed at and employing older people they usually stiffen up and go right off the rails.

There are, as always, a few exceptions, among them a gentle gem for McDonald's in which an older man and woman shyly meet and share a table. And the Lottario and SuperLoto commercials seem to irritate some viewers but do have lots of zest and a nice sense of the ridiculous.

But usually the "senior citizen" ads look wooden and the dialogue sounds forced. Or the tone is all wrong, as it is in the commercial for chewing gum for denture wearers in which a belligerent guy who looks like an aging ex-boxer delivers a hard sell like a punch in the face.

The Ontario government didn't do too well, either, in its well-intentioned attempt to counteract the negative stereotyping of older people in a 60-second spot. It was apparently meant to be taken in a spirit of fun, but not all of us saw the humor in the trendy older couple hastily turning themselves into shabby, doddering old fogies because that's apparently what their visiting daughter and her family expected.

The whole ill-conceived family was a pain in the neck, particularly the ridiculous parents who seemed to reinforce all the worst stereotypical aspects of senior citizens instead of demonstrating how inaccurate they are.

It's probably too much to expect that attitudes can be changed in 60 seconds of institutional TV time. It's likely to be far more effective to nudge attitudes in the desired direction through product commercials and programming.

If we can judge by a number of recent magazine and newspaper stories about the graying of North America, we're likely to see moves in this direction in the not-too-distant future. As the numbers of affluent retired people increase, lifestyle commercials, for instance, may include not only tanned young people gathering for a beer after some strenuous sail-boarding, but tanned older couples enjoying a cool glass of something on the 19th hole or waving goodbye as they board a plane for Tahiti.

It's true that the attitudes that need to be changed have little to do with the healthy/wealthy older people and everything to do with the lonely, ailing old folk in shabby rooms and nursing homes. This is the ugly side of aging, the side we don't want to think about because it scares us to death. That's why the senior citizens who do show up in TV programs and commercials so often look

Relic (Robert Clothier) is an independent senior on CBC's *The Beachcombers.*

incredibly fit and buoyant, reassuring us that old age is really a heck of a lot of fun.

But we can't expect television to solve problems that society itself tries to ignore.

The most effective place to begin opening minds and modifying attitudes is in popular drama series, and right now the most credible senior citizen on TV is Wilford Brimley, the grandfather in *Our House*. He has aches and pains that sometimes make him irritable, he can be brutally blunt, and he and his best friend (Gerald S. O'Loughlin) can get pretty cranky with each other on occasion. But they're also wonderfully irreverent and full of affection, and have no doubt contributed enormously to the image, and self-image, of older members of the population.

Robert Clothier's cantankerous and grubby Relic in *The Beachcombers* strikes a blow for uninhibited independence and so, in her own way, did Ruth Springford in *Hangin' In*. Roland Hewgill's grandfather in *Airwaves* showed lots of promise of getting beyond the twinkle-and-quip stage but seldom did, though he was a very strong and appealing presence.

Whether it's the high artifice and flashy style of *The Golden Girls* and the *Cosby* grandparents or the sweet old pair smiling tentatively at each other over a hamburger, the range of older actors and actresses is virtually unlimited and so is their appeal.

It's going to be interesting to see how the look of television changes as the increasing number of healthy, confident senior citizens begin to exercise their power. They're probably not going to be much taken with programs about the down side of aging, but if television is going to be used to change attitudes and improve the acceptance of older people in society, you can bet your boots that the citizens of 60-plus aren't going to tolerate any nonsense about active, tuned-in grandparents pretending to be old fools just to satisfy somebody else's mistaken notion.

— Joan Irwin
The Toronto Star
June 20, 1987

EXPLORING IDEAS

1. Discuss the following as a class. Whenever possible, back up your views with references to specific ads you know.

   (a) How would you define a *stereotype*?

   (b) What are some of the ways in which advertising has stereotyped women? In your opinion, are such stereotypes still common? Are these portrayals realistic? fair?

   (c) *"...advertisers seem to have eased off on women as stereotypes. Their creative genius has come up with a new target for their 'slice-of-life' reflecting society as they believe it is: the Yuppies."*

   Assess the validity of this statement. What other groups or individuals are stereotyped in commercials and ads? How are these people portrayed? Are the portrayals accurate? fair?

   (d) *"Some of it (advertising) has gone underground, and that's even worse. It's gotten more insidious, with two or three hidden meanings."* Evaluate this statement.

2. What is your response to the claim that it is "*not advertising's job to change society in the direction a vocal minority would like to see it changed*"? Comment in your journal.

3. ***(a)*** Share your views on how realistically seniors have been portrayed in advertisements and on television programs.
(b) The increasing numbers of 60-plus citizens "*aren't going to tolerate any nonsense about active, tuned-in grandparents pretending to be old fools just to satisfy somebody else's mistaken notion.*"
Assess this comment. Suggest ways in which the image of older persons must change if the media are to keep up with the "graying of North America."

INVESTIGATING THE MEDIA

1. Form groups to investigate TV commercials and print ads such as those on the following pages. Collect data and comments on topics such as the following:
(a) What image is presented of
    - men?
    - women?
    - children?
    - senior citizens?
    - minority groups?
    - yuppies?
    - other individuals, groups, or professions?

(b) How accurate or fair is each portrayal? Note particularly harmful stereotypes *and* portrayals which you consider realistic, fair, or helpful in changing negative attitudes in society.
(c) Note and comment on specific design decisions and media techniques that help create these images and messages.
(d) How, do you think, would various special-interest or pressure groups respond to each of the portrayals you noted in ***(a)***?

Appoint a representative from your group to present your findings, comments, opinions, and conclusions to the class.

YOUR TURN

1. Compile print ads that you find
(a) offensive because of their stereotyping of some group in society
(b) commendable for their efforts to present people realistically or to help change negative attitudes in society.
As a class, vote on nominations for the "best" or "worst" ads of this year.
As a group or individually, write to one company that produces a product or service featured in your "worst" ads. Write another letter to a company associated with one of your "best" ads. Explain your reasons for admiring or disliking the ads, and offer any suggestions for improvement you may have.

2. Select a print ad you consider stereotyped. Redesign it — both copy and visuals — to eliminate the offensive stereotyping.

3. Create a visual presentation illustrating a common image in print advertising, for example:
    - women: the physical ideal
    - men: the physical ideal
    - images of motherhood/fatherhood
    - the "new male"/the "new female"
    - superkids — hip consumers
    - yuppies: the perfect lifestyle
    - tuned-in seniors — "gray power"

Accompany your presentation with a commentary on any patterns or new trends you have found in advertising.
or
Write a humorous description of "real men" or "real women" as portrayed in advertisements.

THE COLOUR OF

LIFE

ANNOUNCING THE MOST ACCURATE, REALISTIC COLOUR IN PRINT FILM.

NEW KODACOLOR VR-G
THE COLOUR OF LIFE

Kodak Canada Inc.

Kodak. The official film.

When you're expecting company,
everything has to be perfect.

The Fisher-Price Magic Vac is the best way to keep all your housekeeping from feeling like a chore.

It's a lot more fun than Mom's vacuum cleaner. Just as sturdy. And it's a lot easier to use.

The Magic Vac not only looks real, it sounds real, too. It even lights up when you push it. Of course, it must be magic, because it does all of that without any batteries.

The Magic Vac from Fisher-Price®. It's just one of over 300 toys we make that make childhood a little more special.

Fisher-Price

Because you're only young once.

Kristina Koehler
Kindergartner, Age: 5
Quentin Huillard
Nursery Schooler, Age: 3
Living in Hong Kong

I'm only 5, but I've already been to 7 countries in S.E. Asia to swim competitively. I train 6 hours a week and I'm the youngest swimmer they've ever had from Hong Kong. I have an octopus, Elena, that I named for my best friend, and a white and silver rabbit, Lace. We all play in my garden where there are fig trees and mango trees. Quentin and I just met and he started singing to me right away. He could be a writer because he has a big imagination and likes telling funny stories. When I'm older I want to be a woman because I like to go everywhere by myself.

CLAIROL
Nice 'n Easy
CLAIROL
Nice 'n Easy
"Who wants to be someone else? That's what's so great about Nice 'n Easy.* You can make your hair lighter, brighter, deeper, whatever. You just shampoo it in and pouff! It's still you, only better."
You. Only better.

The lady's staying dry.

Lady Speed Stick anti-perspirant does something that no wet and sticky anti-perspirant can do. It glides on fast and dry and keeps you dry all day.

Lady Speed Stick. The same wide stick protection as men's Speed Stick, but it's made especially for you, so it's gentle.

And that's what staying dry is all about.

ALSO IN NEW ALOE FRESH AND SOFT LILAC SCENTS.

lady speed stick® pour femme
Anti-perspirant
Antisudorifique
by/par MENNEN®
SCENTED/PARFUMÉ

PROTECTS YOU LIKE A MAN. TREATS YOU LIKE A WOMAN.

by **MENNEN**®

UNITED COLORS OF BENETTON.
benetton

From Benetton's "United Colors of Benetton" ad campaign

According to the author of the next article, sexism and stereotyping are not limited to advertising. Program content in television is another powerful source of imagery.

Prime Time Women

If prime-time network television in 1986 was "a women's world," as *US News and World Report* observed at the beginning of that year's new season, the question remained: What kind of women, and whose world?

Despite the ever-growing panoply of nontraditional roles for women on TV in recent years, prime-time series continue to rely on clichés, pat formulas, and stereotypes in depicting female characters.

Take Claire Huxtable, for instance. The beautiful wife-mother-attorney on the immensely popular *Cosby Show* has managed to raise five children while pursuing a high-powered career in law. Her husband, an M.D., still finds her wildly sexy after all those years and all those babies; they never appear too tired for a little romance after a hard day at the office. But what's a hard day in the Huxtable household? On one episode Claire's biggest gripe was discovering that the handle on her favorite coffee mug had been broken and sloppily glued back together — not by one of the little darlings, but by her husband, who quelled his wife's irritation with some kissy-face to make it all better again.

Like Claire's coffee mug, the lives of most prime-time women are full of cream and sugar, and short on credibility. Can we really buy the fact that an attorney, distracted by her latest court case, would make a broken mug handle the major issue of her day?

Real women with real concerns are not only in short supply on the small screen: according to an ongoing study of television by sociologists at the Center for Media and Public Affairs (CMPA) in Washington, D.C., there aren't too many behind the scenes either. Television's leading writers, producers, and executives belong to an exclusive club whose membership is 99 per cent male.

It's not that the other one per cent doesn't account for much of what viewers see and hear about women on prime time. Television's off-screen leading ladies include Susan Harris, creator of 1986's big Emmy winner, *The Golden Girls*, who is avowed to be the finest writer in the industry today. Barbara Corday, wife of producer Barney Rosenzweig, with whom she created *Cagney and Lacey*, is now president of Paramount TV. Terry Louise Fisher, co-creator with Steven Bochco (*Hill Street Blues*) of *LA Law*, is now producer of that show. And executive producer Juanita Bartlett (*The Greatest American Hero, Scarecrow and Mrs. King*) was responsible for giving ABC's macho detective series, *Spenser For Hire*, a lighter touch. Yet these women represent only a very few who have managed to break through network management's glass ceiling into higher-paying, decision-making positions in prime-time programming.

Ironically, what management may lack, prime-time shows make up for. The new breed of TV superwomen include working moms, single women with exciting careers, hard-driving lawyers, no-nonsense parole officers — all of whom are largely "stereotypes that exist in the male psyche," says Robert Lichter, co-author of the CMPA study, "From *Lucy* to *Lacey*: Hollywood's Dream Girls." Lichter, along with his wife and CMPA co-director Linda Lichter and Smith University professor Stanley Rothman, examined the personality traits of more than 2000 female characters on prime-time shows over 31 seasons. They concluded that television is presenting viewers with mixed signals about women's roles in contemporary American society.

"Male writers want to make a positive liberal statement about women," Lichter notes, "and so in

1950s TV woman — Lucille Ball (*holding dog*) in *I Love Lucy*

the past decade we've seen lots of shows that reflect a progressive stance on women's issues."

While television has finally caught up with the notion that women can have successful careers and exciting personal lives, the creators of these characters still tend to portray women against a mostly "traditional landscape" of home and family.

The CMPA study, while noting the rising popularity of women stars on prime-time hit series, observes that the majority of TV's female characters are neither stars nor continuing members of the cast. More common are women making one-episode appearances as "housewives, secretaries, and damsels in distress."

Nowhere are significant, three-dimensional roles for women less evident than prime-time drama and action-adventure series. *Miami Vice*, for instance, one of TV's highest-rated shows, regularly casts a bevy of beauties whose actions are usually motivated by some underlying evil. And while Crockett and Tubbs wheel around the city stalking the evil, their female counterparts on the squad can be found back in the word-processing department, or out on the streets posing as prostitutes.

"Women are invisible, irrelevant or victimized," blasted a 1985 report by the National Commission on Working Women, criticizing prime time's make-believe world in which men are in charge.

It is no secret that Hollywood's 'old-boy network" has kept women in their place in TV's creative process. The lack of representation of women in the creation, production, writing, and directing of network television is reflected by employment statistics recently compiled by the Writers Guild of America West (WGAW). Preliminary figures show that of prime-time shows only 13 per cent were created by women; for hour-long shows, women were responsible for 7.5 per cent.

Early employer of women writers — The 1970s *Mary Tyler Moore Show*

Not considering what their exact titles may be (and most likely those begin with "assistant"), less than 300 of the Directors Guild West's 1611 members are women. Less than 5 per cent of all episodes on prime-time television are directed by women.

Carolyn Miller, co-chair of WGAW's Women's Committee, cites a number of programs that have held "a consistently bad record for hiring women writers." *The Fall Guy*, now in syndicated reruns, whose advertisements in *TV Guide* feature actress Heather Thomas in a wetsuit unzipped to her navel, had less than 10 per cent of the credits represented by women. Surprisingly, the highly respected *Hill Street Blues*, whose public defender character Joyce Davenport has been one of the most sober and cool-headed feminists on TV, also had less than 10 per cent of its credits comprised of women over a four-year period.

"It's a matter of economics," says Miller, a television writer and member of the Guild since 1971. When money and power are involved, she points out, women usually get pushed aside.

While women were once regarded by the industry as incapable of writing comedy, that attitude has been extended to action-adventure and drama series, which also happen to be some of TV's most-profitable and highest-paying genres. Only recently have women's names been appearing in the credits of prime-time sitcoms; women writers are most often working in less-profitable, lower-status genres such as daytime soaps and after-school children's specials.

According to WGAW statistics, women writers average 70 cents to every dollar paid to a male writer with similar experience. Should one be lucky enough to have a hit, a male writer will be able to command a higher price than a woman writer for future scripts.

Dixie Carter (*seated*) plays one of four career-oriented *Designing Women*.

"But with the numbers being so inflated, it's hard to complain," says Sherry Coben, creator of CBS' hit series *Kate and Allie*. "When you're being paid $10 000 per show, who's going to argue?"

Coben, whose desire to bring "real" women back to television was inspired by the kind of writing produced by women on the *Mary Tyler Moore Show*, speaks of an industry "dominated by white males in their 50s and 60s" who are out of touch with the kind of characters women viewers can relate to. Coben, who is 33, recalls one show she wrote in which Kate admitted she wanted to have another baby.

"Allie responded, 'I want Mel Gibson.' The producers didn't know who Mel Gibson was," Coben laughs. "I spent a lot of time trying to convince them that Robert Redford and Paul Newman are not who younger women are going for these days."

No longer involved with the show, Coben says she used to have nightmares in which her characters would beg her for help "because the producers were making them do things they didn't want to do."

In relative terms, TV has come a long way since the days of *I Love Lucy* and *Father Knows Best*. There are no more Samantha Stevens (*Bewitched*) and Jeannies (*I Dream Of Jeannie*) clad in Arabian pajama outfits who call upon the supernatural to manipulate their "masters" (although Barbara Eden still puts on that silly costume for special anniversary episodes). Prime-time series no longer serve us a platter of obedient, submissive housewives whose main objectives are getting food on the table for their husbands.

When MTM Productions and Norman Lear first brought viewers a glimpse of more-realistic female characters in the early '70s, prime time finally began addressing contemporary problems women like Mary Richards and Rhoda Morgenstern were facing, such as sexism in the workplace, and juggling career with personal life. Larger social issues became story lines for highly-rated, two-part episodes: Maude was the first to have an abortion while Edith Bunker faced the discovery that she had breast cancer. While critics may have contended that Maude was too bossy, and Edith too batty, these women broke the mold that set up women as foils and props for male stars.

Then, when the stars of *Charlie's Angels* made the cover of TIME magazine in 1976, network executives knew they had a winning formula on their hands: more cleavage, bigger profits. With 23 million Americans tuning in every Wednesday night to the capers of the three lissome undercover detectives, 30-second commercial spots were selling for $100 000 (in 1976 dollars). When Farrah Fawcett's cheesecake bathing-suit poster outsold supermodel Cheryl Tiegs', the age of the pinup girl had finally made it to TV.

Todays nighttime soaps—*Dallas, Dynasty, Falcon Crest, Knots Landing, The Colbys*—espouse that winning formula. The likes of Joan Collins, Linda Evans, and Donna

Mills have proven that sex — albeit over-40 sex — still sells big.

Yet, with the success of *The Cosby Show* and *Family Ties*, more families moved in in *Our House*, ALF, and *Together We Stand*. The female stars of *Jack and Mike, My Sister Sam, Kay O'Brien, Surgeon*, and *Designing Women* were all aggressively career-oriented.

"Women want to watch shows about women," says Coben, who is currently at work on four new pilots. And the more shows that feature women in leading roles the better it is for advertisers, for whom women have always been the primary target.

But whether any of these shows deal with real issues on more than just a superficial level is left up to TV's majority of male producers and writers. And what they know, or pretend to know, about women is very different from what women know about themselves.

"Until more women are in a position of power within the industry," Coben notes, "we won't be seeing more credible female characters on television."

— Jeannie M. Barnett
January 1987

EXPLORING IDEAS

1. Working with a partner, assess the criticisms the author makes of television's prime-time women. Evaluate current TV programs. Are these criticisms still justified? Discuss this issue in small groups.
2. **(a)** Why, do you think, "*women were once regarded by the industry as incapable of writing comedy,...action – adventure, and drama series*"? What, then, was left for women script writers?
   (b) What difference do you think more women writers and directors would make in the content and the images presented in television programs?
3. What, in your view, could be considered an "innovative image" of men and women? Are there any TV programs that model such images?
4. A study published in 1986 declared that "*too many TV women are affluent.*" (*The Toronto Star*: November 22, 1986)
   (a) How true is this criticism today?
   (b) How do you explain a preference for the rich, sophisticated woman in television programs?
   (c) Do you think this "distortion" would have a positive or negative impact on a viewer's perception of the world?

INVESTIGATING THE MEDIA

1. **(a)** Use the following chart as the basis for a small-group discussion on the topic of the images of men and women presented through film and television. For each word in the left-hand column, select characters from current TV shows and movies whom you would identify with the word. Add words of your own to the word list column.
   (b) What messages about roles and lifestyles are communicated through the movies and programs you have named? Do the characterizations reflect *real* men and women? Is there a difference between images on television and those in the movies?

Roles and Character Traits	Men and Women on TV Shows	Men and Women in the Movies
1. leadership		
2. courage		
3. authority		
4. nurturing		
5. aggressive		
6. warmth		
7. provider		

2. Make a point of reading the credits for the television programs you watch. Note those programs that are written and/or directed by women. Prepare a comparative study. In your view, what differences — if any — are there in the story lines, characterizations, and images in programs created by women and those created by men?

Despite recent sensitivity to sexism, some films still display, as "normal," attitudes that may be considered degrading to women. The authors of the next two articles tell us that if we are to eliminate offensive images in the media, we must speak up to help create a "simultaneous change in attitude in the people we meet and deal with every day."

Men have to speak up in battle against sexism

On a recent Sunday night, I was watching a pay-TV movie with friends — two women and a longtime male friend — when an ugly incident of sexism caused an argument among us.

It made me think about the way men, including me, relate to other men — especially on issues of gender equality.

The movie was Ron Howard's *Gung Ho*, about a Japanese takeover of an American auto plant. In one scene, three Japanese couples and an American couple are having a dinner party, and at meal's end the men decide to discuss their business plans.

Without prompting, the Japanese wives in this scene silently leave the room. But the American woman insists on staying to hear her boyfriend talk shop (to his obvious annoyance). And in mid-conversation, when she voices her opinion, the boyfriend snaps at her to "Shut up!"

I was shocked by the nastiness and aggression of his command. So were the two women in the room, and one commented that the boyfriend was a jerk. My male friend, however, sprang to his defence, arguing that the boyfriend had every right to tell her to "shut up," because she wasn't a part of the men's business plans.

"But he was very rude and that's no way to treat anyone," said the other woman.

"Well, he made it perfectly clear, earlier, that she wasn't wanted in the discussion anyway, so she should have known her place and kept quiet," my friend retorted, his voice rising — and soon three people were talking all at once in a heated way. My male friend was cornered.

Meanwhile, I stayed out of the fray, a passive spectator.

To make matters worse, after that the film grew even more sexist.... Yet, after boyfriend goes through a personal crisis at the factory, girlfriend returns to dutifully console him. And on and on.

By the end of the movie, I was feeling guilty for not taking sides when the issue first came up — so I raised the point again, and suggested that the boyfriend had been way out of line.

"Well," said my male friend, "I can see it's three to one."

I had made my point. But I waited too long.

Later, in a private conversation, the woman with whom I was spending the evening suggested I had been gutless. "You didn't want to be seen taking sides with a woman against your longtime male friend on an issue of sexism," she said.

She was right.

In this male-dominated society, men can get very cliquish about our unfair positions of power. Even if we appear to maintain balanced and equal relationships with the women in our lives, when men band together as a group we can quickly revert to downright piggishness.

When will we stop doing this?

As my female friend explained to me, men will stop doing this when we begin to see sexism in the way that most of us now see racism.

Unlike a few decades ago, today it is widely unacceptable to degrade people on the basis of their color.

For example, most white men today would be embarrassed to see films or magazines that, to gratify racist appetites, feature black people being battered, bound, or beaten. That's because, however racist people may be, most nevertheless pay lip service to race equality. We've been socialized to understand that racist statements or jokes are (at the very least) in bad taste.

Yet sexism like that in the film *Gung Ho* remains the stuff of comedy for many men.

But in the coming years, the vast majority of us (we can hope) will look with disdain to our forefathers who devised and promoted the oppression of women. And it's an important step in that direction for all of us — when gathering among fellow males — to stop being silent, to break up the cliques, to be vocal about equality, and to join women in speaking up for their rights.

True friendship will survive it.

— Fred Kuntz
The Toronto Star/April 11, 1987

Fighting popular sexism

***Sexism** — prejudice or discrimination based on sex; discrimination against women; behavior, conditions, or attitudes that foster stereotypes of social roles based on sex (from Webster's Ninth New Collegiate Dictionary)*

That's a simple definition of a not-so-simple problem.

And what makes the problem of discrimination against women so difficult to tackle is that sexist attitudes are so ingrained in our society.

Little by little we are managing to legislate such discrimination out of hiring practices, out of the workplace, but we are still left with rampant, ingrained sexist attitudes everywhere we look.

One of the places I looked recently, although that wasn't my intention when I went to see the film, was the popular film sequel *Beverly Hills Cop II*.

Films and television are often guilty of depicting a poor and unrealistic image of women, but I've always considered them too unimportant in the grander scale of arguing for things like equality to be overly concerned about the prevalence of "dumb blonde secretaries" in movies.

But the depiction and treatment of women in *Beverly Hills Cop II* is so radically sexist and so alarming in one instance that it left me stunned.

There is only one female human being in *Beverly Hills Cop II*, and by that I mean someone who walks, talks, feels emotion, and lives a life we might recognize. But even she, the daughter of the cop that is shot at the beginning of the film, is given a stereotyped passive role. She sits weeping by his bedside for a few frames, then gathers some information on the suspect from her place of employment to give to the male cops so they can solve the crime.

That's it, that's all — passive girl-next-door type fades to black.

In the rest of the film we see a couple of pretty receptionists, a clinging vine who scuttles away obediently from her man's side when told to do so, a couple of strippers, a couple of hooker look-alikes in a Ferrari, and a bunch of faceless bouncing body parts during a volleyball game at Hugh Hefner's mansion.

The only woman who plays a major part in the film is a six-foot blonde, who is chief assistant to the top criminal in the film. She is a cold, ruthless criminal and an essential element in the action.

But what happens to her is something else.

The film naturally comes to a big shoot-'em-up at the end, complete with munitions explosions and trucks blowing up and three good guys holding an entire team of bad guys at bay.

While main character Axel Foley, played by Eddie Murphy, creeps around in a dusty barn looking for the last of the bad guys, including the six-foot blonde, he hurts his leg. The blonde appears while he's lying on the ground, but she gets shot by someone off-screen before she gets the chance to finish off Foley.

The cop who has killed her steps into view, looks with disdain at the woman on the ground, grins at Foley, and says, "Women!"

I was appalled.

After expressing my outrage to someone who had also seen the film, I was asked what difference it makes. The woman is killed, but a lot of other male criminals in the film are also shot.

That's not the point. The point is that when the male criminals are shot, they are shot because of crimes committed. When the woman is shot, her killer refers to her gender as if that is explanation for her demise.

If you still don't see the outrage, try making the top criminal's assistant a black male.

When he is shot from off-screen, the cop who does the shooting hovers into view, grins at his partner, and says, "Blacks!"

Imagine the gasps of outrage in the theatre. Imagine the controversy. Imagine the mess on the editing-room floor when the scene was cut long before it ever saw public viewing.

As a friend said after the film, we are now sensitized to the insult and outrage of racism and deem it unacceptable. But we are not likewise sensitized to the insult of sexism.

There were no gasps at the showing of *Beverly Hills Cop II* when the cop made his remark.

The audience was too busy laughing, and applauding.

We may be making inroads into "officially" eliminating sexist biases by making such practises illegal in hiring, but without a simultaneous change in attitude in the people we meet and deal with every day, we still have a long, long way to go.

— Christine Stanton
Burlington Post
June 10, 1987

YOUR TURN

1. Have *you* had an experience similar to that described by either of the authors? If you have, describe the incident, as well as your thoughts and feelings about it when it happened, and now, as you write.
   or
   Respond in an article to the suggestion that men have to join women in speaking out in support of equality.
2. "*...we are now sensitized to the insult and outrage of racism and deem it unacceptable. But we are not likewise sensitized to the insult of sexism.*"
   Why, do you think, has society been so slow to recognize the insult of sexism? Write a letter to Ms. Stanton, or an article for a magazine, in which you respond to this question.
3. "*...ingrained sexist attitudes [are] everywhere we look.*"
   Form a small group to discuss this issue as a panel. Invite questions and comments from the class following the discussion.
4. Write a letter to the president of a television network in which you praise or criticize the portrayals of men and women on that network's prime-time programs.

TELEVISION FAMILIES

"What TV tells us about material goods and human beings influences our feelings, behaviour, and judgments before we are taught by life experience. Many programs give a distorted view of family life and expose youngsters to values not espoused by parents. A child can end up with a disturbing, alienating picture of the world he is learning to face. Affluence portrayed in posh sets can make some children feel like have-nots while the image of certain lifestyles, family relationships or the lack of them, sex and race stereotypes all affect the vulnerable values children are forming."

— Dr. Harold and Margaret Breen
"What's TV Doing to Our Kids?"
***Today's Parent*, January 1986**

Television is undoubtedly one of the most powerful image-makers of all the mass media. And since family-oriented series have always been included on network program schedules, evaluating the view of family life presented on television is important. Do television families reflect our own families? Do we want them to?

Should television reflect the contemporary family as it really is, or is the major role of the medium to simply entertain and amuse? Is it possible that today's audiences would rather not *see a realistic portrayal of modern family life? Some media commentators contend that the resolution of these issues need not be an "either-or" situation; they see room for shows that are primarily entertainment but offer "learning through laughter." The following two articles focus on the issues surrounding the family as seen on "the box."*

Children defy reality with the flick of a dial

Children on television bear little resemblance to children in the real world, according to a study by the National Commission of Working Women.

The commission, a Washington group representing women in nonprofessional occupations, studied all prime-time network programs during the 1984-85 season that featured characters under 18. Those children were more likely to be wealthy, white, and the product of divorced parents than their real-life counterparts, the study concluded.

The study also found that, although most television mothers work outside the home, such problems as finding and paying for childcare, juggling job and family, and stretching the budget to meet family needs were rarely discussed.

Similarly, the report said, bigotry and racial discrimination are rare on television and, when those problems exist, they are solved by the end of the show. Young children are shown as self-reliant and either need no childcare or are cared for by live-in help.

"Viewers deserve more from this medium than repetitious portrayals of affluent families where mothers work as spies, corporate presidents, and oil tycoons," said Alexis Herman, chairperson of the commission, when issuing the report. "Television has a social responsibility not only to entertain viewers but also to mirror back the significant aspects of our lives."

Wealthy household — The TV family on *Who's the Boss?*

"This report confuses the purpose of comedy entertainment programming," said George Schweitzer, a spokesman for CBS. "Situation comedies can't be expected to reflect the harshness of reality. Comedy is there to poke fun at social issues and to give us relief from them."

According to the report, television and reality fail to intersect at several points. Among them are:

Few situation comedies, *The Cosby Show, Family Ties*, for example, contain children who live with both parents. Two-thirds live with one parent (usually their father), stepparents, or legal guardians. But in fact, four out of five children in the United States live with both parents.

Nearly half of all television families are upper middle class or wealthy, with *Dallas* and *Dynasty* among the most glittering examples. Yet the median income for a family with two parents working outside the home was just over $30 000 in 1984.

All the single mothers on television were middle class or wealthier. The title characters of *Kate and Allie*, for example, lead middle-class lives, while the divorced mother on *Who's the Boss?* is obviously wealthy. Though no television family is poor, 69 per cent of real households headed by women are currently below the poverty level.

No black television children, except those on *The Cosby Show*, live with their natural parents. On *Webster*, for example, a black child is adopted by white guardians. This show is an example of the fact that 80 per cent of black television children are upper middle class or wealthier. In reality, black children in the United States live in a variety of family settings, and one of two black children lives in poverty.

Childcare centres do not exist on television, where children are independent enough to care for themselves or lucky enough to be cared for by live-in relatives or hired help. In *Gimme a Break*, for example, a live-in housekeeper becomes part of the family.

In reality, however, almost all families with working parents depend on some form of childcare and as many as seven million children under 14 are left unsupervised while their parents work.

— Lisa Belkin
The Globe and Mail
September 1986

Creating Cosby

Can a loving, supportive television family successfully replace its more familiar images of wisecracking children and inept parents — and be a commercial hit at the same time?

Ranked as the number one television series for several seasons in the United States, *The Cosby Show* is also immensely popular in Australia and South Africa, and a weekly hit in Norway and Sweden.

Such an impact of successful comedy in an arena usually associated with global powers has its responsibilities. "I think Bill knows that he has a power, and that he thinks of it very judiciously. He is conscientious and sensitive to the minds of people who watch the show. And he is very respectful of their intelligence," said John Markus, co-executive producer/head writer of *The Cosby Show*. "He sees that a more powerful tool in education is to entertain and engage the audience in a delicate manner rather than to hammer home a message. He wants to educate, but he never wants to sermonize."

Underlying this vision for the show, Markus and producer/writer Carmen Finestra outlined four equal operating principles for creating the weekly show.

Playful affection — Cliff and Claire on *The Cosby Show*

First, the show looks at problems from a fresh perspective. Cosby's loose style inspires a refreshing break from crusted formulas in scripting, Markus indicated. "Bill is a big jazz fan, and I think his approach to comedy is very much like a jazz musician. He doesn't want to hear the same notes every time. He wants to know there are chords in the background, but he wants some room to play with that."

Secondly, the family faces their various situations in a loving and supporting fashion. One of the most favorable audience reactions, according to Finestra, is towards the playful affection displayed between the parents, Claire and Cliff. "There is a real feeling for a couple being married 23 years still maintaining a tremendous physical attraction and love for each other."

And that love is extended to the children by simply allowing them "to be," said Markus. "The Huxtables do not try to control their children. They allow them to make mistakes while providing them with a safety net so they don't kill themselves."

And that sometimes makes for irritations. One of the truths of family life is that "perfectly good, intelligent children that you love can be very annoying. I like the fact that we show the parents getting annoyed with the kids. They laugh at and with them, and that to me is real," Markus commented.

As Cosby himself stated to a meeting of NBC affiliates, "I'm a parent with five kids. Those of us with real children know it is possible to have a precocious child who's not a snot."

But with all the differences between personalities and ages running about the same brownstone, it makes for "endless possibilities," Markus concluded. "Events that might sound trivial — a goldfish dying, a son's first shave, a fight over a hairbrush — there's poetry there if you look closely."

This poetry takes a "slice of life" approach that allows the various ages to laugh at their own and others' preoccupations without the belittling humor of other sitcom families. While Vanessa's age causes consternation over a pimple in the middle of her forehead, Denise's seventeenth birthday fuels a wish for wheels in New York City. But with only $1600 in savings for a clunker, the Huxtable safety net instructs Denise in a responsible purchase that includes the items few wheel-bound teens consider: upkeep and insurance.

Theo's slice provided a story on drugs that won a coveted Humanitas Prize for humanizing achievement in television for the 1984-85 season. "We did a show in which the parents discovered a marijuana joint in their son's schoolbook," explained Markus. "Now, audiences may be trained to think right away: 'Uh oh, this is a show about drugs.' But it became a show instead about trust — the parents' trust of their son, and the son's concern about what his parents thought about him.

"At the end of the show, there was a very subtle anti-drug speech that was over very quickly and simply reflected Bill's personal attitudes. The drug problem hadn't been 'solved.' It had just been experienced, in a constructive way that real-life families could relate to."

That real-life approach is the third underlying principle of the show. It simply must be real and honest. "We never sacrifice reality for a joke. Life does not unfold three jokes at a time (according to the classic theory of sitcom writing in Hollywood), and it doesn't unfold with cliffhangers at the break and things don't get tied up at the end with a neat little bow," Markus says.

"Bill's philosophy — and it's an immensely challenging one for all of us — is that in true situation comedy, you can put the characters in a funny situation and let the humor evolve naturally.

"At one point, I remember, he held up a tennis shoe and said: 'I'd rather that you held up the tennis shoe, and instead of telling a joke about the tennis shoe, just say: this is a tennis shoe.' What he meant was that a joke should work from the inside out — not as an unrealistic tag-on."

And lastly, comedy must be funny! "If it's comedy, it's funny and real, human, intelligent, and compassionate," said Markus, encapsulating each of the four operating principles of the show. "The people who are watching us all have families of their own — and are quite smart enough to learn *with* us, not from us," concluded Finestra.

According to Nielsen, that power of learning through laughter is medicine not to be underestimated.

— Allen Eisenach
Media & Values

EXPLORING IDEAS

1. As a class, compile a list of children or teenagers featured on current TV shows. Brainstorm words and phrases that describe these characters. In your experience, do they behave as real people do? Share your ideas and opinions.

INVESTIGATING THE MEDIA

1. *"Beaver and Dennis and the whole* Father Knows Best *brood were fundamentally innocent. Today's television children are not. They are, in fact, miniature adults who know everything about everything."*

— Simi Horwitz
Channels/January/February 1982

(a) Test the validity of this accusation. Form your class into two groups. Members of the first group are to view "classic" TV sitcoms such as *Leave It to Beaver, Father Knows Best, Family Affair*, and *Dennis the Menace*. Students in the second group view current shows that feature children and teenagers. Take notes on the ways in which children are depicted.
(b) The members of each group should meet to compare notes and discuss the image of children presented in the shows, commenting on the behaviour, personality, and physical appearance of the children portrayed in the various shows.

(c) As a class, compare and contrast the image of children and childhood as it is reflected in classic and in current TV. *Has* this image really changed? If so, which image of childhood — past *or* present — is the most accurate? the most appealing? Offer evidence from your viewing experiences to support your observations, opinions, and conclusions.

2. Are the observations made in these articles still true today?
(a) Form into groups. Each group will evaluate family-life series on one network. Use a data-collection sheet such as the one modelled below. Appoint one member to report your group's findings and conclusions to the class.
(b) Compile all the data collected and present a summary of current television families.
(c) Which of the shows studied were American? Which were Canadian? Is there a difference in the image of the family as presented on American and Canadian shows?

Program	Economic class	No. of parents	Ethnic origin	Employment	Childcare

3. Study the way in which problems are resolved in several shows about family life:

Program	Problem or conflict	Resolution

(a) What evidence did you find of "the phony treatment of real-life issues"?
(b) Which programs, in your opinion, treat issues realistically?
(c) Which shows exhibit instances of "learning through laughter"?

Use your data as the basis for a report entitled "The Best and Worst on TV."
or
Write a list of recommendations you would make for revising scripts to show more realistic TV treatments of family conflicts and related problems.

4. Invite a group of adults to share in an examination of television with you. Each person should agree to watch and take notes on the same selection of programs. At the end of the survey period, present a panel discussion for the class on the issue of accuracy in the portrayal of family life on television.
or
Invite a group of adults to your class to participate with a selected group of students in a more general panel discussion about family life as television presents it.

YOUR TURN

1. Choose an episode of a family-life program in which an issue has been resolved in a manner with which you disagree. Rewrite the ending so that it portrays events more realistically or more successfully helps the audience learn through laughter.
   If possible, present a summary of the ending the show actually presented, followed by a taped or "live" depiction of *your* ending.
2. Compose a poem or article entitled "The Lies TV Tells Children."
3. Hold a class debate on the following issue:
Resolved: "To subject children to adult issues is not necessarily immoral: to lie to them about those issues is."

Adam by Brian Basset.

Author Jerzy Kosinski focuses on the effects television has had on its other children — young people who have grown up with the medium as a normal part of their daily lives. As a member of an age group that has been exposed to TV from earliest childhood, do you consider Mr. Kosinski's assessment fair, or accurate?

TV Children

With the advent of television, for the first time in history, all aspects of animal and human life and death, of societal and individual behavior have been condensed on the average to a 19-inch diagonal screen and a 30-minute time slot. Television, a unique medium, claiming to be neither a reality nor art, has become reality for many of us, particularly for our children who are growing up in front of it.

Imagine a child watching this little world within which Presidents and commoners walk; mice and lions, kissing lovers and dying soldiers, skyscrapers and dog houses, flowers and detergents, all are reduced to the same size, mixed together, given the same rank, and set in the same screen to be looked at. The child watches this crowded world as he or she pleases, while eating, yawning, playing. What is the outlook of such a child? What does it expect of the world? What can it expect?

It expects all things to be as equal as on television: neither bad nor good, neither pleasant nor painful, neither real nor unreal, merely more or less interesting, merely in better or worse color. It is a world without rank. To such a child, the world is to be looked upon; it is there to entertain its viewer. If it doesn't, one alters it by switching the channel.

In the little world of television, all is solved within its magic 30 minutes. In spite of the commercials, the wounded hero either rises or quickly dies, lovers marry or divorce, villains kill or are killed, addicts are cured, justice usually wins, and war ends. All problems are solved again this week, as they were last, and will be next week. Life on TV must be visual. This means single-faceted, revealed in a simple speech and through the obvious gesture. No matter how deep the mystery, the TV camera penetrates it.

Parents leave their children in front of the TV as babysitter, because many feel it is infinitely safer to watch the Sesame world of television than to walk in the world outside of their home. But is it?

Unlike television, the child grows older. One day it walks out of the TV room. Against his expectations, he's finally put in a classroom full of other children. A child who has been trained to control the little world, by changing the channels when he didn't like it, and was accustomed to maintaining the same distance between himself and the world televised for his amusement, is naturally threatened by the presence of people he cannot control. Others push him around, make faces at him, encroach. There is nothing he can do to stop them. He begins to feel that this real world unjustly limits him; it offers no channels to turn to.

In this unpredictable world of real life, there are no neatly ordered thirty-minute private slots. Here, in life, the child brought up only as viewer must feel persecuted. Ironically, our industrial state offers few things that can be resolved in thirty minutes. But the teenager keeps expecting it; when it is not, he grows impatient, then adamant, disillusioned, oscillating between the revolutionary scream, "Now," and a political cool "So what?" He is easily depressed and beaten down. In this world of hierarchy and brutish competition, he is challenged and outranked by others. Soon he believes he is defective; instead of coming of age, he's coming apart. This breeding of weak and vulnerable beings knows few exceptions. The kids of the upper classes counteract TV by being involved with real events — real horses, real forests, real mountains — all things they have seen, touched, experienced. They have been given an opportunity to exist outside the television room. However, many middle-class children, and almost all from poor families, are at the mercy of five or six hours of television a day.

My own attitude toward television is neutral. The medium is here to stay. The danger is in the use we make of it. I'm involved with TV the way I am with the motor car. The motor car has been with us for over 50 years, but it is only recently that we learned its exhaust pollutes our very environment.

In today's atomized, disjointed technological society, with so little attention paid to the individual, man needs more than ever the inner strength to carry him through the daily pressures. This strength should come from early exposure to life at its most real — its sudden pleasures, joys and abandonment; but also its violence, its lack of justice, its pain, illness, and death. There is subtlety to man's fate which lies beyond the television channels.

— Jerzy Kosinski
NBC Broadcast
September 3, 1972

EXPLORING IDEAS

1. Discuss the childhood impressions of the world you recall forming from watching TV. How, and when, did your views change?
2. To what extent do you agree with Jerzy Kosinski's point of view? On what evidence are you basing your response? Share your opinions in a class discussion. What is the consensus on this issue?
3. Mr. Kosinski describes ways in which TV distorts reality, and outlines some of the consequences of this distortion. In your experience, are there any *other* ways in which television distorts reality? Record these additional distortions and some possible consequences in your personal-response journal.
4. Mr. Kosinski compares television to the motor car. Write a brief report or journal entry to explain why you think the comparison is either a good or a poor one.

YOUR TURN

1. In his novel *Being There* (later adapted as a film starring the late Peter Sellers), Jerzy Kosinski tells the story of an elderly man who confronts, and is confronted by, the real world after many years in which his *only* link with the world has been through watching TV. Kosinski's rather simple, naive "videot" actually becomes the darling of politicians and the media, and is seen as a brilliant, original, and prophetic thinker.

   Write a short story or outline a proposed film that describes what happens when a person whose only experience of the world comes from TV finally confronts real life. Alternatively, write the dialogue from a key scene in your film.

   You may wish to borrow Mr. Kosinski's term as the title of your work: "The Videot."

Joanne Ostrow presents her observations on "a TV journey from Mrs. Cleaver to the post-modernist spouse." Just how realistic is TV's image of the modern mother?

The incredible changing tube mom

Like breakfast foods and tennis shoes, styles of motherhood are constantly updated.

These days, prime-time mothers must be as hip as their kids. They must steer their children through a morass of social issues, sometimes without a partner, often while wearing aerobic gear.

June Cleaver had her problems — when the Beav slacked off on homework or told a white lie — but her motherly duties were ordained. As long as she had sugary, high-cholesterol snacks ready when the kids came home from school, June (Barbara Billingsley) was on top of the job.

Since then, TV moms have advanced in the power struggle with their neurotic husbands. Laura catered to Rob Petrie, Harriet coddled Ozzie, now Maggie Seaver (Joanna Kerns) offers transactional analysis for her house-bound psychologist husband, Jason (Alan Thicke), when she returns from the tumultuous outside world to share *Growing Pains*.

After four decades of television-style motherhood, the trend out of the kitchen and into the workforce continues into single parenthood and debt. Also into group therapy and rehabilitation, family-style. Increasingly, Mom is more worried about crack than snacks.

Dennis the Menace's mom taught him to say "I'm sorry" to Mr. Wilson. Webster's mom teaches him to say no to drugs. Contemporary TV parents regularly discourse on teenage pregnancy, child abuse, and drugs. Margaret Anderson (Jane Wyatt) of *Father Knows Best* knew best about measles, but she would have been at a loss to explain sexually communicable germs.

Common sense is not good enough in the computer-interactive age. Moms must know dyslexia when they see it.

It was not always so. For a time, in the late '50s and early '60s, TV put Mom on hold. Wifeless TV dads fumbled for a '60s modern image of what wife and mother should be.

The relevance comedies of the '70s attempted to re-humanize Mom. Suddenly we saw such allegedly liberated women as Julia, a widowed (black!) nurse and her young son, and Alice, a widowed singer with a smart-aleck 12-year-old. The most advanced mom of this period was Bea Arthur's Maude (1972-1978), who lived with her divorced daughter and grandson and endured precedent-setting traumas, but not without viewer protests. Once Ronald Reagan took office, TV moms followed the rest of the population back to traditional values (i.e., "conservativism").

"Once upon a time there was a supermom: Jane Wyatt of* Father Knows Best. *She was pretty, practical, in control and all-round nice. What tamed the '50s suburban fantasy was that mom looked older than her children. Zap to the '80s: now, mom on TV is sexy, successful in her career — and as young as her kids.

***No, there's been only one convincing TV mom since actress Sada Thompson and* Family *were cancelled in 1980 — Barbara Bel Geddes's Miss Ellie on* Dallas *is kind, patient, suffering, omniscient. And, thank God,* old."**

— Gina Mallet
Chatelaine
October 1986

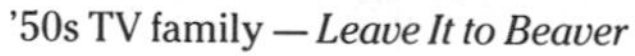

'50s TV family — *Leave It to Beaver*

'80s mom — Tyne Daly (*right*) in *Cagney & Lacey*

As the real-world divorce rate climbed, TV moms began to pursue professional careers. They aimed to be superwomen, steering their offices or squad cars by day, serving their families at night.

Life was more difficult. Safe sex was in, saturated fats were out. Instead of hanging by the kitchen sink waiting for school to let out, Mom left to fight crime, litigate, and decorate, often as a single parent.

Mrs. Cosby (*The Cosby Show*), the era's most-watched mom, is an exception. Claire Huxtable espouses 1950s-style family values with a Superwoman spin. She is fashion plate, lawyer, loving wife, understanding mother, cheerful daughter-in-law, and tidy homemaker. Only incidentally is she a double minority (black female).

We await her nervous breakdown, but it will not happen. Claire embodies that elusive baby-boomer value: having it all, with time out to jam with Stevie Wonder.

Tyne Daly (*Cagney & Lacey*) is a more realistically bedraggled Superwoman. Christine Cagney's support system, Mary Beth Lacey, is wife and mother of three, but she is also a devoted cop, with a cop's hectic homelife.

Meredith Baxter Birney represents the burned-out mom. She exchanges wifely one-liners with Michael Gross on *Family Ties*, but shrugs off certain motherly duties. Michael J. Fox relieved her of some of the burden of child-rearing when a little brother was added to the cast; aging hippie Elyse Keaton rolls her eyes as Alex teaches her youngest the intricacies of mutual funds.

When they are not confronting issues, '80s moms give themselves permission to whine. Susan Saint James and Jane Curtin are almost-bitter divorced mothers on *Kate & Allie*. Meanwhile, Valerie, put-upon mother of three teenaged boys with an airline pilot husband whose lines were of the "Hi, honey, I'm home" variety, was virtually a single parent without benefit of alimony, keeping the place clean in case her husband drops in.

Happy-face moms are out. Overburdened juggling-act moms are in. The post-modernist mom is downtrodden but free. Witness Carla on *Cheers*.

Rhea Pearlman plays the tart-tongued Tortelli, a blue-collar waitress who is hip to her decade. She alternately resents men for being such unreliable louses and casts about for her next catch. Her reproductive talents have been compared to those of rabbits. Her maternal outlook, in brief, is "Oh no, not another one." Meanwhile, Carla works tirelessly to support the brood.

At least TV no longer insists that Mom strive to have it all. As real-world moms explore their options in the '80s, so do TV moms. Everywoman is not a Superwoman. We do not expect Carla to become a career gal with a handsome hubby to share the microwave.

— Joanne Ostrow
The Spectator
June 12, 1987

EXPLORING IDEAS

1. ***(a)*** Analyze the image of the 1980s television mom as this writer describes her. Is it realistic? fair?
   (b) What additional images of mothers, if any, do you see emerging on current TV programs?
2. *"Like breakfast foods and tennis shoes, styles of motherhood are constantly updated."*
   What social and economic trends do you think will soon be reflected on TV? What should television mothers be like as we move toward the year 2000?
3. Who fares better on TV — mothers or fathers? Discuss this issue as a class.

INVESTIGATING THE MEDIA

1. ***(a)*** As a class, brainstorm a list of normal family routines and obligations.
   (b) Using a chart like the one below, collect data on which family members assume these responsibilities on television.
   (c) At the end of the survey period, compile all the data.
   (d) How accurately and realistically does television portray family life? Discuss your findings as a class.
2. Evaluate the images of men presented in the current season's programs. Is there a "preferred" image? In your judgment, is there a positive balance in the roles for men? Present your conclusions in the form of an article or report.
3. Watch several current family-life shows, paying close attention to the way in which fathers are portrayed.
   (a) What images of fathers are portrayed on contemporary TV?
   (b) If TV fathers truly reflected fathers in real life, what would they be like? Work with a partner to develop, write, and present a profile of this more-realistic character.

YOUR TURN

1. Arrange to view some "classic" family-life programs from the past, such as *Leave It to Beaver, My Three Sons, Father Knows Best, Make Room for Daddy, Ozzie and Harriet,* and *The Dick Van Dyke Show.* Focus on how the fathers are portrayed.
   Respond to the following statement in your journal and, if you wish, exchange entries with a partner.
   "...today [TV fathers] are at least more easy going — maybe too much."
2. Write a poem entitled "Moms, Dads, and Kids According to TV" in which you present your impressions of families as they are portrayed on television.
3. Create an anthology of cartoons about television families and the "lessons" we learn from watching family-oriented TV programs.
4. Write an article entitled "The Most Believable Parents of All" in which you evaluate the image of parents on current television programs.

	Program Title:			
	Who is responsible? (check one)			
Routines/ Obligations	*Mother*	*Father*	*Children*	*No one*
e.g., picking the children up from daycare				

IMAGES OF CANADA & THE WORLD

One media observer has called television "one long commercial for the American way of life." There is no question that most of the magazines, movies, and television programs Canadians consume are American. Does the lifestyle depicted in the American mass media differ from our own? How accurately is our society depicted in *our own* productions?

Many of the images we form of our own country come to us second-hand. For the fact is, as Canadians we are major consumers of movies about Canada made in the United States.

Perils of the Royal Mounted

Of the 575 motion pictures that Hollywood has made about Canada, 256 have featured the Royal Canadian Mounted Police or their predecessors, the Royal North West Mounted Police, or *their* predecessors, the North West Mounted Police. Hollywood hasn't always got its nomenclature straight. Some movies refer to the Royal Mounted Police, or the Canadian Mounted Police, others to the Royal Canadian North West Mounted Police, or even the North West Canadian Mounted Police; but the movie industry's unrequited love affair with the force has been passionate and long-standing.

The number of Mounted movies noted above covers only those in which the mounted police are central to the story. In most pictures about Canada there's at least one Mountie to be seen somewhere, and always in his scarlet uniform. In the opening scene of *The Happy Time*, for instance, a whole gallop of Mounties passes by, almost knocking Charles Boyer to the ground. In *Scandal at Scourie* one turns up on a railway platform in western Ontario, an unlikely place to find a member of the force at the turn of the century. In *I Confess* Mounties form a kind of background frieze.

To an international audience, Canada and the mounted police are inseparable. Hollywood has banished them from the screen only in those pictures where shoot-ups were required and the presence of the law would wreck the plot. Even then, as in *North of Hudson Bay*, sometimes a stock Mountie — shoes glistening, dress uniform brushed — pops in and out of the movie long enough to register the fact that this is indeed the Northwest, and then conveniently vanishes, allowing the wicked factor to get on with his dirty work.

The movie Mountie was almost invariably brave, noble, honourable, courteous, kind, and trustworthy — all the standard Boy Scout qualities, to go with the hat. There have scarcely ever been any bad Mounties or even droll Mounties in the motion pictures, at least not intentionally. In a comedy like *Dangerous Nan McGrew*, the Mountie gets the straight lines. He is the quintessential hero and he always wins. He gets his man and he usually gets his girl (or nobly gives her to another). "All Canadian heroes belong to the Royal Mounted," one reviewer commented in 1919, with only the tiniest touch of irony. For half a century that was Hollywood's credo.

"It wasn't that way at all . . ."

No one, of course, expects motion pictures to be historically accurate. American studios have distorted and mythologized their own history and that of other countries just as much as they have twisted the Canadian past. Playwrights do it all the time; Shakespeare, of course, did it — although Shakespeare never went around boasting that his version of history was absolutely authentic.

All the same, it's an unfortunate accident that just as Canada was emerging from the colonial shadows the most powerful educational medium of all was developed by a friendly but alien power. We can't blame Hollywood for ignoring the Canadian character and lifestyle. But there's little doubt that the bludgeoning effect of the motion picture first distorted our image by making us appear as a nation of primitives, and then it blurred it by confusing it with the American image. No foreign myth-makers could be expected to reveal to us our own distinctive identity; that must be the task of our own mass media. Hollywood made it hard for us to recognize the Canadian identity because its movies masked it so effectively.

The American producers, of course, were making commercial pictures mainly for U.S. consumption. There was no reason for them to act like Canadians. We ourselves never required them to use any of their Canadian profits to make a different kind of movie or to subsidize a home-grown industry. The idea of government control was seen as a semi-totalitarian measure, and not just by Hollywood lobbyists; Canadian officials such as Donald Gordon, whose successful careers were based entirely on state-controlled enterprises (the Bank of Canada, the CNR), were opposed to state interference in the foreign-controlled motion picture industry. Our leaders, dazzled by the idea of untold publicity in the movies and buttered up by studio heads, were more concerned with paying homage to a free market and a free flow across the border, at least in the entertainment industry. They didn't realize that the flow has always been one way. What the world got was not the publicity that the Canadian Co-operation Project promised but the Hollywood image of Canada as an American appendage.

The Hollywood attitude to accuracy, as Garth S. Jowett has pointed out in *The Journal of Popular Culture*, has been to *material* things — to sets, costumes, and props, rather than to interpretive matters. DeMille probably believed his own press releases when they lauded his passion for authenticity. His sets *were* authentic. The backlot replica of Fort Carlton in *North West Mounted Police* was faithful in every detail to the original. So were the mounted police uniforms, except for the hats. He went to considerable trouble to make Walter Hampden, the Broadway actor, actually look like Big Bear, even to the extent of fitting him with brown contact lenses. It didn't occur to him to have Hampden act as Big Bear would have acted; in spite of a superficial resemblance, the noted thespian sounded just like any other Hollywood Indian, grunting away in his deep, mellow voice and carefully trimming all the definite and indefinite articles from his sentences.

In movies about the Canadian frontier — and most of the movies have been about the Canadian frontier — everything is right and everything is wrong. The small-town sets are often works of art — the wood on the false fronts carefully seasoned, the paint peeling to give an impression of age and decay — but they are American sets. The costumes are beautiful and, in the big productions, lovingly made, but they are all wrong because they, too, are American — cowboy outfits in the Canadian north, for instance. The fights are carefully staged, especially the gun-fights. Attention is paid to making the weapons fit the exact historical period — DeMille sent all the way to England in the middle of a war to get 1885 Enfields — but they are American gun-fights; Canadians don't go around with six-shooters on their hips. The saloons, with their familiar bat-wing doors, their gilded mirrors, their oil paintings, and their long polished bars, are exquisite replicas of American saloons. The saloon is not really part of the Canadian style. For most of its frontier history, Canada has been dry; when the railway was being built, navvies furtively gulped bad whisky in log hovels hidden from the mounted police. That genuinely Canadian institution, the beer parlour of the twenties, thirties, and forties, has never been shown.

What Hollywood did for over half a century was to superimpose its vision of the old west, itself a mythological anachronism, onto the Canadian northwest. Hard-riding posses, men in cowboy outfits, necktie parties, covered wagons, painted Injuns, boot hills, vigilantes, and even tin stars were moved across the border with scarcely a change in the plot except for the presense of the movie Mounties who, all too often, acted like American town marshals.

It didn't occur to Hollywood and it didn't occur to Canadian audiences, either, that the Canadian concept of order imposed from above clashed with the American idea of rough frontier justice administered at grass-roots level by the people's choices. Nor did the moviemakers understand that in Canada the law arrived before the settlers did, in

American movie mountie — Alan Ladd starred in *Saskatchewan* (1953).

direct contrast to the American experience.

Although Hollywood exaggerated American frontier violence, the western society south of the border was demonstrably less stable than its Canadian counterpart. Shootings on the Canadian frontier were almost unknown. When a Texan on an Alberta ranch shot an adversary in the stomach in 1895, The Fort McLeod *Gazette* reported that it was only the second such killing since the paper was established in 1882.

These contrasts suggest that there is a difference between the American and the Canadian approach to frontier problems. Yet, as *The Daily Telegraph*'s critic remarked of *The Canadians*, "Saskatchewan might as well be in Texas, so traditional is the style." Almost two generations before, an American reviewer said much the same thing about a Hoot Gibson picture, *The Calgary Stampede*: "This is a typical Western with all the snap of the best examples of this class.... The action takes place on a ranch in Western Canada, which seems just like our own ranches...." And why shouldn't it? The gun-play was there along with the ten-gallon hats.

It's a little ironic that the movies with the most Canadian-sounding titles are among the most American in style. A good example is a picture called *'Neath Canadian Skies*, produced in 1948, which, if it wasn't for the movie Mounties, could just as easily have been called 'Neath Montana Skies. Everything about it, including the mountains and the trees, is American: the hardrock mine in the wrong place, the villains with gunbelts who shoot strangers on sight, the townspeople all dressed like Mississippi gamblers and, of course, the inevitable saloon. Even the Mounties in this film act like an American posse, thundering along on their horses firing aimless volleys from their smoking pistols; and, when one of them goes undercover and disguises himself as a typical Canadian westerner, *he* wears a gunbelt too.

— Pierre Berton
from *Hollywood's Canada*

Jeers

To CBS's *Murder, She Wrote*, for the preposterous episode that saw Jessica Fletcher in Quebec City, matching wits with "the top lawyer in Canada," played by the very British Patrick McGoohan. The writers, who seemed bent on providing a new chapter to Pierre Berton's *Hollywood's Canada*, would have us believe that everyone in the capital of *la belle province* is British, from the legal secretaries to the judge, better known as "me lord." There was one exception to the British invasion: a motel owner from Brooklyn. The last straw was the Mountie in full-dress uniform lowering the Canadian flag (what, no fleurs-de-lis?) outside the Quebec National Assembly. Like, who wrote this, a couple of hosers? Take off, eh?

Murderous errors

Dear Editor:
Here is a copy of the letter which I have sent to the executive producer of the CBS series, *Murder, She Wrote*, regarding the jarring inaccuracies contained in the Oct. 4th episode.

Dear Mr. Fischer,
My family and I have regularly enjoyed watching *Murder, She Wrote*, ever since its debut on CBS. Until Sunday evening, Oct. 4th, that is.

We are certain that you didn't set out deliberately to alienate several million Canadian viewers. But by sending Jessica to a Quebec that could only have come from the uninformed imagination of an American writer, that is exactly what you have done.

Thanks to Jessica's little excursion that night, there are now millions of Americans who wrongly believe:

1. That criminal trials are conducted in Quebec in English. In fact, the official language of that province is French, and any court procedure, by law, must take place in French. An Anglophone defendant would have an interpreter appointed to assist him, but the trial itself would be wholly in French. Similarly, the exit signs in a Québécois courtroom would be in French — "Sortie" instead of "Exit."

2. That Canadian lawyers advertise themselves as "attorneys-at-law." The sign on a Canadian lawyer's door will read "Barrister & Solicitor," or "Law Office" — *never* "Attorney at Law," as appeared on Mr. Quayle's office door. Furthermore, in Quebec, again by law, that sign would be bilingual, first in French, then in English.

3. That red-coated Mounties regularly raise and lower the Canadian flag in front of Quebec courthouses. Our RCMP officers wear that uniform only for high ceremonial occasions. At other times, the RCMP is a working police force, dressing and functioning very much like your FBI. *Please*, stop perpetuating that tired Nelson Eddy stereotype!

4. That Quebec is filled with people who have French names but who speak either with aristocratic English accents or with broad New York accents. The vast majority of the people in Quebec have a regional *Canadian* accent. The Québécois accent is quite distinctive; but not once in the Oct. 4th episode did we hear that accent. Would you set a story in the Ozark Mountains and then have all the natives speak like Shakespearean actors?

Too often on American television, Canada is portrayed as either a British colony or the 51st state in all but name. We ask you to remember that Canada is a sovereign country, a *foreign* country because of how little your people know about us, therefore, it requires the same scrupulous background research as any other foreign place.

We sincerely hope you will bear this in mind the next time you consider a Canadian locale for your otherwise excellent series, *Murder, She Wrote*.

Arlene Marks
Richmond Hill

— From "Your Letters"
Starweek
November 28 to December 5, 1987

EXPLORING IDEAS

1. ***(a)*** As a Canadian, what are your feelings when you see Mounties, our legal system, and other aspects of Canadian life portrayed inaccurately in movies or on TV?
(b) How do you think the Hollywood image of Mounties has influenced the attitude of Canadians towards the RCMP?
(c) What impression would someone who has never visited Canada likely form of our country based on the kind of movie or TV show mentioned in these articles?

2. *"What the world got was... the Hollywood image of Canada as an American appendage."*
(a) What other distinctly Canadian traditions and details of our history have been "Americanized" by Hollywood, in your experience of the media?
(b) Are the Canadian character and lifestyle generally ignored by the media? Use examples from movies, television, and advertisements to support your point of view.
(c) What are the consequences of the Americanization of Canadians by the media?
3. *"No foreign myth-makers could be expected to reveal to us our own distinctive identity; that must be the task of our own mass media."*
How successful have our own media been in revealing Canada to Canadians? Give examples to support your opinion.

YOUR TURN

1. **(a)** What differences do you think there are between the Canadian character and lifestyle and the American counterpart? Discuss this question in small groups and keep a record of your ideas.
(b) Use your notes to help you draft a proposal for a new television series called *Borders*, about a family with relatives living in both Canada and the United States. Your proposal should include
    - a list of the main characters who will appear in the series, along with brief descriptions of their characterizations
    - a description of the main settings to be used in the series
    - an outline of the story line for the pilot episode of the series.

Joan Irwin believes that Canadian TV generally misrepresents the multicultural "mix" of our contemporary society.

It's an all-white world on Canadian television

The people who run Canadian television networks, and the private producers who make many of the prime-time programs, must be color-blind.

Or maybe they just lead incredibly cloistered lives. If they ever ride the subway, stroll the main streets of any city, or shop in supermarkets and department stores you'd think they'd notice that Canada is not entirely the color of cream cheese.

Everywhere we look there's a variety of skin tones and bone structures: Oriental, East Indian, West Indian, Middle Eastern, native peoples...the faces of Canadian society. But when we turn on our TV sets for an evening of information and entertainment we're in a white, white world.

Television catches up with changes in society at the stately pace of a glacier (radio is not much better). It's only in the past half-dozen years or so that we've actually heard "foreign-sounding" names on the air outside sports programs, so it's probably optimistic to expect TV to climb the color barrier and begin to show us this country as it really is.

Well, perhaps not entirely absurd. There are some signs of steps being made in the right direction. News departments have at last begun to hire people from visible minorities as reporters and news readers. It's more frequent at the local level, but that at least means qualified people get experience, so reluctant managers won't be able to get away with the old excuse: "I'd love to hire someone from a visible minority but I simply can't find anyone with the right background."

Somehow or other CTV news reporter Bodine Williams and CBC's business reporter Der Hoi Yin got the right background and made it to on-air jobs with network TV news departments. It took a while, but it's a start.

Most of us, however, watch entertainment shows and there the situation is pretty dismal.

In prime time the number of series we can count on to show us the country as it is doesn't make a handful. There's *The Beachcombers*, which features young Indians in continuing roles. *Seeing Things* was reliably realistic in reflecting Canadian society. CTV's *Night Heat* features a black cop, played by Gene Clark, as a regular cast member. And CBC's series, *Street Legal*, actually included an Oriental actor with a few lines of dialogue.

CBC's *Hangin' In* takes place at an inner-city drop-in centre which in real life would be racially mixed. But the series is not.

Otherwise you might catch a glimpse of a non-white face in a crowd scene, and every now and again a member of a visible minority will emerge from the background for a scene or two. But any of us can watch television night after night for considerable time without being aware that we live in the midst of a very rich racial mix.

— Joan Irwin
The Toronto Star

EXPLORING IDEAS

1. As a class, share your comments on the following:
   (a) *"Television catches up with changes in society at the stately pace of a glacier...."*
   (b) Entertainment shows lag behind news programs in *"showing us this country as it really is."*
2. If Canadian television *does* fail to represent the country's "very rich racial mix" accurately, who is at fault — the industry, the public it serves, or both? Discuss this as a class.

INVESTIGATING THE MEDIA

1. **(a)** When we turn on television for an evening of information or entertainment today, what do we find? Form small groups for the purpose of surveying current Canadian television programming. You will want answers to such questions as the following.

Canadian prime-time programs:

- How often are performers from visible minorities featured as
  regular characters?
  single-episode characters?
  background characters?
  main characters?
  secondary characters?
- If the performer plays a role other than one of the leads, what is the relationship between the program's main character(s) and this person?

Canadian news programs:

- How often are people from visible minorities featured as
  news anchors?
  reporters/correspondents?
  sportscasters?
  weather forecasters?
  entertainment reporters?

Canadian children's programs:

- How often do people from visible minorities appear as
  host(s)?
  performers?
  featured guests?

Canadian vs. U.S. programs:

- Is there a difference in representation of visible minorities?

   (b) Compile your data and use it as the basis for a report on the current status of visible minorities on Canadian television.
2. Investigate the representation given to visible minorities in other media — for example, advertising or children's books.

Soon adults may start believing that the world is dangerous and that it's safer inside.

Images of a Depraved New World

"Children who don't distinguish fantasy from reality get the idea that the world is a dangerous place."

— Dr. Harold and Margaret Breen
"What's TV Doing to Our Kids?"
***Today's Parent*, January 1986**

A man and a woman walk down a city street at 2 a.m., in a not very nice neighborhood. A car stops across the street. Someone in the car calls out. He wants to talk to the man. The man leaves the woman standing by herself on the sidewalk and crosses the street to the car. "Don't do that," murmurs a spectator, pulling the covers a bit tighter around himself and reaching for the converter button. "Don't leave that woman alone on that 2 a.m. city street. An awful thing is going to happen to her."

Even though the man and the woman and the city street are on television, nothing awful happens. The man, Ernest Borgnine, finishes his conversation with the people in the car and walks back across the street to join the woman, Betsy Blair. She is unharmed. The movie is *Marty*, the scene is Brooklyn, the time is 1955. You can't do that today. You haven't been able to do that for at least 15 years in the movies. If it isn't a gangster getting you, it's some friend of John Travolta.

The same goes for television. You had better not be out at 2 a.m. on television either. Even in a small town. Even at 10 p.m. Even at 10 a.m. Even in Canada. It doesn't matter that more people are murdered on U.S. television in one day than in Canada in one year. Canada sees the same television, watches the same movies. Canada even makes movies, and they wind up on U.S. television, very late at night, on Tuesdays. In Canadian movies the world is just as ugly. It has to be, so that U.S. television will buy the movies. The only difference is that behind the ugliness you can see the CN Tower. In the Bronx or in Ottawa, Los Angeles or Swift Current, step out your door and TV can't guarantee your safety.

It's scary out there. Better to stay at home. Better not to chance it. Television tells you that. Movies tell you that. In case you missed the message at the movies, television shows the movies too. There's rape out there. Muggers. Random violence. White slavery. Child pornography. Bands of berserk dope fiends. Psychopathic Vietnam War veterans. Bad cults. People who have had their souls invaded by demons. Demons.

Television produces documentaries about these threats. In case nobody watches documentaries, which nobody does, television also makes sure that its dramatic series pay a lot of attention to the beasts that lurk out there. Motorcycle policemen chase them. Hillbillies crash their cars into them. Female detectives lure them into a trap. Medical examiners dissect them. Private detectives, who work near luxury hotels with girls in bikinis lounging around the pool, are enlisted to help.

It is hard for our TV heroes to keep up with the horrors, new examples of which spring up nightly.

Images of violence — TV's *The Equalizer* (Edward Woodward)

In their matter-of-fact, present-tense way, the TV listings tell the story. Police break up a stolen car ring run by a tough high school gym teacher. The nurses threaten to go on strike. A teenage girl discovers that the eight-year-old boy that she babysits is a victim of child abuse. A disgruntled newsman plots the takeover of a nuclear power plant to launch his political career. A daughter defends her mother when she is arrested for putting on a Las Vegas Night at a nursing home.

Las Vegas Night at the nursing home? The weekly catalogue of evil continues. A rookie working on a stakeout is killed. A controversial physician is suspected of being responsible for the death of a wealthy socialite. The calm of a late-night poker game at the hospital is shattered when the victim of a shotgun blast and a Chinese boy with spinal meningitis demand immediate attention. A baby alligator, which has been flushed into the sewer, grows up and develops a monstrous appetite for people. A village choir seems to be hiding something when a man is hunted to death over the edge of a quarry. A group of workers at a plutonium processing plant becomes aware that the site's safety conditions are dangerously inadequate.

Thus does the list of reasons to stay home grow. Hungry alligators, high school gym teachers, striking nurses, plutonium, controversial physicians, village choirs. The more you watch, the more you stay home; the more you stay home, the more you watch.

Could anyone be happy about this situation — a siege mentality driving families into the bunker, the television set serving as their Big Board, their way of charting the advance of the enemy? Well, yes. Sponsors are happy. The more you stay at home, the more TV you watch, the more commercials you see. The more commercials you see, the more commercials the networks sell. The networks are happy too.

New industries arise to supply the bunker: video games can be hooked up to the television set; your children need not go to video-game arcades to play. Arcades are full of junkies and pushers, as you have seen on television programs. More and more video games are being invented. They become more realistic. Video-game advertising on television is high. Hmmm.

Videotape cassette players are also heavily advertised on television. With a videocassette player, you can sit in the bunker and watch movies about how dangerous it is outside. Pay TV advertises heavily on television. With pay TV you will be able to watch uncut movies on television. Some of them, the advertising slyly points out, are pretty raunchy. Life outside is pretty raunchy. A lot of people are taking their clothes off out there at the drop of a hat, and you wouldn't want to see it in person.

In this Depraved New World not much is going on outside. While you hide in the bunker, gasping at the urban, suburban, and rural decay shown on your screen, the best tables at the best restaurants become available. Video-game manufacturers are seated at them. Pay-TV executives have the frontrow seats at the theatre. Videocassette tycoons are having no trouble finding parking spaces.

Only those funny people next door, the ones with no TV set, are out. They are going for a stroll. They walk for miles, never seeing an alligator or a controversial physician.

— Charles Gordon
Maclean's
January 31, 1983

EXPLORING IDEAS

1. The writer states that television presents stories in "a matter-of-fact, present-tense way." What effect would this style have on viewers?
2. ***(a)*** In a single paragraph, evaluate Charles Gordon's point of view in terms of your own experiences and feelings. Indicate clearly whether or not you agree with Mr. Gordon, and explain why you feel the way you do.
   (b) Form small groups and read your paragraph aloud. When everyone has had a turn, compare the opinions expressed and discuss whatever differences emerge.
3. Mr. Gordon implies that sponsors are at least partly responsible for the amount of violence in television shows. This is a common accusation to which sponsors frequently respond by saying they're simply providing the type of programs the viewers want to see. Debate this issue informally in class. *Do* audiences want to see this kind of action described in the article, or do they watch because there are few alternatives?

YOUR TURN

1. If people really do come to view the world as dangerous, as films and television say it is, what might society be like in the future? Write a short story or an editorial on this subject.

Choose from the following or develop your own activities and research projects to investigate further the images and issues presented in this unit.

Students drawn to 'glamorous courses,' colleges say

What the young and the restless really want is to be upscale and glamorous.

Ontario students are flocking to learn how to be private investigators, legal secretaries, and nurses, but shying away from less-glamorous technology programs.

College administrators are puzzled by the fickle tastes of their students. They say the Nielsen television ratings may be the best indicator of what young people want to study.

"A lot of people are influenced by images that come out of television shows and what they perceive as glamorous," said Trevor Massey, registrar of Centennial College in Scarborough, Ont.

Mr. Massey said that when Love Boat, *a TV series about romance on the seas, was popular, there was a surge of interest in courses for cruise directors; and interest in ambulance care increased when* Emergency, *a drama about paramedics, was on the air.*

"If you brought in a series tomorrow and the hero happened to be an electronics specialist, then we're rolling," Mr. Massey said.

— Margaret Polanyi
The Globe and Mail
July 28, 1987

1. Make a list of the professions that are represented in current TV programs. Identify people in your community who work in these professions. Arrange interviews with some of them and find out how they feel about how their work is portrayed on television. Does television distort reality? Are the people you talk with concerned about the image the public may have of their profession? Prepare a report on this topic for the class.
2. How realistically are children and adolescents portrayed in literature? Survey a variety of novels written for and about teenagers. Write a report in which you present your views and conclusions about the image of teenagers in books — their feelings, the problems they face, and the solutions they find to those problems.
3. Focusing attention on film, television, and advertising, prepare a presentation for the class on the changing image of the "ideal" man and woman. Include in your commentary a discussion of the relationship between the images projected in the media and the characteristic values of society.
4. Lynn Johnston is a Canadian cartoonist who has gained an international audience for her work. Her comic strip *For Better or For Worse* has been praised for its realistic portrayal of family life. Prepare a report in which you evaluate the images of parents, children, and family living in Lynn Johnston's comic strip in comparison with that presented in other comics.
5. Has the media industry in Canada done an adequate job of presenting Canada to Canadians? Do some research on the problems facing the Canadian television, movie, or publishing industry and present a report on the problems they face and possible solutions.
6. Interview teachers who work with children and young teenagers. Record their impression of how the images their students see in the media affect their attitudes and behaviour. Ask specifically about the kinds of stories students write, the games they play in the schoolyard, and their social interactions generally. Prepare a report based on your interview investigations.
7. Arrange to interview a number of adults to find out how portrayals and images in the media shaped their expectations when they were adolescents. Write an article based on your investigations.
8. Legal procedures in Canada and the United States are quite different, yet many Canadians are unaware of this because of exposure to American police and courtroom dramas. Arrange interviews with people who work in a variety of professions connected with our legal system. Prepare an oral presentation on the topic of the misconceptions people in Canada may have about the law.

UNIT SEVEN:

THE MAKING HERO

OF A

Heroes, the old saying goes, are made not born. Although rather shopworn, this statement is seen by many commentators as an accurate description of the relationship between heroic figures and the mass media. Do the media actually have the power to make — and break — heroes?

From our earliest days, humanity has always craved heroes. Every civilization has celebrated the exploits of great figures in oral and written epic poetry, song, prose, and the visual arts. Today, novelists, filmmakers, journalists, and television script writers play a major role in satisfying our need for heroic figures.

No matter what the source of our images of heroism, most of us grow up with a vision of what it means to be heroic. Who are today's heroes; what do they have in common with those heroes in myths and legends developed hundreds of years ago? How do modern-day heroes differ from their heroic antecedents? What do they reveal about our values and attitudes? In answering these questions, it is essential to analyze the ways in which media affect the image of the hero.

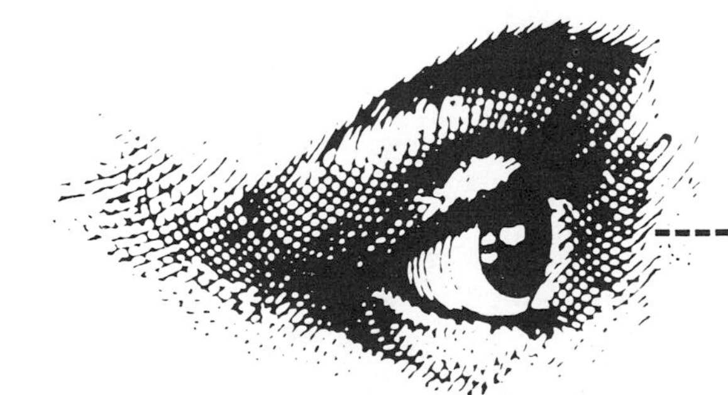

YOU & THE MEDIA

1. How many heroes — real people and fictional characters — can you name?
(a) Develop as long a list as you can. In addition, try to identify where or how you learned about each

individual on your list. Here are some possible sources:

- movies
- television series
- novels
- comic books or comic strips
- school textbooks
- news items
- sports
- recordings and concerts

Work in small groups to complete a data sheet such as the following:

Hero	Source (TV, film, pop song, sports, etc.)	Heroic character traits	Character flaws	Symbols/images associated with hero

(b) Compare your list with those of the other groups in the class.

- What names come up most often?
- What characteristics are typical of a hero?
- What is the source of most names?
- What does this suggest about how ideas concerning heroes are formed and influenced?

2 (a) What is your personal definition of a *hero*? Jot down key words and phrases in your response journal.

(b) What is the difference, if any, between a hero and a *star*? Is a hero also a star? Is a star also a hero?

(c) What function do you think heroes fulfill in society? Why do people appear to *need* heroes?

Record your views, and any evidence you can provide, in your journal. Share your ideas with the class.

3 The following statement appeared in an article in *Maclean's*.

"There are some . . . that fame kills off before they can really establish their right to it. Before they become immortal, they become bores."

— Allan Fotheringham
Maclean's
January 1985

Discuss the following as a class:

(a) How can fame "kill" people off?

(b) Name some individuals who you think would be examples of what Mr. Fotheringham means. Why, do you think, did the public become bored with these individuals?

(c) In your judgment, what must an individual do to establish a right to fame?

4 Maintain a personal or class file on people that are presented as heroes in the media. Clip photographs, articles, editorials, news items, and so on. Include real-life public heroes and the so-called "new" or "invented" heroes in movies or on television. At some point, review your file and discuss as a class the attitudes and values that are being popularized today.

"By knowing someone's role models you get some idea of that someone's values and attitudes." What do high school students' heroes reveal about their values and attitudes?

List of heroes a glimpse into future

A short news item appeared in *The Star* not too long ago. From it we learned that the top 10 heroes of American high school students, in order of popularity, are Bill Cosby, Sylvester Stallone, Eddie Murphy, Ronald Reagan, Chuck Norris, Clint Eastwood, Molly Ringwald, Rob Lowe, Arnold Schwarzenegger, and Don Johnson. If a similar poll were taken of Canadian high school students I suspect that the only major difference in the result would be that Reagan's name would disappear and Wayne Gretzky's would be added somewhere in the lower half.

What does that have to do with looking into the future?

By knowing someone's role models you get some idea of that someone's values and attitudes. By knowing the heroes of this generation of high school students we can get a glimpse of the values and attitudes of the future generation of voters, parents, teachers, and leaders.

Of course, one's heroes as a high school student are not necessarily one's heroes later in life. All of us have grown out of many likes and dislikes, but I still admire many of my earlier heroes and I have no doubt that you do too.

What can we draw from this present list of heroes?

The most striking fact, without question, about this high school list is that only one woman made it. To be more precise, a teenaged actress who plays "vulnerable and sensitive characters" made it, as noted by Mark S. Hoffman, the editor of *World Almanac*, the publication that conducted the poll. So much for women's liberation at the high school level. Clearly, much work is still left to be done.

Regrettably, although not surprisingly, no historical or foreign figures made the list. The Canadian list would certainly include foreigners (Americans), but would probably also lack any historical heroes. Our future will certainly not be very bright if we continue to restrict our thoughts in this way.

Yet, another significant fact is that nine of the 10 most admirable people, as far as American youth are concerned, act, more or less, and the 10th (Reagan) was an actor, more or less.

But how does one get into movies and television? What qualities appeal to our future generation of voters, parents, teachers, and leaders?

Four basic patterns spring from the list: good looks, humor, tremendous physical power evidenced by one's ability to kill a great number of people, or some combination of those.

Great physical power has always been a formula for capturing hero status, but it is depressing to note that all the representatives of this formula on this list prove it through the killing of others, many others. Gone are the days when four gold medals, 40 homers, or 50 goals could catapult you into the top 10. How can such mere mortals compete against someone who can single-handedly defeat the entire Vietnamese army and still have enough left over to defeat Russian giants? Only someone like Gretzky could even come close and only in a hockey-mad society.

Friedrich Nietzsche argued that "the will to power" was a natural and admirable drive which should be nourished as much as possible. It is precisely this sort of philosophy that the Stallone, Schwarzenegger, and Norris "die-foreigner-die" genre of films is legitimizing. So, for example, what sort of foreign policy will those who idolize these three men condone in the future? What sort of criminal justice system will result from the demands of a generation that made Dirty Harry and Sonny Crockett top-10 heroes?

However, the picture I see in the crystal ball is by no means as bleak as the above might suggest. To begin with, cheering a certain behavior in a movie does not necessarily mean that such behavior will be demanded or condoned in reality.

More importantly, however, I draw great satisfaction and hope from the fact that Bill Cosby topped the list of heroes. I doubt that such gentle, caring humor has ever put anyone at the top of the list before. Now that it has happened perhaps it will encourage others and perhaps the Cosby types will soon crowd the Stallone-Schwarzenegger-Norris types off the list. Predictably, at this point the crystal ball grows dim.

— Rocco Rossi
The Toronto Star
March 10, 1987

EXPLORING IDEAS

1. Earlier, your class identified the most popular heroes for your group. How accurate was Mr. Rossi in predicting the names that Canadian high school students would pick for their honour roll of heroes?
2. If your class's list is significantly different, discuss some of the possible reasons for the differences.
3. In small groups, discuss the issue of heroes and personal values. Look over the names on the list of personal heroes you developed earlier. To what extent do these people reflect your personal goals, values, or beliefs? What do they reveal about the attitudes and values of your generation?
4. Most of the heroes identified in the article are creations of film and television. Why, do you think, do these two media have such a powerful influence?

YOUR TURN

1. Write a brief article — similar to the one you have just read — about what today's heroes reveal about our values and attitudes.
2. Design a collage that makes a visual statement about heroes in popular culture today.
3. Talk to your parents and grandparents about the men and women who were popular heroes of their generation. What role did the media play in creating these heroes? What values and attitudes were modelled by these heroes? Write a poem or an article about "Heroes Then and Now."

FASTER THAN A SPEEDING BULLET

Action comics, with their unique artwork and storytelling techniques, are the source of many heroic figures in popular culture. The forces of evil seldom face stiffer opposition than they do from these comic-book superheroes. The popularity of comics and their superheroes declined in the 1970s, but once again these larger-than-life figures have a devoted following on TV, in films, and in print. When the creators of comic-book fantasies responded to demands for "new-and-improved" superheroes, a new generation of fans became hooked on their tales of mighty deeds.

The "Man of Steel" — Superman — is the most enduring superhero of them all. Recently the "Caped Crusader" has gone through some changes now that he has passed his fiftieth birthday.

Superman goes back to the drawing board

The revamped Superman debuted in 1986.

THE FAR SIDE By GARY LARSON

Dang!.. Now where was I going?

Superman in his later years.

A New York publisher has finally achieved what legions of mad scientists, sinister aliens, and bloodthirsty monsters have failed to do: Knock some of the super out of Superman.

Ironically, by weakening one of the greatest fictional heroes of all time, DC Comics Inc. is hoping to make him stronger where it really counts — on the magazine rack.

And by the time the character's 50th anniversary is observed in 1988, fans will have witnessed a complete reforging of the Man of Steel.

The upheaval is part of a monumental cosmic housecleaning that DC began to streamline, modernize and, in some cases, even eliminate dozens of costumed heroes clogging a badly crowded comic-book universe.

But Superman required especially sensitive treatment, because he remains one of the truly mythic figures of pop culture, despite several years of gradually declining sales.

His poor performance in the ledger books is the cumulative result of decades of superficial, innocuous, or outdated details — super-pets, silly enemies, simplistic behavior quirks — which were innovative in their day, but now threaten to drag the legend down.

Readers have also grown bored with a hero so powerful that nothing fazes him. Human qualities and the all-important sense of challenge are severely diminished in a man who can ignite suns with his x-ray vision, punt a planet out of orbit, or fly to Alpha Centauri in the blink of an eye.

The solution — a colossal gamble on DC's part — is being attempted by one favorite and former Marvel writer, artist John Byrne, a Calgary native who has recreated Superman as a hero who is forced to sweat to succeed.

Byrne is returning to the concept pioneered in 1938 by Toronto-born artist Joe Shuster and Cleveland writer Jerry Siegel, who envisioned Superman as incredibly strong and gifted, but hardly omnipotent.

He'll still be faster than a speeding bullet, more powerful than a locomotive, and able to leap tall buildings in a single bound, but he may have to think twice before braving a nuclear blast. Costume and general appearance remain unchanged and reminiscent of Christopher Reeve who starred in the Superman movies.

Among the other changes:

- Superman will be the only survivor of the destruction of his home planet, Krypton. This should restore his one-of-a-kind status which faded with the proliferation of Kryptonian refugees, including a super-dog, super-monkey, and an army of super-criminals.
- Superboy, the adolescent Superman, will cease to exist. The new story calls for an un-super baby to be rocketed to Earth and raised as a normal child. Only in his late teenage years does his battery-like body absorb and modify enough solar energy to transform him into Superman.
- Clark Kent, Superman's alter ego, will shed his unrealistically shy personality and become both self-sufficient and assertive, as befits a top reporter at the Metropolis Daily Planet. Byrne is modelling him on the Kent portrayed by George Reeves in the 1950s *Superman* TV series.
- Instead of dying while Superman is a teenager, his adoptive Earth parents will stay alive and give Clark emotional support through manhood. For this reason, Superman will no longer seek refuge in a remote Arctic fortress.
- Lois Lane will express casual curiosity about Superman's double identity, but will no longer be

obsessed with uncovering his secret. Nor will she display her traditional gushing adoration for Superman and withering contempt for Kent. She'll be a more mature, balanced, 1980s woman.

- Kryptonite, the deadly radioactive mineral created during Krypton's explosion, became too plentiful in the past and was used too often as a weapon against Superman. In the revised story, only one small piece finds its way to Earth.
- Luthor remains Superman's arch-enemy, but he won't be a half-crazed criminal genius. In a nod to realism, he'll mastermind a vast corporate empire that shields him from direct implication in his attacks on Superman.

This redesigning of Superman is causing quite a fuss, because DC has dared to tinker with much more than just another fantastic character from the funny pages.

Superman is the archetypal super-hero — the first to don cape, boots, longjohns, trunks, and stylized insignia to face challenges undreamed of by Tarzan, the Shadow, Doc Savage, and other earthbound heroes who preceded him in pulp fiction of the 1930s.

Most important, Superman served as the catalyst for millions of hours of wistful, childhood reverie. So powerful were these daydreams that they transformed tens of thousands of young fans of the 1940s, '50s, and '60s into today's adult comic-book collectors, while attracting a new generation of young recruits.

And it is they who will respond with a wrath more venomous than Luthor's if Byrne and DC prove unequal to a task that would have taxed even the old, unrestrained power of the Man of Steel.

— Henry Mietkiewicz
The Toronto Star
June 21, 1986

EXPLORING IDEAS

1. Did you read comic books as a child? Do you enjoy comic books now? What childhood heroes provided *you* with "hours of wistful, childhood reverie"? In your journal, describe them and what they meant to you as a child.
2. Think about the formula that is used to create comic-book superheroes and their heroic adventures. What elements, common to all, can you identify? For example, what are the characteristics of the superhero? the villain? the hero's origin?
3. What are some of the conventions and techniques you associate with comics? What is different about the way heroes are portrayed in comics and in other media? Share your observations and conclusions with the class.
4. Consider the changes in today's comic-book heroes. What do these changes suggest about current-day values and our concept of heroism? In a class discussion, tell how you would account for these changes.
5. Why would it be difficult to unmake a hero such as Superman who has been popular with readers for decades?
6. Discuss the following statement: "*(Superman) remains one of the truly mythic figures of pop culture....*"

INVESTIGATING THE MEDIA

1. **(a)** Spend some time watching television programs that feature cartoon superheroes for children. What formula is evident in these programs? What values are communicated?
(b) How do various media, manufacturers, and retailers work together to increase the popularity of cartoon superheroes?
As an individual, or in small groups, visit stores in your community. Note and jot down brief descriptions of toys and other spin-off items that promote various superheroes. What are some common features shared by superhero action toys? How are they advertised to children? (Survey in-store displays, TV commercials, toy catalogues and magazine advertising, and the packaging of the toys.)
(c) Prepare and present an oral or written report based on your findings and conclusions.

YOUR TURN

1. **(a)** Working with a partner, design your own comic-book superhero. Consider the following story features in your planning:
- character's name
- positive character traits and trademarks of the hero
- character flaws or weaknesses of the hero

- costume and any signs or symbols associated with the hero
- hero's mission or purpose
- hero's personal history/origins/birth legends
- character who is the superhero's everyday counterpart/identity (for example, Clark Kent = Superman, Bruce Wayne = Batman)
- hero's archrival

(b) Describe toys and other spin-off items that could be marketed to promote your superhero. (For example, action figures, buildings, T-shirts, shoes, watches.)

(c) If you can, use modelling clay, papier mâché, styrofoam, and so on, to create a model of one or two of these spin-off toys.

(d) If possible, present an outline of your superhero along with the complete marketing package to a group of young children. Ask this "target audience" to comment on the appeal of your superhero package. You may wish to revise your treatment based on the audience feedback.

2. Role-play a TV game show in which all of the participants are superheroes.

3. Videotape a series of interviews with superheroes in improvised role play.

Never heard of this Canadian Forces pilot and his deeds of derring-do? Seems that the rest of the world has.

Dan Cooper All-Canadian Hero

In 30 arduous years of ridding the skies of bad guys, Maj. Dan Cooper, Canadian Forces pilot, has aged not a single day. He has relentlessly winged from one adventure to the next in Canada, Europe, Australia, Africa, the Arctic, *and* outer space — but nary a stress line mars his craggy handsome face.

He has chased spies and assassins, shadowed sinister satellites, fought off aerial pirates, rushed supplies to earthquake victims, and smoothly herded errant Soviet fliers back into their own airspace. Yet his hair is as jet-black, his eyes as clear blue, his smile as dazzling white as the day he flew his first CF-100 Canuck. Although happiest when flying such interceptors as the CF-104 and CF-18 Hornet, the indefatigable Dan can turn his hand to anything: helicopters, old-fashioned Dakotas, Hercules transports, or even the American space shuttle. He handles them all with consummate skill and, although occasionally shot at or forced down, has never been wounded.

All this is easy for the dashing major. He is imaginary.

Dan Cooper, all-Canadian hero, is the wildly successful cartoon creation of Belgian artist Albert Weinberg — successful, that is, nearly everywhere but where English is the main language. Since 1954, 32 full-color Cooper cartoon books have sold 11 million copies in 24 countries and in 17 languages, including Yiddish, Arabic, Vietnamese, Nepalese, and Greek. A French version is marketed in Quebec. Bootleg copies are even sneaked into the Soviet Union. But to Weinberg's puzzlement, Major Dan has never caught on in English.

"Albert is a brilliant artist and his work is technically excellent," says

Peter Morris, assistant manager of The Toronto Star Syndicate. "But it's very difficult and rare for a cartoon to make the jump from Europe to North America. It is not just a matter of translation. Tastes and styles are different."

Meanwhile, bilingual members of Air Command (successor to the Royal Canadian Air Force) — especially those who have served or are still serving overseas — remain Weinberg's major Canadian fans. But *such* fans.

"It's a wonderful portrayal of an honest-to-goodness Canadian hero who exudes those qualities that we like to tell our young airmen and airwomen are good ones," says Lt. Gen. Paul Manson, head of Air Command. "Things like integrity and courage, skill, chivalry. I guess he appeals to our sense of pride."

Dan Cooper is a clever blend of cartoon-adventure and genuine airforce lore. Weinberg, 62, a slender, courteous man with thinning brown hair, has a passion for detail. He regularly prowls Canadian air bases here and abroad, and NATO bases all over Europe, with a tape recorder, sketch pad, and three cameras. A wide-angle lens gives him complete views inside cockpits; a motor-driven camera captures each split second of landings and takeoffs.

Every aircraft serial number is authentic (indicating whether Dan is flying out of, say, Bagotville, Que., Cold Lake, Alta., or Lahr, Germany). Every rivet and decal is in the right place; every movement of man or machine is accurate. Weinberg even knows how long it takes Dan to unsnap his parachute.

Every exchange among Cooper, his fellow pilots, senior officers, and the control tower is true to life. Even the slang is contemporary (this year Cooper's mates are saying, "Go for it!"). Sometimes the faces of the characters are those of real Canadian airmen, with fictitious names. They enjoy their celebrity as "models."

Weinberg fans delight in the realism. He gets hundreds of letters from all over the free world, often from young people who want to learn more about Canada or aviation. Sometimes fliers tell him, "I'm a pilot because of you. I read Dan Cooper as a kid, and wanted to grow up like him!"

"Sometimes I think of a certain young man who is up in the air because of Cooper," muses the conscientious Weinberg, "and I hope he is okay."

Weinberg studied law, but before he even practiced a case, his hobby, cartooning, took over. It began with a few documentary newspaper strips on such historical figures as the explorers Cortez and Magellan, and scientist Albert Schweitzer. Then one day in 1952, he attended a film on the breaking of the sound barrier. It was Weinberg's first glimpse of a jet plane and he was captivated by "the beauty of the shape and movement."

He based a cartoon strip on the film. His editor called for more, and then for a book. Weinberg had admired Canada since school days — to him it epitomized freedom. His hero would be a Canadian.

That first book, *The Blue Triangle*, described the testing of a new jet in Australia, where the hero was a colonial attached to the Royal Air Force. (At the time, Weinberg didn't know that Canada had its own air force.) He tried dozens of names before settling on Dan Cooper, because it "felt right." Some years later a French-Canadian reporter demanded why French-speaking Weinberg had picked an English name for the character.

"Ah, his father is from Toronto, it is true," Weinberg explained diplomatically, "but his mother is from Chicoutimi!"

Cooper's bicultural parentage is part of his carefully constructed profile. The major is also a muscular six-footer, a nonsmoker, and a moderate drinker (just a few beers with the boys after a hard day in the clouds). He is cheerful, articulate, kind to widows and orphans, and a role model for the young.

His frequent companions are French-Canadian Captains Gagnon and Tremblay, Captain Chattanooga, a full-blooded Cree (who, oddly, wears his hair in braids while in full uniform), and Captain Louverture, a Black. Usually one or two attractive women figure in the story, but there is no hanky-panky. Dan's mates may utter some macho hoots at the sight of the female form, but the major himself is straight-arrow.

For years his heart belonged to Randi, a gorgeous blond Norwegian, sister of a NATO officer friend. Through many a book Dan pined for Randi, who professed love for him but persistently eluded him. Now, alas, Randi is no more. In book No. 32, *Viking Connection*, Cooper flew in pursuit of drug traffickers, unaware that Randi was a hostage aboard the fugitive aircraft. Cooper's warning shots disabled both engines. But instead of landing, the panicky drug smuggler turned his floatplane, instantly engulfing it in flames. Only after it crashed into the sea did Cooper learn that his beloved Randi had also gone down.

"*Major Cooper, Major Cooper, répondez!*" pleaded the control tower. But the heartbroken major did not answer.

It was a dramatic — and accidental — turn for the Cooper books.

Weinberg had planned the attack right down to the second, as it would have happened in real life. He hadn't intended to zap his heroine.

"Then I realized the other plane would *have* to crash," he says. "I had various actions coming together and if I changed any of it, I must change the whole story. I said to myself, 'It is impossible that Randi be killed!' Then I said, 'Why not! Maybe life must be so.'"

Weinberg often dips into real life for his stories. In *Space Shuttle*, his graphic details of the American shuttle are an entertaining but accurate lesson on spacecraft. He built another story around a sonar system set up to detect Soviet submarines off the coast of Norway. His book *Operation Kosmos 990* was based on the crash of the satellite Kosmos 954 in northern Canada in 1978. Averaging a 15- to 16-hour workday, sometimes going 40 hours nonstop, Weinberg divides his year between homes in Brussels and Switzerland, his studios in each one crammed with reference works. When not drawing, he pores over science, aviation, and business magazines (the last to keep him abreast of trends in politics and strategy).

He grosses about $100 000 a year. A reporter told him, "You could make a lot more if you turned Dan Cooper into an American." Although Weinberg knew it was true, he was mildly offended. "Dan Cooper will always be a Canadian," he says firmly.

What lies ahead for the all-Canadian hero? For one thing, he will probably stay a major. Promotion would move him into administration — making him a poor candidate for heroism.

In the newest book, as he grieves for Randi, the major withdraws for a while to a little island. Returning to his squadron, he realizes on his first day aloft that the memory of that last tragic flight still haunts him. He cannot squeeze the trigger even to fire at the drone being used for aerial target practice.

Weinberg thinks he'll let Randi's memory always linger with Dan Cooper; the major will remain devoted to one woman for life. Perhaps, says his creator, the cartoon hero will ease his sorrow by helping some young pilot with deep problems of his own.

One thing is certain: There will always *be* Dan Cooper as long as there is Albert Weinberg. "I will never retire," the artist says fervently. "And" — echoing his millions of readers around the world — "I cannot live without Dan Cooper!"

Robert Collins and others
Reader's Digest
November 1984

EXPLORING IDEAS

1. *"You could make a lot more if you turned Dan Cooper into an American."*

   In your view, what is unique about the Canadian image of public heroes? Collect your own thoughts on this issue and present them in a short essay.

YOUR TURN

1. Working with a partner, design an all-Canadian comic-book hero that you think would be successful in Anglophone Canada. Develop a series of marketing strategies to promote this new comic-book character. Present your ideas to the class for their comments and suggestions.

Wonder Woman

1980s Wonder Woman

Where did she come from? How did she get such superhuman powers? Like most good comic book creations, Wonder Woman had a birth legend that dramatically answered all such questions. Her inventor, a psychologist named William Moulton Marston, combined Greek myth and Amazon speculation to produce the first and classic Wonder Woman adventure in 1941. Marston was proud of Wonder Woman and the purpose for which she had been invented: to provide an alternative to the "bloodcurdling masculinity" of most comics by showing that strength could be used with love and justice.

Wonder Woman's character was set by this first story, but her costume immediately changed from skirts to shorts. "It was too darned hard to draw in action pictures," remembers the creator's widow, Elizabeth Marston. "Besides, it would have been up over her head most of the time."

The change made this first comic book a collector's item. Never again would Wonder Woman be seen in skirts.

Comic books were not quite respectable, which was a large part of the reason I read them: under the covers with a flashlight, in the car while my parents told me I was ruining my eyes, in a tree or some other inaccessible spot; any place that provided sweet privacy and independence. Along with cereal boxes and ketchup labels, they were the primers that taught me how to read. They were even cheap enough to be the first items I could buy on my own; a customer whose head didn't quite reach the counter but whose dignity was greatly enhanced by making a selection (usually after much agonizing) and offering up money of her own.

If, as I have always suspected, children are simply short people — ancient spirits who happen to be locked up in bodies that aren't big enough or skillful enough to cope with the world — then the superhuman feats in comic books and fairy tales become logical and necessary. It's satisfying for anyone to have heroes who can see through walls or leap over skyscrapers in a single bound. But it's especially satisfying if our worldview consists mostly of knees, and tying our shoes is still an exercise in frustration.

The trouble is that the comic book performers of such superhuman feats — and even of only dimly competent ones — are almost always men. The female child is left to believe that, even when her body is as grown-up as her spirit, she will still be in the childlike role of helping with minor tasks, appreciating men's accomplishments, and being so incompetent and passive that she can only hope some man can come to her rescue. Of course, rescue and protection are comforting, even exhilarating experiences that should be and often are shared by men and boys. Even in comic books, the hero is frequently called on to protect his own kind in addition to helpless women. But dependency and zero accomplishments get very dull as a steady diet. The only option for a girl reader is to identify with the male characters — pretty difficult, even in the years of childhood. If she can't do that, she faces limited prospects: an "ideal" life of sitting around like a technicolor clothes horse, getting into jams with villains, and saying things like "Oh, Superman! I'll always be grateful to you," even as her hero goes off to bigger and better adventures. It hardly seems worth learning to tie our shoes.

I'm happy to say that I was rescued from this plight at about the age of seven or eight; rescued (great Hera!) by a woman. Not only was she as wise as Athena and as lovely as Aphrodite, she had the speed of Mercury and the strength of Hercules. Of course, being an Amazon, she had a head start on such accomplishments, but she had earned them in a human way by training in Greek-style contests of dexterity and speed with her Amazon sisters. (Somehow it always seemed boring to me that Superman was a creature from another planet, and therefore had bullet-proof skin, x-ray vision, and the power to fly. Where was the contest?) This beautiful Amazon did have some fantastic gadgets to help her: an invisible plane that carried her through dimensions of time and space, a golden magic lasso, and bullet-proof bracelets. But she still had to get to the plane, throw the lasso with accuracy, and be agile enough to catch bullets on the steel-encased wrists.

Her creator had also seen straight into my heart and understood the secret fears of violence hidden there. No longer did I have to pretend to like the "Pow!" and "Crunch!" style of Captain Marvel or the Green Hornet. No longer did I have nightmares after reading ghoulish comics filled with torture and mayhem, comics made all the more horrifying by their real-life setting in World War II. (It was a time when leather-clad Nazis were marching in the newsreels *and* in the comics, and the blood on the pages seemed frighteningly real.) Here was a heroic person who might conquer with force, but only a force that was tempered by love and justice. She converted her enemies more often than not. And if they were destroyed, they did it to themselves, usually in some unbloody accident.

She was beautiful, brave, and explicitly out to change "a world torn by the hatreds and wars of men."

She was Wonder Woman.

— Gloria Steinem
from *Wonder Woman*

EXPLORING IDEAS

1. *"It's satisfying...to have heroes who can see through walls or leap over skyscrapers in a single bound."*
   Form small groups to discuss the value of comic-book superheroes. What emotional and psychological needs do such heroes satisfy?
2. *"The trouble is that the comic book performers of such superhuman feats — and even of only dimly competent ones — are almost always men."*
   (a) Is this still true today? If so, what are the reasons?
   (b) What type of female hero is no longer acceptable? Why have tastes and styles changed, in your opinion?

INVESTIGATING THE MEDIA

1. How are women portrayed by writers of contemporary superhero comics? Form small groups and evaluate the characterization of women both in newspaper comic strips and in comic books. Consider
   (a) women as helpmates for superheroes
   (b) women as superheroes
   Prepare a report based on your findings.

HEROES OF THE SILVER SCREEN

In the 1980s, movie reviews proclaiming that "heroes are back!" began to appear in magazines and newspapers. Once again, movies about people of action and courage, men and women dedicated to keeping the world safe for the rest of us, had become fashionable. Such movies hadn't always been popular; let's examine the image of heroes and heroism presented in movies and how that image changes to reflect the ideals and values of the people who line up to see them.

"Love him or hate him, Sylvester Stallone has brought the hero to the forefront of American Mythology." How do Rocky and Rambo measure up to your image of what a hero ought to be?

Rocky & Rambo

Forget homework. Forget school troubles and boy troubles and parent troubles. For Carmen Smith, 19 years old, World War III was being waged in a prize ring onscreen at the Sack Cinema 57 in Boston, and Russia, in the person of a blood-doped bionic giant named Ivan Drago, appeared to be winning. "You gonna get ... whipped, boy," Carmen was muttering half in prayer, but the punches were raining down like MIRV'ed missiles on her champion and America's, and she and most of the kids around her were squirming deeper into the dusty red plush of their seats, waiting for the end. And then, suddenly, the good guy — *our* guy — was on the attack again, answering the Russian blow for blow, and Carmen bounced to her feet with the others, screaming, *"Go, Rocky, go! Go, Rocky, go!"*

Rocky, or course, was an up-from-the-canvas palooka named Rocky Balboa, and he and his blood brother John J. Rambo, a Green Beret machine-tooled to kill in Vietnam, are the twin icons of a flag-waving, Red-bashing new nationalism in our mass culture. They are the creatures of one Michael Sylvester Stallone, an actor, writer, and director of otherwise unexceptional gifts; his face droops in key places like a melting waxwork, his voice sounds by his own estimate like a Mafia pallbearer's, and his announced notion of the ideal screenplay would consist of a single word of dialogue. But his *Rambo: First Blood Part II*... and *Rocky IV*... brought the mythic American hero downstage center again, standing tall after years in hiding, ready to take on the world with guns, knives, gloves, or bare knuckles. Their breakaway success at the box office is, in the eyes of Rocky's chief hypester, Irv Ivers, marketing president of MGM/UA, a case of simple hero worship. "America has always wanted a hero it can identify with," he enthuses. "It *was* John Wayne. It *is* Sly Stallone."

Ivers is, of course, an interested party, and his reverence for his property is not widely shared among critics, cinematic or social. *Son of Rambo* was widely dismissed as a revenge fantasy and *Great-Grandson of Rocky* as the burned-out end of a spent series; the daily reviewers called it empty, crude, primitive, boring, bloated, hollow, mush-headed, butter-brained, elephantine, witless, redundant and, in one Hobbesian spasm in *The Baltimore Sun*, "loud, stupid, nasty, brutish, and short." Vietnam veterans attacked Rambo for his war psychosis. Feminists savaged Rocky for his unregenerate machismo. Psychologists worried about the romanticized violence in both film cycles — the implicit message that the problems of today can be solved in the manner of the frontier, by hitting or shooting them.

Ticket sales: Nobody much likes Stallone or his works, that is to say, except the people, and not, as widely supposed, just teenage boys; nearly half the cash customers, after the opening rush, are over 25, and nearly half are women. *Rambo* rang up $32 million in ticket sales in its first six days, the third best launch in history, and has grossed $150 million thus far. *Rocky IV* did $32 million in five days, the strongest nonsummer opening ever, and pushed the total domestic take for the series over $400 million. The numbers owed much to shrewd marketing strategies — to saturating screens with trailers long in advance and rushing the films to theaters ahead of the seasonal competition. But their deeper source was Stallone's own intuitive — or, as some prefer, cynical — feel for the *Zeitgeist*. He taps the same wellsprings as Bruce Springsteen, say, or Ronald Reagan; he is filmmaker to a blue-collar America that doesn't want to take it anymore.

He is suitably modest, for publication, about his folk genius; he likes to say it was his characters who were at the right place at the right moment in our history. He thinks of himself as an artist, and receiving a caller last week, he sat surrounded by the appurtenances of art — a Diego Rivera and a Chagall, a copy of *Ulysses* cheek by jowl with a biography of Rocky Marciano and the leatherbound scripts of his own growing *oeuvre*. But art to him is instinct rather than cerebration, "like playing football in the dark," he says. "You don't know when you're going to get tackled — you just have to go for it." First Rocky and then Rambo arrived to him on the wash of patriotism — even jingoism, he concedes — that swept the country beginning in the Bicentennial year of 1976 and crested in the Age of Reagan. "And I happened to get caught in it," he told his visitor. "It's like a guy who goes out fishing and gets caught in a tidal wave."

He was not the first to ride that wave, and he is not swimming alone in it now; a generation of cinematic pop artists also sensed America's weariness with the angst-ridden antiheroes of the '60s and '70s and its thirst for an older style of champion a white hat in city clothes, this time, or combat khakis. The worship of the warrior hero is at least as old as Hercules, and in America it has grown its own frontier strain: the "legitimate savage," historian Stan K. Schultz calls him, who operates outside the laws and strictures of civilization and uses violent means to worthy ends. Some scholars see Clint Eastwood's *Dirty Harry* as the precursor of his return to the popcorn circuit after a long absence; others nominate other stars in other star vehicles. Suddenly the silver screen seems crowded with lone-wolf heroes dispensing politics and justice out of the barrels of .357 magnums — Charles Bronson stalking muggers on the subway. Chuck Norris hunting MIA's in Vietnam. Arnold Schwarzenegger standing off an army in *Commando* with weapons including a severed arm.

But Stallone's ingenious comic-strip artistry has zapped them all; his success with two series at once, and with two grunt heroes, is unprecedented in the industry. That success has become a bit of a prison for him, spoiling practically everything else he tries in the movies; his Rambo/Rocky persona is too powerful for ensemble playing. Yet he cannot seem to escape it . . .

Kidvid hour: Thus, for the moment, he is trapped inside his brainchildren and crying all the way to the bank. . . . Rocky dolls and Rambo water guns are in the toy stores. A cartoon series about Rambo — a nonviolent, nature-loving Rambo, its *auteurs* insist — is in production for the Saturday-morning Kidvid hour. A New York modeling agency ran a Rambo look-alike contest; the winners got to dress up (or down) as Rambo and deliver gag "Rambo-Grams," with the warning to the recipient, "Take it or else." In Houston, a new saloon named Rambose opened, with camouflage nets for décor and a buffet served from an army stretcher. Even the president wished aloud for a Rambo to send to the next hostage crisis, and Fritz Mondale played the theme from *Rocky* whenever he won a primary from Gary Hart.

Stallone's climb to the top of the hero business was roundabout, begun before heroics were fully back in fashion. There were trace elements of the antihero in the Rocky Balboa we first met . . . years ago — the struggles of the Hollywood equivalent of a gym rat hanging out around a practice ring and hoping for the big break. Rocky was a club fighter of 30 at the time, a "ham-and-egger" by his own thick-tongued estimate; there was trouble in his pedigree (19 juvenile arrests, seven schools in two years) and nothing in his pro record (44 wins, 20 losses) to indicate much more than a capacity to absorb punishment. "I'm at least half a bum, y'know?" he told his lady Adrian, a plain-Jane shopgirl until she took her glasses off and became beautiful. Rocky was a product, culturally, of the Age of Limits, and when he was chosen by whim to fight a Muhammad Ali clone named Apollo Creed for the heavyweight title, his expectations were suitably low. "All I want to do is go the distance," he said. "...When that bell rings and I'm still standing, I'll know for the first time in my life, see, that I weren't just another bum from the neighborhood."

The rest is folk history. He went the distance that time, won the championship in a rematch, lost it to Mr. T, won it back, bore a son, buried friends, wrestled with self-doubt, and — in contrast to the neurasthenic '60s heroes — invariably won. ("'Cause I'm a fighter," he concludes in *Rocky IV*. "I didn't ask to be one, but that's what I am. That's the way I'm made.") In the process, he knocked the rust off the whole canon of traditional American values and became their exemplar. He loved his family. He was loyal to his friends. He was kind to animals. He believed in the American Dream of opportunity for all, and achieved it by hard, unremitting labor. He raised the work ethic to a nearly religious plain; his training for his fights became a saintly mortification of the flesh, a rite of purification requiring his retreat to various wildernesses — a meat-packing plant, a hostile ghetto gym, and finally, in *Rocky IV*, the frozen steppes of Russia.

Where next? The stories took on a relentless sameness from sequel to sequel, as Stallone himself was acutely aware; there were no surprises anymore. "Where do you go?" he asked himself, and his answer was deeper into minimalism — shorter films, flashier images, louder music, less talk, more action and longer flashbacks to earlier installments in the series. Rocky became less a character ... than a checklist of virtues and a balance sheet of pain, given and received. The predictability of the Rockys had always been one of their attractions, "like going to McDonald's for dinner," David Marc, a Brandeis professor of American studies, says. "You know you're not getting gourmet stuff, but it's fun and safe." By *Rocky IV*, the experience had become nearly ritual, like mass at San Vitale in Ravenna; the players had been worn as smooth and flat as the saints in the mosaic, and the story line was as dependable as liturgy.

The difference, this time, was that *Rocky IV* emerged from Stallone's brow at a time of resurgent Russophobia in the land and allowed him to politicize his vision; the ham-and-egger from Mighty Mickey's gym in Philly had been transmogrified into the ultimate cold warrior, taking on the best the Soviets had to offer in gladiatorial combat. A president of the United States had declared Russia the Evil Empire. A deep chill had settled over U.S.-Soviet relations and had spread into popular culture at a pitch unheard since the 1950s — into sports, movies, comedy, and even television commercials. A particularly crude promo for Wendy's hamburgers pictured a Soviet fashion show with a single stout model in a babushka and a dowdy gray frock. For evening wear, the same woman modeled the same dress with a flashlight; for resort wear, the same ensemble again, this time with a beach ball.

Rocky was preceded into politics by his doppelgänger Rambo, who had been mopping up commies while Rocky was still stopping punches at the Resurrection Athletic Club. John J. Rambo is Rocky as he might be after a plate of bad clams — or, more precisely, after one extended tour in Vietnam and another in an American prison quarry doing hard time for blowing up an unfriendly town. Rocky's theater of war is the prize ring; the combat there, while brutal, is contained by the ropes and ordered by the rules. Rambo's is the bush, and the law of the bush is the law of the jungle. "To survive war, you have to *become* war," he says, and he has. He was a Medal of Honor winner in a war that was, in the politics of his movies, a lie, and when he is sent back in to find a campful of American POW's, that is a lie, too — a mission betrayed from birth by his own government. "Sir, do we get to win this time?" he asks when he is recruited for the job. "This time it's up to you," his ex-CO says.

It isn't, not really, but Rambo wins it anyway, running up a Russo-Vietnamese body count that would have made a battalion proud in the real war. His contempt for politicians remains murderous; his regard for America survives. "Hate?" he says. "I'd die for it...[I want] what every other guy who came over here and spilled his guts and gave everything he had wants — for our country to love us as much as we love it."

In the iconography of the Stallone movies, Rambo is a man of the past shooting up the past — those days of shame when America lost a war, witnessed the disgrace of a government, knuckled under to mullahs, sheiks, and tin-pot dictators,

"Jingo-Jangle" — A triumphant Rocky (Sly Stallone) stands in the ring in Moscow on Christmas day (*Rocky IV*).

and seemed immobilized by the difficulties of doing something about anything. His last paroxysm of violence, this time around, is directed not at the men who betrayed him but at the machines lining their cybernated command post; the computers stand for complication against common sense, for bureaucracy against people, for paralysis against action. His rage is meant to be cathartic, for himself and, Stallone guesses, for all those guys out there with their own wars to fight. It works for the audience, or seems to in their deep, visceral response to the movie. It does not for Rambo; he is imprisoned in history, his own and America's.

It is instead Rocky Balboa who stands for the future in the world according to Sly; standing in the ring in Moscow on Christmas Day, the flag around his shouders and the slain Drago at his feet, he is the apotheosis of a new America, open, tough, disciplined, confident, and unabashed at having and using power. Stallone had written scenes aligning the American establishment against Rocky; the boxing commission, in one, forced him to give up his title if he insisted on fighting Drago, and the government, in another, threatened to revoke his passport if he tried. But those perfidies belonged to the Rambo, not the Rocky canon, and they were left on the cutting-room floor. In *Rocky IV* East-West politics is reduced to parable or even fable. Rocky is the self-made champion of freedom, Drago the machine-made product of the state. The outcome, even for newcomers to the formula, is a foregone conclusion.

Jingo-jangle: What the early box-office returns suggest is that America was ready for such a fantasy, though only up to a point; the roar of the crowd gives way to titters, in some theaters, when Rocky uses the moment of his triumph to plead for peace and gets the whole Soviet house applauding, even the Gorbachev look-alike in the Politburo box. It is what one scholar calls the conquistador spirit that people come to see.... The jingo-jangle Stallone admits is at the heart of the work is, in his eyes, not a bad thing — not after the shoving around America took in the world of the '70s. "They just pushed," he mused, "until finally the giant said, 'Wait a minute, I'm big and strong, but I haven't done anything that's *that* atrocious.' ...There's nothing wrong with being fit and strong and powerful and, if necessary, to flex some muscle. We're back to geopolitics on an even keel. We're not coming in there quaking, 'What do I do?' We're coming in as an equal. We're now in the proper weight class."

Rocky's victories and Rambo's do not count for much even in their own terms and do not live long after the 90-minute running time of Stallone's reductionist late works. But the two of them descend from a long bloodline of warrior heroes in America's popular culture — soldier heroes who do battle under the codes and conventions of war and outlaw heroes who use private violence when armies, posses, or policemen fail. They date at least to the Minutemen, to Davy Crockett and Dan'l Boone, and they have recurred in cycles in many guises — as cowboys and cavalrymen, as private eyes and rogue cops, as space travelers and supermen — and now in the unlikely personae of a ring-worn fighter and a stressed-out soldier. They are nearly as much a part of the symbolic furniture of Reagan's America as the president himself — a can-do America re-emergent, in his vision, from a can't-do past. "America thinks it's about time John Wayne got back in the saddle again," says historian Schultz, a professor at the University of Wisconsin — only this time the Duke is Sly Stallone.

Not all students of our mass culture are happy with what the Rambo/Rocky phenomenon says about the state of our communal fantasy life. The Rocky movies teach the traditional values of grit and hard work, but when Robert Fillman, a 10-year-old in Boston, was asked what he liked about them, he answered readily, "He always *wins*." The Rambo cycle is bloodier and more nihilist, the chronicle of a nearly mute hero whose natural state is war and whose vocabulary is sudden death. At a recent class on war films at Notre Dame, a student asked Prof. Patrick D. Anderson where he would put Rambo. "In the trash can," Anderson replied. To his astonishment, a sizable share of the class rebelled. The body count seemed not to matter, or the amoral framing of the war. Rambo, for the dissenters, was a *hero* — a kind of noble savage who got fed up with a system that reduces men to numbers and who took arms against it with wit, cunning, and skill.

Collective past: Yet Rocky and Rambo are figures of redemption as well after the anti-heroics of the recent past, a trend in mass culture that reflected a nation's fallen regard for itself. Our fantasy heroes are less mirrors of what we are than windows into what we might like to be. Rambo and Rocky are archetypes of our collective past, and if one was disfigured by it, the other is its champion — the underdog who went for it and made good. "If I could unzip myself and step out and be somebody else," Rocky's brother-in-law, Paulie, tells the champ just before his fight with Drago, "I'd wanna be you." So, by the evidence of his success, would a lot of us.

— Peter Goldman
Newsweek
December 23, 1985

EXPLORING IDEAS

1. **(a)** *"It was his characters who were in the right place at the right time."* Based on the information in the article and on your own experiences, suggest why Rocky and Rambo were right for their times.
   (b) What type of hero is right for today? What trends in movie heroes are evident in films that are box-office smash hits now? Share your views in a class discussion.
2. *"Our fantasy heroes are less mirrors of what we are than windows into what we might like to be."*
   (a) What does the success of Rocky and Rambo reveal about how we would like to be?
   (b) In what way is Rambo a "limited" hero? What is lacking?
3. **(a)** Stallone's heroes represent a type of movie hero some have identified by the labels "warrior hero" and the "legitimate savage." Create a list of movie heroes, both past and present, who suit these labels. Develop a profile of the "legitimate savage as hero" in movies.
   (b) In what ways, if any, does the "legitimate savage" dispensing justice differ from the hero in
   - television or movie Westerns?
   - science-fiction movie series such as *Star Trek* and *Star Wars*?
   - television or movie crime dramas?
4. **(a)** The writer of this article uses the terms "mass culture" and "folk hero." Explain or define these

concepts in your own terms.

(b) What are the differences, if any, between mass culture in Canada and in the United States? What personal qualities and characteristics would a *Canadian* movie folk hero have?

Record your responses in your journal.

5. *"Rocky's victories and Rambo's do not count for much...and do not live long after the 90-minute running time of Stallone's ... works."*

   What influence do you think heroes like Rocky and Rambo have on society? What *does* linger on long after the film is over?

6. The author suggests that watching Rocky movies *"had become nearly a ritual"* and that the story line was *"dependable."*

   As a class, discuss other movies about heroes and heroics that you have seen. What conventions of character, plot, and film technique are common to all of them?

INVESTIGATING THE MEDIA

1. The success of Stallone's films and heroes owes much to "shrewd marketing strategies."

   How have other heroes been created, packaged, and marketed for the public? Working in a small group, select a movie or television "hero" and research and prepare a report that describes how the mass media have worked collectively to create and sustain the character as a hero.

YOUR TURN

1. When one college professor suggested that Stallone's movies belonged in a trash can, his students rebelled. Which side are *you* on? Write your own article about either the Rocky/Rambo movies or other movies like them.
2. Working in a small group, script and present a scene that is a parody of the "noble savage" type of hero.
3. Imagine you are a Canadian film producer or that you work for an advertising agency. Create the next hero for movie audiences in the 1990s. Invent a profile for your character that includes
   - details of the character's background
   - the character's personality traits
   - the values and ideals the character will symbolize
   - the typical enemy or antagonist the hero will do battle against

   Present your ideas to the class. Following your presentation, invite comments and questions from the class.

   or

   Present your ideas, complete with drawings and sketches, to the class. Invite comments and questions from your audience.

After Rocky and Rambo, what next? — Eliot Ness for one. He carried a badge and a gun and he was "very moral. He was like your neighbour next door, who when you lend him your lawnmower it comes back to you cleaned and filled to the brim with gas." (Kevin Costner in Premiere*: July/August 1987)*

Untouchables feeds desire for moral certainty

The Untouchables, Brian De Palma's movie about gangsters and G-men in Prohibition-era Chicago, fast became a summer hit in 1987. The reasons go deeper than its engaging performances, fluid camerawork, and wry script.

With the exception of films about cartoon-like figures (Dan Aykroyd's spoof of straight-arrow detective Joe Friday in *Dragnet* or the super-hero squad of *Buckaroo Banzai*), *The Untouchables* is perhaps the only adult movie in recent memory with characters who view real-life events with absolute moral certainty.

In this respect, it's a throwback to the self-assured pictures of the 1930s, '40s, and '50s, when anti-heroes such as Paul Newman's Hud or Dustin Hoffman's Benjamin Braddock (in *The Graduate*) were yet to be created.

During Hollywood's golden age, a great many melodramas, Westerns, thrillers, and screwball farces took a solid moral stance and rarely wavered in finding the proper means of achieving a desirable end.

Only a few extraordinary movies — *Citizen Kane, All The King's Men, Modern Times*, or *King Kong* — exposed an element of ambiguity in the characters' motives. At the same time, they warned us we might have difficulty in categorizing the heroes' decisions as right or wrong.

The Untouchables, on the other hand, never falters from its assertion that bootlegger Al Capone is evil, federal agent Eliot Ness is good, and there is nothing unseemly about enforcing the law against the sale of alcohol.

Judging by the box office response, today's audiences obviously feel the need to escape into this moral universe, since it provides relief from the uncertainty and the ethical gray areas of contemporary society.

The world of *The Untouchables* is not, after all, one where a fundamentalist preacher would commit adultery and lose his ministry, where a top U.S. federal official would secretly sell arms to an enemy nation, or where a frustrated subway rider is hailed for gunning down four youths who taunted him.

No, this is a near-mythical Chicago where a savior like Eliot Ness can declare with grim confidence: "I'll tell you how I feel about Prohibition: It's the law of the land."

To be sure, his statements were often greeted with snickers of derision from the press. And, at the movie's end, Ness acknowledges his strange dilemma by explaining what he'll do when Prohibition is repealed: "I think I'll have a drink."

But he also reminds us that there is some point in laying one's life on the line in defense of goodness. Even more crucial, he implies that the noble ideal of justice can be achieved through unswerving loyalty even to admittedly imperfect laws and a rickety political system.

"We must be pure, and I want you to stop (drinking)," Ness tells Chicago policemen who practise the double standard of arresting bootleggers but drinking on the sly.

"It's not a question of a harmless drink, which it well might be. We are here to enforce the law and we must do so by example."

In this way, Ness aims to make his hand-picked team untouchable — if not physically, then spiritually. And it is this purity of purpose that gives David Mamet's script its urgency.

In fact, when death finally does come to two of the Untouchables, it is a result of a moral lapse in which Ness's commandment against drinking is broken. Charles Martin Smith is murdered after sipping from a barrel of illicit liquor, while Sean Connery is machine-gunned at home after taking a slug of whisky from a bottle hidden in his oven.

Such black-and-white terms of reference, while hardly new in modern movies, are usually confined to the realms of fantasy. For instance, it is sexually permissive teenagers who are usually the first to be slaughtered in what passes for divine retribution in slasher films.

And we would never think to doubt James Bond's mission to eradicate unspeakably evil villains like Dr. No and Goldfinger, let alone question Superman's devotion to truth, justice, and the American way.

But amusing though these fanciful heroes might be, they lack the ring of authenticity. *The Untouchables*, however, draws a surprising amount of power from the fact that Ness, Capone, Prohibition, and the Untouchables really existed.

In a rare moment of doubt, Ness does break down and wonder whether his single-minded approach and strong-arm tactics may somehow be diluting the purity of his moral make-up. "I have forsworn every law, I have promised to uphold," he tells a shocked judge. "I have become what I have beheld."

But then, without a flicker of hesitation, he adds: "I am content that I am right."

Few current movie characters could make such a remark with complete confidence.

So convincing is Ness's belief in his own ideals that we're even tempted to cheer when, just before a raid, he rallies his fellow policemen with the cry: "All right, men! Let's do some good!"

— Henry Mietkiewicz
The Toronto Star
July 4, 1987

EXPLORING IDEAS

1. ***(a)*** Evaluate the view of life and morality presented in De Palma's movie, according to Henry Mietkiewicz. What type of hero was Eliot Ness in the film?
   (b) Why was Ness the right kind of hero for audiences in the late 1980s? What other factors would likely influence the public's acceptance of this kind of hero?
   (c) Why, do you think, is the vision of life presented in this film most strongly associated with cartoonlike characters and films with mythical or near-mythical settings?

INVESTIGATING THE MEDIA

1. In *The Untouchables*, Eliot Ness symbolizes the type of law enforcement officer and hero who believes "that the noble ideal of justice can be achieved through unswerving loyalty to...the laws."

   What images of heroes and law enforcement are presented in today's popular films and television programs? Form small groups to discuss this question. Prepare a group report which includes your conclusions on the issue of the image of morality, justice, and the hero presented in the movies and on TV. (You may include programs and movies you remember from the past if you wish, in order to make comparisons and identify trends.)

YOUR TURN

1. How satisfied are you by movies that "view real-life events with absolute moral certainty"? Respond to this question in your journal and share what you write with a partner.

"James Bond is one film hero who has survived over the years."

James Bond: 007

Good grief, I grew up with James Bond. The realization comes as something of a shock. What's more, I think he deeply affected my adolescence or at least served as a marvellous escape from its constraints. So now that the movie Bond is celebrating 25 years of informing everyone's most dangerous fantasies, it is perhaps time to come to terms with him.

It goes without saying that James Bond, British Secret Service agent 007 (the 00 prefix means he is licenced not, as it turns out, just to kill, but to make money), has become a phenomenon; an indestructible movie hero, who has long since outlived his contemporaries, and who has eclipsed that other long-running British celluloid hero, Sherlock Holmes.

Counting the latest Bond opus, *The Living Daylights*, there have now been 15 Bond adventures produced first by the team of Harry Saltzman and Albert R. Broccoli, and latterly, by Broccoli himself. There have been pretenders to Bondom, *Casino Royale*, a lavish, mostly misfired sendup, and *Never Say Never Again*, a remake of *Thunderball*, that somehow fell out of Broccoli's purview. Neither film is considered to be the real thing.

For the record, the movies collectively have earned more than a billion dollars at the worldwide box office, making the series far and away the most financially successful in film history. There have been four Bonds to date: Sean Connery, certainly the most fondly remembered of the Bonds (counting *Never Say Never*, he did 007 seven times); George Lazenby, the former model who played Bond only once in *On Her Majesty's Secret Service*; Roger Moore, the most criticized but, ironically, the most popular Bond at the box office (seven times); and now Timothy Dalton, 40, the Welsh actor who is introduced in *Living Daylights* and is said to be a throwback to the dark and dangerous days of Ian Fleming's novels.

The original Bond film, *Dr. No*, was released Oct. 6, 1962. Fleming, a newspaperman who was a former intelligence officer himself, had been writing the books since he introduced *Casino Royale* in 1953. Ironically, he was to die in 1964, at the age of 56, just before the release of *Goldfinger*. Fleming never knew just how popular his hero was to become.

Dr. No was made on a low budget, just over $1 million. Albert Broccoli says today that originally he and Saltzman offered the part of Bond to Cary Grant. However, Grant turned it down and the producers chose instead a 30-ish Scottish actor named Sean Connery who was almost totally unknown at the time, and who had hair everywhere on his body, except on his head.

Broccoli now says he always expected the Bond films to be a success. It's the *amount* of the success that continually dismays him. Viewed today, *Dr. No* has the look and feel of a B-movie. Only Connery, with his darkly dangerous good looks, really stands out. He is whipchord thin, wearing his own hair for the first and only time, and you can't take your eyes off him. Watching *Dr. No* 25 years later, you have to conclude that if a lesser actor had played Bond, no one would have noticed, and the series would never have gone anywhere.

But propelled by Connery's incredible screen presence, it of course did. The first movie was successful enough to inspire a sequel, *From Russia With Love* (1963), the film that Bond aficionados maintain is the best in the series. The year after that there was *Goldfinger*, and in a sense it became the benchmark Bond film, the mold from which all the others have been struck. *Goldfinger* got Bond's combination of humor, action, and sex just right. The films have never been quite so good since.

By the time *Thunderball* appeared in 1965, Bond had become a worldwide obsession. You could buy 007 shaving cream and 007 cologne, and everyone and his brother was writing a spy novel or making a spy movie *(Our Man Flint*, and the Matt Helm movies, to name but a couple of imitations).

Sean Connery played Bond seven times.

Eventually, the world tired of 007 hair spray, but the movies endured. Fleming once said he wrote the novels as fairy tales for adult readers. But actually Bond is *the* hero of the baby boomer adolescence in much the same way *Terry and the Pirates* or Boston Blackie might have been a hero to kids of an earlier time.

As a kid, I read all the hard-boiled private detectives,

Latest 007 — Timothy Dalton

Philip Marlowe, Lew Archer, Mickey Spillane's Mike Hammer. But Marlowe and Hammer and his ilk were poor and rather miserable. You would not want to actually be those guys. But Bond. Who would not want to be James Bond?

He travelled to exotic places, lived in first-class hotels, drove the fastest cars, ate the finest foods, consumed the best wines, defeated the most interestingly deformed villains ever imagined.

The impact of reading this stuff amid dull adolescence, locked into the ennui of a small town, cannot be overstated. I devoured the novels, and the movies that came out of them. Bond was not just a character; he was a means of escape. The magic carpet ride to adventure.

It is often forgotten today because most of the attention is now focused on the films, but Fleming, for all his seeming nonchalance about churning them out, really was a fine thriller writer. His imagery is vivid, his characters absolutely unique, and the plots moved along at such a pace that I could never turn the pages fast enough.

The movies after *Thunderball* gradually became less intriguing. Their ever-increasing success — the discovery of Bond by a whole generation of kids weaned on *Star Wars* — caused them to become outsized, hugely expensive cartoons that bore almost no relationship to the Fleming novels. This is not to say they did not have merits of their own. One can only admire the slick, almost delirious speed of the later Bond films, *The Spy Who Loved Me*, for example with that wondrous opening sequence in which Bond, escaping on skis, goes over a cliff, only to be saved by a parachute emblazoned with a replica of the British flag.

But 007 himself had become lost somewhere in the undeniable excitement of the action sequences. Roger Moore, it was contended, became the stand-in doing closeups for the stunt doubles. Moore finally gave up after *A View to a Kill*. He was close to 60; the actor who for years defeated age with boyishness was himself finally beaten.

So now there is a new Bond, and a new Bond movie. Albert Broccoli, late into his 70s and still going strong, recently told the Los Angeles *Times* that if *The Living Daylights* makes even a dollar, there will be more Bond movies, despite the fact the producers now have exhausted every Fleming title extant.

Somewhere along the way, 007 stopped being the magic carpet for me, the way of escape. I guess I no longer needed it. Bond long ago taught me there was a world out there, and now I was all grown up, and could buy my own ticket. Thanks, James. For everything. I don't think I could have gotten through adolescence without you.

— Ron Base
The Toronto Star
July 26, 1987

EXPLORING IDEAS

1. James Bond *"has become a phenomenon; an indestructible movie hero, who has long since outlived his contemporaries...."*

Why has James Bond been more durable than other movie heroes and superheroes?

2. Ron Base claims that *"James Bond is* the *hero of baby boomer adolescence."*

(a) In your opinion, how valid is this comment?

(b) Who will be *the* hero for your generation? Why?

3. Ron Base suggests that Sean Connery's "incredible screen presence" contributed to the durability of James Bond as a movie hero. How important, do you think, is the actor's presence in making a movie hero? What other movie heroes have, in your view, captured the imagination of audiences because of the performer's aura? Which have just missed because the performer lacked the right charisma? Discuss this issue in small groups, or as a class.

INVESTIGATING THE MEDIA

1. *"...the discovery of Bond by a whole generation of kids weaned on* Star Wars *caused (the films) to become outsized hugely expensive cartoons...."*

(a) Form small groups and arrange to view some of the later Bond movies. Evaluate the characters, plot elements, and film techniques. What qualities, if any, do you think the movies have in common with cartoons?

(b) How do you react to the portrayal of women in Bond films? Is it good-natured fun or degrading sexism? Share your views.

(c) What values are revealed through the characterization and the action in Bond movies? Write an article in which you evaluate James Bond as a hero and role model.

Norman Bethune was a Canadian surgeon who died on the frontlines of the Chinese Revolution in 1939. Considered a genuine hero in contemporary China, Dr. Bethune has only recently come to be recognized as a hero in the country of his birth. A film about his life was co-produced in 1987 by China and Canada.

Making a Legend

Bent over the operating table, he deftly cuts away at a special-effects wound with a pair of scissors. As he works, he describes each manoeuvre to his listeners, Chinese actors, with convincing authority: "Wash it out with saline solution, remove the devitalized muscle tissue, ligate the blood vessels." The actor wears a blood-stained apron and rubber gloves sticky with synthetic gore. As he glances up, rimless spectacles refract a piercing, blue-eyed gaze. Only a pair of yellow high-topped sneakers — safely out of the camera's frame — mar the illusion for the onlooker. Otherwise, Donald Sutherland, with his head shaved to look almost bald, bears an uncanny resemblance to Dr. Norman Bethune, the Canadian surgeon who died a hero on the frontlines of the Chinese Revolution.

The mere fact that the movie was made is something of a miracle. *Bethune* is the product of deep-rooted obsessions: screenwriter Ted Allan, co-author of the 1952 Bethune biography *The Scalpel, the Sword*, spent 45 years trying to bring the surgeon's story to the screen. And Sutherland, who portrayed Bethune in three TV productions, has talked about starring in a Bethune movie since the early 1970s. One of Hollywood's most versatile talents, the mercurial actor accepted the role despite serious doubts about the health of the production. "But because I am Canadian," Sutherland said, "I couldn't have lived with myself if I hadn't done it."

The story itself has a quintessentially Canadian ring to it — an idealistic doctor who becomes national hero for one billion Chinese while remaining an obscure enigma

Canadian legend — Dr. Norman Bethune as played by Donald Sutherland

in his own country. But until recently it was assumed that only a Hollywood studio could make a movie on the scale of the Bethune story. Allan first sold a 180-page biography of Bethune to 20th Century-Fox in 1942. Over the years executives at both Columbia Pictures and Warner Bros. have taken a run at producing it, and stars such as Robert Redford, Warren Beatty, Richard Dreyfuss, and Sean Connery have expressed interest in playing the lead. But in the end, said Allan, Hollywood "seemed politically afraid of making an epic about a Canadian Communist doctor." The project died.

Then, in 1984 Filmline International Inc., a Montreal-based production house, revived it. And although *Bethune* is one of the most expensive Canadian movies ever made, its $16-million budget is threadbare for a three-location epic with a five-month shooting schedule — about half the budget that Hollywood spends on such pictures.

— Brian D. Johnson
Maclean's
August 10, 1987

EXPLORING IDEAS

1. *"...(the story) has a quintessentially Canadian ring to it."*

   In your view, why did Canada take so long to make a film about Dr. Bethune? In what ways does Norman Bethune differ from the typical Hollywood hero? Share your ideas in a class discussion.

YOUR TURN

1. Identify other Canadian heroes that might be appropriate subjects for a film or television mini-series.

   Create a poster and publicity blurb advertising the story of "________________ : a Canadian Legend."

   or

   Write a paragraph describing the opening scene of your movie, *or* do some research into the life of your subject and script an important scene from the movie.

REAL-LIFE HEROES IN THE MEDIA

Terry Fox has been acclaimed by almost everyone as the first *true* Canadian hero of our times. Public response on Terry Fox Days throughout the country is vivid testimony of the spark he ignited in the hearts of Canadians. It wasn't always that way, however. Terry Fox endured many lonely days with little recognition before the media focused attention on him and his heroic cause. Even genuinely heroic individuals seem to need the mass media to spread their message of hope.

The Terry Effect

Ontario, at dawn. An unseasonable chill creates a dense Brigadoon ground fog that hides the highway, lets evergreens float rootless, and makes a mystery of the familiar. As his car crested the hill, the driver saw a blurred red glare in the distance that resolved into the flashing red lights of police cruisers heading a procession half a mile long. At the last moment, just as he was passing, the driver saw the figure of Terry Fox lurching from the fog, the thin steel shaft where his right leg should have been catching the light of the headlights behind. "I just caught a glimpse, you see, as I passed, but there he was, with that queer hobble, pumping and hopping, his fists clenched. I blubbered. I just blubbered..." This is how it began, with the queer lurching run. And the blubbering.

On the shady side of Parliament Street in Cabbagetown, the Canadian Cancer Society has set up a couple of card tables just outside the liquor store, and for hours on a hot September Sunday hundreds of people in various states of exhaustion stumble up to them to pant out their triumphs: 10 kilometres "for Terry," with pledges ranging from a nickel to hundreds of dollars a kilometre. Whatever Olympian snobbery had formerly floated about those *serious* daily joggers dissipated under the sheer weight of earnest amateurs.

On Terry Fox Day it wasn't how easily you knocked off those kilometres but how grindingly *hard* it was, how many times you wanted to fold into a patch of cool shade...but didn't. So the constant straggle of finishers who were finding the last few metres the hardest of all began to look like a scene from a Fellini film, full of wild, unplanned color and eccentric people. "*Sure* I finished," drawls a teenager with I Love Terry printed on her T-shirt. "But... I'm nearly dead." While the reporter from the *Toronto Sun* asks for details, she sits on the curb, dirty socks stuffed into tight jeans pockets, battle-worn Adidas slung around her neck, and rubs her bare red feet. After every answer, she blows a satiny pink globe of bubble gum, like a miniature Goodyear blimp. "Listen, I saw Terry running on University Avenue with Darryl Sittler. And at City Hall. And I have all his speeches..."

Across the road at the restaurant where the runners start out, a clown is flapping, leaping, his white face scaring the dickens out of small children. Off trots a woman, to the scattered applause of onlookers, pushing a stroller in which a perfect little red-headed baby wears a Tots for Terry shirt. A 77-year-old man chugs up, eyes gleaming with the old remembered proverbs from the *Boy's Own Annual*, to proclaim his best personal time: 10 kilometres in three-quarters of an hour.

If it weren't so impulsively, exuberantly happy, it might be bizarre. The Cancer Society volunteer, who checks everyone in, puffs one du Maurier after another. A man with asthma sails past on roller skates, noiseless and graceful as a dancer. Parked against the curb is a marvellously mysterious woman whose black T-shirt proclaims Dangerous Lady; she wears huge dark sunglasses and talks softly from her wheelchair, a cigarette tilting elegantly from her lips. There are kids so poor their running shoes flop and gape, and a man rich enough to wear dazzling tennis whites and have a troika of Afghans trotting delicately beside him. The band at the outdoor café, the Runyonesque cab driver who cruises by in a fan-fendered Studebaker, the pop cans and the shrieks of delight when someone else starts out or staggers in — it all has the hectic but pleasant air of a neighborhood carnival. Except that it has been meticulously planned, organized, and brought to life to honor Terry Fox.

After a couple of hours, the charge of emotion just his name engenders becomes overwhelming. Buttons, T-shirts, banners, balloons ... I'm for Terry, I'm Running for Terry, Support the Marathon of Hope. And the slogan that probably best explains why so many people pushed themselves to their limits and beyond: Terry Fox Lives!

Not that this was a Cabbagetown phenomenon alone. Far from it. By the end of the day, Richard Munro, of the national committee heading up the various events, was predicting that Ontario's contribution alone would reach $1 million, and the CBC's coast-to-coast television coverage that afternoon was revealing just how massive the Canadian response was to Terry Fox Day. From bleak St. John's, where Fox had started his now legendary run, to Victoria, the teacup among the fiords, the 24 hours of September 13 became an outpouring of emotion — and money. Coming three months after Fox's death, after a summer of government wrangling, galloping inflation and soaring interest rates, the response was phenomenal. For the Cancer Society, just barely recovered from the millions that had rolled in during the Marathon of Hope and subsequent benefits, this fresh surge of generosity was boggling. "Not that Canadians aren't generous," says the Society's national special events chairman Ron Calhoun. "In fact, among the nations of the world, Canadians have always been the top contributors to cancer research fund-raising drives. But this went past generosity, past anything we've ever dreamed would happen."

That's why there were no quickly computed figures trailing across our TV screens. What we saw instead were droves of people running, walking, biking, skating, bowling, horseback riding, and even swimming, not just for pledges, but for Terry Fox. Again and again, during the Cabbagetown run and elsewhere, the comments were about him and his effect on the country. "To us, he's legend," said a Quebecker, jogging along the newly named Terry Fox Path. *We're all Canadians today. He restored my faith in human nature. He brought us together.*

Then, later in the day, something more mystical began to filter into the comments. Proudly wearing their blisters and bruises like medals, people dropped the past tense, almost with relief. *He is our hero and believe me, I know he was with me today. Look, I couldn't have done it without him. Terry gets all the credit.* Long before September 13 and the first annual Terry Fox Day, Canada had acclaimed him a hero. Now he was legend as well, one who could be mystically restored to us, whole and happy, whenever things got tough and we needed inspiration.

Back on Parliament Street, out of nowhere spins an incredible little woman who has taken more than two hours to propel her wheelchair along the Cabbagetown course. Her cotton blouse is splotched with sweat across the shoulder blades, but there is an ecstasy when she extends her arms, hands upwards, to show the bloody cuts along the palms. "It's nothing," she says cheerfully, "compared to what he went through." It was her sacrifice, making her hands do what her lifeless legs would not, and someone trundles her across the way to a good lunch and maybe a cold beer under the sun umbrellas at the restaurant.

This is how it ended: with the slogans, Terry is with us, and the stigmata of the woman in the wheelchair. How did we get here *from* there?

Not everyone is willing or able to separate the hero from the phenomenal effects of his heroism. Maybe it's because all our previous "heroes" have been fast-frozen in history books or are glued to hockey sticks that we protect our one full-blooded and contemporary hero with such prickly zeal. Between the time Fox began his run westward from St. John's, Newfoundland, and Terry Fox Day on September 13, 1981, the young runner's image was transformed from cripple to hero in a media campaign both dizzying and dismaying in its relentlessness. The first time Fox was seen on national television, most viewers had gut reactions ranging from cynicism to outrage. Abby Hoffman, who knows the gruelling test of marathons, admits that her first sight of Fox hobbling through a sleety rain both astonished and disgusted her. "I thought... here's another crackpot! How did this guy get on the CBC news?" Reporters made the Marathon of Hop a newsroom joke, and suspected the Cancer Society was exploiting him. Among those who turned out to support his cause there was always the sprinkling of people drawn by the macabre, the freak show titillation of peeking at a cripple.

Later, the reaction changed so completely that even positive criticism was buried under pure hysteria, with everyone from Irving Layton, who delivered his sentimental poem ("On one metal leg, dear boy, you hopped into our hearts and immortality") to Mr. Peanut, Standard Brands' top-hatted symbol, getting into the act. For every sincere supporter, there appeared to be 10 bandwagons clattering close behind.

Once Fox crossed into Ontario, the media blitz became self-sustaining as it fed off the emotions it both sensed and caused in ordinary people who turned out to watch Fox run. The *Toronto Star* covered the marathon in minute detail: every time Terry Fox breathed out, the *Star* breathed in. But possibly the low point was *Maclean's* January 12, 1981 issue: on the cover, within the garish circle of a stylized halo, Fox looks for all the world like a plaster saint being carried through the streets of Seville. Inside, writer Roy MacGregor wrestles valiantly with his impossible assignment, striving to delineate the nature of Canadian heroism, comparing Fox to Wayne Gretzky and Lester Bowles Pearson.

Perhaps this is the saddest result of mass worship: it always dismisses the hero's frailty, the human qualities that make his act of heroism heroic. Terry Fox was a wholesome young man, fairly conservative in his view of women and life, not terribly profound, and stubbornly, obsessively brave. These qualities came through in early reports, and traces of them stayed in the coverage by Leslie Scrivener in the *Star* and Arthur Johnson in the *Globe*. But generally, these flaws, as much a part of Fox's persona as his flawed running, were either entirely submerged, or were mysteriously transmuted into virtues. Soon, the public, too, had so mixed his virtues and faults that the ordinary man disappeared and the hero made his triumphant entry — pure, superhuman, untouchable. When he stood before the crowds, face as fetching as a Norman Rockwell character, modest and unassuming, he *looked* the role we'd cast him in. But just how much of this was real and how much was hype may never be known. While it drew from us the warmest empathy and generosity, it points out how susceptible we are to the manipulative techniques of hysteria so neatly controlled by the media.

There is another element in the Phenomenon of Terry Fox, and that is the nature of the disease that killed him. Cancer is a very potent symbol, and symbols are what make heroes. Not too many of us have lost loved ones who were amputees or have suffered the death of someone close who was a cripple. But we all know someone who was struck down by cancer. Cancer does the same work in our society that forest devils did in others: it causes random terror, striking seemingly at will; it reminds us of our vulnerability; it is a source of dread and confusion. When did you last hear a standup comic do a routine on tumors? Who remembers now that it was the War Amputations of Canada Association that built and paid for Terry's artificial leg, that made him two new ones and kept him going with advice, prosthetics, and money, at a time when the Cancer Society was not as involved? Amputees don't have the potency of cancer victims. It was not the sight of Fox hopping across Canada but his defiance of the dread killer that stirred the emotions. If he'd been an accident victim instead, he'd have run as far, maybe further, and he'd have collected $43.34 for the War Amps.

If there was one moment, and one place, where everything that defined the legend of Terry Fox came together, it was crossing into Ontario. From the morning that the Marathon of Hope's small caravan crept across the Perley Bridge linking Quebec to Ontario, the media was ready, the Ontario Provincial Police had an escort waiting, and the response of ordinary people was so electric that it began a brushfire that later spread to the rest of the country. Even British Columbia, where Fox was born and where he died, was never quite as enmeshed in the emotional surge as Ontario. Why *here*?

Less than a month before, in Charlottetown, Fox had jotted in his diary: "Many people are congratulating me, and I can't figure out what for." Bill Vigars, the campaign coordinator from the Ontario division of the Cancer Society, who stayed with the marathon throughout Ontario, remembers when so few people knew what the run was about, or who Terry Fox was, that the van crew laughed over the things they had to do to get attention. "They were saying they were beginning to feel like apostles, running ahead to announce the Second Coming."

The Maritime segment of the run had been a jumble of high hopes, frequent letdowns, and physical hardships caused by the moody uncertainty of the early spring weather. The weather, however, was never so depressing as a poor

Actors Eric Fryer (*centre*) and Robert Duvall (*arm extended*) portray Terry Fox and Bill Vigars, respectively, on film.

turnout, which could either depress Fox or bring out a crusading zeal: *I try so hard and get let down. I am going to run right into this city's main street. We will be rebels. We will stir up noise. People will know that Terry Fox ran out of his way to Saint John for a reason!*

By June 10 he had run 2386 kilometres, 48 kilometres on that day, to reach the Quebec border; there began in the diary a series of entries that had become increasingly bitter. *We learned that there would be very little done in Quebec. Apparently they don't speak English* — no one on the marathon spoke French — *maybe they also don't get cancer.* In one long stretch of 161 kilometres, only $35 was collected, while they'd heard that Newfoundland had collected $25 000. Cysts had formed on Fox's abused stump; his unpredictable temper had been reduced to flinty sensitivity by awful weather and the depressing apathy of Quebec toward his run.

Why this apathy? No one has the temerity to think Quebeckers less warm than Ontarians to the causes they embrace. Nor, as Fox peevishly muttered, do they get fewer cancers than the folks further upstream toward the Love Canal. Nor is the Quebec media less prone to hysteria. Possibly there are many reasons. For one, the Quebec press is not geared to making heroes of outsiders, not if they can help it. And at that point, many of the critical ingredients necessary to stir up interest — direct information, public curiosity, and the fissile element, awe — simply weren't there to set off the chain reaction that keeps a good news story self-sustaining. In Quebec, there just wasn't *enough* of anything to draw crowds and compassion. In Ontario, already fired up by Scrivener's coverage of the marathon in the *Star*, and fuelled by the Cancer Society's complete co-operation in scheduling events, the marathon became a steamroller that barely paused for Fox's death. Even without him, the Event rolled along, and we were treated to the seamy spectacle of TV networks squabbling over coverage of the funeral.

The Making of the Hero was complete long before Fox's death. Trudeau, having ignored Fox's first visit to Ottawa, caught up with the country and adopted him as a symbol. From a hobbling cripple, Terry Fox had been transformed into a superathlete. "After Terry had run more than a thousand miles," Abby Hoffman told a CBC reporter, "I realized what an incredible athlete he was."

Before Fox died, the media coverage had turned to awe, even reverence. Typical was a *Globe* report:

"On the surface, the 3000 people at Nathan Phillips Square last night had little in common.

"But they were bound together by a belief in miracles. They had come to a candlelight vigil for Terry Fox, the 22-year-old Marathon of Hope runner whose survival now depends on prayers.

"They raised their candles and their banners in the air. 'You'll run in our hearts forever, Terry.' 'Keep fighting Terry, we are rooting for you.' 'God loves you Terry.'

"Their eyes expressed sadness and fear and hope and together they turned to God to save the life of the man who, as Metro Chairman Paul Godfrey told them, is our true Canadian hero.

"'He can't die, he isn't going to die,' said Susan Heiner, 21, 'because if he dies there isn't a God.'"

Fox's achievement was really being described as an act of moral courage, instead of the physical ordeal it was. Writer June Callwood, in a moving tribute, wrote of his "determination to be two-legged again." His refusal to acknowledge death was praised everywhere; he had to fight back fears and bitterness, but then, so do the aged, and with far less support.

Says Bill Vigars of the Cancer Society, who is neither cynical, or naive: "I really believe Canadians were sensitive to something special about Terry himself. In a lot of ways he was a normal 21-year-old who liked pretty women, a few beers, and even an occasional dirty joke. He had a very bad temper and he had it all his life. Yet his Spartan self-discipline and that almost innocent dedication to what may have become old-fashioned virtues touched everyone. Sometimes it was hero worship, but whatever it was, we could see people changing right before our eyes."

As the marathon gathered momentum in Ontario, the possibility of cashing in on Fox's popularity brought out the fast operators seeking commercial tie-ins and spin-offs. It was the Cancer Society's Ron Calhoun who screened these, a job he found a little easier, because Fox himself had set two unbreakable rules. "First," says Calhoun, "he would accept no money for himself, only for the Society. He refused new cars, a boat, a motorcycle that would have been specially fitted out for him, even a college scholarship. The second rule was that no one was to make money, ever, by using him commercially."

In her book on Fox, Leslie Scrivener quoted Fox as saying he was happy with what he'd done. "If he felt any bitterness, it was because some business people had tried to use him to sell their products."

Every cent, every dollar, of the money Fox raised went to cancer research. "Everything that looked like commercialism infuriated him," says Cancer Society executive vice-president Robert Macbeth. "You know, it was almost unsettling to have someone that young be your example." The Cancer Society, partly as a result, has kept scrupulous records on all money received, information it will happily show to anyone who asks. The Society is still honoring its promise that the money will go to research, though there have been suggestions that education, new equipment, and new hospitals be considered as well.

If the Fox phenomenon had its tasteless moments, its commercial ripoffs, its element of high-wire hysteria, something in the hero himself — old-fashioned dedication, generosity, and altruism — provided the positive side. The sight of that lurching run and the pugnacious, defiant expression on Fox's face combined to touch many people in a very direct way. It was this that inspired artist Ken Danby when he painted Fox — and then gave the painting away. And certainly it was this that is taking super Cabbagetown fund raiser, Bill Mole, to Israel to plant trees for Terry in a Jerusalem square ("Terry goes international," said the *Star*, inadvertently using the present tense, like the other hero worshippers.)

From the clipping files come the sort of results that Terry Fox didn't expect, the *Run, Terry, Run* song, written by a Kitchener high school student. There's an eight-foot granite statue of Terry, thumbs upturned, as they were during his run, to be erected at B.C. Place in Vancouver. The R. Vincent Beauty Salon in Willowdale offered a Free Manicure for Terry. Five thousand prints of an original oil by Cliff Kearns of London, Ontario, have been sold for $100 each. Near Nipigon, where Fox's last valiant running days were witnessed by many, there's the Terry Fox Courage Highway. There are three new cancer research programs actually named for Fox. A Boeing 737 carries his name for the Nordair Fleet, and a mountain in the Rockies is now Terry Fox Mountain. Rod Stewart had a song titled *Never Give Up on a Dream* on a recent album ("It'll be a long, long time/For to fill your shoes/It'll take somebody who's a lot like you"), and his Canadian trip in February 1982 was called the Terry Fox Tour.

At the CNE, the day after Labour Day, over a year after the stunned driver caught his glimpse of Fox in the foggy dawn: a freezing north wind slams across the vacant picnic tables and down the alleys, sorting litter and spinning it against the empty buildings; enormous caravans have taken the place of crowds — loading equipment, stripping signs, striking the annual circus of games and rides. Two very different symbols remain, one for Terry Fox, and one that represents the Fox Phenomenon.

For Terry Fox, there is a special place in the Canadian Sports Hall of Fame, where the relics of grief and triumph rest without comment or exploitation. His jersey, his shorts, his running shoes, the Lou Marsh Trophy, the Order of Canada. And in eloquent sequence, 52 pictures of the hero taken during the marathon.

To see the symbol commemorating the phenomenon, I had to go to the CNE Coliseum, near the TTC streetcar tracks — a vast echoing place smelling comfortably of wet cardboard and horses. It took a while, but I found it at last. Terry Fox, seven feet high, 800 pounds, caught in mid-run and meticulously carved — from familiar grimace to Adidas shoes — in solid butter. How lonely and colorless he seemed, too big for the refrigerated case, turned around so that he looked, ironically, as if he were running away. "Oh," said the lady in the main office, "I think they'll just cut it down into pounds, or recycle it for nursing homes or something."

— Margaret Drury Gane
Toronto Life
January 1982

EXPLORING IDEAS

1. How do we know that an individual has become a public hero? Pick out details from the article that describe some of the things people have done as evidence of their belief in Terry Fox as a hero.
2. The writer says that Terry has become a *legend* as well as a hero. What is the difference between a legend and a hero?
3. ***(a)*** The author suggests that certain ingredients are necessary to create a hero. Working in small groups, identify these elements and discuss how they contributed to the transformation of Terry Fox from an ordinary individual into a hero.
   (b) Note the qualities the writer has called "flaws" in Terry Fox's character. Do you agree with her judgment on this point? Why might the writer have considered these qualities to be flaws in a public hero?
4. Compare Terry Fox's campaign to that of his "successor," Steve Fonyo. Is Steve Fonyo any more of a hero because he succeeded in his quest? Or, any less of a hero? (If so, why?)
5. What does this article tell us about what people want a hero to be like? How does this match up with your own definition of a hero?
6. Could Terry Fox have become a public hero *without* media coverage? Did the media make him a hero, or is heroism independent of the media?

INVESTIGATING THE MEDIA

1. If possible, view the film *Terry Fox: His Story*. Write a review of the movie in which you focus on the image of Terry Fox as a hero. Did the movie portray Mr. Fox as you imagined it would? What is the message?
2. Some people believe that the media invent heroes, then shape and sell them to the public.
   (a) If there is some basis for this belief, what are the implications?
   (b) Working with others in a small group, make a list of individuals who have become media heroes in the past few years. What role did the media play in bringing these people and their stories to the attention of the public?

   Were the individuals genuine heroes, in your view, or inventions of the media? Prepare a group report in which you explore answers to these questions.

Media Facts & Techniques

Rick Hansen — Making the "Man in Motion" a Media Hero

Five years after Terry Fox began his Marathon of Hope, Rick Hansen emerged as another genuine Canadian hero. Mr. Hansen's Man in Motion World Tour brought the public out again to cheer and encourage the efforts of a heroic individual.

To reach a better understanding of how the media shape our image of the individual as hero, let's examine how separate aspects of one medium — newspaper journalism — worked together to promote successful Rick Hansen media events.

April 13, 1986: Rick Hansen wheels up a steep incline on the Great Wall of China.

A. *Newspaper Headlines*

You are likely already well aware of the importance of a headline in a newspaper. As people glance at their newspapers, it is the headline that attracts their attention. Attitudes formed by a reader are often based on the first impressions created by a headline. Consider these headlines that appeared during Rick Hansen's Man in Motion tour:

Metro gets ready to open up its heart to wheelchair hero
Man in Motion: The Rick Hansen Story
Wheelchair marathoner pursues 'what is in my heart'
Hansen keeps wheeling despite pain, frustration
U.S. media ignoring Canada's wheelchair hero

All of these headlines appeared at various times during the fall and winter of 1986, in the *Toronto Star*. What specific words and phrases contribute to the reader's image of Mr. Hansen as a "real-life hero"? Note these in your personal-response journal.

B. *News Photos*

The following news photos appeared in Toronto papers when Rick Hansen's tour reached the city. Examine them carefully and note in your personal-response journal the effect each has on you.

TORONTO: Nov. 31, 1986: *Man of the Hour* — Rick Hansen waves to the largest crowd on the Canadian part of his Man in Motion global tour. An estimated 6000 people cheered their hero, who so far has banked $2 235 000 for spinal-cord research.

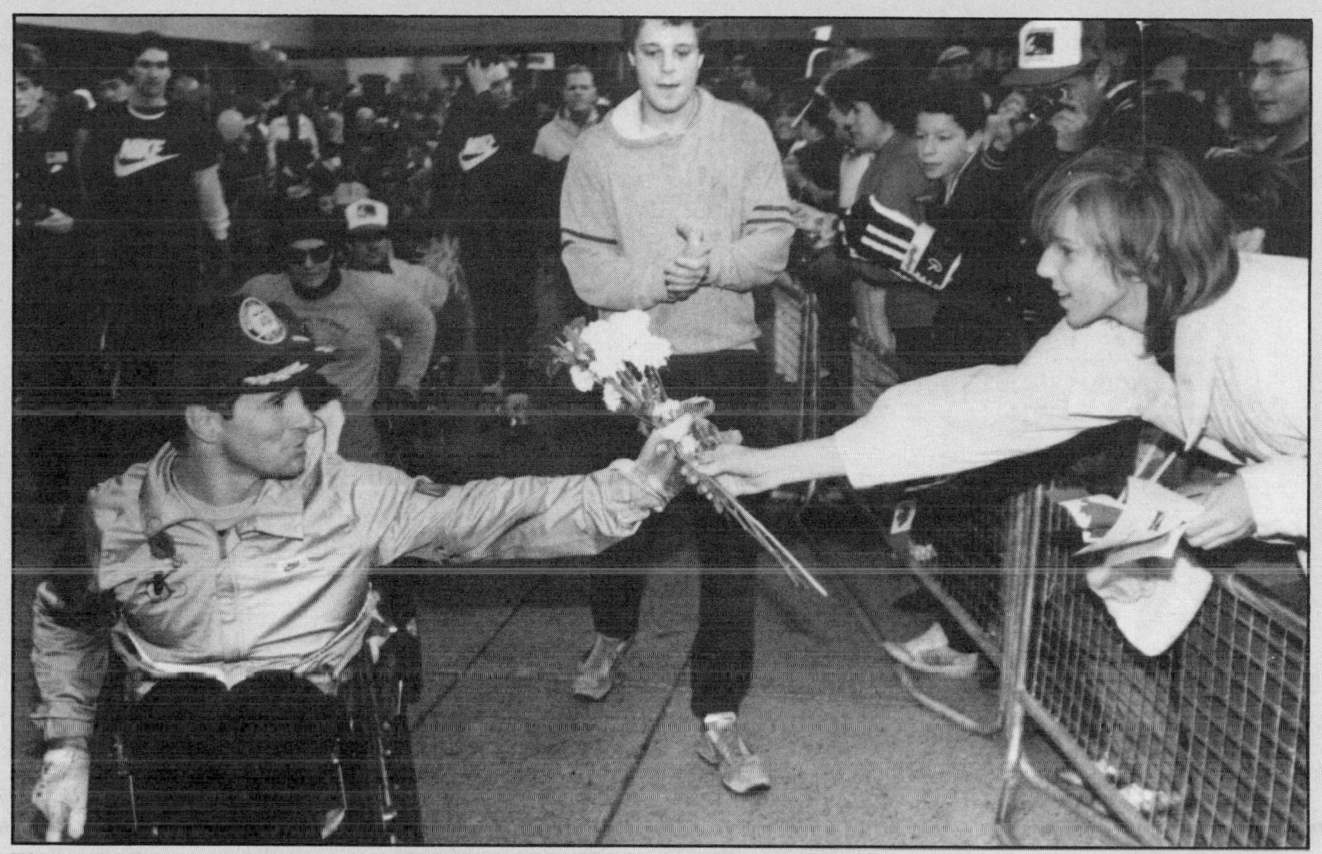

TORONTO: Nov. 2, 1986: *Flowers for Rick* — Rick Hansen is handed some flowers by a supporter at City Hall in Toronto where he was welcomed to the city.

NEWMARKET, Ont., Dec. 4, 1986: *A kiss for Rick* — Wheelchair athlete Rick Hansen receives a kiss from 4-year-old Christine Smith during a visit to Newmarket, just north of Toronto.

C. Feature Story and Editorial Commentary

In the next section you will find a feature story and a newspaper editorial published at the time the Man in Motion tour reached Toronto. Evaluate how each article contributes to the making of a hero. Record your responses in your journal.

An open letter to Rick

Open letter to Rick Hansen, Canada's Man in Motion:

Welcome to Toronto, Rick!

I read in this fine newspaper that you don't like to be called a hero. The title embarrasses you, and you worry that it will detract from your efforts to promote the handicapped.

That was a revelation. There aren't many people these days who turn back the title of hero, and we do tend to bestow it on a lot of people who don't deserve it — such as rock stars and surly Hollywood actors.

I reached for my Webster's dictionary to see if I could shed some light on the subject. It said a lot:

Hero: *A man of distinguished valor, intrepidity or fortitude; a central or prominent personage in any remarkable action or course of events; a man admired and venerated for his noble deeds or qualities; one invested with heroic qualities in the opinion of others; the principal character in a poem, story, or play, or the like....*

Except for the part about the poem, story, or play — all of which I think will soon follow — I'd say there's no question you're a hero, Rick.

My Webster's even has a "classical mythology" definition of hero: *"A man of superhuman strength, courage, or ability; an immortal being intermediate in nature between gods and man; a demigod."*

That's rather pompous, and you would doubtless agree that only an egotist would like to be thought of as a "demigod." But there's also no doubt you've shown "superhuman strength, courage, and ability" in your 20 000-mile trek around the world.

I would add to this by saying that you are a truly Canadian hero, Rick, because we see you as a very modest, happy, and engaging fellow.

We Canadians like that, because we are a very suspicious lot. We don't like people who put on airs, or appear to be doing so. Remember Steve Fonyo's unhappy fall from grace?

Toronto Archbishop Emmett Cardinal Carter said it very well in his address to his annual fund-raising dinner the other night: "As soon as one of us stands a little higher than the crowd in the United States, Americans cheer. We (in Canada) shoot at him."

All too true. You are painfully aware that there are a few cynics out there who think you're a Johnny-come-lately on the charity scene, stealing the thunder of Terry Fox and Steve Fonyo. It's been tough raising money for Man in Motion.

And you've had to put up with stories by righteous newshounds who think there's some kind of ethical problem with the fact you've got McDonald's, Coca Cola, Nabob, and other firms supporting you.

These same newshounds will likely turn around six months from now and write stories asking why it is that big corporations aren't doing more to help the poor and needy. We in the media frequently fail to recognize our own hypocrisy.

Another good thing about rejecting this hero status, Rick, is that you won't have to feel guilty when your human side begins to show.

I'm sure that in 20 000 miles worth of rough roads, bad food, ripoffs, fatigue and boredom you've had more than a few instances where there's been rough language, fights with your roadies, and snubs given to roadside supporters and town mayors.

It will all come out in the press, and you'll just have to live with it. Poor Steve Fonyo was crucified because of a dumb remark about Wayne Gretzky.

As much as you deserve the title of "hero," Rick, I'd say you're right to keep fighting it. Let it be a title that simply lives in the hearts and minds of the people who stand on the roadside and applaud you, as I will be doing today.

You are maintaining a Canadian tradition of quietly helping out your fellow man. You have a job to do, and you are doing it well.

Godspeed to Vancouver.

Yours Truly, Peter Howell.

— Peter Howell
The Toronto Sun
November 2, 1986

D. Sponsor Advertisements

As Rick Hansen has stated in interviews in the media, his fundraising tour would have been impossible without corporate assistance — "Without them, I wouldn't be here."

Evaluate these ads used by two of Rick Hansen's corporate sponsors. In your journal, comment on the effectiveness of these "advocacy ads" in developing the heroic image of Mr. Hansen — and the image of the *sponsor*. *See next page also.*

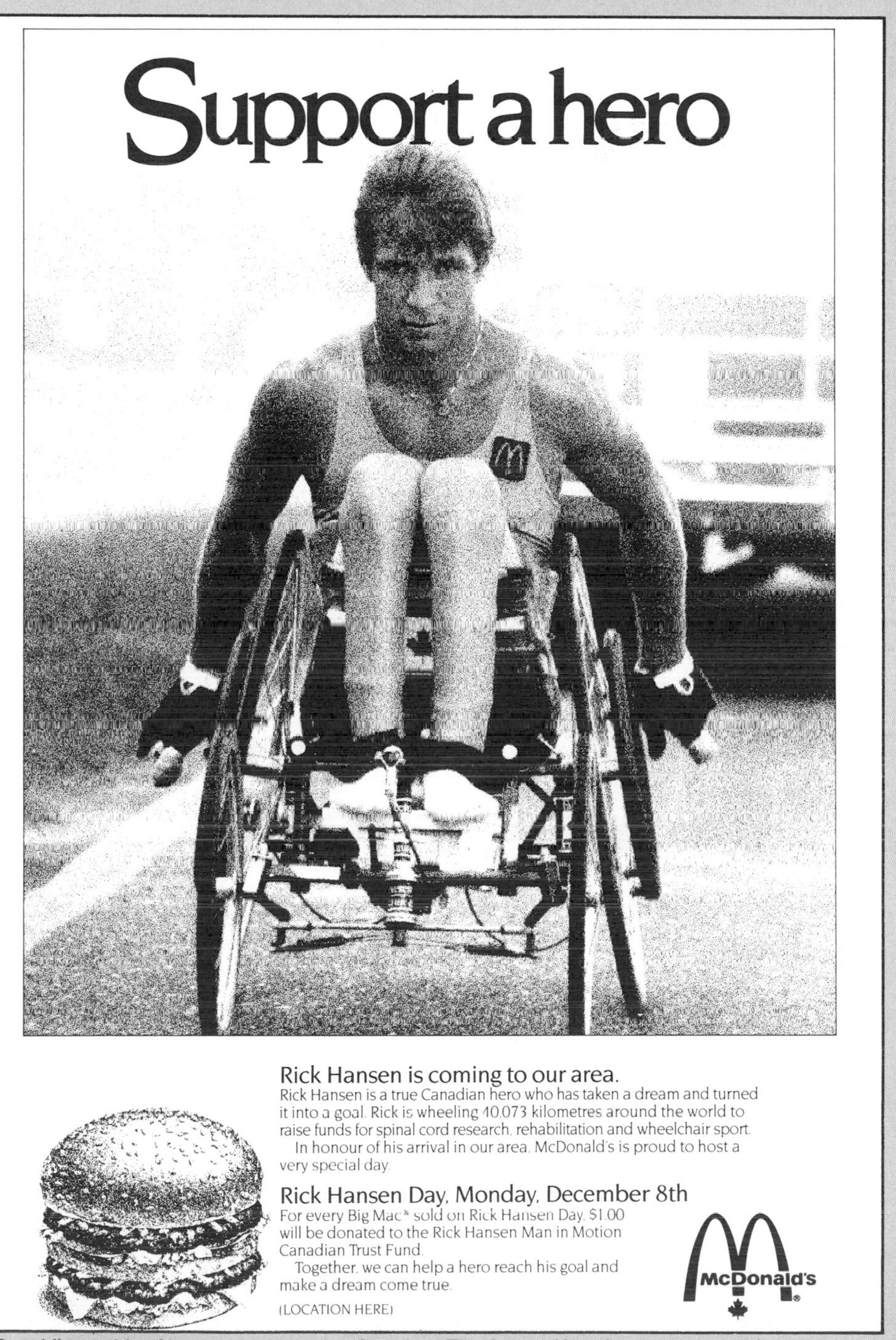

McDonald's ran this ad in newspapers across Canada — The date and location were changed accordingly. *The Sunday Star,* November 2, 1986

SO NEAR. YET SO FAR.
LET'S ALL GIVE
RICK HANSEN THE PUSH
HE SO DESERVES.
For almost 2 years and more than 20,000 miles, Rick Hansen has used his arms so others may use their legs again. And now he's almost home.
But his quest to change attitudes to physically disabled people, to have all people realize their full potential has barely begun.
Money. So much money.
One day, the funds raised for spinal cord research will enable people to walk away from their injuries. In the meantime, before that wonderful day comes, disabled people will be able to rebuild their lives through rehabilitation and wheelchair sport.
But research requires money. A great deal of money. Just think what it would mean if each and every Canadian gave just one dollar to help.
Coca-Cola Ltd. is helping.
For each one of our employees and each one of the employees of Coca-Cola bottlers across Canada, Coca-Cola Ltd. has donated $1 to Rick's cause.
And you can help, too.
If you'd like to help, you can. Simply stop in at any branch of The Royal Bank of Canada and deposit a dollar, or more if you can, into Rick Hansen's Man In Motion account.
Together, we can make Rick's impossible dream come true.
Coca-Cola Ltd.

Wheelchair marathoner pursues 'What is in my heart'

Rick Hansen was 15 years old, sitting in the back of a pick-up truck on his way home from a weekend fishing trip, happy and secure in his place in the world.

He was a star athlete. He had ambition and spunk. He loved hiking in the rugged and wild country around his home in Williams Lake, B.C.

In the blink of an eye, that world was shattered.

He'd hitched a ride in the truck with his buddy Don Alder. It seemed to be moving day, because the truck was filled with suitcases and boxes. The driver didn't know the roads well and as he rounded a corner, the truck skidded. He regained control for a moment, but oversteered. The truck slid out across the highway again and flipped.

Alder was thrown clear. Hansen, who was on the underside, heard a sickening crunch. It was his back breaking.

"I lost consciousness for a minute and I thought I was going to die. But then I rolled away and thought. 'I'm okay.'

"The first thing I noticed was that my legs had turned to jelly. They were numb. Then I felt shooting pains in my back."

In the Williams Lake hospital he was told he probably wouldn't walk again. His parents, Joan and Marv, were weeping.

It would be years before he would accept this twist of fate, years before he could say: "It was just a matter of understanding that life could go on, that it was not the end of the world...that I could still pursue what is in my heart."

In following the call of his heart, Hansen has traversed the world in a wheelchair. His most important contribution, perhaps, has been his example. His mere presence has been a symbol of hope.

From the vineyards of Portugal to the Great Wall of China, people have seen a man in motion, full of strength, not a man imprisoned by his wheelchair.

Brian Rose, a Vancouver sporting goods salesman, was Hansen's advance man for three months in Australia and New Zealand. He saw Hansen at close range in the most difficult conditions.

"The thing I found most amazing was that Rick does this unbelievable physical effort every day. It's immense and he'd done it day after day for a year and a half. In the midst of this, people come up to him constantly — the media, school children, police, all with some story to tell him.

"I can't remember a case when he wasn't unfailingly polite. He realized when he was in a foreign country that he was a representative of Canada.

"He made an effort to be positive and to make a good impression in the midst of all this wheeling. You or I could be lucky to be graceful under such pressure.

"He made you proud to be a Canadian."

The idea of living with a disability had never occurred to Rick. "Being an athlete, I'd had injuries before. They put a cast on you and in no time you're back on the road again," Hanson said.

His spinal cord was severed, however, and there was talk about an operation in Williams Lake. Hansen insisted that he be taken to Vancouver to see a specialist.

The operation went well, though there seemed little hope that he could ever use his legs again. Hansen didn't accept that prognosis. Coaches and friends came to visit him and he'd say: "Don't worry, I'm going to be there in the starting line-up. Don't replace me."

He was told that the next 18 months were crucial to his rehabilitation. "I worked really hard. One of the things that kept me going, even though I was devastated, was that I wouldn't believe I was not going to walk again. I never stopped trying until the 18 months were up."

In the meantime he set goals, such as building up his arms, learning to use a wheelchair and how to move his body without the use of his legs.

"I was stubborn, single-minded and full of purpose. For some I was a model patient; for others, I was a pain in the butt."

He couldn't be fitted with braces until he was admitted to the G.F. Strong Rehabilitation Centre — a three-month wait. He asked the hospital to make casts for him so he could learn to walk again.

Some tried to encourage him to take occupational therapy. He wasn't interested in make-work projects such as cookie baking or wood working. They only diverted him from his goals.

When he returned home, he hated using the wheelchair — it was the sign of a disability. "I hadn't realized it was an important functional tool," he said. Though it was winter, Hansen manoeuvred himself to school on crutches.

Hansen was becoming interested in girls before his accident. "That was taken away from me. Who was going to be interested in a guy with no legs? After my accident I lost 35 pounds, my legs were beginning to atrophy. I wouldn't go swimming, or do anything so that my legs would be shown.

"I became a watcher. I was feeling sorry for myself.

"Then I got mad. This wasn't the way I wanted to spend the rest of my life. I couldn't keep looking back at what could have been. The key was to move forward and start adapting."

Encouraged by his coach, Bob Redford, Hansen learned to be an athlete in a wheelchair. He started coaching and training able-bodied athletes.

"I was always moving forward. There were many internal battles, but I was always setting goals — to get out of the hospital, to get out of the rehabilitation centre, for example. I started to gain confidence and realized I could achieve things, that life wasn't over."

Before his accident Hansen had set his mind on being a physical education teacher. Redford kept nudging him — what was he going to do about it?

The University of British Columbia had never had a disabled student in its physical education faculty. When Hansen applied he was told to try one year of arts and science and then he'd be considered for physical education.

"At first I took that as an insult, being narrow-minded as I could be." He eventually accepted their conditions and was the first disabled student admitted to the faculty.

In Vancouver he discovered the world of wheelchair sport. It gave him the athletic focus he needed.

The Vancouver Cable Cars wheelchair basketball team, he soon discovered, was no "pansy rehabilitation activity. It was very competitive. To make the team I had to work very hard." It was also one of the top wheelchair basketball teams in North America.

It was Hansen who recruited an unhappy and dispirited Terry Fox to the Cable Cars. A basketball player at Simon Fraser University, Fox had lost a leg to cancer and responded immediately to Hansen's invitation and fine example.

Their values were similar. Both were articulate, self-possessed, and pushed themselves to excellence. They were full of competitive spirit and stars of the basketball team which, in six years, won five national championships.

It was significant when Hansen set out from Vancouver's Oakridge shopping centre that Terry's parents, Betty and Rolly Fox, were among the well-wishers. As Betty Fox said, "they were so alike in their thinking, in their sincerity. The basis of his tour was the same as Terry's."

When he saw the impact of Terry Fox's cross-Canada run and how, in a few months, Fox had changed our perceptions of the disabled, Hansen's dream began to take a different shape.

His objectives changed. He began to see that he could make a contribution to the public good and that he, too, could change the way most of the world looked at the disabled.

Hansen won the wheelchair section of the Boston Marathon in 1983 and while training for the race in 1984, crashed while wheeling downhill, dislocating his shoulder and destroying the new racing chair he'd been testing.

As he told Vancouver *Province* columnist Jim Tayler: "I told the doctor at G.F. Strong (Rehabilitation Centre) if I was going to need a physiotherapist, get me a good-looking one. I was kidding, but he wheeled me in, I saw this girl and thought, 'Aw, I couldn't be that lucky.' But I was."

The physiotherapist was Amanda Reid. They became, as the saying goes, friends, and saw each other occasionally as he trained for his world tour. When he left in March, 1985, he thought he wouldn't see her again until he returned 18 months later.

But only days after setting out from Vancouver he suffered an injury and called for Reid to join them in Oregon. She'd planned to stay only for her two-week vacation. It turned out to be for keeps. Except for one short break they've been together 24 hours a day since the tour began.

In Shediac, N.B., Hansen asked Reid to marry him. "Our relationship was forged in the heat of battle. There have been so many battles, so many difficult times. Living with other people, having no time."

He stresses that the tour always was the top priority. "We didn't talk a lot about our relationship as it was developing. We were afraid people would misinterpret and we didn't want to lose the focus of the tour.

"But what little personal life I did have, I wanted to enjoy. The time was right for me to do it."

When he speaks of Reid, tired as he is at the end of the day, his voice lifts. It's full of joy.

"She's been my backbone, in many ways. We make a great team. We've learned how to love one another for who we are, to accept and understand one another, and to be there when we need someone."

— Leslie Scrivener/*Toronto Star*

EXPLORING IDEAS

Review the notes you have made in your personal-response journal and quickly skim the photos, articles, and ads you have commented on.

Form small groups to discuss your reactions and to draw some conclusions on how the various aspects of the newspaper medium combined in developing the image of Rick Hansen as a genuine Canadian hero. The following questions will help focus your discussions. Appoint one student to record and report your group's observations and conclusions to the class.

1. Discuss the following in relation to the *news photos* on pages 314-315:
   (a) What immediate effect does each photo have on you? How does this effect contribute to the making of a hero?
   Comment on the basic photographic techniques used to create this effect.
   (b) What basic human needs or emotions are appealed to?
   (c) What attitudes towards Mr. Hansen are expressed or implied through each photograph?
   (d) In your view, do the photos make their message clear *without* the use of captions? What, if anything, do the captions add to Rick Hansen's heroic image?
2. Review the *articles* on pages 316-320 and your journal notes on them. Share your observations and opinions.
   (a) In your judgment, what is the purpose of each item?
   (b) Consider audience appeal. What types of information are included in the feature article? What basic human needs or desires are appealed to in each article? What reader response is called for? (Refer to the language the writers use and the details included in each piece.)
3. Analyze and evaluate the *corporate advocacy ads* (pages 317-318).
   (a) How effective is each of the ads in developing an impression of Rick Hansen as a hero? Refer to specific techniques: the content of the ads, the size, the composition, camera angles, and the text, or copy.
   (b) How do the visual techniques in the first ad differ from those in the second? What emotional response is called for in each? Which has the stronger impact on you? Why?
   (c) What reasons might corporate sponsors have for supporting the Man in Motion tour? Is such support necessary or valuable? Support your views.
   (d) The corporate sponsors are proud of their support of Mr. Hansen's cause. In making their support known, what image of *itself* does each sponsor wish to convey? Express your views on the validity of corporations using sponsorship-related advocacy ads to enhance their own public image.
4. Terry Fox chose the *slogan* "The Marathon of Hope"; Rick Hansen's tour was identified with the slogan "Man in Motion." What emotions do each of the slogans arouse? What associations do they bring to mind? Explain.
5. Individuals can be said to become symbols.
   (a) What is *your* definition of a symbol? In your view, what is the difference between a hero and a symbol?
   (b) What, in your opinion, do Terry Fox and Rick Hansen symbolize? Explain and support your views.
   (c) What is the value of such symbols in our society? What function do they seem to serve?

YOUR TURN

1. Working with a partner, or in a small group, choose a character from a novel or an individual you have studied and present this individual as a public hero. Design a newspaper page to bring her or him to the attention of the public. Write headlines, an editorial, and a news feature that would achieve this goal. Describe the photographs you would include and any sponsor ads you think would be suitable.
   Present your newspaper coverage to the class and lead a discussion to help you evaluate its effectiveness. Based on the audience comments, are there any ways to improve your coverage?
2. What cause or issue might ignite Canadians in the future? Working with a partner, develop a media campaign that will promote an individual as the *next* media hero. What marketing strategies will be effective? (Consider slogans, sponsorship, logos, layouts for ads, songs, jingles, and so on.) Select a group of students to role-play your hero's organizing team. Present your ideas to this group and be prepared to respond to their questions and comments.

HEROES IN THE REAL WORLD

"His lip occasionally quivered. His eyes at times misted over... his boyish tenor alternately rang with defiant indignation or broke with emotion. He tugged on the public heart strings by invoking the spectre of a threatened terrorist attack on his 11-year-old daughter, [and] he cast himself as a fearless action man willing to risk self-destruction in carrying out secret foreign policy initiatives."

— from "Hero or Outlaw"
by Marci McDonald in *Maclean's*,
July 20, 1987

At first glance, you might think the writer of the above is talking about some fictional movie hero. These words were used, however, to describe Lt. Colonel Oliver North, who electrified television viewers during his testimony before a congressional committee in the United States. In six days, "Ollie" was catapulted to the level of a national folk hero — despite admitting to having broken the law in "service to his country." A new word entered the vocabulary: *telegenic*. The events surrounding the North testimony provided a sharp reminder of the power of the media — in this case television — to transform ordinary women and men into heroes ...the power to shape public opinion almost overnight.

As the following writer points out, the media's role in creating public heroes may not always be a positive one.

America has topsy-turvy idea of heroism

The image of heroes and heroism is badly worn in American culture; it suffers mightily from celebrity hype and political expediency.

The renewed interest in creating an Age of Heroes is evident from Rambo to "The Refrigerator," Chuck Yeager to Lee Iacocca. Some attribute this new hunger for heroes to Ronald Reagan, his celluloid genesis as Notre Dame's Gipper and his continuing popular appeal as a real-life president.

The appetite of television for new faces is another factor, according to experts in various fields. It is also a radical departure from only a decade ago when anti-heroes were popular in movies and literature in the wake of the Viet Nam war.

"Every hero mirrors the time and place in which he lives," Marshall Fishwick wrote in *The Hero, American Style.* "He must reflect man's innermost hopes and beliefs in a public way."

When American children wore coonskin caps and sang "Davvvvy, Davvvy Crockett, King of the Wild Frontier" they were still, it seems, in a world of innocence, a less complicated land.

People and events are more blurred and distorted now to accommodate the mass media's hunger for celebrity figures and political leaders' hunger for symbols which, they hope, will reflect glory on them.

The issue threads through society. In the current anxiety and vexation about terrorism and national helplessness, there is an eagerness to discover, maybe even invent, new heroes.

Nearly 9000 medals were given out to U.S. military personnel after the Grenada invasion in October, 1983. That represents approximately 15 medals for each Cuban military man and civilian construction worker present on that small island before American troops moved in. And just as surely as Rocky IV wraps himself in the American flag, political and mechanical mistakes such as the Marine deaths in Beirut are wrapped — and buried — in the flag of heroism.

The influences that are altering American perceptions come from many sources, from the White House to comic books and scriptwriters. John Wayne movies created their own vision of America. Somehow Elvis Presley has taken on heroic proportions since his death. Writers and artists are now in the process of "revitalizing" Superman for the late 1980s, said Peggy May, a spokesman for DC Comics.

President Reagan, in a much more somber vein, referred to navy diver Robert Stethem, who was killed in the TWA plane hijacked to Beirut, as an "American hero."

Others slain by terrorists get the same accolade, but surviving victims of the terrorists strongly denied that any heroism was involved.

One of the TWA passengers was Dr. Arthur Toga, an assistant professor of neurology at Washington University School of Medicine in St. Louis, who said after his safe return, "I'm not a hero. I don't want any ticker-tape parades. I'm just a little guy who was in the wrong place at the wrong time and on the wrong plane."

Another hostage, Thomas Cullins, said simply, "We did nothing that was in my definition of a hero."

But that doesn't stop others from capitalizing on tragedy. New York Senator Alfonse D'Amato proposed the congressional gold medal award for Leon Klinghoffer, who was killed by terrorists and thrown overboard in his own wheelchair from the Achille Lauro cruise ship.

Gen. Chuck Yeager, who is now retired and promoting batteries, warplanes, and seatbelts, is perhaps one of America's most famous and genuine heroes. He described the nomination of Klinghoffer as "the most stupid remark for a U.S. congressman to make. It sort of degraded every American who gave up his life for his country. They should sit back for 10 days or so before they start talking. People who are victims (of hijackings) are simply that, victims, just the same as people who get killed by drunk drivers. Nobody calls them heroes."

The urge to commercialize is omnipresent in American culture. A family spokesman said recently that Klinghoffer's widow, Marilyn, had been talking with producers about selling her story for a television movie or serial.

Lenny Skutnik, the clerk who jumped off a bridge into the freezing waters of the Potomac to rescue a woman from the Air Florida crash in 1982, complained recently that he and the woman he saved can no longer speak to each other because of a contract dispute on selling the story.

"People, before the 19th century, did not charge for their names or characteristics...that is one of the features of mass culture," says Neil Harris, a professor of history at the University of Chicago. He says there are now several lawsuits in California brought by the estates of actors to retain their styles and characteristics claiming that "celebrities have the right of publicity, just as others claim the right of privacy."

In an earlier essay on mythical figures and copyright law, Harris wrote: "In this country during the past hundred years manufacturing energies, advertising ingenuity, and media appetites have combined to create a powerful post-industrial folklore...in effect, modern mythic heroes are franchised on a for-profit basis, rented out to sell products, experiences, or values."

This is not the first time the image of heroes has raised concern. Thomas Carlyle, a Victorian man of letters, lamented that Napoleon was "our last Great Man" because the modern age, he wrote in 1841, "denies the existence of great men; denies the desirableness of great men." Hero worship, he claimed, had "finally ceased."

A contemporary historian of Charles Lindbergh noted in 1940 that "In the mill of modern publicity, heroes are worn out quickly." Chap Freeman, who teaches the history of filmmaking at Columbia College in Chicago, echoes that: "We are creating and discarding heroes at a fairly rapid clip. Our society is unable to agree on values long enough to be able to agree on heroes." A hint of that may be in the treatment of even Congressional medal of Honor winners who returned from Viet Nam and who are only recently being acknowledged.

Twenty-five years ago, Daniel J. Boorstin, now the Librarian of Congress, in his book *The Image*, made this distinction: "Celebrity-worship and hero-worship should not be confused. Yet we confuse them every day, and by doing so we come dan-

Heroes or victims? — TWA hostages arrive in the U.S.

gerously close to depriving ourselves of all real models."

The classic definition of a hero describes someone who shows extraordinary bravery, who is known for a noble deed or his own "greatness of soul." The hero had no self-serving motive and was admired and revered for his courage and willingness to risk his life or reputation for some greater good.

Jay Ogilvy, a philosopher who directs a program on values at the Stanford Research Institute in Palo Alto, Calif., says the installation and impact of values is hard to pin down, "but we do know there are some factors that make a difference now... Throughout the centuries father was the model for how to be a man for a male child. Now through television there may be hundreds of models and with the increasing pace of technological change — there was a time when the elders knew more than the young — now, at least in a technical sense, many younger people know more than their elders."

Hundreds of television roles do impress young children, but the problem becomes even more complex than that. Some critics have worried recently that there are few live actors anymore on Saturday morning programs. They see the likes of Sky King and Mr. Wizard, the Lone Ranger, Roy Rogers, and Hopalong Cassidy replaced largely by figures like the dog Scooby Doo and robotic Transformers.

The impact of television and other forms of mass culture on advertising, movies, and magazines appears to have accelerated the topsy-turvy idea of heroism.

"Heroes today are not born. They are packaged," wrote Mark Gerzon in *A Choice of Heroes.* "They are thrust upon us by marketing strategies. In place of legends, we create personalities. Instead of gods, we manufacture superstars. Instead of admiring greatness, we worship celebrity.

"It is a consumer's heroism, and the shelves of our cultural supermarket are crammed to capacity with competing brands..."

Yeager, who broke the sound barrier on Oct. 14, 1947, in the X-1 rocket plane that now hangs in the Smithsonian Air and Space Museum, said when he was growing up in the hills of West Virginia, "a hero, for me, was if a man was a good shot or a hunter or a guy that could make furniture on a machine.

"The movies and Hollywood distort what is a real hero. People who watch Rambo — I've never seen it myself — and all the other shoot-'em-up kinds of movies, they don't live up to it (the film image). Hell, nobody can live up to it."

— Timothy J. McNulty
Chicago Tribune

EXPLORING IDEAS

1. Form small groups and select *one* of the following quotes for discussion. Appoint one person to keep notes and present your group's ideas to the class. The suggestions below will help you to organize and focus the discussion:
   - Re-state each comment in your own words.
   - Discuss examples from your own experiences that either support or disprove the comment.
   - Decide whether you agree or disagree with the comment — and why.

   (a) *"The renewed interest in creating an Age of Heroes is evident from Rambo to 'The Refrigerator.'... The appetite of television for new faces is another factor, according to experts in various fields."*

   (b) *"In this country...in effect, modern mythic heroes are franchised on a for-profit basis, rented out to sell products, experiences, or values."*

   (c) *"We are creating and discarding heroes at a fairly rapid clip. Our society is unable to agree on values long enough to be able to agree on heroes."*

   (d) *"Celebrity-worship and hero-worship should not be confused. Yet we confuse them every day, and by doing so we come dangerously close to depriving ourselves of all real models."*

   (e) *"Heroes today are not born. They are packaged. They are thrust upon us by marketing strategies. In place of legends, we create personalities. Instead of gods, we manufacture superstars. Instead of admiring greatness, we worship celebrity."*
2. **(a)** Do you agree with writers who present good athletes as examples of heroes? Explain why or why not.
   (b) Do Canadians and Americans idolize athletes to the same degree? Why or why not?
3. Timothy McNulty writes as an American describing the American cultural scene. To what extent do you think the statements apply to Canada and the Canadian public?

INVESTIGATING THE MEDIA

1. **(a)** Review your personal definition of a hero, taking into consideration the issues you have examined in this unit. Draw up a list of criteria for a *true* hero.
   (b) Examine your media file for clippings about people the media present as heroes. Which of them, in your opinion, are true heroes? Which are not?
   (c) Select one subject and write an article in which you tell why you feel he or she is — or is not — a hero.

YOUR TURN

1. Compose a poem or song entitled "Where Have All the Heroes Gone?" that deals with heroes who have come and gone in the media. Include sufficient details in your writing to evoke vivid memories of those heroic people or fictional characters.

Can too much publicity turn a criminal into a folk hero? Two journalists try to answer a question that has been with us since the days of Jesse James and Billy the Kid.

Computer hackers, are they folk heroes or common criminals?

Early in November, 1987, a Burlington high school student was charged with "theft of communications."

For those who may not know the story, a computer hacker is alleged to have used his home computer to break into and make unauthorized calls from computerized telephone systems of a number of large companies in the area.

The story was given a tremendous amount of publicity and I even heard some people indicating they thought it was "kinda neat" that a young kid should be able to pull a stunt like that.

After all, goes the rationalization, a big corporation is fair game for a computer rip-off, isn't it?

By giving too much publicity to an act in which someone uses electronic means to deliberately defraud, and therefore steal, from someone else, the offender, particularly if he or she is young and bright, can easily, and wrongly, acquire a sort of romantic folk-hero status.

In this electronic age, we have seen a number of Hollywood movies and television programs with similar themes. A likeable computer whiz of a "David" takes on, albeit illegally, an establishment "Goliath."

There is all too often a tendency to be impressed by and admire the audacity and ingenuity of such a criminal mind.

But except in the obvious matter of degree, a thief is still a thief whether he uses a computer or a gun...and that is how he should be treated by the public, the media, and the law.

— Vic Hyde

Yeah, but...

Nobody is trying to make a modern-day Robin Hood out of the accused. The media is simply doing its job, giving the public the facts about an unusual theft.

The story warrants being on the front page or the lead report on a news broadcast because it is quite different. It's not every day a 17-year-old hacker is charged with "theft of communications" from a large firm.

In this case I would have to say the media has handled the story in a responsible manner, unlike what some well-known rags would do.

It was only two months ago a boa constrictor was the talk of the province when he slithered away into the plumbing system of his owner's apartment building in Hamilton, only to surface in another tenant's bathroom. The snake story received a lot of play, because it was so unusual.

This is a similar case. The crime is not being glorified, it is being reported on. There have certainly been no editorials or commentaries supporting the accused.

I also don't think the Burlington youth has acquired folk-hero status. The accused is just the focal point in a very intriguing story.

— David Rashford
Burlington Post
November 15, 1987

EXPLORING IDEAS

1. What is the difference between "reporting on" a crime and "glorifying" it in the media? Do the mass media exhibit a tendency to giving some types of criminals "romantic folk-hero status"? Discuss these issues in small groups. Select one member to take notes and report to the class.

YOUR TURN

1. Write an editorial in which you express your own views in response to one of the viewpoints in the article on "hackers."
2. Using the material you have collected in your file as a starting point, prepare an outline for *either* a film documentary *or* a television drama based upon the life of one of today's media heroes. Select a group of students to role-play production executives. Present your ideas to this group and be prepared to respond to their questions and suggestions.
3. Write a song lyric or poem to honour one of the individuals you have been collecting information on in your file.

Choose two or more of the following suggestions or develop your own activities and research projects to investigate further "The Making of a Hero."

1. Who are the heroes of popular culture today? What new heroes have been invented for public consumption? What values are implied or promoted by these heroes? View some recent films and current television programs and prepare a report for the class. Your report should include some conclusions you have drawn from your viewing.

2. In his column about Rick Hansen, writer Peter Howell mentions Steve Fonyo's "unhappy fall from grace." Do some research into Fonyo's marathon across Canada. As you collect information, try to answer the following questions:
   (a) Given that Steve Fonyo accomplished what Terry Fox was unable to do, why did he not capture the imagination of the public to the same extent as Terry Fox did?
   (b) What role did the media play in influencing the attitudes of the public to Steve Fonyo?
   (c) In interviews published in the print media, Mr. Fonyo has stated that, given the chance to do it all over again, he would have gone about presenting his cause — and his public image — in quite different ways. "My appearance would be different...my answers to the media would be different....It would be slicker." (Steve Fonyo as quoted in the *Toronto Star*, January 5, 1988, by Tim Harper).

   Imagine you are Steve Fonyo's public-relations adviser and that Mr. Fonyo *does* have the opportunity to turn back the clock. What changes would you advise him to make in packaging his 1984-'85 cross-Canada trek, and in creating an improved image that would gain for Steve the same hero status as a Terry Fox or a Rick Hansen?

3. **(a)** Do some research into the heroic myths and legends written for other cultures in other times. (North American Native myths, ancient Greek, Roman and Egyptian myths and legends are some possibilities.) What patterns are evident in the personality traits of mythic or legendary heroes and in their exploits? Assuming that the tales reflect the culture they represent, what conclusions can you draw about the values and beliefs of the society? What aspects of modern heroes can be traced back to very early patterns?
   (b) Prepare a report in which you focus on the similarities and differences that are apparent in myths and legends from different cultures — both ancient and modern.
   or
   Write your own ancient — or modern — myth or legend. Apply the patterns you have identified through your research to the development of the heroic character central to your myth and to the story line.

4. How have the styles and images of film heroes changed over the years? How do these changes reflect both the values and the social and political climate of the different eras? Do some research on this topic. If possible, arrange to view a variety of feature films. Prepare a report based on your investigations. Your report should include your predictions about the types of heroes and heroic stories that will be "right" for the 1990s.

5. Prepare a report on Ken Taylor, a Canadian diplomat who was heralded as a hero for helping American families escape from Iran when hostilities erupted between that country and the United States in 1979. Your report should focus on the kind of media coverage given to Mr. Taylor by both American and Canadian news media.

6. Research the tradition of the antihero in film. What are the particular characteristic traits of this type of hero? Why were films featuring the antihero popular during the 1960s and '70s? The following are a few film titles to get you started:
   Hud
   Rebel Without a Cause
   Easy Rider
   Cool Hand Luke

7. Select a hero from the present day or from history. Research the hero's life and deeds carefully; then role-play the hero in a "live" interview for the class.

8. Create a new chapter for this text. The focus of the chapter will be the influence of the media on an individual's career. Some possible titles are "The Making of a Politician," "The Making of a Superstar," or "The Making of a Media Event." Consult a variety of news media and collect photos, feature stories, editorials, headlines, and so on that you would include in the new chapter.

UNIT EIGHT:

FUTURE-WATCH

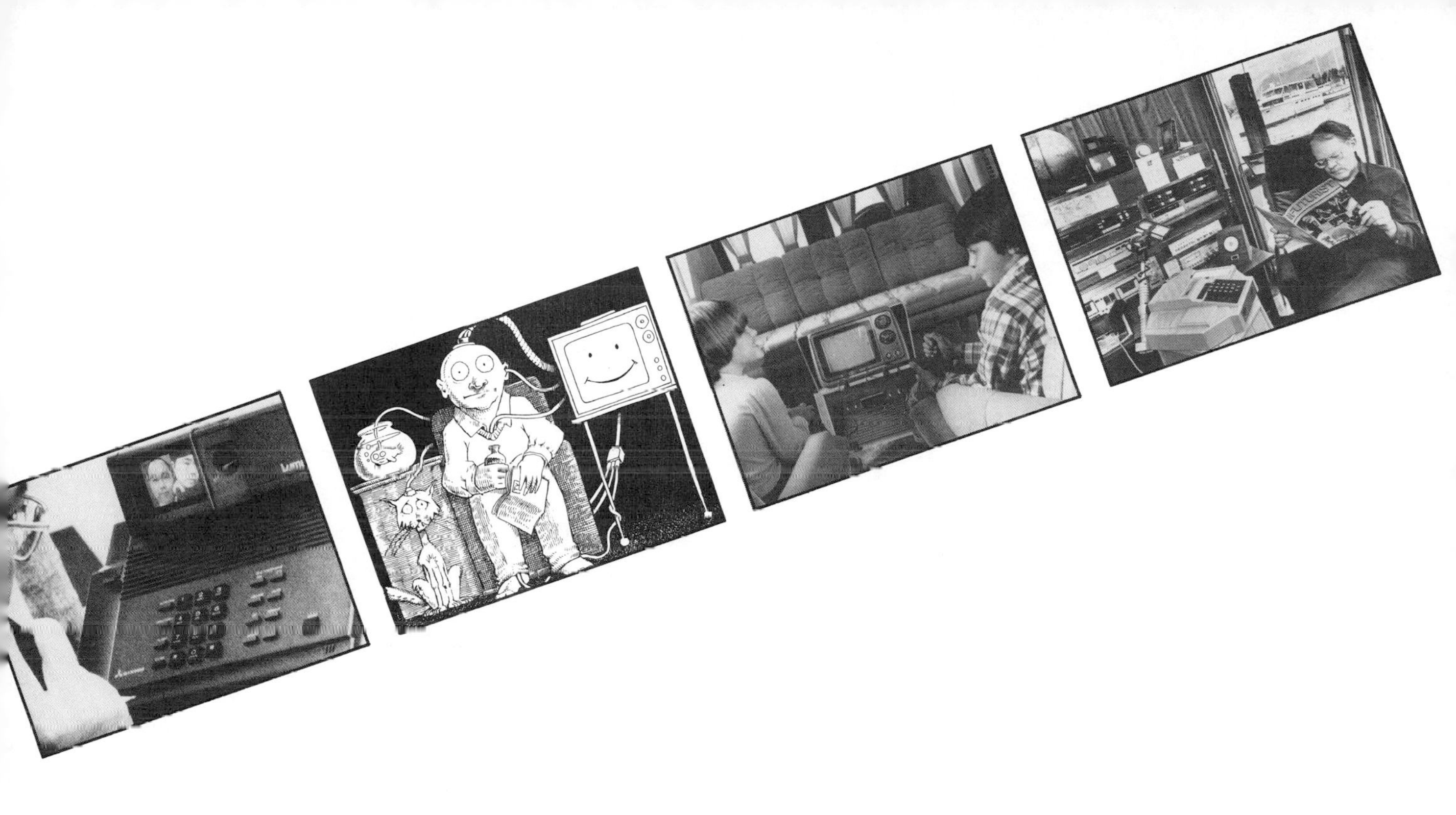

> “What appears on the surface to be a set of unrelated events
> turns out to be a wave of closely interrelated changes
> sweeping across the media horizon from newspapers
> and radio. . .to magazines and television.
> New, de-massified media are proliferating, challenging,
> and sometimes
> even replacing the mass media. . . .”
>
> – **Alvin Toffler, *The Third Wave***

The revolution known as "mass media" began in the mid-1400s when Johannes Gutenberg and others developed the process of printing from movable type. The mass media brought a wave of information to millions of ordinary people. This wave has been remarkable not only for the amount of information it contains but also for the fact that people living thousands of kilometres apart have access to the same information at about the same time; in many ways, the "global village" predicted by early media prophets is now a reality.

But this revolution is undergoing transformation — today's media analysts talk about the "de-massification" of the media. The new de-massified media offer more and more individuals the opportunity to be entertained, learn, shop, and work without leaving their homes. Will the new wave of de-massified media bring greater personal choice and freedom — or as some analysts fear, bring us isolation from each other and our environment?

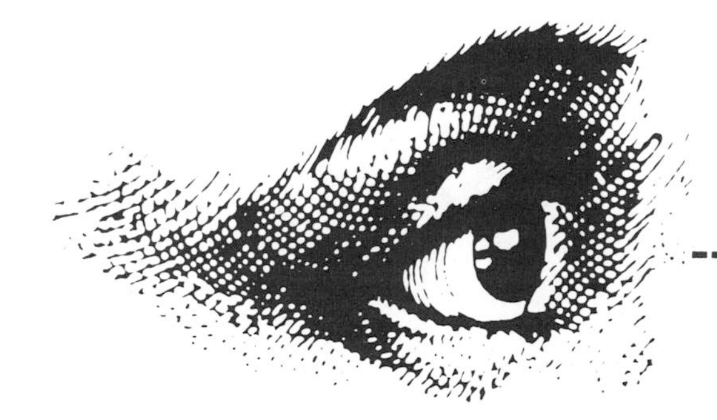

YOU & THE MEDIA

For I looked into the future
Far as human eye could see
Saw a vision of the world
And all the wonders that would be.

— Alfred, Lord Tennyson
"Lockaby Hall"

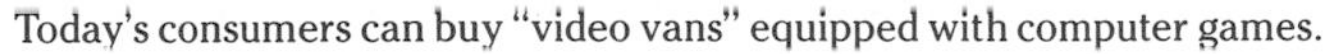
Today's consumers can buy "video vans" equipped with computer games.

A walking, talking Canadian robot toured Britain to promote Expo '86.

1 What technological achievements are "just around the corner"? What impact will they have on our lives and our society? As a class, develop a list of "inventions-for-the-not-too-distant-future" you have read or heard about. Focus on innovations that relate to the mass media and communications technology. Consider:
(a) Which item or innovation on the list is the most exciting to you personally? Why?
(b) Which seems the most threatening? Why?
(c) Which achievement, do you think, will affect you most strongly? Explain.

Uncertain steps into the future

They're off.

The first grads of the year 2000 are in school.

They can barely print their names, but Ontario's 183 058 kindergarten children have just taken the first steps of a 14-year mystery tour that will thrust them into a different world.

But are they the right steps?

As Ontario starts to educate the first wave of the 21st century, there is growing fear that it is not training our young people to find a focus in the blur of high-tech change.

The public is worried, and experts are worried.

— Louise Brown
Toronto Star/April 25, 1987

2 Record your response to the following questions in your journal. Then share your ideas in a class discussion.
(a) In what ways might the schools the next generation attends differ from the schools you have attended? Which subjects, if any, might be dropped from the curriculum? Which might be added?
(b) What will your daughter's or son's classroom look like? What media and kinds of technology do you think could become regular features of education?

3 Begin a media file of advertisements and articles about new media-related products and services. Throughout this unit:
(a) As a class, discuss the impact these innovations may have on the way we live and work in the future.
(b) In your journal, explore your own feelings about the future — and about trends in the media.

LIVING IN THE 21ST CENTURY

As the year 2000 draws near, it is likely there will be some fundamental changes in how we communicate with each other, in how and where we do our jobs, in how we spend our leisure time, and possibly even in how we are governed.

Edward Clifford looks forward to the year 2010 and expands our vision of what a computerized future may actually be like.

Computer gets day up and running

Barely awake, Tom shuffles down the hallway and opens the delivery locker. It is 7 a.m., and the morning paper is waiting, as usual, along with the complimentary container of hot coffee (two milk, one sugar — just the way he likes it).

He carries the paper into the living room and sits beside the commterm, punching in his personal code. The voice synthesizer immediately responds in a wide-awake woman's voice: "Good morning, Tom." He prefers a woman's voice first thing in the morning, but he usually switches it to that of a man before his wife stirs out of bed.

Nothing unusual here. The newspaper and coffee service is typical of what a guest at a first-rate hotel received in 1985. In 2010, it is available at home. The communications terminal (commterm) was already old hat in 1985, but interactive voice synthesizers still had a few bugs to be worked out.

Tom opens the paper to the sports pages. As usual, the scores from the night games on the West Coast have not made it into the paper. He tells his commterm: "news data base, Page 47, update score, Vancouver-San Diego."

After brief pause, the voice comes back: "Vancouver Mariners 7, San Diego Padres 6; winning pitcher Jones in relief, his fifth; home runs Ripken for the Mariners and Thornton for Vancouver; Mariners take over sole possession of second place."

On the front page, there is a report of an earthquake in Pakistan. The story puts the number of dead at 746. Tom says: "News data base, Page 1, update earthquake." The commterm quickly comes back: "Latest reports indicate more than 1000 dead. Red Cross flying in emergency supplies of food and shelter."

Then he asks for the traffic report. "Allen Expressway jammed to Lake Shore, Don Valley crawling, Gardiner impassable, 401 a disaster, Scarborough a writeoff," the commterm replies. Then it adds (somewhat gratuitously, Tom thinks): "If you're going to the office, better take the train today."

Contrary to some prophesies in 1985, the daily newspaper is still alive and well in 2010, for the simple reason that it remains a cost-effective advertising medium. Its embrace of technology gives it what could be a stranglehold on news dissemination. Newspapers can, for example, take over traffic reports — which in 1985 were the sole province of radio stations — because these provide

Million-bit chip—Tiny computer memory chips are able to pass through the eye of a needle

news in its purest form — information that is instantly usable.

Someday, Tom wants to find out who programs these things. He suspects the railway transit authority pays Info-Util an extra fee to promote the commuter service. Sold years ago to the private sector, both are regulated provincial utilities.

Tom finishes his coffee, a courtesy provided by the newspaper for every home subscriber who also buys access to its newsbase from Info-Util. The whole package adds $1000 a year to his information bill, but it is probably as good a news service as he can get.

He hears a soft beeping noise from the front hall. Probably the laundry and dry cleaning, he says to himself. Checking the locker again, he finds his freshly pressed suit and two clean shirts hanging inside. At least, he thinks, somebody has figured out what he should wear today.

There has been a huge increase in the nighttime workforce since 1985. The change makes more efficient use of roads, stores, utilities, and capital equipment, allows many services to be performed more effectively at night (such as pressing Tom's suit) and accommodates the growing economic interdependence of the highly developed nations, letting each respond to the needs of customers around the world, regardless of where the sun happens to be shining at any particular moment.

Tom remembers his grandfather telling him that, up to the middle of the 1960s, all kinds of goods were delivered to the home — bread, milk, butter, eggs, ice — things that would last only a day or two and needed to be replaced continually. Squads of young boys were employed by drug stores, grocers, and meat markets to rush telephone orders to customers. These services all but disappeared by 1960.

Now, of course, food items can be stored almost indefinitely and, in any event, are kind of fun to buy at Carnival Place, the huge market and recreation centre. The time-consuming side trips — getting a newspaper, taking in dry cleaning, picking up beer — can, however, be eliminated by hiring a fetchit service. These number in the hundreds, with adults, not youngsters, doing the work. Some believe the fetchit industry is poised on the brink of nationalization as larger companies move into this lucrative labor-intensive field.

Of course, it was necessary to install the delivery locker, to which the various fetchits had punch-code entry. His grandfather had scoffed when he had it installed. "Nothing more than an oversize milk box. Some things never change."

Not completely true. In the 1920s and 1930s, milk boxes were built into the sides of houses, usually by the side door — traditionally the tradesmen's entrance. For the sake of convenience and in keeping with the egalitarian nature of society in 2010, delivery lockers are beside the front door.

Robotic helper — Frank Ogden of Vancouver relaxes while robot Nabu changes a videotape. Nabu speaks several languages, tells jokes, and can summon help in case of burglary.

Tom switches the commterm over to the man's voice, turns on the video and says: "Office message centre."

He has the old-fashioned work ethic. He checks in with the office at least once a day, including weekends, and it is not unusual for him to work a 30-or 32-hour week. The commissions that make up a large part of his compensation package are one incentive.

Nonetheless, he enjoys his job, selling package tours of Canada in overseas markets. He is assigned southeast Asia and, last year, single-handedly sold $30-million worth of vacations and business trips to customers in Singapore, Malaysia, Thailand, and Indonesia.

Tourism accounts for 20 per cent of Canada's foreign exchange earnings in 2010, 10 times the percentage in 1985, surpassing mining and primary manufacturing together in providing jobs for Canadians.

Part of Tom's success is undoubtedly because his territory embraces some of the world's most prosperous countries — the nouveau riche of the Pacific. His sales pitch for these markets revolves around experiencing Canada's wide-open spaces, but he sets up the tours knowing full well that two or three days in the remote Rockies or Northern Ontario are about all the isolation most visitors from these populous lands can handle.

Tom knows they will then rearrange their schedules to spend more time in the cities, which is just fine with him and his employer, Pacifican Inc., because it usually means more commissions.

Pacifican also has interests in restaurants, bars, and theatres to serve the tourists and makes sure that a substantial number of visitors are steered there.

Tom makes frequent trips to his client countries to develop contacts in the travel industry. His wife, Cheryl, can usually accompany him without much inconvenience since her own job — an experience designer for Pacifican — involves short concentrated periods of work and long periods of leisure.

Experience design was a small but growing trade in 1985. People playing military games in the woods with paint-pellet guns were using the services of experience designers, even if they did not know it. By 2010, the experience designers can put together a wide range of vaca-

tion packages, such as being a baseball player, actor in an off-Broadway play, or captain of a seventeenth-century barque.

While both Tom and Cheryl can do virtually all their work without leaving the house, they enjoy going to the office three or four times a week. These visits are more like social occasions than work. They find personal contact with colleagues to be among their most productive activities, enabling them to trade ideas and experiences or just plain gossip.

In their early 30s, they talk occasionally about having a child — "most of our friends have one" — but are in no hurry to make a decision. In any event, there is a huge international traffic in legal adoptions, so babies are readily available to qualified couples or single people who have the requisite training to be parents.

As Tom lounges in the living room, Cheryl yawns her way toward the kitchen, where the coffee is already perking. The self-disciplined member of the household, she is soon by Tom's side at the commterm and activating her own code. "Schedule on the screen, please." She always says "please," even to a machine, and has programmed it to respond in kind.

One of the petty irritants in using 1985-style bank teller machines was that they flashed little messages like: "Thank you for using Instant Teller," yet had no button for the customer to answer: "You're welcome." The whole exchange seemed to end on a vaguely uncivil note, a problem that has been eliminated by 2010.

Cheryl's daily schedule pops up, and the first item is "Bills Due." It lists three or four bills that have to be paid in the next two days and three others that should be paid within the next week. Postponing a bill past one week is almost unheard of. The time-value of money has taken on critical importance in the flowering of fully computerized financial services, and interest on unpaid bills is onerous.

In seconds, she calls up the couple's bank balance, authorizes the bank to pay the current bills, transfers some funds to a medium-term (seven-day) savings account, and reviews the net worth of their stocks according to current trades on the 24-hour world market.

Next, she calls up a list of stocks trading at 10 per cent or more above what they paid for them, and notes there is an outstanding offer at a 12 per cent premium for some Zambian Copper shares acquired two weeks before. She calls up the offer and notes that it was made by a powerful Harbim farming co-operative. Cheryl pushes the "sell" key and, three seconds later, the sale is concluded. The proceeds of $3700 are credited to her trading account.

She spends it immediately on Aeroflot shares, but makes no other trades. Cheryl does not feel sufficiently nimble to make much money today, especially since it is so nice outside, a fine day for gardening. She says, "Thank you," to the commterm, and it says: "You're welcome. Have a nice day."

Existence of a single world trading market, with transactions being made directly between buyers and sellers, rather than through brokers, was hardly expected back in 1985. Nor was it widely expected that the Soviet Union would sell off part of its state enterprises to foreign investors.

There were, however, suggestions that, by the time the twenty-first century was 10 years old, a substantial number of Canadians — probably the majority — would treat the pursuit of wealth as secondary to what they felt were rewarding leisure activities.

— Edward Clifford
The Globe and Mail

EXPLORING IDEAS

1. ***(a)*** Working alone, or with a partner, identify and evaluate — from a personal perspective — the changes predicted by Mr. Clifford in each of the following:
   - family life and daily routines
   - the work force generally and the workplace for the individual
   - mass media
   - the character of society as a whole

   Decide which changes would improve the quality of our lives, and which would not.

   (b) Personalize the vision of the article. Brainstorm a list of daily routines you perform at home and in school. Select one or two items from your list and suggest how *you* would like future technology to alter these routines. How accurate might your predictions be? Explain.

   (c) What questions does this vision of the future raise in your mind? What would you like to know more about? Share your ideas in a small-group discussion.
2. Do you find this vision of a "brave new world" thrilling? somewhat frightening? a little puzzling? Respond to this issue in your journal.

INVESTIGATING THE MEDIA

1. Survey print ads and employment opportunities in the "Careers" section of the newspaper. What trends are evident that will affect the workplace and life at home? Prepare a written report or visual display on this topic.

YOUR TURN

1. Look into the crystal ball. You are seventy years old and have seen lots of changes throughout your lifetime. Script and perform "live" or on tape a monologue entitled "I Remember When..." in which you describe life as it is in your 70th year and as it used to be when you were younger.
   or
   Using the same theme, either script and perform *or* write a short story involving two characters — an elderly man or woman and that person's grandchild. Imagine the two characters are alone and the child is asking questions about how things used to be.
2. Expand the vision in the article. Brainstorm a list of additional services that might be available in 2010. Working in small groups, script, rehearse, and perform a series of commercials describing the benefits of these innovations.
   or
   Using the same theme, write a short story set sometime in the future. The action takes place in your community and should reflect the technology and services you imagine will be available to us in 2010. Your story may be serious or may present a tongue-in-cheek vision of the future.
3. Present a series of cartoons or comic strips on the theme of mass (or de-massified) media and the future.

The following article looks at the goods and services that have revolutionized our lives in the past...and ones which will change our lives in the future — notably the "PC," personal computer, and its many applications.

The way we were and the way we will be

If you're old enough, cast your mind back to the mid-1940s and remember what life was like back then. If you're not old enough to recall the forties, just try to imagine life without antibiotics, without air conditioning, without automatic washers and dryers, without commercial air travel, never mind fast food, color television, and credit cards. In the 1940s there weren't the conveniences of today's state-of-the-art technology; indeed, life was a lot tougher 40 or 50 years ago. But the wonders of the consumer age, which began in earnest back then, have made day-to-day living in the eighties immeasurably easier. As the Second World War drew to a close, the industrial era was in its death throes, while the information age was merely dawning.

What might the next 50 years of the consumer age mean to our existence? On these pages we take a look at the future and examine what's new on the market and which products and services could alter our lives.

It would be hard to examine the latter half of the 20th century without looking, first and foremost, at the revolutionary microchip. It, of all developments of this century, offers infinite possibilities of change. Microchips are found in everything from pocket calculators, digital alarm watches, and programmable dishwashers and washing machines to high-tech audio systems and advanced camera equipment. The mass production of these tiny miracles brings modern-day technology within reach of the average consumer.

Above all, there is one microchip product of undisputed importance to both this century and the next: the computer. Whether we like it or not, computers are here to stay. They come in all shapes, sizes, and levels of complexity, and they already influence the way we do busi-

Mighty microchips — These IBM memory chips are able to control memory storage in large computers and can read the entire contents of 75-volume encyclopedia in one second.

ness and the way we live. And it won't be too far into the future before each household, nay, each person in a household, has their own personal desktop computer. New "user friendly" models are even simple enough for children.

There is home computer software to play games, to teach languages, to prepare a household budget. You can do almost anything with a home computer these days: shop, bank, get up-to-date information on the stock market, order plane tickets, even finish up some office work at home. Industry benefits too, particularly with quantum advances in desktop publishing which allow average Canadians to print anything from a newsletter to a magazine.

There are lightweight, portable computers which run on battery power, so you can literally take the office on the road. Imagine row upon row of business people working madly away at their lap computers on planes, in restaurants, or on the beach while on vacation. That's what could be in store, when portable computers become the traditional briefcase of the future.

Now that computers are portable and personal, it makes sense for other office machinery to follow suit. Photocopiers are a prime example. Portable models, no bigger than an attaché case, are ideal if you're on the road, and they come with different color cartridges. Larger more sophisticated photocopiers are even used creatively by artists.

Tremendous advances in electronics have brought about the possibility of a home that's able to think for itself. All you'll have to do is program the "brain," and you'll be living in a James Bond movie. You will be verbally greeted as you walk in the door, drapes will open and close automatically when the room reaches certain preset temperatures, sensors worn on the dog's collar will open and close doors for the family pet, appliances will turn on and off by remote control, and sophisticated motion and noise detectors and outdoor lights that turn on as strangers approach the house will be sure to discourage even the boldest burglar.

In the interim, there's the Smart House, a home that's electrically wired to make your life easier. There is no central computer, rather individual microchips automatically turn lights on and off, let you know when the baby's crying or help you monitor a sick person in bed when you're in the basement, and even flash a signal on your television when the washing needs to be put in the dryer. Smart House technology already exists today and will likely be available in Canadian homes in the next year or two.

More and more, it's important to protect your home these days, especially as our entertainment tastes turn to expensive gadgetry. Televisions now boast superior audio and visual technology, and programming features such as channel memory let you directly access your favorite channel, a handy feature to sort out the 22 cable and nine pay TV channels.

Grabbing a snack is one of the only reasons to leave your armchair these days, because the entire home entertainment system — from the television and the videocassette recorder to the stereo and even the lights — can be digitally or electronically controlled by one remote-control unit. Electronic entertainment knows no boundaries: as books and magazines are transferred onto tapes and videocassettes, the TV becomes a visual library, and as products are displayed catalogue-style on the screen, the TV becomes an in-home shopping mall. (Rogers Cablesystems Inc. in Toronto already has a nationwide shopping system on the air.)

The early eighties saw the arrival of the compact disc (CD) player, a sophisticated, laser-operated piece of equipment which offers distortion-free sound reproduction. Early models were in the $1500 price range, but now that the cost has dropped drastically — to about $300 for some models — CDs are being built into cars, portable stereo units, and even into individual portable units. The CD music library in North America, which currently offers about 5000 titles, is growing rapidly. Moreover, in 1986 Motown Records announced that it would stop production of conventional LPs in favor of CDs.

CD technology is also being used for computer memory: a CD-ROM (Compact Disc-Read Only Memory), for example, can store vast quantities of information such as an entire encyclopedia on a single disc for very little cost. Needless to say, the potential benefits for any information-gathering organization are phenomenal.

The advances in communications technology since Alexander Graham Bell invented the telephone in 1876 are mind-boggling. We already take such telephone conveniences as automatic redial, call waiting, and speed dialing for granted. Some added features for the coming year include calling line information display, which shows the phone number of the person calling you on a digital display on the phone; extended call fowarding, which forwards calls received by one phone number to other preprogrammed phone numbers when you're away from home; and automatic call set-up, which eliminates the frustration of redialing when you get a busy signal (your phone rings when the line is free). There are other possible applications not yet in effect: different rings for each member of the household and a screening system which blocks preprogrammed calls from selected individuals or businesses by not ringing.

Bringing the office with you — Portable cellular telephones make it possible to carry out business anywhere at any time.

Cellular phones have also revolutionized the telecommunications industry. They use radio frequencies rather than telephone wires to transmit messages, so calls can be made anywhere in the world from a car, a boat, or even a briefcase. Portable models which can be removed from the car and locked to prevent unauthorized use are currently available, and in the future, miniaturization of phone batteries may produce even smaller phones which require no installation at all. Imagine a phone that fits into your pocket or purse which can be answered in the park or on the bus. Such transportable models would certainly satisfy our obsession to be close to a phone day and night.

In the meantime, answering machines are invaluable devices for those times we must be separated from the telephone. Sophisticated models can be used by remote control from anywhere in the world. Couples, who are constantly on the go, often use answering machines to communicate with each other about who should pick up the milk or what time to meet that evening.

"Photophone" — In 1987, Japan's Mitsubishi Electronic sold 10 000 TV phones in the U.S. The American-made "Lumanaphone" transmits still images of its users.

The latest breakthrough in cameras is the filmless camera. It uses a floppy disk and takes pictures which can either be viewed immediately on a television screen or monitor, printed out with a color printer, or transmitted via telephone lines to a distant location. The technology is invaluable to newspapers, magazines, and newsphoto agencies as it enables them to file photographs with the story.

The general public, on the other hand, probably has more use for a camcorder, a compact videotape camera-recorder. The small, lightweight, easy-to-use camera makes video movies for instant TV viewing. It's a budding movie producer's dream. Several models of camcorders are on the market — some weigh as little as four pounds; some are only six or eight inches long — and all come with different size tapes. They're even light enough to bring on vacation without paying excess baggage.

Years ago we would have scoffed at the idea of traveling to far-off places faster than the muzzle velocity of a bullet, but we now take it for granted, just like many other developments we once believed to be impossible. We don't think twice about communicating with anyone, anywhere, from a car, a bus, or a boat, and we don't look askance at the idea of shopping at home on our television set. We use gadgets for eveything: working out, cooking, even entertaining. And now that we're beginning to make our homes work and think for us, suddenly the even *more* impossible becomes possible.

— Carol Jamieson
Goodlife
October 1987

EXPLORING IDEAS

1. Form small groups to share your ideas on the following. Select one group member to record your ideas and to present them to the class for feedback.
(a) Brainstorm a list of possible implications of advances in telephone technology. Evaluate each item in your list: will it lead to positive or negative changes in the way we live?
(b) An innovation *not* mentioned in the article is the "photophone." With it, callers are able to transmit still pictures of themselves to the person receiving their call. It is also possible to transmit images of documents or photographs by simply holding the article in front of the photophone's camera.

How might the photophone change the way we use telephones in the home? at work? How might the photophone continue to evolve?

(c) Explore ways in which CD technology could revolutionize the way we work, learn, and play in the future.

(d) *"Cellular telephones and the communications revolution will make this an even smaller world."*

— Ron Starr, "The Cellular Solution"

In what ways might the world get "smaller" in the future? What are your reactions to this concept?

(e) Are the changes portable computers are making in *how* and *why* we conduct business good or bad, in your view? What other predictions can you make about the impact of PCs in the workplace of the 21st century?

(f) In a recent survey, 85 per cent of business people polled indicated there was no reason for them to travel to work every day as all their business dealings were conducted on the telephone or through computer networks.

Many futurists predict that soon homes will be transformed into electronic workplaces.

- Explore the implications of the *home* becoming the workplace. How will family life be affected? What aspects of the general economy will be affected? Can you see any similarities between this new "post-industrial" society and the "pre-industrial" societies of the past?
- What are your personal reactions to computerized, home-based work?

YOUR TURN

1. Working with a partner, or in a small group, create a print ad or TV commercial for one of the products or services mentioned in the article. Display or present your advertisement to the class. How successfully did you "sell" this new technology?
or
Create an advertisement for a new product or service *you* imagine will soon be available that relates to or extends the potential of one of the high-tech innovations in the article. Encourage audience feedback on the impact of your ad.
2. Write a short story or a poem in which you set the action in the "Smart House" of the future.

BRAVE NEW TV TECHNOLOGY

It's difficult to keep up with the rapid advances in video technology that are changing our entertainment, information-gathering, shopping, and working habits. As we rush to buy state-of-the-art technology, some experts anxiously wonder where the new media will lead us, while others offer marvellous images of the video culture of the future.

The next article tells us that "the taped medium is the message. Video has become our teacher, seller, and storyteller."

The Age of Video

Let's call him Video Man. Of course he's just as likely to be a she, but that's how anthropologists have traditionally christened an evolutionary jump — and, who knows, this one could prove as momentous as any in the ages B.V. *(Before Video).*

Tonight finds Video Man in the favorite corner of his habitat (the recliner he ordered from a video catalog) as he looks back — literally — on the past decade of his life. The electronic artifacts whir through his time machine. The video of his 80-yard run for South Seawash and of his valedictory address at State. The video from Telegenic Imaging that taught him how to tape the job pitch that got him into MegaGlam (was his voice that shaky?). The video of his wedding (for an extra fee, the videographer spliced in the theme music from "Chariots of Fire" and the fireworks scene from "To Catch a Thief"). The video of the birth of his child (did his grip on the camcorder really flutter that badly?). A dozen more cassettes bring him to the video recently received from his lawyer, which demonstrates how a client can make a video of his will. A perfectly fitting notion, he quickly decides, albeit one with a melancholy hitch: he won't be around to videotape his loved ones watching him bequeath them his videotapes. That, he ruefully concludes, will be the first video event of his adult life over which he will not have the remotest control.

• • •

Say this for our man: as a planetary trend setter, he made it big astonishingly fast. Social scientists estimate that it took nearly 500 000 years for Homo sapiens to move from oral communication to writing, another 5000 years to progress, if that is indeed the word, from print to television. Video Man first flitted into view during the '60s, when a few avant-gardists began experimenting with tape as a medium for far-out small-screen art. Then, a scant 10 years ago, the introduction of the videocassette recorder launched him into our mass consciousness. In the beginning the VCR was regarded as little more than a plug-in toy. But as the machines seized our enthusiasm — they now hold sway in nearly 30 per cent of all North American households with television — so did the realization that the new technology could be applied in ways far beyond time-shifting Bill Cosby or renting *Beverly Hills Cop*. The explosion in how-to cassettes offers

"Perfect gift" — The camcorder, a miniaturized video camera, makes recording home movies for VCRs almost as easy as taking snapshots.

the most obvious evidence. Besides attending shiatsu classes and sharpening their golf and tennis strokes, today's VCR owners can learn how to do massage and apply makeup, care for their plants and train their pets, relieve back pain and cope with stress, whip up coquille Saint-Jacques and pick up the opposite sex.

To fully appreciate the technology's revolutionary impact, however, you've got to get out of the house. These days video permeates virtually every corner of our culture, inexorably and irrevocably transforming the mechanisms by which millions of us define who and what we are. Just look around. It's in classrooms, courtrooms, board rooms, and operating rooms. It's on the floor of Congress and above the supermarket checkout line. It looms large on stadium scoreboards and hangs from the ceiling in fashion emporiums. It has swallowed the music industry and, in the process, gotten the generations at it again, this time over the content of rock videos aimed at the young.

For the true videophile, the preferred gift is a camcorder, a miniaturized, lightweight camera that makes producing home movies for VCRs almost as easy as shooting snapshots. The camcorder has already spawned the video Christmas card — homemade tapes of family members imparting holiday greetings. Or perhaps sentiments not so sentimental. According to the operator of a video-card service in New York, one female Scrooge recently used his gear to dispatch a Dear John missive to her live-in boyfriend.

As the video generation fast-forwards toward what conceivably could become an all-videoized culture, social analysts are only starting to address the fundamental conundrum: is all or even any of this *really good for us?* Whether they lean toward the Utopian or apocalyptic, most agree that we're witnessing what futurist Alvin Toffler calls the "de-massification" of the media, a shift from broad distribution of a few images to all of us (e.g., via the networks) to narrow distribution of many images to select groups (via video). If such diversification has a downside, it is the erosion of that commonality of experience — that communal vision, if you will — that binds a heterogeneous society.

Academics, meanwhile, fret that today's undergrad, nurtured by video at home, school and play, has grown addicted to action at the expense of thought. Reports Michele Lamont, an assistant professor at the University of Texas-Austin: "Students are becoming more and more visual. In sociology classes, when they're asked to read something even a bit complex, they get no pleasure out of it." Others fear that the formidable expense of plugging into the new video environment will further widen the educational breach between socioeconomic classes. "The poor," predicts University of Pennsylvania communications Prof. George Gerbner, "are going to be left out of it."

Hopeful futurists: Alvin Toffler, for one, opts for the bullish perspective. "We're reinventing the printing press," he declares. "[Video] makes for a greater variety of symbols and it encourages individualism. That doesn't mean a left-wing cult will have a million viewers, but it will have a niche. The political impact of video appears to be limitless." John Naisbitt, the author of "Megatrends," sounds even more upbeat. "I don't see any [drawbacks to video]," he proclaims. "It's part of the unfolding of human experience. The chief benefits are access to information a lot of people wouldn't otherwise get. What we're doing is creating more and more options — more and more *ways* of doing things." At the same time, Naisbitt cautions that any prognostication risks being instantly outdated: "The technology is really exploding, with every step in fluency. I don't think any of us have any idea where it's all going to end up."

Master Teacher

Initially, video arrived at the business office as part of elaborate multimedia presentations designed to train and motivate employees. "First you entertain them, then they'll learn," explains Herb Bass, cofounder of San Francisco's largest multimedia production firm. "It's like teaching the ABC's with Big Bird and the gang on *Sesame Street* instead of repeating after the teacher." With Bird & Co. seeming a bit passé of late, the most revolutionary breakthrough promises to be the adaptation of computer and video technology to "interactive" training programs. Ford Motor Co., for instance, is testing an interactive system that will impart the latest information on car repair to its 40 000 far-flung auto mechanics. On the left side of a split screen, the system flashes an underhood shot of, say, a carburetor; on the right side, it presents an array of tools needed to service it. Using an electronic "light pen," the mechanic transfers the tools over to the other screen, connects them, and begins making adjustments. (Look Ma, no grease.) All the while an audio track carries the appropriate sound of the engine running smoother or rougher. "This is like a flight simulator that gives hands-on training," says Tom Kubeshesky, a Ford planning supervisor. "It's amazing the way our technicians took to it. They love it."

More esoteric interactive experiments are under way in the Massachusetts Institute of Technology's "Athena Project." One of the most intriguing is designed to teach foreign tongues. For example, an aspiring linguist might learn French by watching a video in which a Parisian couple visits a real-estate brokerage in search of a suitable apartment. Playing the role of the broker, the student translates the couple's specifications and then, using detailed computerized listings and an electronic map of Paris, "interacts" with the couple by typing in recommendations in French on his keyboard. "Interactive video isn't a passive medium," says Janet Murray, the language project's director. "It requires a response."

Ultimately, the MIT researchers hope to apply computer-assisted video to the production of "electronic reference books" for students, but let's be sure to keep a wary watch on this one. By automatically recording how much time students actually spend hitting the "books," the computer can keep track of how diligent they are about their homework — an innovation that might have delighted Mister Chips if he hadn't read Mister Orwell. MIT research fellow Rus Gant predicts the system will be able to tell a professor, "This student comes in an hour a day or that one works 48 hours at a stretch and then disappears for two weeks." Nevertheless, Gant is convinced that the educational payoff will compensate for any unease about electronic surveillance. Interactive teaching courses sponsored by corporations and the Pentagon, he reports, have indicated that "students learn two to three times faster than with books and retain nearly triple as much information."

The thing is, as the young are discovering every day, that video is *there* just about everywhere. You don't have to be a psychotherapist to sense that there is a radical recondi-

Hands-off training — A Ford auto mechanic practises on an interactive video system.

tioning process at work on how the generations regard one another. If seeing is indeed believing, then our progeny can now be confronted with an illuminating new perspective on what it means to become old. For children to witness, courtesy of a family video, their parents conducting their courtship or a mother in her first ballet recital adds a dimension to their perceptions of human growth far beyond reach of any still camera. "There is no better way of preparing people to age," observes the University of Pennsylvania's Gerbner, "than to expose them to the phases of life before they get to them."

As video acquires more and more cachet, educational institutions are witnessing a rush to learn to *do* it rather than just learn from it. Would-be Spielbergs and Lucases, having discovered that a degree from a film school rarely pays the rent, are now turning to university video courses. "Film will always be around, but video is the medium of the future," explains David Johnson, a professor at the University of Southern California School of Cinema-TV.

Top Salesman

It's a tradition as American as concocting a plastic container that keeps the burger hot and the lettuce cold: the first to sniff out the potential of any techno-leap are usually those with a product to pitch. Or in the words of Jackson Bain, an executive at a Washington, D.C., public-relations agency: "The second guy who used the telegraph was trying to sell something."

Bain may be jesting, but there's little question that video has emerged as the delivery system of choice for today's sales messages. Real-estate agents now put together "video brochures" for prospective buyers. Perhaps the busiest and most inventive is Mike Glickman, whose real-estate operation in the vast San Fernando Valley does nearly $300 million in annual business. Whenever Glickman receives a new listing, he sends still shots of the residence to a video company that inserts them into a laser-disc system linked to a computer, producing an electronic brochure that house seekers can screen at his firm's headquarters. "Buyers love it because they don't have to spend days trudging from one inappropriate house to another," says Glickman. "And sellers love it because they don't have a lot of people who won't buy come through their homes criticizing their carpets."

Showing duds: Since we can't resist looking at it, video seems ideal for selling what we put on. In the apparel industry, fashion videos are currently luring the ready-to-wear shoppers along with the haute couture crowd. "FTV," as the new style was quickly christened, is designed to create more than just a buying mood. At a department store in Washington, D.C., visitors to the young-women's section are enveloped by 15 TV monitors playing rock videos. "We don't want to just sell clothes," explains Joe Consolo, a store executive. "We also want to entertain the customer."

It may seem a considerable jump from marketing things to selling people, but not for the true techno-hustler. Looking for a job? Better get with it and drop by The Corporate Interviewing Network, Inc. For a fee of a few hundred, the network develops lists of interview questions submitted by employers and bounces them off preselected job candidates during videotaped sessions at one of the firm's 20 U.S. franchise offices. While both parties save time and travel costs, the system seems to be loaded in favor of the telegenic smoothie — but then, as they say, that's showbiz.

All of this brings us to Wayne Fisher, a Houston personal-injury attorney. Fisher's specialty is the settlement brochure, which can include a taped presentation designed to persuade the other side to settle out of court. While Fisher is hardly the only claims lawyer to use video in such brochures, few invest as much care and ingenuity in their creation. With the help of $500 000 worth of state-of-the-art video gear and two full-time technicians, Fisher turns out productions that could stimulate the tear ducts of Ivan Drago.

'I miss Daddy': Consider one of Fisher's "day in the life" videos, which vividly illustrate how a client's injury or death has affected his life or those of his relations. The 40-minute tape opens with the key fact: a man, the narrator somberly informs us, perished in a plane crash in a swampy area of Florida. Dozens of pictures from his family albums — old snapshots of the victim fishing or presiding over holiday dinners — weave in and out of on-camera reminiscences by his loved ones. His widow recalls their courtship. ("He wrote me poetry," she says. "He sent me a dozen roses every month the first year we were married.") Several of his colleagues at work laud his character ("He had a very special sensitive core that he was not frightened to let anyone see"). Then comes the heart of Fisher's case: the death's devastating impact on the victim's young daughter. As his wife testifies to his fatherly devotion, more snapshots fill the screen: the child playing on Christmas morning with the dollhouse he built her. Fighting back tears, the widow reports that her daughter tells her, "I miss my daddy...I miss his jokes." Cut to a drawing made by the child at school. It shows a house capped by a black rainbow and a boxlike car. "It's almost like a hearse," observes her teacher.

Fisher estimates that he has used settlement brochures to win a half a dozen multi-million-dollar awards. To some in the judiciary, however, the emotionally manipulative content of such presentations may constitute prejudicial evidence. As video emerges as a new legal tool, it has set off a complex debate over its applications. Today some prosecutors in child-abuse cases spare the young victims from testifying in court by videotaping their descriptions of what happened for the jurors to study. Video, like any high-tech innovation, is, of itself, morally neutral. How we judge its usage as a new medium of persuasion hinges entirely on what the user is selling.

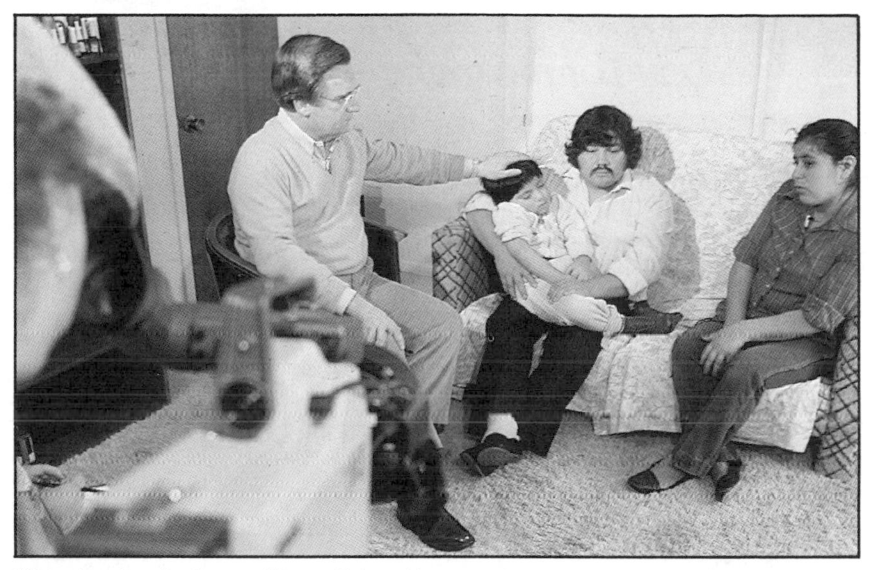

"Video brochure" — Lawyer Wayne Fisher videotapes the injured party's testimony.

Personal Historian

Now for the fun stuff. As the camcorder, with its instant-playback gratifications, usurps the hegemony of the home movie camera, fashioning family video albums is burgeoning into something of a national pastime. Births, graduations, weddings, class plays, bar mitzvahs, that first haircut and that last will and testament — name it, and odds are there's an amateur documentarian lurking about to capture it all through his viewfinder.

Taping marriage ceremonies is fast becoming the sine qua non for a classy nuptial (according to one estimate, 10 per cent of all U.S. weddings end up on cassettes). The videographer's bill can run as high as $3000, depending on whether the newlyweds desire such special-effect insertions as narration, captions, or Barry Manilow crooning Their Song. Yet to many couples in the video age, the chance to preserve those priceless moments — the bride's mother heading for the church with her daughter's honeymoon suitcase or that seven-second kiss at the altar — compensates for the extra expense as well as for whatever disruptions the camera crew may create. Sometimes the unexpected disaster provides the most cherished footage. Judy Onthank, vice president of a Connecticut videography firm, remembers taping a wedding at which the bride suddenly developed a nosebleed before her final vows. The entire scene, including the groom and the bridesmaids offering her Kleenex, remained in the final edited version — to the couple's everlasting delight. "It was a real human moment," chuckles Onthank.

There you have it. Video, like television itself, has taken on an irresistible momentum. Indeed, what we seem to be witnessing is the invention of an instrument for which we will conceive now-unimaginable applications as it sweeps us along. As the technology continues to penetrate every niche of our culture, futurists envision it enhancing creativity, enriching leisure habits, bringing us more closely in touch with our traditions by allowing us to relive birthday celebrations and holiday gatherings, even spawning its own modes of social intercourse.

Video Man. He communicates in a language we can see.

— Harry F. Waters
Newsweek
December 30, 1985

EXPLORING IDEAS

1. **(a)** Explain in your own words the concept of "de-massification" of the media.
   (b) Will the consequences of de-massification on society be positive or negative? Explore this issue in a class discussion.
2. **(a)** In your opinion, why have VCRs been the fastest-spreading consumer electronic product since the TV set?
   (b) What social uses might there be for home videos in the future?
3. **(a)** If interactive video *does* become standard in most schools, how will education be different? Discuss as a class.
   (b) Brainstorm as a group additional ways video might be used in schools of the future. Consider each of the following:
   - instruction
   - evaluation
   - monitoring

   (c) Evaluate the ideas in your list. Which are positive? negative?
   (d) Would you want to be there? Present a summary of the ideas that have been discussed along with your personal reactions to them.
4. **(a)** Comment on the claim that family videos have a reach far beyond that of the still camera and photos in a family album.
   (b) *"Film will always be around, but video is the medium of the future."*
   What advantages has video over film? What disadvantages?
5. *"Video...is, of itself, morally neutral."*
   (a) In addition to the examples given in the article, what other uses can you imagine for video in the process of law and justice?
   (b) Is video "too manipulative" to be used as a legal tool? Debate this issue in class.

INVESTIGATING THE MEDIA

1. What impact, if any, does/would owning a VCR have on your family? Share your observations in a class discussion.
2. Conduct a survey of how retailers in your community are using video both to sell to and entertain the customer. Prepare a presentation on this topic for the class.
3. *"The thing is...video is* there *just about everywhere."*
   Investigate the role of video in your community and in our society now. Who is using it? How is it being used? Prepare a report to the class.

YOUR TURN

1. Write an editorial in response to *one* of the following statements.
   (a) *"It's bad for the culture. People are retreating from the public world. VCRs are making domestic space a sponge that sucks in the occupants to movies."*
   (TIME: December 4, 1984)
   (b) *"If the medium is really the message, (VCRs) could ultimately mean new forms and styles of television programming."*
   (TIME: December 4, 1984)
   What new forms and styles might the VCR revolution create?
2. Working in a small group, create a "video brochure" designed to "sell" your school to parents who are shopping around before deciding where to send their children to school.
   or
   Imagine your parents have just put your home on the market. Create a video brochure to be used by the agent who will be selling your home.
3. Create your own series of video greeting cards.
4. The critical issue for the future seems to be *the use* we make of video. What are some of the potential abuses of video in society? What can and should be done now to prevent these possible abuses? Explore these questions and present your ideas in the form of an editorial or a news article.
5. *"...what we seem to be witnessing is the invention of an instrument for which we will conceive now-unimaginable applications as it sweeps us along."*
   What might a video society of the future be like? Present your ideas in the form of a short story, poem, or article.

Reprinted with special permission of King Features Syndicate, Inc.

Video Review magazine invited some of society's leading observers and artists to comment on how video has "reshaped our lives and touched every facet of our culture."

Video Shapes Your World

Finally, the future is here. The VCR has worn out all the clichés. No longer a "revolution in the making," the VCR now sits comfortably in almost a third of all North American homes. It has become a fact of our cultural lives, an appliance as familiar as our TV sets. And video as a medium is no longer a stepchild to television or an afterthought to the movies. It's right up there with books and magazines in conveying information and entertainment. Video has reshaped our lives and touched every facet of our culture. To get a deeper sense of that impact, some of society's leading critics, cultural observers, and artists were invited to help fine-tune the focus. Here's how they see it.

— Michel Tcherevkoff
Video Review
April 1986

LIFE

Edward Cornish
President of the World Future Society and editor of The Futurist.

The VCR is making possible the exportation of American cultural products around the world and bringing people in developing countries into the global communications network. The desire to get a VCR will begin motivating them to produce for the global economy.

You can't get televised movies everywhere, but with a VCR a movie just made in Hollywood can be seen immediately in the African jungle or in Calcutta. VCRs are already being used in Bombay to set up little movie theaters. Someone gets one, usually on the black market, and then charges his neighbors admission to come see a film. Once the machines have penetrated the Third World, they can be used for other purposes, including education.

Joseph Coates
President of J.F. Coates, a futures research firm

The VCR is going to displace the babysitter. Instead of going out Friday night, more families will rent films which they will watch with their children. But people are not foolish; they won't retreat from the world because of VCRs. They will simply have more discretionary time and income at their disposal. When they can have an evening's entertainment at home for 2, 5, or 7 bucks, they will have more money left to do other things on different nights. They will find more diverse ways to use their leisure.

Arthur C. Clarke
Author of 2001: A Space Odyssey, *and the acknowledged "father" of satellite communications resides permanently in Colombo, Sri Lanka. To get his views on the current impact of home video,* Video Review's *publisher Richard Ekstract flew to Colombo for this exclusive conversation.*

VR: You have an extensive array of TV sets, computers, and video gear here in your home. How does this aid you in your work?

AC: The VCR is one of the most important inventions of the 20th century. I've lived in Sri Lanka for 30 years but I don't know if I could have remained here and kept up with current technological developments these past 10 years without my computers, satellite-TV dish, and home-video gear. They keep me in touch with the world.

VR: How active is your involvement in video?

AC: More than might be expected of a man of my age. For example, I was personally involved in linking Sri Lanka by satellite with the worldwide Christian Crusade. This was an even more massive satellite linkup than the Live Aid concert.

VR: How is home video affecting your part of the world?

AC: Home video is growing in popularity everywhere. We have video shops right here in Colombo. Home video is a worldwide phenomenon. Do you know how many VCRs they have in Poland?

VR: Poland? I understand there are a million VCRs in *India*.

AC: It's just the beginning. But I'll tell you what alarms me. It's the piracy that's allowed to thrive in Southeast Asia. We had the latest Rambo releases here before the official sale date in the U.S. (Turning on satellite receiver.) Look, this is a transmission from Russia.

VR: Video recorders are a hot item in Russia, too.

AC: Indeed. And they'll help bring about political change — as will home computers. Governments can't restrict information when the population has electronic information sources.

Gene Roddenberry
Creator of Star Trek

Video certainly has a wider impact than *Star Trek*. I think what we're seeing is really only the beginning of what video will do. Instead of having to carry cassettes around with us, I think that within years, the entire nation will be wired with fiber optics, or some other material. We'll all have directories the size of the New York City phone book in our homes, and we'll be able to call in whatever we want to see on video. Maybe it'll be movies, or the evening news — regardless of the time of day — or weather or recipes or travel information. Every human being will be able to have the combined knowledge of all humanity at his fingertips, something made possible by video. That's pretty exciting.

MUSIC

Paul Shaffer
Musical director of Late Night with David Letterman

Video has changed people's semantics. People ask me now if I've *seen* a certain song, not heard it. And I've had that experience — seeing a great song, seeing the video of a song, and then really liking it. Then when I'm just hearing the song — say, on a jukebox in a restaurant — I realize that it wasn't as good as I thought. That's happened a few times. No, I will not name names.

Not a video fan — Musician Frank Zappa

Frank Zappa
Music pioneer, father of Moon

Basically, when it comes to what is commonly known as videos, I don't like them at all. They've become effective sales tools, sure, but they're just commercials for albums. No different than TV commercials. And I hate what they've done to the music business, which is to basically cut the options of anyone who isn't videogenic. I know a lot of musicians whom you don't want to look at but who really sound good and these people can't get anywhere. But then this is a society that wants to stay forever young. Eventually, we'll get what we deserve.

Ronnie Milsap
Country music star

Video has been of great help to my career. Some people might find it unusual that I've done seven music videos and that I'm blind. But, that exposure nationwide and even worldwide on the many video networks and shows cannot but help an artist's career. Video is also a creative outlet, adding to the music. Images on video can make a song very special and fun to do, even if the hours get long while you're *making* the video. But I even like that.

I think video has had a tremendous impact on artists' stage shows, too, because there's so much video now, whether it's tapes or videodiscs, that folks can have in their home. So you can't just get up on stage and say, "This is my latest record and it goes something like this." Those days are gone. You have to have a show that really means something now, or you're not a part of the business anymore. You get phased out pretty quickly, and it's a constant challenge to come up with something that's new.

Music video in general has had a positive influence because videos tend to convey positive thoughts and images, whether they're about politics or love or just plain fun. In addition, video is an art form that should be encouraged, as any art form should be, whether it's painting, writing, songs, poems, sculpture — whatever.

Bill Graham
Concert impresario

I think video has had an awesome effect on our lives in general and I know it's had a tremendous effect on the music business. For one, the age range for rock 'n' roll has expanded a great deal. Before video, the age of the typical rock fan was anywhere from 15 to 40. But now, because of MTV being on in the house, the fans on the lower end of the scale are now nine, or five, even four. Very young children are now watching rock 'n' roll. Whether that's necessarily a good thing, I could talk about for several hours at least. But it is definitely a fact.

One good side of video that I've seen is that it can increase a performer's success significantly. Because people have seen the performer in videos and heard all of the songs, they may be more eager to see him when he comes to town in concert. And, of course, a video success is going to sell records. Someone like Michael Jackson is going to sell 10 million records after those videos, instead of the three or four million he would have sold without them. Obviously, that's a very big difference.

That's the good side. There is also a down side with videos. For one, not everyone is going to have video success and that's going to affect their careers negatively; those performers who do succeed on video will get the attention. And, even those who succeed on video run the risk of not living up to their own success when they go out onstage to perform live. Remember, some artists do very tricky, technically sophisticated and inventive videos and that's what audiences have seen. They've also seen the finished product, not the 77 takes it may have required to get that final result. But onstage, performers can't duplicate those same tricks as easily and if they try, they only have one take in which to accomplish it. If they fail, the audience feels a major disappointment. I've seen this happen a couple of times and it's terrible. You want the performer to be as good as he can be. You don't want to see him be less than the video version.

PRINT

Robert Bernstein
Chairman of the board and president of Random House

We've done, and will continue to do, videocassettes that seem natural to the book business. Is there an uneasy relationship between video and books? I don't think so at all. When radio came along everyone said that was going to eliminate reading. When TV came along, everyone said that was going to eliminate reading. Now the videocassette: Everyone says it's going to eliminate reading. I don't think any of it is true. They all widen the world for reading, because they whet people's appetites to know more about something, and that always leads to books. The book remains principal; it is the most portable, it offers the widest choice, it packs the most information. Other media condense information; books expand it.

Ken Kesey
Author of One Flew Over the Cuckoo's Nest

I'm beginning to work on what I call an electronic novel, written for video, not to be read on the page, but one-to-one like a book instead of one-to-an-audience as most television is. It's just another form literature is going to take, just as the book was a new form that emerged from the printing press. I imagine a whole library of books that are in an absolutely new form. Usually a reading, since there are certain books that have more detail than you can put into a movie, such as *Moby Dick*. If I were doing my own book it would be: Me, seated there, looking at the camera, reading. But, when it comes to scenes you could play out you'd have two actors to read the lines. And then you would swing back into the narrative of the writing. Cheaper than videos trying to make everything look like *Star Wars*.

Mary Higgins Clark

Author of A Stranger Is Watching

Because of videos, people are impatient with long, endless description. Our minds are moving faster. As a result, I have tried to be very lean in any descriptions in my books, and I always advise budding novelists that they're not going to be given time to go from tip to toe with every little freckle and movement and gesture — you *must* get to your story fast and learn to create a word picture in a sentence or two.

With my VCR I will study a movie, say something by Hitchcock, and try to analyze why it's a classic. One of the reasons Hitchcock is infinitely more dramatic than the current blood-and-guts stuff is he never shows any explicit violence; he leaves it all to your imagination. I've always written on that basis and the premise is underscored when I watch some of the really fine old movies.

MOVIES

Carl Reiner

Director of Summer Rental

Anyone who has made movies would have to agree that the only reason you do it is to get them to the people. Some people will go out of their way for the experience. They'll go to theaters when a movie opens, but others don't want to do that. They don't want to have to get into their cars and drive there. So videocassettes have opened up a whole new avenue for motion picture viewers — they've given people access to movies right in their own homes.

The experiences aren't always the same, however. In the cases of comedies, it probably doesn't make much of a difference; a funny scene is going to be a funny scene anywhere. And in the cases of movies with deep, emotional content, they may even work better on home video because it's a personal medium, made even more personal because it's in your home. But I think there will always be large theaters, because some movies need the size of the screen, the sweep that goes along with that experience. I've been meaning to rent *Amadeus* for my wife, for example, because I know she wants to see it and she missed it in the theaters, but I've stopped myself because I think you really should see it on a big screen. I don't think it will be as powerful if you see it on a small screen.

Jerry Bruckheimer and Don Simpson

Producers of Top Gun, Flashdance, *and* Beverly Hills Cop

It's important to us that our movies can be seen more than once — and videocassettes can do that. Kids watch them over and over, stop them and go back to their favorite parts. So they have to be good; they have to stand up to that kind of scrutiny. We're also fortunate that such young, talented performers as Eddie Murphy, Jennifer Beals, and Tom Cruise seem to want to be in the kind of movies we do. These performers hook an audience, get them to watch a movie over and over. And that's another element that helps, our characters. They are the ones who sell those movie tickets and those videocassettes.

Sherry Lansing

Independent producer, former executive at 20th Century-Fox

I've always had this theory, and it seems to be true, that the home-video market was not taking away from the boxoffice, but, in fact, was adding to the boxoffice potential for a movie. By that I mean, there always seemed to be two audiences: the moviegoing audience, which for the last 10 years has been predominantly under the age of 25; and those over 25 who simply were not going out to see our movies.

I'm convinced that you could release a picture in the theaters and the audience that usually goes — the kids who want to get out of the house--will go. You could release it the same day on videocassettes and the over-25 audience that wants to stay home will get it that way. Videos, to me, have been the means to capture this lost audience.

Similarly, I've seen movies that didn't do well in the theaters go on to do well on videocassette — usually the movies that were intended for adults. *Racing with the Moon* had moderate success in theaters, but it had enormous cassette sales, because the theme was more nostalgic; it appealed to older audiences.

Film producer Sherry Lansing says that home videos actually help movie boxoffice sales.

It gave us the confirmation that you could still make movies for adults.

Home-Video Software Market

	1983	1988
Total Revenues	$1 billion	$5 billion
Program type		
Movies	67%	50%
Adult	14%	8%
Music	4%	25%
Instructional/ Informational	7%	6%
Children's	7%	8%
Other	1%	3%

EXPLORING IDEAS

1. Comment on the positive and negative consequences of exporting North American culture worldwide through video technology.
2. If people *do* have more "discretionary time and income at their disposal" because of video technology, how might the social and economic patterns in our country be altered?
3. In what ways do you think video technology will contribute to political change?
4. *"Every human being will be able to have the combined knowledge of all humanity at his fingertips...."*

   In the society of the future, how might attitudes and approaches to learning and education be different from what we know today if this prediction becomes a reality?
5. *Has* video had a positive influence on music? Debate the issue in class.
6. ***(a)*** Robert Bernstein believes that videocassettes will not eliminate reading. What do *you* think? Will everyone learn to read in the future? Describe your vision for the future of books, and reading in general.

   (b) Suggest some possible uses for the electronic novel.
7. ***(a)*** If Sherry Lansing is right in her assessment of the relationship between movies and videocassettes, how might this affect the movie industry? What will be the impact on society?

   (b) Do *you* watch movies in the way the producers of *Top Gun* describe? How have videocassettes influenced the relationship between teens and movies? Discuss this as a class.

INVESTIGATING THE MEDIA

1. Compare novels written in the late 19th and early 20th century with those being written today. What differences are apparent in the kind and amount of description, in the author's use of dialogue, and in the way action is presented? Do you agree that video is affecting the form of books as Mary Higgins

Clark suggests? Present your conclusions in the form of a report.

2. Conduct a poll in your school to find out which are the 10 best-selling videocassettes in your community. When you have collected the data, suggest explanations for the popularity of the videos on your list. Present a market research report to the class.

YOUR TURN

1. Working with a partner, or in a small group, select a section from a novel and create your own "electronic novel." Present your video to the class.
2. Write a poem or an article entitled "I Can't Wait!" in which you explore the potential of video in the 21st century.

   or

   Write a poem or an article entitled "Is This Progress?" in which you present some of the more negative aspects of a futuristic video society.
3. What is the difference between *seeing* a song and *hearing* a song? Write an article suitable for a video or music magazine in which you describe your own experiences with music and video.
4. Create a series of cartoons presenting your ideas on the humorous side of life in a video society.

Cable TV was almost universally hailed as a way of providing audiences more freedom of choice. Lately, however, some observers have been worrying about the consequences of more specialized programming on cable — "electronic cocoons" as Roy Shields puts it.

TV technology is wooing viewers into electronic cocoons

It is possible to spend years as a critic and observer of television and yet miss the most obvious and significant thing of all about the medium.

That's what happened to me. Either I had not thought about it, I told myself, or having done so, dismissed it as too self-evident to note. But now it rattles around in my brain and won't go away.

It is the memory of a program called *The Television Explosion* in the fine PBS series *Nova*.

Here we had the usual parade of industry experts, ranging from Les Brown, editor of the television magazine *Channels*, to Mark Fowler, chairman of the U.S. Federal Communications Commission. Most of the talk was about the new video technologies — 100-channel cable, videocassettes and discs, home satellite dishes, the works. They told us little that we didn't already know.

Then, in the midst of them, came a pert little lady whose words reverberated like the sudden clash of cymbals. She was Rose Goldsen, a professor of sociology at Cornell University.

"When the medium was first launched," she said, "we were told that it would bring families together, that the television set would be sort of like the central heart around which the family would gather.

"But, you know, today in the United States, more than 40 per cent of us have more than two sets in the home and many, many families have three, four, and five sets in the home — one in the kitchen, one in the family room, the children have a set of their own, and so on.

"People watch television alone. It is mainly an isolating experience in American society.

"Moreover, the interacting goes from you to the screen. Even if you're sitting there watching in unison with other people, the dominating presence in the room is the television screen."

That fundamental fact must now be considered in the light of further isolation. Soon young people will have their own cable channels, old people theirs, and all the ethnic groups, the businessmen, the sports fans, women over 30 but under 35, and so on.

Add to this the cassette libraries and personal computers linked to the TV screen and you have a situation in which people can almost avoid each other entirely except to mutter "Good morning" over the breakfast table.

What's more, this isolation in your private world, protected from human contact by electronic distance, has great attractions. There doesn't have to be any inane small talk with friends, family, or associates, any emotional clashes, wounds, or waste of time. Why even leave the house to mingle with the masses and endure the traffic?

Nova concluded its program with this observation about television: "It has brought us together in times of national triumph and tragedy. And yet at the same time it has driven us apart, even in our own homes. Of its role in the future only one thing is certain: It will be larger than ever before."

The last words were left to Prof. Goldsen: "It means (it will affect) not just you and me, those of us who are on the face of the earth at this moment, it means (it will affect) the future generations...(who) come and inherit a world they never made.

"And we have to make the kind of a broadcasting system that will not contaminate what I call the 'thought environment' for future generations, but on the contrary, will bring out not the worst in people, but the best in us."

What is troubling about those words is the gnawing feeling that it is already too late, that we are beyond the point of no return. We will watch programs ranging from porno-pay to college courses alone in silence.

It will be a sad world indeed if future generations are born into electronic cocoons from which they rarely leave to eat, bathe, make love, or do violence, then retreat to the warmth of their isolation.

Are there no answers to this grim scenario?

— Roy Shields
Starweek

EXPLORING IDEAS

1. How many students in your class live in homes where different household members have their own TV set? In which rooms are these sets located? What led to the decision to buy separate TVs for individuals? How has this viewing pattern affected family life? Discuss as a class.

2. **(a)** Write a paragraph or journal entry in which you express your views on each of the following statements:

"People watch television alone. It is mainly an isolating experience in society.... What's more, this isolation in your private world, protected from human contact by electronic distance, has great attractions."

"Of (television's) role in the future only one thing is certain: It will be larger than ever before."

(b) Form small groups to read your paragraph or entry aloud. Invite members of the group to comment on your ideas.

3. **(a)** *"Are there no answers to this grim scenario?"* In small groups, brainstorm some possible solutions to the scenario presented in Mr. Shields's article. Focus on ways in which we might help bring people *together* and encourage a sense of responsibility for the welfare of others.

(b) Select one or two ideas from your list and elaborate on them.

Present your expanded proposals to the class and seek your classmates' comments.

YOUR TURN

1. How do you imagine television might be used in the future by the individual? — by society? Explore your ideas about this in a short story or an article.

2. Do you think people will ever use, and interact with, their televisions in the way this writer describes? Present your thoughts on this issue as an editorial or news article.

Television viewing in the future need not be simply a passive activity. Retailers are already developing TV we can "talk back to" — interactive television will soon be finding its way into more and more living rooms...and pocketbooks.

Interactive TV opens new retail market

If tests now under way prove successful, two interactive-television technologies may add a significant new twist to retailing. The systems — J.C. Penney's Telaction and Symonds Associates' TV Answer System — provide instantaneous two-way communication between viewers and a central computer that downloads video signals to home televisions.

Practical interactive television has long been a dream of retailers such as Penney and Sears which want to offer shoppers the convenience of ordering merchandise at home with the touch of a button. Other businesses want to offer services such as pay-per-view TV and television on demand, which allows a viewer to order a movie or TV show from a video catalog.

Earlier attempts at interactive television have failed to efficiently handle millions of people interacting with a central control point. Attempts to use cable failed because few cable systems are capable of two-way communications. Operator-based telephone systems have proved expensive, clumsy, and easily overloaded.

Telaction's solution is to wed telephone and cable in an interactive service that users control with ordinary Touch-Tone telephones. Telaction will be tested in more than 125 000 homes. If the test is successful, the Penney subsidiary Telaction Corp. plans to establish regional "electronic malls" nationwide.

The system will require local cable-television networks to dedicate a channel for Telaction. With the channel tuned in, a viewer will telephone a local number and punch in an identification code, which accesses the control computer. Selecting from menus on the television, a user will register choices on the telephone keypad. The selected image — perhaps an item offered for sale in the system's electronic catalog — will appear as a still picture with background sound and narration.

At the receiving end, the requests will be filled by computers controlling the system, which will package the appropriate images — stored on laser disks — for electronic transmission. The signal will then be sent to the customer's cable system via microwave transmission, terrestrial lines, satellite, or other existing data-communications network. The cable system will automatically route the signal to a decoder located on a utility pole near the viewer's home. The decoder will convert the signal for television and pipe it into the user's home. Telaction Corp. expects this selection process to take only a second or two.

While it will offer shoppers more convenience, Telaction will give merchants greater flexibility. It will be an economic way to sell in far-reaching geographic areas, shipping out of a central warehouse rather than stocking many separate stores. Further, Telaction will regularly provide computer-generated reports indicating merchandise sold, plus the demographic profile of the shoppers — valuable marketing information that is often hard to obtain.

— G. Berton Latamore
High Technology
August 1987

EXPLORING IDEAS

1. If electronic shopping becomes the normal way of doing business, how will employment, the economic structure, and social patterns be altered? Make a list of possible consequences and evaluate each of them. On the whole, do you think electronic shopping will be good or bad for society? Present your conclusions in a summary paragraph and share your response with a partner.

2. ***(a)*** In small groups, generate a list of *other* possible applications of interactive television. Select one member to record your group's ideas and to present them to the class. Focus on future applications in

- entertainment
- education
- the workplace
- the marketplace.

(b) Evaluate a few of your class's most intriguing suggestions. What consequences will there be for the individual? for society as a whole?

THE NEXT WAVE IN ADVERTISING

Retailers and people who work in the advertising industry cannot afford to stand still. Styles and tastes in society are constantly changing — as consumers adapt to changing time constraints and lifestyles. Manufacturers have been quick to make use of brave new technologies. How will these new techniques and processes affect you, as a consumer, as we approach the 21st century?

Adam

Shopping channels are now promoting their products almost 24 hours a day. This form of interactive TV seems to be a vision of future retailing — the ultimate way to get to the largest potential market... at relatively low cost but high profit.

Shopaholics just tune in for a spending fix

Like that voracious, burping plant in *Little Shop of Horrors*, video shopping pulses forth. Via cable television, it's already projected into five million Canadian living rooms, chomping thousands of piggy banks, well on its way to taking in wads of cheques, plastic, and good cash.

But just ask higher orders of old Toronto television what they think of this Canadian Home Shopping Network, this monopoly for video shopping, and the answer shouted down by our aristocrats is, "disgusting."

Pay no mind. Video shopping is one rich idea.

The inspiration for the Canadian cable shopping channel is Home Shopping Network, with annual revenues of $208 million, based in Clearwater, Florida. From down there last year, it netted $22 million and saw its revenue increase 988 per cent. Clearwater owns 14 per cent of CHSN's Castlefield Avenue enterprise.

There, in a sprawl of lighting and silicone plants, CHSN's franchised assets include $4 million in brilliant American-designed computer software used to woo and remember its audience, as well as acres of inventory, phones by the hundreds, networks of conveyor belts, a spread of studios, fleets of delivery trucks and, of course, a single satellite link activating Anik, over the equator, to beam bargains down to the television viewer-buyers in every province.

CHSN's fusion of computers, market research, communications, and gab powers a special, radical television that enables viewers miles and miles away to talk back to its broadcasters, to feel motivation, to make decisions, and to accept public praise, that rare Canadian commodity.

This franchised CHSN approach to its audience is — can we see it? — influencing behavior, educating at a distance.

The use of technology to motivate more active audiences is very alive on cable channels and will further influence commercial broadcasting. The shopping network leads French- and English-speaking viewers coast-to-coast to decide on "club" membership, to buy, and to compete with one another to acquire low-inventoried items which, presumably, they value highly. Thousands of viewers are participating, peaking during the soap operas and after 7 p.m.

They will get merchandise they order (most of it tested for shelf life in Clearwater), as well as small gifts sent later through computer memory of birthdays and anniversaries. The network currently ships 5000 purchases daily. CHSN has found it pays to have audiences learn from the two-way dialogues.

The network studio roisters like a midway. On separate stages, show hosts — one Française, the other English — rivet separate cameras, glance occasionally to computer-displayed scripts, sound clown horns, and cue swells of applause from records when a viewer blooms into a buyer. Facing these frantics stretch 200 booths with gabbing "network operators," using phones and computer keyboards to take down marketing data from the customers.

Hosts frequently break the pitch to chat with people in Victoria or Victoriaville who call in, cheque books at the ready. Unlike service at most Toronto stations, someone always talks to CHSN callers, 20 hours daily.

So far, nabobs bedded elsewhere in broadcasting consider all this beneath notice. Not for long. You could lay a $208-million bet on that.

— David Walker
Broadcast Week
October 31, 1987

EXPLORING IDEAS

1. In small groups, discuss the following and report your conclusions to the class.
   (a) *"...the answer shouted down by our (television) aristocrats is, 'disgusting.'"*

   Do *you* consider the home shopping channels "disgusting," or a valid use of the media? Explain your responses.

   (b) *"Most viewers think of these shows in terms of a TV program — like a game show."*

   — Susan Kastner
   Starweek
   August 22, 1987

   What are the possible implications of this viewing mentality?

INVESTIGATING THE MEDIA

1. If possible, arrange to watch the Canadian Home Shopping Network on cable TV. Identify the advertising and selling techniques employed. Use your observations as the basis for a "Viewpoint" article on the topic of "Non-stop Commercials on TV."

Manufacturers and retailers have found a new way to boost sales of consumer goods: "PoP" — point-of-purchase advertising uses the latest in flashy technology and advertising techniques to woo impulse buyers…right in *the store.*

Supermarkets woo impulse buyers

North American consumers are surrendering a long-standing inclination to budget and plan their purchases in favor of a more relaxed, impulsive style of spending — and nowhere is the change more evident than among supermarket shoppers.

According to early returns from a nationwide survey last fall by a U.S.-based advertising association, more than 80 per cent of all supermarket brand buying decisions are made in the store. That is up 15 per cent from only three years ago.

Sponsored by 20 major packaged-goods companies such as Proctor & Gamble Inc. and Pepsico Inc., the survey found that about 15 per cent of all purchases begin as generic searches. About 5 per cent are switches from one intended brand (an in-home decision) to another (in-store). More than 60 per cent are not planned at all.

Convenience mealtimes, radically altered shopping roles among men and women, and market fragmentation are some of the factors that have shifted decision-making from the home to the supermarket — from the in-home selections based on brand preferences to last-minute, in-store choices based on impulse.

However, none has influenced the trend more than the in-store environment itself, according to research experts who monitor the marketplace.

"It has become more powerful than ever in the past. Stores are offering more life, more flavor, more pizzazz. They have become or they are becoming events," said John Kawula, president of the Point-of-Purchase Advertising Institute, which is based in Fort Lee, N.J., and commissioned the survey.

In 1986, food marketers in Canada and the United States spent more than $9 billion (U.S.) on point-of-purchase hardware and promotion materials, 22 per cent more than they spent in 1985.

In Canada, half a dozen new methods of in-store advertising have been introduced in the past five years. These include audio messages, product and general literature booths, grocery-cart ads, and sponsored television.

They have been added to a formidable arsenal of shelf ads — "talkers" — posters, point-of-purchase promotions, unpublished discounts, aisle specials, and product demonstrations.

With computer-based automated kiosks, electronic coupons, and interactive video-display systems on the way, supermarkets, along with other types of retailers, should develop even more of a carnival atmosphere, one consultant said. They are becoming "destinations, places to go."

Among the novel applications on the way are kiosks that can analyze shopping tastes and preferences, then make appropriate buying suggestions to customers.

"They can do a better, more thorough and accurate job than a clerk could possibly do," New York ad agency Ogilvy Group Inc. said in a report to its clients. "They cost less to retain, they never call in sick, and they rarely get nasty."

Other novelties.

- Video-Q Market Place Television has monitors in 67 Toronto-area supermarkets and sells product spot commercials to run between travel tips, weather, sports, and time reports.
- The video wall, pioneered in Japan and Europe and being produced commercially by NV Philips, will be able to beam messages at shoppers from a wall assembly of nine to 108 computer-controlled monitors.
- Low coupon redemption rates might be overcome by the use of computer-based machines at supermarket checkouts to provide coupons for only the types of products a shopper is buying. Only a buyer of detergent, for instance, would get a coupon for a competitive product. Early tests of the system show unusually high response rates — up to six times the redemption rate of conventional couponing.
- Point-of-purchase radio is being tested as an alternative to canned music. Packaged radio programs can be used for special sales or coupled with advertising and other time-sensitive promotions.

Video-disc terminals will allow

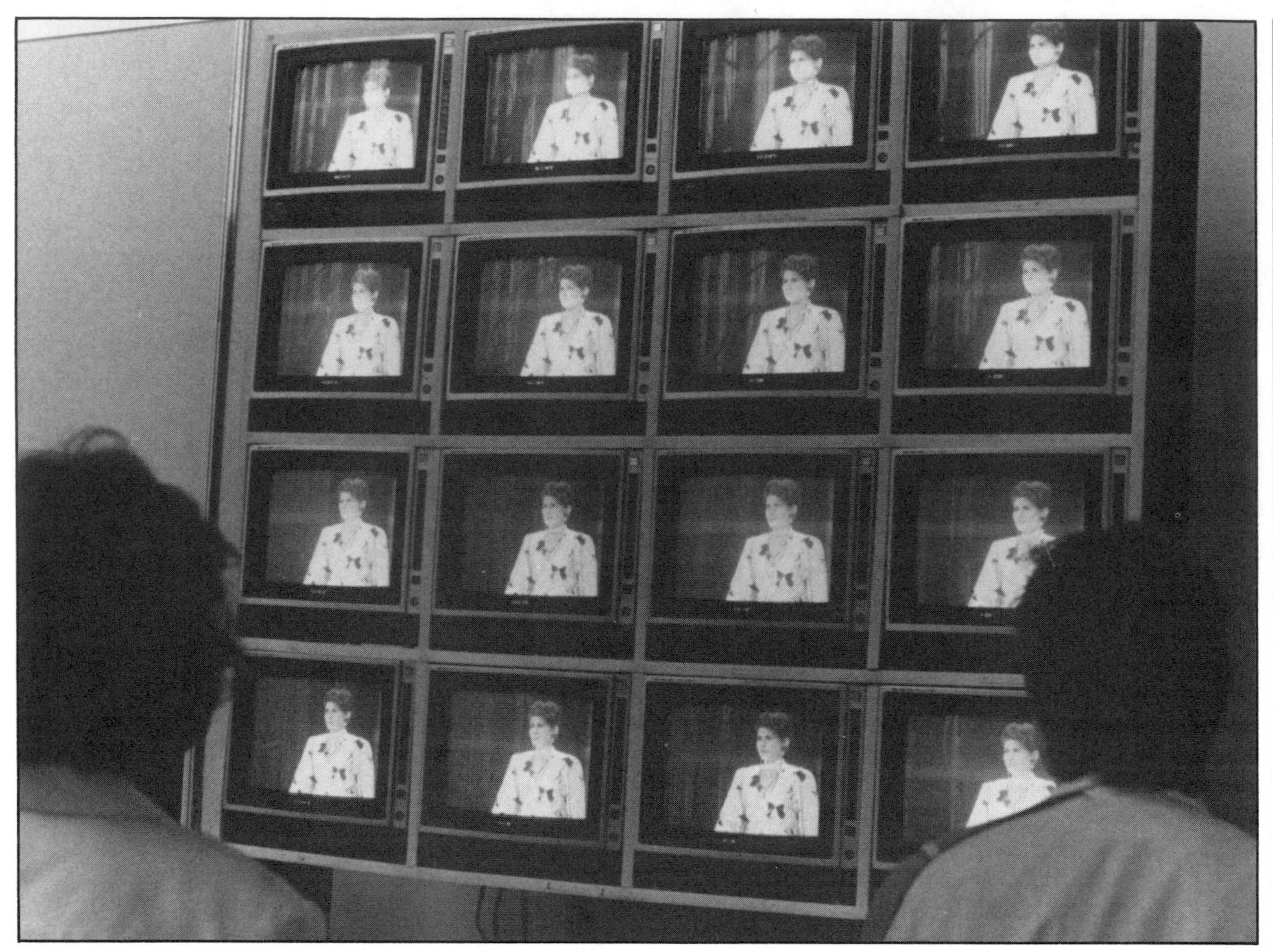

"Video wall" — A bank of TV monitors was used to promote a Toronto fashion show. Soon, larger video walls will beam messages to consumers from 108 computer-controlled monitors.

shoppers to scan shelf goods and other merchandise without having to walk the aisles. Such machines can retrieve thousands of pages of food-related information, or data about product lines not usually carried in the outlet.

One in-store unit developed by a U.S. shop-at-home service occupies less than 40 square feet of space and offers 92 "upscale" products that can be ordered through a credit or membership card.

An ultrasound device detects an approaching customer and switches the system from a self-advertising message to an interactive mode with the company's warehouse terminal in another city.

Simpsons Ltd. of Toronto has been using a system that promotes applications for the department store's credit card. Part of the data collected finds its way into the retailer's market research.

U.S. management consulting firm Touche Ross & Co. estimates that the number of video-disc terminals in U.S. retail outlets alone will increase to 30 000 by 1990 from 1500 today. A New York consultant, Link Resources Inc., expects merchandising applications for interactive video discs to account for almost a quarter of the entire market by 1990.

Interest in Canada is also deepening. Media Videotex Corp. of Vancouver has been running tests on a video-disc system since 1985, and Alphatel Videotex Directories Ltd. of Edmonton, which operates a 20-unit public-access system, is preparing to move into in-store placements as well.

Laser video disc technology — a system that provides exceptionally high-quality full-motion and color video stills as well as sound — is still prohibitively expensive for some in-store applications, Alphatel president Murray Richmond said. All creative shooting has to be carried out in a single pass, and editing flexibility is still limited.

Keelson Electronic Marketing Inc. of Halifax said it will invest about $25 million in a system for 300 supermarkets across Canada. High-resolution overhead video-display terminals will use commercially sponsored, animated graphics to show in-store and community events, and interactive videotex terminals on the ground will enable shoppers to call up coupons, recipes, and other promotional printouts.

The company, which rolled out a 100-unit, 50-store system for Sobeys Stores Ltd. of Stellarton, N.S., is about to conclude deals with chains in the Toronto and Montreal areas, said president Tom Murdoch, a former food merchandising executive.

The company, which describes itself as an electronic publisher, will sell national advertisers time on its "electroboards" and "space" on its information terminals to reach a total audience of five million consumers, Mr. Murdoch said.

Because Keelson's deal with its retail market gives the company access to checkout sales records, it "can tell the advertiser — the food manufacturer — exactly what's working and what isn't."

This sense of immediacy is the essence of point-of-purchase effectiveness, the U.S. point-of-purchase association said. "Product success or failure now depends on the last 5 per cent of the marketing effort, not the preceding 95 per cent."

As a result, the association said, the traditional domestic shopping list — historically the critical short list for brand-name manufacturers — is no longer relevant to marketers as a bellwether of product performance.

A number of advertising agencies agree.

Vicky Fitzpatrick, media supervisor for Toronto-based McCann-Erickson Advertising of Canada Ltd., tells clients that "the war (for brand supremacy) is fought on many fronts. However, the point-of-sale represents the final boundary. It is the last chance for a brand to reign supreme by being chosen over its competitors. Understandably, the fight at this level is a vigorous one."

Everything is up for grabs, Ogilvy Group said, because no advertiser has a lock on the customer's buying preferences.

"Rather than a single brand, most customers have a menu of brands that are acceptable within a category. While we all like to think of our customers as exclusive users of our brands, in reality, we're merely on their menus."

— Ben Fiber
The Globe and Mail
January 10, 1987

EXPLORING IDEAS

1. In small groups, explore the implications of each of the following PoP advertising techniques:
- a "video wall" beaming commercials to shoppers
- personalized electronic merchandise coupons
- electronic kiosks where customers can go for purchasing suggestions
- electronic detectors of approaching shoppers
- interactive terminals that allow shoppers to call up recipes, coupons, and so on.

INVESTIGATING THE MEDIA

1. Form small groups in order to survey the supermarkets and shopping malls in your community. Keep records of any PoP advertising techniques you see as you walk through. If possible, talk to store owners and clerks about the impact PoP is having on sales. With the manager's approval, talk to customers in the stores about the impact PoP has on their buying decisions. Prepare a group report for the class.

YOUR TURN

1. *"Supermarkets...should develop even more of a carnival atmosphere. They are becoming destinations, places to go."*

You are a member of a design team that has been hired to submit plans for a new supermarket or mall in your neighbourhood. Working in a small group, use the ideas presented in the article as a starting point for your designs for a shopping mall or supermarket of the future. Present your ideas to the class, who will act as your clients. Be prepared to answer their questions about your design.

ISSUES & ETHICS OF FUTURE-TECH

The high-tech world of the computer-assisted information explosion is already upon us. How are the new electronic technologies transforming our lives? Will we view the ever-increasing innovations in media as simply tools to make life easier and more enjoyable — or will we become more cautious as we respond to new waves of "wired-up" technology? "Futuretech" promises major advances in our access to information, but it also poses some ethical questions that are often difficult to answer.

Do you agree with Andrew Osler, that "individual privacy could become as archaic as medieval bear-baiting"?

Warily into a wired-up world

I've been looking at the development of videotex interactive television, with Canada's Telidon system acclaimed internationally as the best of the breed, and what I see scares me. It's the social equivalent of an atomic bomb with the potential to blow society, as we know it, wide open, and few people seem to be worrying about what to do with the fallout. This new technology could wipe away whatever scraps of individual privacy remain to us, and that's the least of our worries. It also contains the capacity to fine-tune public mind manipulations in a way that makes George Orwell's *1984* scenario look bush league by comparison. Yet Orwell didn't know about computers, with their capacity to sort and filter vast amounts of detailed information about us, when he first imagined the awful future use of two-way television as a social control mechanism. And computers are what videotex is all about.

The problem is simple: information is power, and when you have a vast amount of information, especially about people, as videotex will give to its planners and operators, then you have a vast amount of power. It looks benign at first glance. What we have is the marriage of a computer, perhaps thousands of kilometres away, to the familiar family TV. System details vary, but the only new technical wrinkle visible to the living room Telidon user is a push-button control box. By pushing the right sequence of buttons, you can talk to that computer and do such things as comparative grocery pricing, catalogue shopping, personal banking, and looking up Aunt Martha's phone number.

Eventually, you'll be able to order library books or personalized news summaries; haul in financial advice from a trust company; have your gimpy heart monitored 24 hours a day; or even find a job in the Canada Employment Centre listings and apply for it electronically. And that's Telidon from the bright side, the side the federal department of communications and its many private-sector collaborators at places such as Bell Canada want us to see. A bottomless cornucopia of electronic goodies.

Unfortunately, there's a darker view. If interactive television is to work, it will have to know an awful lot about us. If it is to monitor Great Uncle Charlie's heart, it will need his medical history. If it is to help with our financial planning, it will need to know everything about our income and spending habits, and if it is to help us find jobs, it will need our full employment and educational records. And there will be nothing to stop the system from acquiring such

Reprinted with permission: Charles Jaffé

things as lists of our department-store purchases and library books we borrow, or from logging all the phone numbers we look up in its directory.

And here comes the catch. If someone should ever decide to put all that information — and much, much more — into one computer (which with satellite and fibre-optic transmission systems is no big deal), then that person, or agency of government, or political party, or multinational corporation could learn more about us than we know about ourselves. The scenario develops. Individual privacy in tomorrow's wired-up world could become as archaic as medieval bear-baiting. Sophisticated surveillance of individuals (not just of those with medical problems), and the talented massaging of public opinion become terrifying possibilities. Voter manipulation prospects make today's pollster politics look naïve, and heaven knows what an enterprising ad agency could do to our buying habits with access to an interactive data base. Of course, it doesn't have to happen this way. Electronic blocks could be built into that computer labyrinth, and we could have protective legislation. Something could even be said about permissible uses in our constitution.

We still have some precious time, a very little bit of it, to think and plan and to pressure our political representatives into formulating legislation to prevent such abuse. In its first few years, Telidon will be expensive. One estimate indicates you'll need a $70 000-a-year income to be first on the block with Telidon. But the price will plummet once manufacturers figure out the logistics of cheap mass production, and then there'll be no time left. In the meantime, I wouldn't bet on politicians taking any initiatives on our behalf. Not when you look at the record of public computer systems now in place. Every April, when the taxman takes his annual chunk from my backside and I insert my social insurance number (SIN) at the top of the tax-return form, I remember how Prime Minister Lester Pearson stood in the House of Commons in April, 1964, to promise that our SINs were for social welfare bookkeeping, and never, never, would be used for such things as personal income tax. Not to mention the banks and other private-sector concerns that use our SINs so cheerfully at the expense of our privacy.

A 30-member committee of government and private-sector people, the Canadian Videotex Consultative Committee serves as an advisory board to Telidon. But only four members represent groups such as the Consumers' Association of Canada, which might be expected to worry about our rights in tomorrow's wired world. Overwhelmingly, Telidon is in the hands of bureaucrats, businessmen, and engineers, not the sort inclined to see beyond profit-and-loss columns and technological nuts and bolts. Some of us will have to do a bit of worrying for them about this electronic monster, and we'd better start now.

— Andrew Osler
Maclean's
1984

EXPLORING IDEAS

1. How do *you* define "personal privacy"? Explore this issue in a class discussion.
2. How much do you know about what others know about you? Discuss the following as a class:
   (a) What kinds of information can be collected about each of us?
   (b) How can this information be collected?
   (c) What individuals or groups might be interested in knowing these facts about us?
   (d) What are the future social implications of all this?
3. ***(a)*** Working with a partner, develop a list of daily, routine tasks that could be managed through the marriage of computer technology with television.
   (b) Determine the impact this new way of doing things might have on society as we know it now. For instance, how will the job market change? Will our social interactions be different in any way? Share your ideas on this issue with the class.

4. Form small groups to examine the concept of "the talented massaging of public opinion."
   (a) Create a scenario that explains how computerized television might be used to manipulate voters.
   (b) *"It's the social equivalent of an atomic bomb with the potential to blow society, as we know it, wide open...."*
   Brainstorm additional potential uses for futuristic television systems. For example, what impact could this technology have on the way we are governed? Select one member of the group to present your ideas to the class.
5. Through the use of credit and debit cards, social insurance numbers, membership card numbers, and so on, it is possible to "track" the behaviour of any private citizen. In small groups, decide what groups or individuals — if any — should be permitted access to the following information:
   - an individual's medical records
   - an individual's credit records
   - an individual's record of motor vehicle violations
   - records of magazines an individual subscribes to
   - records of charitable and political organizations an individual supports with financial donations
   - records of brand name foods an individual purchases
   - records of the movie titles an individual rents through video stores

YOUR TURN

1. Develop a set of guidelines that will help assure the privacy of the individual while providing public access to vital information.
   Compare your guidelines with the following federal guidelines proposed to the private sector in 1987 regarding data collection and the individual's right of privacy.
   - Informed consent from data subjects for the use of information about themselves, where appropriate.
   - The collection of only relevant, accurate, and timely data, related to the purpose for which they are to be used.
   - Advance identification for the purposes of data collection.
   - Restrictions on the re-use of data for new purposes without the prior consent of data subjects or without legal authority.
   - Reasonable security safeguards.
   - Openness about practices with respect to collection, storage, or use of personal data.
   - A right of access for individuals to information about themselves.
   - The accountability of the data controller for compliance with data protection measures.
2. Imagine a future society in which the vision presented by Andrew Osler becomes a reality. What are some of the implications of this for manufacturers, advertising agencies, television program developers, politicians, and the general public? Together with a partner, create a scenario for the society you imagine. Share your scenario with others in a small group.
   or
   Write a short story about a futuristic society that reflects the ideas you have been discussing.
3. Create a series of print ads or television commercials designed to raise the public's awareness of the potential dangers of indiscriminate data collection.

As Michael Miller points out, "computers have made the technical manipulation of someone else's art easy. But is the product legal? Is it real?"

The questionable ethics of modern creativity

Tom Lord-Alge is a hot young rock-music recording engineer, and one reason is his enormous collection of other people's sounds. He has them neatly organized on 10 reels of tape.

He has Phil Collins drumming, James Brown shrieking, the Tower of Power horn section blaring, Bruce Springsteen yelling "whoa," a little piece of a Japanese television commercial, and about 2000 other noises.

When he works on new records, computerized recording gear lets Mr. Lord-Alge dip into his collection as if it were a palette of paints. He recently slipped the James Brown scream into a record by Orchestral Manoeuvres in the Dark.

For a song by The Cars, he pasted in the sound of TV's cartoon character Road Runner running. In 1987, the 25-year-old engineer won a Grammy for his work on Steve Winwood's latest album, where he adorned one song with Diana Ross and the Supremes clapping and stomping their feet in "Where Did Our Love Go?"

Rock records today are made this way all the time. "We're all blatantly stealing from everyone else," says Mr. Lord-Alge. "Any record is fair game, no matter what it is... That's just the way it's done in the '80s."

New technology is making the '80s a strange and lawless time to be a creative artist. Not only musicians but also photographers and movie makers are grappling with the advent of computers that let their works be manipulated by other people in powerful new ways.

The computers are stirring up big disputes in the arts world, pitting artists against producers and publishers — and sometimes against other artists.

All this raises questions that strain the modern boundaries of law, morality, and esthetics.

Are Madonna's rights infringed when another record uses her trademark squeal electronically raised an octave? Who gets to decide whether *The Maltese Falcon* should be reissued in color? Is it wrong to lift the sunset from a magazine photo, play around with the colors, and use it for the background of another picture?

As the anti-computer faction sees it, much more is at stake in this debate than the way rock records sound or TV movies look. This faction says the new arts technology sends a dire message about artists' place in society, by overpowering their basic right to control their own work.

"Just as in other fields — in the sciences and weaponry — our technological capabilities here are far in advance of our intellectual development or our moral development," says director and actor Woody Allen, who emerged from his customary reclusion to speak out against colorizing movies.

"The problem," he said in an interview, "is that the solution in the United States always comes down so heavily for the side where the money is."

The high-tech advocates think computers open up exciting new avenues for artists. Like their opponents, some of them base their case on artists' rights. Artists, they say, have the right to use any new artistic techniques without restrictions.

"This is a new form of music, just like collages," says Arthur Baker, who runs the Shakedown Sound recording studio in New York and is known as one of the kings of audio cutting and pasting. "The technology has developed to the extent that if you like the sound, you can have the sound."

The tool of his trade is a device called a digital sampler. It can take any "sample" of recorded sound, convert it into a series of numbers, and manipulate it in virtually limitless ways by changing the numbers.

It can raise or lower its pitch, give it more or less echo, repeat it in any rhythm, combine it with other sounds, and perform dozens of other tricks that a simple tape recorder could never do.

Samplers once cost tens of thousands of dollars, but now a cheap system sells for $700 (U.S.). The odds are good that any pop song you hear on the radio today has sounds that came out of a sampler.

Engineers feed their samplers all manner of sounds: new ones made by studio musicians or electronic synthesizers, and old ones gleaned from other records. Using old sounds is easier and cheaper, and it has a certain renegade allure in the rock-music world.

Figuring out who gets credit for sampler music is messy. A few years ago, David Earle Johnson, a jazz drummer, brought his rare Nigerian conga drums into a producer friend's studio and played a few patterns into a sampler. Months later, he flipped on *Miami Vice* and heard his drumming running through the entire theme song.

Mr. Johnson couldn't persuade the producer, Jan Hammer, to pay him for the use of the samples. He also couldn't persuade the musicians' union to take up his case. "My mistake was I didn't have any kind of written agreement," he says.

"Now the computer has my sound for life." Mr. Hammer's manager, Elliott Sears, comments that Mr. Johnson simply wanted "money for doing nothing."

Frank Doyle, a New York engineer, recently plugged into his sampler the sound of Madonna screaming "hey!" on her song "Like a Virgin," raised it an octave, and dropped the new sound into a few parts of a song by Jamie Bernstein.

He took a horn blast from a James Brown song and turned it into a lush, mellow tone for a Japanese singer's love ballad. "I didn't feel at all like I was ripping James Brown off," he says.

Soul-music pioneer James Brown — Computer sampling makes him furious.

That's not the way James Brown sees it. "Anything they take off my record is mine," says the soul-music pioneer, speaking from his Augusta, Ga., office. "Is it all right if I take some paint off your house and put it on mine? Can I take a button off your shirt and put it on mine? Can I take a toenail off your foot — is that all right with you?"

So far, the U.S. copyright law, which was last updated in 1976, hasn't been much help in untangling the questions that digital sampling raises. It prohibits knockoffs that "directly or indirectly recapture the actual sounds" of a recording, but lawyers disagree as to whether that language applies to sampling and there hasn't been a court test.

One rock star trying to put up his own legal roadblocks against sampling is Frank Zappa. His album *Jazz from Hell* bears the unusual warning in small print on the cover: "Unauthorized reproduction/ sampling is a violation of applicable laws and subject to criminal prosecution."

New technology has photographers embroiled in a similar dispute. At its centre are million-dollar graphics computers — made by Scitex Corp. and others — that scan photographs and convert every tiny point into computer information. Ad agencies and publications routinely use them to do jobs that would take too long or look sloppy without a computer.

National Geographic stirred a debate in the photo world when it used a Scitex machine in 1982 to move two of the pyramids of Giza closer together to fit on a cover. It used the Scitex again for another cover that year, to add a little chunk to the top of a Polish coal miner's cap that had been cut off by the camera in the original photo.

Two years ago, *Rolling Stone*'s editors faced a last-minute crisis over a cover photo that displeased the magazine's publisher, Jann Wenner. The picture showed the two stars of *Miami Vice* clowning around near the ocean.

A grinning Don Johnson wore a pistol in a shoulder holster slung over his pink sleeveless shirt. Mr. Wenner, an anti-handgun activist, refused to go to press with a gun on the magazine's cover.

Putting the picture inside a Scitex computer solved the problem. An artist sitting behind a keyboard and a big monitor carefully overlaid the gun with little pieces of pink fabric electronically copied from the photo of Mr. Johnson's shirt.

He extended the shadows and wrinkles from the real shirt onto the new artificial patch. When he was finished, there was no trace of the gun left and no detectable seam where the computer had done its work. It was as if Jann Wenner had reached into the photograph and pulled off Don Johnson's holster.

Like digital samplers, photo-rearranging computers are leading into a wilderness of legal and ethical questions. Photographers wonder whether they will lose their copyright on pictures that emerge from a computer-tinkering session.

They also worry about losing money if publishers furtively reuse photos stored in a computer — or pieces of them. (Without a computer, a publisher usually has to use an original negative.)

Most of all, they worry that high-tech tinkering could damage the credibility of journalistic photos. "People have always wondered about writing — if you didn't hear someone speak, you can never be sure if they've been quoted right — but they've always believed photographs," says Ken Kobre, director of San Francisco State University's photojournalism program.

"Now there's no way to prove that a picture is phony," says Michael Evans, a Washington, D.C., photojournalist. Mr. Evans spent four years as President Ronald Reagan's personal photographer.

"I'm a little terrified," he says, "at the prospect of the image makers at the White House having control over a process they can seamlessly put together, like they seamlessly put together press releases."

Of course, photographers have been using artificial means to play around with their pictures for decades, cropping, pasting, using filters, and using bleach in the darkroom to brighten sections of photos.

"I have an old friend who says you shouldn't use a flash — that alters the reality — and if it's dark, you shouldn't photograph," says Rick Smolan, co-director of the *Day in the Life* series of photo books about different countries. "This is just another tool," he says of photo computers.

But it is an extraordinarily powerful tool. Mr. Smolan has used a Scitex to fiddle with the covers of all seven books in his series, usually to adapt a photo to fit a vertical space.

In *A Day in the Life of America*, he moved the moon and a tree in an originally horizontal shot of a preacher riding up a hill. In the forthcoming *A Day in the Life of the Soviet Union*, he added an extra strip of sky to the top of a shot of Red Square at night.

He says he doesn't use the Scitex to "change the meaning of the picture" and would use it only on the cover photo, whose integrity is already spoiled by printing words on it.

The loudest battle in the computer-arts arena right now is over colorizing movies. On the one side are a handful of entertainment companies, led by Turner Broadcasting System Inc. and Hal Roach Studios Inc., that have spent millions of dollars electronically adding color to dozens of old black-and-white movies.

On the other is a loud coalition of filmmakers and critics who think the technique mutilates movies and shouldn't be used without a director's approval.

Meanwhile, movie makers are just starting to line up against another new technology: an electronic device called an audio time compressor. It performs a neat trick on audiotapes: it converts them into computer data and then deletes what the device's makers call redundant elements of sound.

The result, compressor makers say, is a tape that plays faster without turning squeaky or detectably losing any sound. Compressor makers say they can shorten a tape by up to 15 per cent.

The leading compressor maker, Lexicon Inc. of Waltham, Mass., has sold about 150 of these machines to TV stations, which use them to speed up the sound of movies and TV shows.

Last year, the Directors Guild of America asked the Federal Communications Commission to bar or regulate the use of compressors. It argued that the machines let TV stations secretly play movies faster so that they can sell more commercials.

The FCC refused to take action. The guild has petitioned the FCC to reconsider, a request that is still pending.

Lexicon's rejoinder to this debate is that directors are even worse off without compressors. Normally, TV stations just chop up movies that run too long for their time slots.

"We don't live in a perfect world," says Ronald Noonan, Lexicon's president. "Would you rather have the thing be cut with the prejudice of an editor or would you rather have the whole thing compressed?"

— Michael Miller
The Globe and Mail
September 7, 1987

EXPLORING IDEAS

1. In small groups, discuss the following and present your views to the class:
(a) Is electronic sampling and other methods of adapting an artist's creations — without consent — ethical? Why or why not? In what ways, if any, should such manipulation be controlled?
(b) Magazine publishers can now use a Scitex computer or other image-manipulation devices to alter a photographer's work. Who is entitled to the copyright on such altered images, in your view — the photographer or the manipulator? Should photographers (who traditionally have had little control over *how* their images are reproduced) have the right to prevent such manipulation if they wish?
(c) Which do you find *least* objectionable: the "chopping-up" of films shown on TV, or the use of "compressors" to speed up the running times of movies so they will fit into television time slots? Explain.
(d) *Do* television audiences prefer to see films that were originally shot in black-and-white in fabricated colour? What rights, if any, should film directors have regarding the colorization of their work?

INVESTIGATING THE MEDIA

1. Working with a partner, evaluate the differences in the impact that black-and-white and colour photographs and advertisements have on you. Do you notice different details when a picture is in colour? What differences are there in the moods created? What, in your view, are the strengths of each medium?

Create a display of the photographs and advertisements that have the strongest appeal for you. Use your display as a basis for a presentation on the merits of both black-and-white and colour in pictures.

2. Creators of music videos have made extensive use of both colour and black-and-white, sometimes mixing these two diverse elements in the same video. Working in small groups, view several musical videos, cataloguing how each makes specific use of either colour or black-and-white, or a combination of both, to maximize the video's impact.

Prepare a report, for presentation to the class, which attempts
- to generalize or to categorize *how* each of these elements is used,
- to assess the overall effect or impact each of these elements seems to have,
- to judge the *appropriate* use of these diverse elements in adding to the successful presentation of the music.

YOUR TURN

1. As a class, debate *one* of the following issues:
Resolved: "New technology is making the '80s a strange and lawless time to be a creative artist."
or
Resolved: "...our technological capabilities here are far in advance of our intellectual development or our moral development."

— Woody Allen, director and actor

Are you ready for the "futuretech" world of media? Choose from the following or develop your own activities to investigate further how the mass — and de-massified — media will be reshaping your life in the 21st century.

1. Computers made the possibility of using "teaching machines" in education a reality. Investigate the role of teaching machines in the classroom. What kind of curricula do machines provide? What are the advantages and disadvantages of this type of program? Prepare a report based on your research. Conclude the report with your personal views on whether or not you would want this type of education for your child.
2. Make a study of advances being made today in the field of mass media and communications that are of interest to you personally. In a written report, describe the potential uses for the new technologies and provide a critique exploring the possible benefits and hazards to society.
3. Determine the issues related to the future of the media and communications industries that are of the greatest concern to you and your fellow students. Research these issues and prepare a report for the class.
4. Read a futuristic novel such as Ray Bradbury's *Fahrenheit 451* or Aldous Huxley's *Brave New World*. Prepare a written report in which you summarize the writer's vision of the future and discuss the possibilities of the vision becoming a reality.
5. Make a study of trends in the media. What kind of society are we heading towards? Present an oral report on this topic to the class.
6. How is the advent of the Information Age affecting Canada's economy and the workforce? How will education be affected? Conduct an investigation of these issues and prepare an oral report for the class.
7. Explore some of the needs television could serve in the future, beyond the functions it is fulfilling now. Plan a class presentation or a written report on this topic.
8. What media and communications equipment will become "normal household appliances" in the next two or three decades? Do some research into this and let your imagination take flight. Design a high-tech home of the future and present your ideas to the class.

Index

Acknowledgments

Care has been taken to determine and locate ownership of copyright material used in this text. In the case of any errors or omissions, the publishers will be pleased to make suitable acknowledgments in future editions.

Readings

UNIT 1

Average Canadian Sees 24 Hours of TV a Week: Reprinted with permission — The Toronto Star Syndicate.
Making Prime-Time Hits: Copyright © 1985 by The New York Times Company. Reprinted by permission.
What Happens When TV Tries a Little Risk-Taking: Reprinted with permission of Howard Rosenberg.
Today's Morality Play: The Sitcom: Used by permission of The New York Times Syndication Sales Corporation.
Soap Opera 'Disease' Claiming More Victims: Reprinted by permission of *The Globe and Mail,* Toronto.
America Wins Ratings Game: Reprinted by permission of *The Hamilton Spectator.*
Tough Times for the CBC: Reprinted with permission — The Toronto Star Syndicate.
A Long-time Critic (Finally) Counts the Reasons U.S. TV Beats All: Reprinted with permission — The Toronto Star Syndicate.
Roberta Says Mom Doesn't Know Best: Reprinted by permission of *The Spectator.*
Searching for God in the Soul of Man: Reprinted by permission of *Maclean's.*
Stay Tuned: Reprinted by permission of George A. James.
10 Steps to Better Family TV Viewing: Reprinted with permission — The Toronto Star Syndicate.
Radio: The Great Survivor: Reprinted by permission of *Channels of Communication.*
Radio Broadcasting Less and Less Canadian Content: Reprinted courtesy of Teen Generation Magazine, 202 Cleveland St., Toronto, Ont. M4S 2W6.
Golden Oldies in the Year 2017: Reprinted by permission of *Maclean's.*

UNIT 2

Literacy in Canada: One in Four Canadians Functionally Illiterate: Reprinted by permission of Southam News.
The End of Meaning: Reprinted by permission of A. Stephen Pimenoff.
Talking Books: Reprinted by permission of Canada Wide Feature Service Limited.
The Paperback Revolution: "Preface," pp. xi-xii, from *The Two-Bit Culture* by Kenneth C. Davis. Copyright © 1984 by Kenneth C. Davis. Reprinted by permission of Houghton Mifflin Company.
Paperback Best-Sellers: The First 25 Years: "Paperback Best Sellers: The First 25 years," p. 289, from *The Two-Bit Culture* by Kenneth C. Davis. Copyright © 1984 by Kenneth C. Davis. Reprinted by permission of Houghton Mifflin Company.
Packaging Romance: The Harlequin Story: © Harlequin Enterprises Limited. All rights reserved. Reproduction by permission of the publisher of Harlequin Enterprises Limited, Don Mills, Ontario, Canada.
Harlequin Romance: Editorial Guidelines: © Harlequin Enterprises Limited. All rights reserved. Reproduction by permission of the publisher of Harlequin Enterprises Limited, Don Mills, Ontario, Canada.
S.E. Hinton: "S.E. Hinton" from *From Writers to Students: The Pleasures and Pains of Writing* edited by M. Jerry Weiss, copyright 1979 by the International Reading Association. Reprinted with the permission of S.E. Hinton, the International Reading Association, Inc., and Curtis Brown, Ltd.
The News Business: "The News Business" from *Canadian Newspapers: The Inside Story* used by permission of Walter Stewart.
Color: Excerpt from pages 19-21 and excerpt from Chapter 4 from *The News Business* by John Chancellor and Walter R. Mears. Copyright © 1983 by John Chancellor and Walter R. Mears. Reprinted by permission of Harper & Row, Publishers, Inc.
Readers for Sale: Reprinted by permission of Mark Czarnecki.
Maclean's at 80: Reprinted by permission of *Maclean's.*

UNIT 3

The Mission of the Camera: From the book *Successful Photography,* Revised Edition, by Andreas Feininger © 1954, 1975. Used by permission of the publisher, Prentice-Hall, Inc., Englewood Cliffs, N.J.
Dilip Mehta: The Journey of a Photojournalist: Reprinted by permission of John McClyment.
People in Action: Excerpts from *Man in Sport: An International Exhibition of Photography.* Used by permission of The Baltimore Museum of Art.
The Jail — A Photo Essay: Reprinted by permission of Nir Bareket.
Filmmaker Isn't Spoiled by an Oscar: Reprinted with permission — The Toronto Star Syndicate.
Spellbound in Darkness: "Spellbound in Darkness" by Bruno Bettelheim from *Hollywood: Legend and Reality* by Michael Webb reprinted by permission of Random House, Inc.
Magic Moments: Excerpts from *Magic Moments From the Movies* by Elwy Yost, copyright © 1978 by Elwy Yost. Reprinted by permission of Doubleday, a division of Bantam, Doubleday, Dell Publishing Group, Inc.
The Untouchables: Shot by Shot: Reprinted by permission of Jesse Kornbluth.
A Taste for Terror: Reprinted from March ELLE, © 1987 ELLE Publishing, all rights reserved.
Bringing Sci-Fi Down to Earth: Reprinted with permission — The Toronto Star Syndicate.
Lights! Camera! Special Effects!: Copyright 1986 Time Inc. All rights reserved. Reprinted by permission of TIME.
Hollywood's New Vision: Reprinted by permission of *Maclean's.*
Canadian Films Slowly Shucking Their Loser Image. Reprinted by permission of Geoff Pevere.

UNIT 4

Confessions of an Advertising Man: David Ogilvy, excerpted from *Confessions of an Advertising Man.* Copyright © 1963 David Ogilvy Trustee. Reprinted with the permission of Atheneum Publishers, an imprint of Macmillan Publishing Company.

Crisis Time? Don't Touch That Dial!: Reprinted by permission of Jennifer Fisher.

What Advertisers Pitch We Rush to Gobble Up: Reprinted by permission of Joanne Kates, journalist and *Globe and Mail* columnist.

The Case Against Advocacy Advertising: Reprinted by permission of Morris Wolfe.

'Born to Shop' Electronic Age Kids Are Spending Billions on Themselves: Reprinted with permission — The Toronto Star Syndicate.

Do You Know What Your Tots Watch?: Reprinted with permission — The Toronto Star Syndicate.

Commercial Dos and Don'ts: Highlights of the Broadcast Code for Advertising to Children: From *Television and Your Children* published by TVOntario, 1986. Reprinted with permission of TVOntario.

Highlights of the Code of Standards: From *The Canadian Code of Advertising Standards* (May, 1986) reprinted by permission of the Canadian Advertising Foundation.

UNIT 5

Cleopatra and the Messenger: © 1982 by The Reader's Digest Association (Canada) Ltd. Reprinted by permission.

Ann Medina: TV Foreign Correspondent: Reprinted by permission of Robert Collison.

Canadians Favor TV for News, Poll Says: Reprinted by permission of *The Globe and Mail*, Toronto.

Can TV Tell the Truth?: Reprinted by permission of Morris Wolfe.

The Man Who Finds His Son Has Become a Thief: "The Man Who Finds His Son Has Become a Thief" reprinted from *Collected Poems of Raymond Souster* by permission of Oberon Press.

The Honorable Tradition of Not Naming Names: Reprinted by permission of Terry Poulton.

Canada's Crucible: Reprinted by permission of *Maclean's*.

Terrorism & Television: Reprinted from *TV Guide*, July 26, 1986, by permission of Andrew Ryan, Associate Editor.

New Media Guidelines Urged for Coverage of Terrorist Acts: Reprinted with permission — The Toronto Star Syndicate.

You Be the Editor: Reprinted with permission — The Toronto Star Syndicate.

Trial by Media: Reprinted by permission of Canada Wide Feature Service Limited.

Star Blasted for Story of Murderer: Reprinted with permission — The Toronto Star Syndicate.

Reporter Broke Law to Expose Security Flaws, Crosbie Says: Reprinted with permission — The Toronto Star Syndicate.

Mounties Question Ethics of Interview With B.C. Escaper: Reprinted with permission — The Toronto Star Syndicate.

UNIT 6

Advertising's Not-So-Subtle Sexism: Used by permission of Tony Thompson.

Gray Power Altering Face of Television: Reprinted by permission of Joan Irwin.

Prime Time Women: Reprinted by permission of *Playgirl*.

Men Have to Speak Up in Battle Against Sexism: Reprinted with permission — The Toronto Star Syndicate.

Fighting Popular Sexism: "Fighting Popular Sexism" by Christine Stanton is reprinted from the *Burlington Post*, June 10, 1987, by permission of *The Post*.

Children Defy Reality With the Flick of a Dial: Copyright © 1985 by The New York Times Company. Reprinted by permission.

Creating Cosby: The article was written by Allen Eisenach for *Media & Values* magazine, No. 35, "Making the Media Work for You," 1962 S. Shenandoah, Los Angeles, CA 90034.

Perils of the Royal Mounted: Reprinted by permission of the author, Pierre Berton.

Jeers: Reprinted by permission of *TV Guide*.

It's an All-White World on Canadian Television: Reprinted by permission of Joan Irwin.

Images of a Depraved New World: Reprinted by permission of *Maclean's*.

Students Drawn to 'Glamorous Courses,' Colleges Say: Reprinted by permission of *The Globe and Mail*, Toronto.

UNIT 7

List of Heroes a Glimpse into the Future: Reprinted by permission of Rocco Rossi.

Superman Goes Back to the Drawing Board: Reprinted with permission — The Toronto Star Syndicate.

Dan Cooper: All-Canadian Hero: © 1984 by The Reader's Digest Association (Canada) Ltd. Reprinted by permission.

Rocky & Rambo: From *Newsweek*, December 23, 1985 © 1985 Newsweek, Inc. All rights reserved. Reprinted by permission.

Untouchables Feeds Desire for Moral Certainty: Reprinted with permission — The Toronto Star Syndicate.

James Bond: 007: Reprinted with permission — The Toronto Star Syndicate.

Making a Legend: Reprinted by permission of *Maclean's*.

An Open Letter to Rick Hansen: Reprinted by permission of Canada Wide Feature Service Limited.

Wheelchair Marathoner Pursues 'What is in My Heart': Reprinted with permission — The Toronto Star Syndicate.

America Has Topsy-Turvy Idea of Heroism: © Copyrighted 1987, Chicago Tribune Company; all rights reserved, used with permission.

Computer Hackers, Are They Folk Heroes or Common Criminals?: Reprinted by permission of *The Post*.

UNIT 8

Uncertain Steps Into the Future: Reprinted with permission — The Toronto Star Syndicate.

Computer Gets Day Up and Running: Reprinted by permission of *The Globe and Mail*, Toronto.

The Way We Were and the Way We Will Be: Reprinted by permission of Carol Jamieson and *Goodlife* magazine.

The Age of Video: From *Newsweek*, December 30, 1985 © 1985 Newsweek, Inc. All rights reserved. Reprinted by permission.

Video Shapes Your World: Copyright 1986 *Video Review*, reprinted with permission.

TV Technology Is Wooing Viewers Into Electronic Cocoons: Reprinted with permission — The Toronto Star Syndicate.

Interactive TV Opens New Retail Market: Reprinted with permission, *High Technology Business* magazine, August 1987. Copyright © 1987 by Infotechnology Publishing Corporation, 214 Lewis Wharf, Boston, MA 02110.

Shopaholics Just Tune In for a Spending Fix: Reprinted by permission of David Walker.

Supermarkets Woo Impulse Buyers: Reprinted by permission of *The Globe and Mail,* Toronto.
Warily Into a Wired-Up World: Reprinted by permission of Andrew M. Osler.
The Questionable Ethics of Modern Creativity: Originally titled "Creativity Furor: High-Tech Alteration of Sights and Sounds Divides the Arts World," from *The Wall Street Journal* 9/1/87. Reprinted by permission of *The Wall Street Journal* © Dow Jones & Company, Inc. 1987. All rights reserved.

Photographs

P.6 — courtesy of The National Broadcasting Company, Inc.; **p.8** — Shooting Star/Pono Presse Internationale; **p.13** — courtesy of The National Broadcasting Company, Inc.; **p.16** — Rex Features Ltd./ Pono Presse Internationale; **p.19** — Canapress Photo Service; **p.20** — *The Toronto Star;* **p.23** — Bruce MacAuley/Atlantis Films Ltd; **p.25** — Canadian Broadcasting Corporation; **p.35** — The Bettman Archive; **p.38** *(Luba)* — © 1986 Hrair Hawk Khatcherian/Pono Presse Internationale; **p.38** *(Adams)* — Canapress Photo Service; **p.41** — Rex Features Ltd./Pono Presse Internationale; **p.49** — Canadian Give the Gift of Literacy Campaign; **p.52** — Coalition for Literacy; **p.54** — Listen for Pleasure, Inc.; **p.57** — Jeremy Jones; **p.60** — Harlequin Enterprises Limited; **p.64** — David Inhofe/ courtesy of Dell Publishers; **p.65** — courtesy of Warner Bros. Inc. © 1983 All rights reserved.; **pp. 68-69** — used by permission of *The Globe and Mail,* Toronto; **p.72** — *The Toronto Sun;* **p.73** — reprinted with permission/The Toronto Star Syndicate; **p.83** — used by permission of *Maclean's;* **p.84** — © J.B. Porée/ Pono Presse Internationale; **p.85** *(top)* — Canapress Photo Service; **p.85** — Monticeui/Gamma/Pono Presse Internationale; **p.91** *(bottom left)* — Masterfile © Tony Stone Worldwide; **p.91** *(top left & bottom right)* — © 1987 Dilip Mehta/ Contact Press Images; **p.91** *(top right)* — © 1988 Dilip Mehta/Contact Press Images; **p.93** — reprinted courtesy of Andreas Feininger; **p.95** — © 1987 Dilip Mehta/ Contact Press Images; **p.96** — Canapress Photo Service; **p.97** *(top)* — © 1987 Dilip Mehta/Contact Press Images; **p.97** *(bottom)* — Canapress Photo Service; **p.98** — Canapress Photo Service; **p.100** — Canapress Photo Service; **p.102** — Canapress Photo Service; **p.104** *(top left)* — Masterfile/© 87 Roberta Weissman; **p.104** *(centre left)* — Masterfile/© Tony Stone Worldwide; **p.104** *(bottom left)* — Masterfile/© Tony Stone Worldwide; **p.104** *(top right)* — Masterfile/ Harvey Lloyd; **p.104** *(bottom right)* — Masterfile / © Tony Stone Worldwide; **p.105** *(top left)* — The Image Bank/ JaneArt Ltd.; **p.105** *(bottom left)* — The Image Bank/Hank DeLespinasse; **p.105** *(top right)* — The Image Bank/ Michael de Camp; **p.105** *(bottom right)* — The Image Bank/Tim Biebering; **p.106** *(top)* — Masterfile/© 87 Vince Streano; **p.106** *(bottom left)* — The Image Bank/ Jean Anderson; **p.106** *(bottom right)* — The Image Bank/ Anthony Boccaccio; **p.107** — Masterfile/© Tony Stone Worldwide; **p.108** — Masterfile/Allsport/Vandystadt; **p.109** *(top)* — Masterfile/Claus Anderson; **p.109** *(bottom)* — Masterfile/Terry Hancey; **p.110** — Canapress Photo Service; **p.111** — Masterfile/Allsport; **pp. 112-117** — Nir Bareket; **p.119** — Canapress Photo Service; **p.121** — Joel Guthro; **pp. 127-130** — courtesy of Paramount Pictures Corporation, *The Untouchables* © 1987 by Paramount Pictures Corporation. All rights reserved.; **p.133** — Shooting Star/Pono Presse Internationale; **p.137** — Shooting Star / Pono Presse Internationale; **pp. 138-139** — TM & © Lucasfilm Ltd. (LFL) 1983, 1985 or 1986. All rights reserved. Courtesy of Lucasfilm Ltd.; **p.141** — Orion/ Shooting Star/ Pono Presse Internationale; **p.143** — Cinéphile; **p.144** — Lyne Charlebois/ Cinéma Plus; **p.151** — Bill Smart; **p.155** — reprinted courtesy of Lisle-Kelco Limited; **p.157** — Metropolitan Toronto Library Board Picture Collection; **p.158** — courtesy of Carder Gray Advertising for Panasonic; **p.159** — courtesy of Yamaha International Corporation, Piano Division; **p.161** — courtesy of Rubin Postaer and Associates for American Honda Motor Co., Inc.; **p.164** — reprinted courtesy of Ally Gargano for Rose's Lime Juice/Cadbury Schweppes Inc./ **p.165** — reprinted courtesy of Giorgio Beverly Hills; **p.166** — courtesy of NW Ayer Incorporated for AT&T; **p.170** — © Danielle Jones 1987; **p.176** — Jeremy Jones; **p.181** — Vickers and Benson for McDonald's of Canada; **pp. 182-183** — reprinted courtesy of Texaco Canada Inc.; **p.184** — Canadian Mental Health Association; **p.185** *(top left)* — Joseph E. Seagram & Son, Limited; **p.185** *(right)* — Reader's Digest Magazines Limited; **p.185** *(bottom left)* — R.J. Reynolds Tobacco Company; **p.187** — Doug Griffin/*The Toronto Star;* **p.189** — © Yoram Kahana/Pono Presse Internationale; **p.193** — Reproduced with the permission of the Canadian Advertising Foundation; **p.201** — CBC Television; **p.205** — The Journal/CBC; **p.208** — Régis Bossu/ Sygma/Publiphoto; **p.213** — Canapress Photo Service; **p.214** — The Toronto Star Syndicate/ Canapress Photo Service; **p.217** — Canapress Photo Service; **p.220** — Canapress Photo Service; **p.223** — Sygma/ Publiphoto; **p.224** — Canapress Photo Service; **p.225** *(top)* — Alain Nogues/ Sygma/Publiphoto; **p.225** *(bottom)* — Allan Tannenbaum/ Sygma/Publiphoto; **p.230** — Canapress Photo Service; **p.231** — Canapress Photo Service; **pp.238-239** — Reprinted by permission of *Maclean's;* **pp.241** — Metro Toronto Library Board Picture Collection; **p.243** — Canapress Photo Service; **p.244** — Fred Phipps/ CBC, used by permission of Robert Clothier; **p.246** — Reprinted courtesy of Eastman Kodak Company; **p.247** — Reproduced with the permission of Fisher-Price Canada, Division of The Quaker Oats Company of Canada Limited. Copyright holder Fisher-Price, Division of the Quaker Oats Company, East Aurora, NY, USA 14052; **p.248** — Reprinted courtesy of Esprit de Corp.; **p.249** — Reprinted courtesy of Clairol Canada; **p.250** — courtesy of McCann Erickson Advertising of Canada Ltd. for The Mennen Company, Mennen Canada, Inc.; **p.251** — courtesy of Metropolitan Toronto Police; **pp.252-253** — Reprinted courtesy of Benetton Services Corporation; **p.255** — Canapress Photo Service; **p.256** — Canapress Photo Service; **p.257** — Canapress Photo Service; **p.263** — Embassy/ Shooting Star/Pono Presse Internationale; **p.264** — J. Bond/ Shooting Star/ Pono Presse Internationale; **p.270** *(left)* — Shooting Star/ Pono Presse Internationale; **p.270** *(right)* — Shooting Star/ Pono Presse Internationale; **p.274** — Springer/Bettman Film Archive; **p.279** — Universal/Shooting Star/Pono Presse Internationale; **p.288** — SUPERMAN, and WONDER WOMAN (**p.294**), their respective logos and indicias are trademarked and copyrighted by DC Comics Inc. **p.299** — Shooting Star/ Pono Presse Internationale; **p.304** — Canapress Photo Service; **p.305** — Canapress Photo Service; **p.307** — Alan Mackfield/Shooting Star / Pono Presse Internationale; **p.311** — Joe Traver/ Gama/ Pono Presse Internationale; **p.314** *(top)* — Canapress Photo Service; **p.314** *(bottom)* — Toronto Star Syndicate; **p.315** *(top)* — Canapress Photo Service; **p.315** *(bottom)* — Canapress Photo Service; **p.317** — McDonald's of Canada; **p.316** — Coca-Cola Ltd.; **p.324** — Allan Tannenbaum/ Sygma/ Publiphoto; **p.333** *(left)* — Canapress Photo Service; **p.333** *(right)* — Canapress Photo Service; **p.335** — Canapress Photo Service; **p.336** — Canapress Photo Service; **p.339** — Canapress Photo Service; **p.340** — Gabe Palmer/ Masterfile; **p.341** — Canapress Photo Service; **p.344** — Al Harvey/ Masterfile; **p.345** — Jacques M. Chenet/ Woodfin Camp & Associates; **p.347** — © 1988 Herman Kokojan/Black Star; **p.350** — Michel et Philippe Hamon/ Gamma/Pono Presse Internationale; **p.353** — courtesy of Jaffe/Lansing Productions; **p.360** — Canapress Photo Service; **p.366** — M. Ponomareff/ Pono Presse Internationale.